Dietary Patterns and Nutrient Intake in Pregnant Women

Dietary Patterns and Nutrient Intake in Pregnant Women

Editors

Louise Brough
Gail Rees

MDPI

Basel • Beijing • Wuhan • Barcelona • Belgrade • Novi Sad • Cluj • Manchester

Editors
Louise Brough
Massey University
Palmerston North
New Zealand

Gail Rees
University of Plymouth
Plymouth
UK

Editorial Office
MDPI
St. Alban-Anlage 66
4052 Basel, Switzerland

This is a reprint of articles from the Special Issue published online in the open access journal *Nutrients* (ISSN 2072-6643) (available at: https://www.mdpi.com/journal/nutrients/special_issues/Dietary_Patterns_and_Nutrient_Intake_in_Pregnant_Women).

For citation purposes, cite each article independently as indicated on the article page online and as indicated below:

Lastname, A.A.; Lastname, B.B. Article Title. *Journal Name* **Year**, *Volume Number*, Page Range.

ISBN 978-3-0365-9572-6 (Hbk)
ISBN 978-3-0365-9573-3 (PDF)
doi.org/10.3390/books978-3-0365-9573-3

Contents

Preface

This Special Issue brings together some of the latest original research into maternal diets and nutrient intakes during pregnancy from across the globe. Good nutrition in pregnancy is not only vital for the health of the mother but also influences the physiological development and metabolism of the fetus, and it has the potential to determine the future health and disease risk of the offspring. Determining optimal nutrition for different stages of pregnancy and measuring nutrient intake is challenging; thus, this collection seeks to expand our understanding in this important area of maternal and child health.

This Special Issue includes research papers exploring dietary habits/diet quality and the risks of heart defects in the offspring. Individual nutrients of interest in this issue include vitamin D, choline and omega-3 fatty acids. We also include research investigating dietary intakes/distribution of intake and weight gain, and the issue of under-reporting of energy intake. Research is drawn from across Europe, Asia and the United States representing individuals following a wide range of dietary patterns.

Louise Brough and Gail Rees
Editors

nutrients MDPI

Article

Underreporting of Energy Intake Increases over Pregnancy: An Intensive Longitudinal Study of Women with Overweight and Obesity

Katherine M. McNitt [1], Emily E. Hohman [1,*], Daniel E. Rivera [2], Penghong Guo [2], Abigail M. Pauley [3], Alison D. Gernand [4], Danielle Symons Downs [3] and Jennifer S. Savage [5]

1 Center for Childhood Obesity Research, The Pennsylvania State University, University Park, PA 16802, USA; katherinemcnitt@gmail.com
2 Control Systems Engineering Laboratory, Arizona State University, Tempe, AZ 85281, USA; daniel.rivera@asu.edu (D.E.R.); penghong.guo114@gmail.com (P.G.)
3 Exercise Psychology Laboratory, The Pennsylvania State University, University Park, PA 16802, USA; amp34@psu.edu (A.M.P.); dsd11@psu.edu (D.S.D.)
4 Department of Nutritional Sciences, The Pennsylvania State University, University Park, PA 16802, USA; adg14@psu.edu
5 Center for Childhood Obesity Research, Department of Nutritional Sciences, The Pennsylvania State University, State College, PA 16801, USA; jfs195@psu.edu
* Correspondence: eeh12@psu.edu; Tel.: +1-814-865-5245

Abstract: (1) Background: Energy intake (EI) underreporting is a widespread problem of great relevance to public health, yet is poorly described among pregnant women. This study aimed to describe and predict error in self-reported EI across pregnancy among women with overweight or obesity. (2) Methods: Participants were from the Healthy Mom Zone study, an adaptive intervention to regulate gestational weight gain (GWG) tested in a feasibility RCT and followed women ($n = 21$) with body mass index (BMI) $\geq$25 from 8–12 weeks to ~36 weeks gestation. Mobile health technology was used to measure daily weight (Wi-Fi Smart Scale), physical activity (activity monitor), and self-reported EI (MyFitnessPal App). Estimated EI was back-calculated daily from measured weight and physical activity data. Associations between underreporting and gestational age, demographics, pre-pregnancy BMI, GWG, perceived stress, and eating behaviors were tested. (3) Results: On average, women were 30.7 years old and primiparous (62%); reporting error was −38% ± 26 (range: −134% (underreporting) to 97% (overreporting)), representing an ~1134 kcal daily underestimation of EI (1404 observations). Estimated (back-calculated), but not self-reported, EI increased across gestation ($p < 0.0001$). Higher pre-pregnancy BMI ($p = 0.01$) and weekly GWG ($p = 0.0007$) was associated with greater underreporting. Underreporting was lower when participants reported higher stress ($p = 0.02$) and emotional eating ($p < 0.0001$) compared with their own average. (4) Conclusions: These findings suggest systemic underreporting in pregnant women with elevated BMI using a popular mobile app to monitor diet. Advances in technology that allow estimation of EI from weight and physical activity data may provide more accurate dietary self-monitoring during pregnancy.

Keywords: obesity; gestational weight gain; prenatal care; eating behaviors; stress; mHealth

Citation: McNitt, K.M.; Hohman, E.E.; Rivera, D.E.; Guo, P.; Pauley, A.M.; Gernand, A.D.; Symons Downs, D.; Savage, J.S. Underreporting of Energy Intake Increases over Pregnancy: An Intensive Longitudinal Study of Women with Overweight and Obesity. *Nutrients* **2022**, *14*, 2326. https://doi.org/10.3390/nu14112326

Academic Editor: Josep A. Tur

Received: 28 April 2022
Accepted: 27 May 2022
Published: 1 June 2022

1. Introduction

Two-thirds of women enter pregnancy with overweight or obesity [1], and over 60% will exceed gestational weight gain (GWG) recommendations [2]. Women who enter pregnancy with elevated BMI and/or exceed GWG recommendations are at risk for complications including gestational diabetes, preeclampsia, unsuccessful breastfeeding, and postpartum weight retention [3–6], and longer-term risks such as type 2 diabetes and some cancers [7,8]. In offspring, risks include macrosomia, large for gestational age, high blood pressure, and obesity [9–11]. Additionally, many people do not consume key nutrients during pregnancy and improved dietary guidance is warranted to help pregnant people to meet but not exceed dietary recommendations [12].

The Institute of Medicine recommends clinical dietary assessment for all pregnant people [13] and this may be especially beneficial for those at risk of excessive GWG [14]. Clinicians ask patients to monitor their food and energy intake (EI) [13,15]. In the general population, underreporting of EI is widespread [16,17] and is positively associated with BMI, younger age, and psychosocial factors, including cognitive restraint [18–21]. However, studies of underreporting during pregnancy are lacking. Underreporting of EI makes it difficult for health care providers to accurately interpret and monitor self-reported dietary information and may result in ineffective intervention efforts to regulate GWG.

Estimated prevalence of underreporting during pregnancy ranges from 13% to 50%, with the highest prevalence among those with pre-pregnancy overweight and obesity [22–24]. These studies relied on cross-sectional data and used a variety of methods to estimate underreporting (e.g., threshold cutoffs) to exclude "implausible" reporters [25], which collapses quantifiable underreporting (e.g., kcal, percent EI) into categorical groups (e.g., over reporters, under-reporters, "adequate" reporters) based on arbitrary limit values. Threshold cutoffs and cross-sectional data limit our understanding of how EI changes across trimesters in pregnancy as nutritional needs change. In sum, prior research focused primarily on identifying inadequate reporters in cross-sectional studies while the estimated magnitude of dietary underreporting during pregnancy remains unknown.

This study's aim was to describe the extent of energy intake reporting error throughout pregnancy among women with overweight or obesity using an intensive longitudinal data approach [26]. We also examined maternal factors associated with underreporting (i.e., demographics, pre-pregnancy BMI, GWG, perceived stress, and eating behaviors). Based on previous literature in pregnant and non-pregnant samples, we hypothesized underreporting would be positively associated with gestational age [27], income [27,28], pre-pregnancy BMI, GWG [27,28], perceived stress [29], uncontrolled eating [29], and emotional eating [29]. We also expected underreporting to be negatively associated with maternal age [27,28] and dietary restraint [27–29].

2. Materials and Methods

2.1. Study Subjects

Participants were pregnant women in the Healthy Mom Zone study, an adaptive intervention to regulate GWG tested in a feasibility randomized control trial and followed pregnant women with overweight and obesity (n = 21) from early pregnancy to ~36 weeks gestation living in and around State College, PA (ClinicalTrials.gov identifier #NCT03945266) [30]. This was an optimization trial within the multiphase optimization strategy (MOST) framework [31]. Details of the Healthy Mom Zone study intervention have been published previously [32]. Participants were recruited from 2016–2017 through flyers, online platforms, and referrals by local obstetricians at first prenatal appointment. Inclusion criteria were 8–12 weeks gestation and pre-pregnancy BMI = 24.5–45.0 (BMI = 40–45 were enrolled with physician consent). Exclusion criteria included pre-existing diabetes and other conditions known to impact fetal growth or GWG, severe allergies or dietary restrictions, contraindications to prenatal physical activity, and not residing in the area. Thirty-one participants were randomized to either the intervention (n = 15) or standard of care control (n = 16). All participants (n = 31) received usual prenatal health care through their personal health care provider and the intervention offered nutrition and physical activity guidance beyond what was offered in standard care. Regardless of group randomization, participants completed study measures daily, weekly, and monthly throughout the study. From this initial group, one participant was missing all EI data, one dropped out, one was non-compliant (e.g., <70% of measures completed), three had a first trimester miscarriage, and four had BMI < 25.0, resulting in a final sample size of 21 for this analysis. Ethical approval for the Healthy Mom Zone study was granted by the Pennsylvania State University Institutional Review Board (STUDY00003752, approval date: 12/1/15), participants provided written informed consent to participate, and all aspects of data collection and storage were in accordance with standards stipulated by this body.

2.2. Measures

2.2.1. Demographic Characteristics

At baseline, demographics and self-reported pre-pregnancy weight were collected from participants using questionnaires and trained nurses obtained height. Gestational age was defined using the first day of last menstrual cycle.

2.2.2. Weight and Physical Activity Measures

Participants weighed themselves daily from home using a Fitbit Aria Wi-Fi Smart Scale (Fitbit Inc., San Francisco, CA, USA). Weekly weight change was calculated as the average weekly weight minus the average weight of the prior week. Final maternal weights within 10 days of delivery were abstracted from medical records or using Aria Wi-Fi Smart Scale data if medical record data were not available. Total GWG was calculated for participants with a final maternal weight (n = 19) by subtracting self-reported pre-pregnancy weight from last available weight (within 10 days of delivery).

2.2.3. Psychosocial Measures

At study enrollment and every four weeks thereafter, participants completed the 21-item Eating Inventory [33] via online surveys collected with the secure data platform, Research Electronic Database Capture (REDCap) [34]. The Eating Inventory, which has a four point response scale ranging from (1) definitely true to (4) definitely false, measures three eating behavior subscales: cognitive restraint (e.g., "I consciously hold back on how much I eat at meals to keep from gaining weight."), uncontrolled eating (e.g., "Sometimes when I start eating, I just can't seem to stop."), and emotional eating (e.g., "I start to eat when I feel anxious."). Scores for each subscale were calculated by averaging items. Internal consistencies ranged from acceptable to excellent (restrained eating: $\alpha = 0.71$, uncontrolled eating: $\alpha = 0.86$, emotional eating = 0.92). Participants completed the 10-item Perceived Stress Scale [35] at enrollment and weekly thereafter. The Perceived Stress Scale assesses how unpredictable, uncontrollable, and overloaded respondents find their lives ($\alpha = 0.89$).

2.2.4. Self-Reported Energy Intake

Self-reported EI was obtained using MyFitnessPal (dietary intake application). While MyFitnessPal is not a validated method for collecting EI, it was chosen due to its ease of use and acceptability among participants as a tool for self-monitoring [36]. Both intervention and control participants were trained on using the app and recorded all foods and drinks consumed over 24 h on three days per week (two weekdays and one weekend day). Resting metabolic rate (RMR) was estimated daily using quadratic formula: RMR = 0.1976(weight in kg)^2 − 13.424(weight in kg) + 1457.6 [37]. This formula accounts for an assumed increase in RMR across gestation [37,38]. Physical activity (e.g., daily activity time, daily step count, and estimated energy expenditure) was assessed at baseline and throughout the study using a wrist-worn actigraphy device (Jawbone UP 4, Jawbone Inc., San Francisco, CA, USA) [39]. Jawbone UP 4 has been found to reliably predict physical activity, compared with other popular fitness monitors [40,41].

2.3. Calculating Underreporting of Energy Intake

In response to limited accuracy of self-reported EI, we expanded an energy balance model developed by Thomas and colleagues to back-calculate EI from GWG during pregnancy [28] using additional input variables, including measured daily weights (measured from home using Aria Wi-Fi Scale), activity kcal (Jawbone activity monitor), and resting metabolic rate (RMR) [38,42]. K_1 and K_2 are coefficients that map changes in daily energy intake and physical activity, respectively, into maternal weight gain/loss. T is the sampling time (in this case daily). The equation accounts for fetal and placental growth and expansion of the uterus, mammary glands, blood, and extracellular fluid in coefficients as a function of gestational age in days (k).

$$EI_{est}(k) = \frac{-W(k+2) + 8W(k+1) - 8W(k-1) + W(k-2)}{12TK_1} - \frac{K_2}{K_1}(PA(k) + RMR(k))$$

To calculate reporting error, self-reported and back-calculated EI data were matched by date. Unmatched data were excluded from analyses. Reporting error was calculated using the equation: Reporting Error = [(self-reported EI-back-calculated EI)/back-calculated EI] × 100% [43]. This continuous variable represents error in reporting of EI or discrepancy between self-reported and back-calculated kcal. This includes participant error in reporting as well as potential inherent errors in the app database, and is reflective of what users experience when using a dietary tracking mobile app. Negative values indicate EI underreporting and positive values indicate over reporting, with 0 representing accurate reporting.

2.4. Statistical Analysis

Statistical analysis was performed in SAS version 9.4 (SAS Institute Inc., Cary, NC, USA). Sample means were calculated for continuous demographic variables (pre-pregnancy BMI, GWG, and age). Frequencies and percentages were calculated for categorical demographic variables (pre-pregnancy BMI category, race, ethnicity, marital status, employment status, income, gravidity, and parity). Survey data where participants reflected back on a prior period of time (e.g., Perceived Stress Scale) had study week assigned to the week prior to survey completion. Weekly and daily data were merged by gestational age and monthly and daily/weekly data were merged by study week. Restrained, emotional, and uncontrolled eating and perceived stress were mean-centered by participant to disaggregate the effect of within- and between-person fluctuations on reporting error.

Multilevel modeling [44] tested whether reporting error changed over time (i.e., gestational age) and associations with the following: anthropometrics (pre-pregnancy BMI, GWG), treatment group (intervention or control), demographics (maternal age, parity, household income), perceived stress, and eating behaviors (cognitive restraint, uncontrolled eating, and emotional overeating). Repeated observations (level 1) were nested within participant (level 2). Each model used restricted maximum likelihood, compound symmetry covariance structure (CS), and included gestational age was a covariate [45]. Linear, quadratic, and cubic effects of gestational week were considered. Post-hoc group comparisons were adjusted using Tukey method. Intraclass correlation coefficients (ICCs) were calculated as the ratio of between-subjects variance to total variance. Statistical significance was determined at $p < 0.05$.

3. Results

3.1. Demographic Data

Age at study entry ranged from 24–37 years (M = 30.7 ± 3.0). All subjects had overweight or obesity with a mean pre-pregnancy BMI = 32.7 ± 6.8. Forty-eight percent reported having overweight pre-pregnancy (BMI = 25.0–29.9 kg/m^2) and 52% had obesity (BMI ≥ 30 kg/m^2). Most participants were married (90%), primiparous (62%), well-educated (95% with a college degree or higher), affluent (76% reported an annual household income ≥ $40,000), and employed full-time (81%). Mean total GWG for this sample was 21.5 ± 15.4 kg (kg) (Intervention: M = 10.7 ± 7.0 kg, Control: M = 8.7 ± 7.3 kg) (Table 1).

Table 1. Baseline Descriptive Characteristics of Pregnant Women with Overweight and Obesity (n = 21).

Characteristic	N(%) [1]
Maternal Age, years	30.7 ± 3.0
Preconception BMI, kg/m^2	32.7 ± 6.8
% BMI = 24.5–29.9	10 (48%)

Table 1. *Cont.*

Characteristic	N(%) [1]
% BMI ≥ 30	11 (52%)
Gestational Age at Baseline (Weeks)	10.0 ± 1.7
Gestational Weight Gain, kg	21.5 ± 15.4
Race	
White	21 (100%)
Ethnicity	
Non-Hispanic	21 (100%)
Marital Status	
Divorced	1 (5%)
Married	19 (90%)
Single	1 (5%)
Maternal Education	
High School	1 (5%)
College	11 (52%)
Graduate/Professional School	9 (43%)
Gravidity	
1	11 (52%)
2	8 (38%)
3	2 (10%)
Parity	
0	13 (62%)
1	8 (38%)
Employment	
Full-Time	17 (81%)
Part-Time	2 (9%)
Self-Employed	1 (5%)
Other	1 (5%)
Household Income	
<$20,000	1 (5%)
$20,000–$40,000	4 (19%)
$40,000–100,000	8 (38%)
≥$100,000	8 (38%)

[1] Continuous variables (maternal age and BMI: body mass index) data presented as mean plus/minus standard deviation.

3.2. Error in Reporting of Energy Intake

The mean of all reporting error observations (n = 1404) of −38% ± 26 (range: −134% (underreporting) to 97% (overreporting)), representing an approximately 1134 kcal underestimation daily. The ICC indicates about 54% of variation in reporting error variable was within-person, while 46% of variation was between-person. In other words, 54% of variance in reporting error is accounted for by change within participants (e.g., from day to day), while the remaining variation can be explained by characteristics differing between participants, such as pre-pregnancy BMI. Participant mean reporting error was −38% (range: −65–0%); meaning participants underreported EI by 38%. Twenty out of 21 participants underreported 90% of the time or more.

3.3. Change in Reporting Error across Pregnancy

Mean self-reported EI did not significantly differ between first (M = 1792 ± 70), second (M = 1681 ± 67), and third trimesters (M = 1692 ± 68). Back-calculated EI increased by an average of 272 kcal from first (M = 2688 ± 144) to second trimester (M = 2960 ± 141; $p < 0.0001$) and 117 kcal from second to third trimester (M = 3077 ± 142; $p = 0.0005$) (Table 2). There was a between-person relationship between gestational age (in days), when treated as a continuous variable, on reporting error such that underreporting increased as pregnancy progressed ($p < 0.0001$) (Figure 1).

Table 2. Energy Intake (kcal/d) and Underreporting During Pregnancy by Maternal Characteristics and Treatment Group in Pregnant Women with Overweight and Obesity.

Characteristic	Self-Reported EI (kcal/d) Mean ± SD	Back-Calculated EI, (kcal/d) Mean ± SD	Difference between Back-Calculated and Self-Reported EI, (kcal/d) Mean ± SD	% Underreporting Mean ± SD
Overall (n = 21)	1696 ± 481	2950 ± 142	1263 ± 162	38% ± 4
Gestational Age (Trimester)				
First Trimester	1702 ± 70 ^{a}	2688 ± 144 ^{a}	986 ± 166 ^{a}	32% ± 4 ^{a}
Second Trimester	1681 ± 67 ^{a}	2960 ± 141 ^{b}	1280 ± 162 ^{b}	39% ± 4 ^{b}
Third Trimester	1692 ± 68 ^{a}	3077 ± 142 ^{c}	1386 ± 164 ^{c}	40% ± 4 ^{b}
Pre-Pregnancy BMI				
BMI 25–29.9 (n = 10)	1743 ± 97 ^{a}	2537 ± 165 ^{a}	794 ± 190 ^{a}	28% ± 5 ^{a}
BMI ≥ 30 (n = 11)	1637 ± 92 ^{a}	3324 ± 157 ^{b}	1688 ± 181 ^{b}	47% ± 4 ^{b}
Total GWG Classified by Institute of Medicine Guidelines				
Not Exceeding (n = 12)	1736 ± 88 ^{a}	3006 ± 191 ^{a}	1271 ± 220 ^{a}	35% ± 5 ^{a}
Exceeding (n = 9)	1622 ± 102 ^{a}	2874 ± 221 ^{a}	1253 ± 254 ^{a}	41% ± 6 ^{a}
Parity				
0 (n = 13)	1672 ± 86 ^{a}	3000 ± 184 ^{a}	1329 ± 210 ^{a}	40% ± 5 ^{a}
1 (n = 8)	1712 ± 110 ^{a}	2867 ± 234 ^{a}	1156 ± 340 ^{a}	36% ± 6 ^{a}
Annual Household Income				
$10,000–$20,000 (n = 1)	1465 ± 315 ^{a}	4286 ± 613 ^{a}	2821 ± 61 ^{a}	65% ± 17 ^{a}
$20,000–$40,000 (n = 4)	1689 ± 158 ^{a}	2695 ± 307 ^{b}	1007 ± 346 ^{b}	32% ± 9 ^{a}
$40,000–$100,000 (n = 8)	1624 ± 111 ^{a}	2971 ± 216 ^{b}	1348 ± 244 ^{b}	41% ± 6 ^{a}
>$100,000 ($n$ = 8)	1778 ± 111 ^{a}	2888 ± 217 ^{b}	1111 ± 244 ^{b}	35% ± 6 ^{a}
Treatment Group Assignment				
Intervention (n = 11)	1689 ± 94 ^{a}	2902 ± 200 ^{a}	1213 ± 229 ^{a}	37% ± 5 ^{a}
Control (n = 10)	1686 ± 99 ^{a}	3002 ± 210 ^{a}	1318 ± 240 ^{a}	40% ± 6 ^{a}

Values are least squared mean plus/minus standard error from repeated measures models (PROC MIXED). Results of statistical models are represented by a, b, c group comparisons. Values with different subscripts indicate a statistically significant difference between the two values (e.g., $p < 0.05$).

In a separate model, gestational age was examined as a categorical variable where there was a main effect of trimester on reporting error ($p < 0.0001$). Reporting error in the first trimester (LS mean = −32% ± 4) was significantly higher than in the second (−39% ± 4) and third trimesters (−40% ± 4).

3.4. Independent Factors Associated with Reporting Error

A main effect of continuous pre-pregnancy BMI on reporting error showed higher pre-pregnancy BMI was associated with more underreporting ($p = 0.01$) (Figure 2). In a separate model, there was also a main effect of categorical pre-pregnancy BMI status on reporting error between participants with obesity (LS mean = −47% ± 4) and overweight (LS mean = −28% ± 5) ($p = 0.0075$). Mean self-reported EI did not significantly differ between participants with obesity (LS mean = 1637 ± 92) and overweight (LS mean = 1743 ± 97; $p = 0.43$), while mean back-calculated EI was lower in participants with overweight (LS mean = 2537 ± 165) compared with those with obesity (LS mean = 3324 ± 157; $p = 0.0027$).

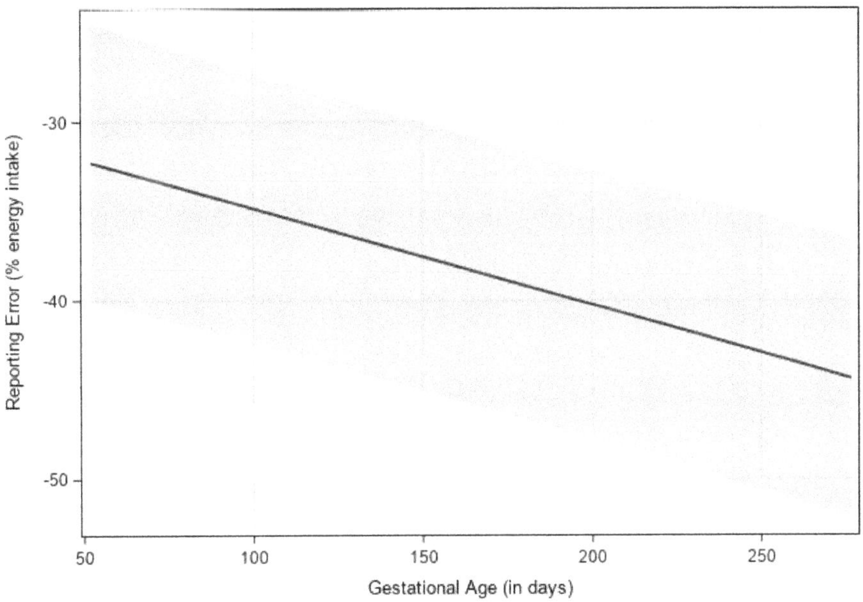

Figure 1. Visualization of estimated reporting error over gestational age (in days), with 95% confidence interval. Estimates were generated by using multilevel modeling (SAS PROC MIXED). Linear, quadratic, and cubic effects of gestational week were considered, with a linear relationship having the best model fit.

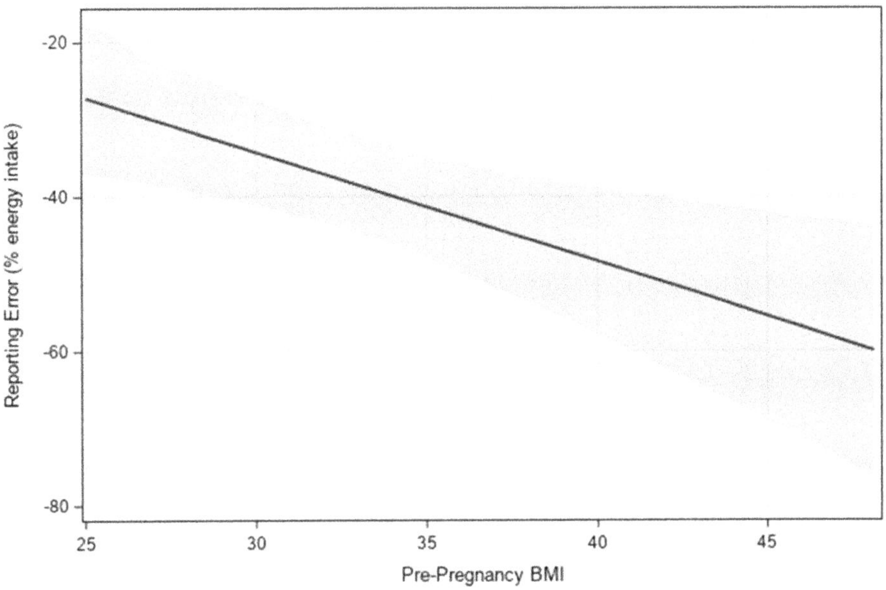

Figure 2. Visualization of the linear relationship between estimated reporting error and pre-pregnancy BMI, with 95% confidence interval. Estimates were generated by using multilevel modeling (SAS PROC MIXED).

While there was no association between overall GWG and underreporting, we observed a positive association between weekly GWG and underreporting ($p = 0.0007$), such that participants with higher weekly GWG had greater mean underreporting (Table 3). Additionally, when examining weekly GWG as a categorical variable, reporting error was lower in participants who exceeded (LS mean = −40.1% ± 4) compared with participants who were below (LS mean = −36% ± 4) weekly Institute of Medicine GWG recommendations based on trimester and BMI category ($p = 0.0009$) (Table 3). Three participants developed gestational diabetes mellitus (GDM) after enrollment in the trial. These women also had the highest pre-pregnancy BMIs of the sample. Sensitivity analyses were conducted excluding these participants ($n = 18$). All conclusions were the same, except that when participants with GDM were excluded, the positive association between total GWG and underreporting became statistically significant ($p = 0.01$).

Table 3. Predictors of maternal underreporting of energy intake during pregnancy in women with overweight and obesity [a] ($n = 25$).

Variable	Model Estimate	Standard Error	p-Value
Gestational Age (days)	−0.05372	0.009664	<0.0001
Gestational Age (by trimester) (reference = Trimester 3)			<0.0001
Trimester (1)	8.0931	1.6027	
Trimester (2)	1.3743	1.1605	
Pre-Pregnancy BMI (kg/m^2)	−1.4144	0.4943	0.0100
Pre-Pregnancy BMI classification (reference = BMI > 30)			0.0075
BMI = 25.0–29.9	19.3786	6.4793	
Perceived Stress (within-person)	0.2561	0.1033	0.0133
Perceived Stress (between-person)	−0.1708	0.6372	0.7915
Emotional Eating (within-person)	7.3520	0.5073	<0.0001
Emotional Eating (between-person)	−0.1734	0.6583	0.7950
Cognitive Restraint (within-person)	0.6897	0.5186	0.1838
Cognitive Restraint (between-person)	−2.7578	3.2976	0.4134
Uncontrolled Eating (within-person)	−0.3294	0.2798	0.2393
Uncontrolled Eating (between-person)	−1.3742	1.1126	0.2318
Total GWG (in kg) ($n = 19$)	−0.5049	0.5856	0.4006
Total GWG (meeting vs. exceeding Institute of Medicine guidelines) (reference = meeting guidelines)	−6.5364	8.3740	0.4458
Weekly GWG (in kg)	−5.4802	0.9972	<0.0001
Weekly GWG (meeting vs. exceeding Institute of Medicine guidelines) (reference = meeting guidelines)			0.0007
Under	5.0148	1.9283	
Over	0.5328	1.9144	
Treatment group (reference = intervention)			0.7294
Control	−2.7539	7.28448	
Maternal Age (yrs)	0.3989	1.3283	0.7672
Parity (reference = 1)			0.6131
Parity (0)	−4.1338	8.0404	

Table 3. *Cont.*

Variable	Model Estimate	Standard Error	*p*-Value
Household Income (yearly) (reference ≥ $100,000)			0.3396
$10,000–$20,000	−30.4517	18.3616	
$20,000–$40,000	2.8334	10.6118	
$40,000–100,000	6.9350	8.6440	

[a] Multilevel model parameter estimates showing independent predictors of maternal reporting error, each in a separate model. All models controlled for gestational age except where gestational age/trimester was the predictor of interest.

Stress increased ($p < 0.0001$), while emotional, uncontrolled, and restrained eating decreased (all $p < 0.05$) across pregnancy. The ICC for perceived stress was 57%, indicating 43% of variability in stress was within- and 57% was between-person. After controlling for gestational age, a main effect of participant mean-centered perceived stress on reporting error showed that on days when participants reported higher stress compared with their own average, reporting error was more positive, indicating less underreporting ($p = 0.02$) (Table 3). The ICC for emotional eating was 81%, indicating 19% of variability in stress was within- and 81% was between-person. There was not a significant association between participants' average emotional eating and average reporting error ($p = 0.8$). However, there was a significant effect of within-person emotional eating on reporting error, such that on days when participants reported higher emotional eating compared with their own average, underreporting was lower ($p < 0.0001$). ICCs for restrained and uncontrolled eating were 58% and 82%, respectively. Cognitive restraint and uncontrolled eating were not significantly associated with reporting error. While there was no significant relationship between treatment group and reporting error, there was an interaction of study group with weight status on reporting error ($p = 0.01$). Post hoc comparisons indicated that, in the intervention group, participants with overweight had lower underreporting than participants with obesity, suggesting that the intervention had a positive impact on underreporting for participants with overweight only. No significant relationships were detected between maternal age, parity, or income and underreporting (Table 3).

4. Discussion

This is the first study to use daily longitudinal data to characterize reporting accuracy in a sample of U.S. pregnant persons with elevated BMI, showing that underreporting increases throughout pregnancy. Further, pre-pregnancy BMI was positively associated with underreporting in the second trimester in this sample of women with overweight and obesity. Data also indicate that weekly GWG was positively associated with underreporting. Finally, higher than average perceived stress and emotional eating were associated with reporting error during pregnancy, but parity, age, income, cognitive restraint, and uncontrolled eating were not associated with reporting accuracy (Table 4). Together, these data suggest that underreporting has complex roots and the extent of underreporting increases later in pregnancy, despite simultaneous increases in recommended energy requirements to support fetal growth.

Across pregnancy, underreporting appeared to be driven by stable, self-reported EI. Back-calculated EI data indicate that participants consumed about 400 more kcal on average in trimester three, compared with trimester one, but self-reported eating the same amount of food across trimesters. This is consistent with a prior study showing EI underreporting prevalence was higher in late compared with early pregnancy [27]. People may tire of logging intake and reporting may become less accurate over time [46]. Dietary self-monitoring can be burdensome, resulting in non-compliance and underestimation [47], potentially explaining the increase in underreporting across pregnancy. Alternative methods of collecting dietary intake data, including remote food photography, are gaining popularity but further validation studies are needed [48].

Table 4. Summary of associations between participant characteristics and energy intake underreporting.

Predictor	Relationship with underreporting
Gestational age	Greater underreporting in later pregnancy
Pre-pregnancy BMI	Greater underreporting with higher BMI
Gestational weight gain	Greater underreporting with greater weekly weight gain
Maternal age	No association
Parity	No association
Household Income	No association
Perceived stress	Less underreporting during weeks when participant indicated higher stress than their usual stress level
Emotional eating	Less underreporting during months when participant indicated higher emotional eating than their usual level
Cognitive restraint	No association
Uncontrolled eating	No association

This study adds to research showing underreporting is associated with pre-pregnancy BMI, with many of the previous studies on this topic including a majority of women with normal weight [27,49–51]. Though there was no significant relationship between total GWG and underreporting in this sample, we observed a positive relationship between changes in weekly GWG and underreporting. Higher weekly GWG may lead to increased underreporting through desirability bias. Meanwhile, underreporting could result in difficulty in self-monitoring and weight management. In contrast, Shiraishi found underreporters had lower total GWG when compared with normal- reporters [52]. More research is needed to elucidate the relationship between GWG and underreporting.

Psychological factors such as social desirability, eating restraint, and history of dieting are associated with underreporting in non-pregnant populations [29]. In addition, Moran found that limiting food intake to lose weight and self-reported dissatisfaction with weight/body shape were predictors of underreporting at 36-weeks' gestation [27]. Very few studies have explored trends in restrained, emotional, and uncontrolled eating across pregnancy. One study found that dietary restraint was lower in the third trimester in comparison with the first, but no change in emotional eating [49].

Less is known about relationships between stress and underreporting during pregnancy, although positive associations were found in non-pregnant samples [29]. Contrary to our hypothesis, within-person fluctuations in perceived stress and emotional eating were negatively associated with underreporting in this sample. Emotionally salient information is typically better remembered than neutral information [53], and individuals with emotional eating have been shown to report greater dietary intake than individuals without emotional eating [54], especially during times of perceived stress [55]. This seems to be independent of dietary intake in non-pregnant samples [56]. For many people, pregnancy is a time of increased psychological distress [57]. Individual differences have been observed in food intake response to stress, with approximately 40% increasing, 40% decreasing, and 20% not changing dietary intake [58]. There may be something unique about prenatal stress that produces a tendency to reduce dietary intake, thus providing less opportunity for reporting error.

A variety of factors have been attributed to poor reporting of EI, including incomplete recordkeeping, conscious underreporting, changes in eating behavior from diet tracking, training, and quality control [29]. Common advice during pregnancy is to snack more often to meet additional kcal needs or combat morning sickness, and this may contribute to underreporting [59]. Future studies should explore additional factors that may influence within-person variation in underreporting which may include day of week (e.g., weekend vs. weekday), types of foods (e.g., snacks, beverages), selective underreporting of nutrients (e.g., fat or carbohydrates), frequency of consumption (e.g., unplanned eating, snacking), and other factors which vary from day to day.

MHealth technologies are increasingly popular among both healthcare providers and patients [60]. While the use of dietary and weight-tracking mobile apps, including MyFitnessPal, for self-monitoring of EI and weight have produced clinically significant weight loss in randomized controlled trials of non-pregnant people [61], our findings suggest users of diet-tracking apps may have difficulty self-monitoring intake due to systematic underreporting. Improving connectivity between weight, physical activity, and dietary mobile data would allow for use of predictive equations to back calculate EI within mHealth apps to give users a better understanding of their actual dietary intake and clinician guidance in counseling women during pregnancy to better manage weight.

In contrast to previous studies [27,28], we found no significant association of reporting error with the following: age, income, parity, or total GWG. Moran found socioeconomic status was an independent predictor at 36 weeks of EI underreporting. McGowan found young women were more likely to underreport than older women during pregnancy [51]. Thomas found higher income predicted higher underreporting [28]. One explanation for lack of association in our study is we had a relatively small, homogenous sample, which reduced our ability to detect relationships with demographics. Further research should explore characteristics associated with underreporting across gestation.

Findings from this study have important implications for behavioral interventions and research on dietary intake in pregnancy. Our data reinforce that underreporting is pervasive during pregnancy, especially in individuals with obesity. Participants in this sample underreported by an average of 986 kcal in trimester one, 1280 kcal in trimester two, and 1386 kcal in trimester three. Prenatal clinicians and intervention specialists should incorporate methods to improve reporting accuracy (e.g., multiple-pass 24 h recalls) [62] and be aware of social desirability bias in underreporting (e.g., higher BMI/gestational age). If self-reported EI is habitual, baseline self-reported EI may be an important indicator of participant consciousness level and sustained intervention efficacy. Finally, using predictive equations to estimate back-calculated EI may be a useful clinical and research tool, considering prevalence and magnitude of underreporting.

Strengths of this study include intensive longitudinal data collected throughout pregnancy, using reporting error as a continuous variable, as well as using measured weight and physical activity to determine back-calculated EI. There are also significant limitations to the results of this study. Limitations to this research include reliance on self-reported pre-pregnancy weight, which can lead to underestimated BMI [63]. In addition, the small sample size precludes the ability to make assumptions at a population level. Differences between actual and reported EI were calculated using an equation of approximation rather than gold standard measures (e.g., doubly labeled water). Although the equation accounts for factors relevant to weight change and gestational age in pregnancy, the equation relies on several assumptions (e.g., fetal physical activity in the womb is negligible) and does not account for all potential factors that can influence GWG (e.g., medications, genetics, obstetric complications). Finally, this was a homogenous sample of participants who were predominantly educated, non-Hispanic white, married, and middle-to-upper income, from central Pennsylvania, and enrolled in a GWG intervention, thus limiting the generalizability of the study findings to other populations of pregnant persons. Future research may extend these findings with a larger, more diverse sample. Research should also continue to explore interventions that promote reporting accuracy during pregnancy to improve patient adherence to EI recommendations to manage GWG.

5. Conclusions

Energy balance is essential for weight management during pregnancy, though this is difficult to monitor due to poor reporting of EI. Using a predictive equation to estimate EI, we found that underreporting using a popular diet-tracking mobile app was positively associated with pre-pregnancy BMI, weekly GWG, and gestational age across pregnancy, and negatively associated with perceived stress and emotional eating. These findings have implications for research and prenatal nutrition counseling and there is a need to develop efficacious interventions that improve reporting accuracy during pregnancy to promote maternal and child health. Research should also continue to explore which tools are most effective in improving reporting accuracy to promote positive pregnancy outcomes in individuals with overweight and obesity.

Author Contributions: K.M.M., E.E.H. and J.S.S.: drafted the manuscript; K.M.M., E.E.H. and A.M.P.: analyzed the data; D.E.R. and P.G.: involved in initial design of the study and energy balance model used for back-calculated energy intake formula; A.D.G. and J.S.S.: involved in study design, selection of study measures, and development of protocols; D.S.D.: designed the study and is the Principal Investigator on the NIH grant that supported the work. All authors have read and agreed to the published version of the manuscript.

Funding: This research was funded by the National Heart, Lung, and Blood Institute (NHLBI) of the National Institutes of Health (NIH) through grants R01 HL119245-01 and R56-HL126799. Additional support was by the National Center for Advancing Translational Sciences and National Institutes of Health (NIH), through Grants UL1 TR000127 and TR002014. The sponsors did not influence study design; data collection, analysis, and interpretation; writing of the report; or the decision to submit the article for publication.

Institutional Review Board Statement: The study was conducted in accordance with the Declaration of Helsinki, and approved by the Institutional Review Board (or Ethics Committee) of the Pennsylvania State University. Approval Code: STUDY00003752. Approval Date: 12 January 2015.

Informed Consent Statement: Informed consent was obtained from all subjects involved in the study.

Data Availability Statement: Data will be made available upon request.

Acknowledgments: We thank the Healthy Mom Zone participants and team who assisted with participant recruitment and data collection for this study.

Conflicts of Interest: The authors declare no conflict of interest.

References

1. Flegal, K.M.; Kruszon-Moran, D.; Carroll, M.D.; Fryar, C.D.; Ogden, C.L. Trends in Obesity Among Adults in the United States, 2005 to 2014. *JAMA* **2016**, *315*, 2284–2291. [CrossRef] [PubMed]
2. Haugen, M.; Brantsaeter, A.L.; Winkvist, A.; Lissner, L.; Alexander, J.; Oftedal, B.; Magnus, P.; Meltzer, H.M. Associations of pre-pregnancy body mass index and gestational weight gain with pregnancy outcome and postpartum weight retention: A prospective observational cohort study. *BMC Pregnancy Childbirth* **2014**, *14*, 201. [CrossRef] [PubMed]
3. Nehring, I.; Schmoll, S.; Beyerlein, A.; Hauner, H.; von Kries, R. Gestational weight gain and long-term postpartum weight retention: A meta-analysis. *Am. J. Clin. Nutr.* **2011**, *94*, 1225–1231. [CrossRef] [PubMed]
4. Vesco, K.K.; Dietz, P.M.; Rizzo, J.; Stevens, V.J.; Perrin, N.A.; Bachman, D.J.; Callaghan, W.M.; Bruce, F.C.; Hornbrook, M.C. Excessive gestational weight gain and postpartum weight retention among obese women. *Obstet. Gynecol.* **2009**, *114*, 1069–1075. [CrossRef]
5. Gunderson, E.P.; Sternfeld, B.; Wellons, M.F.; Whitmer, R.A.; Chiang, V.; Quesenberry, C.P., Jr.; Lewis, C.E.; Sidney, S. Childbearing may increase visceral adipose tissue independent of overall increase in body fat. *Obesity* **2008**, *16*, 1078–1084. [CrossRef]
6. McDonald, S.D.; Han, Z.; Mulla, S.; Beyene, J. Overweight and obesity in mothers and risk of preterm birth and low birth weight infants: Systematic review and meta-analyses. *BMJ* **2010**, *341*, c3428. [CrossRef]
7. Chen, L.W.; Soh, S.E.; Tint, M.T.; Loy, S.L.; Yap, F.; Tan, K.H.; Lee, Y.S.; Shek, L.P.; Godfrey, K.M.; Gluckman, P.D.; et al. Combined analysis of gestational diabetes and maternal weight status from pre-pregnancy through post-delivery in future development of type 2 diabetes. *Sci. Rep.* **2021**, *11*, 5021. [CrossRef]
8. Fu, Z.; Kelley, J.L.; Odunsi, K.; Edwards, R.P.; Moysich, K.; Modugno, F. Gestational weight gain and risk of epithelial ovarian cancer. *Cancer Causes Control* **2021**, *32*, 537–545. [CrossRef]
9. Vesco, K.K.; Sharma, A.J.; Dietz, P.M.; Rizzo, J.H.; Callaghan, W.M.; England, L.; Bruce, F.C.; Bachman, D.J.; Stevens, V.J.; Hornbrook, M.C. Newborn size among obese women with weight gain outside the 2009 Institute of Medicine recommendation. *Obstet. Gynecol.* **2011**, *117*, 812–818. [CrossRef]
10. Hillier, T.A.; Pedula, K.L.; Vesco, K.K.; Schmidt, M.M.; Mullen, J.A.; LeBlanc, E.S.; Pettitt, D.J. Excess gestational weight gain: Modifying fetal macrosomia risk associated with maternal glucose. *Obstet. Gynecol.* **2008**, *112*, 1007–1014. [CrossRef]
11. Schack-Nielsen, L.; Michaelsen, K.F.; Gamborg, M.; Mortensen, E.L.; Sorensen, T.I. Gestational weight gain in relation to offspring body mass index and obesity from infancy through adulthood. *Int. J. Obes.* **2010**, *34*, 67–74. [CrossRef]
12. Bailey, R.L.; Pac, S.G.; Fulgoni, V.L.; Reidy, K.C.; Catalano, P.M. Estimation of Total Usual Dietary Intakes of Pregnant Women in the United States. *JAMA Netw. Open* **2019**, *2*, e195967. [CrossRef]

13. Institute of Medicine. *Nutrition During Pregnancy: Part I Weight Gain: Part II Nutrient Supplements*; The National Academies Press: Washington, DC, USA, 1990.
14. Farpour-Lambert, N.J.; Ells, L.J.; Martinez de Tejada, B.; Scott, C. Obesity and Weight Gain in Pregnancy and Postpartum: An Evidence Review of Lifestyle Interventions to Inform Maternal and Child Health Policies. *Front. Endocrinol.* **2018**, *9*, 546. [CrossRef]
15. Phelan, S.; Jankovitz, K.; Hagobian, T.; Abrams, B. Reducing excessive gestational weight gain: Lessons from the weight control literature and avenues for future research. *Womens Health* **2011**, *7*, 641–661. [CrossRef]
16. Tooze, J.A.; Subar, A.F.; Thompson, F.E.; Troiano, R.; Schatzkin, A.; Kipnis, V. Psychosocial predictors of energy underreporting in a large doubly labeled water study. *Am. J. Clin. Nutr.* **2004**, *79*, 795–804. [CrossRef]
17. Poslusna, K.; Ruprich, J.; de Vries, J.H.; Jakubikova, M.; van't Veer, P. Misreporting of energy and micronutrient intake estimated by food records and 24 hour recalls, control and adjustment methods in practice. *Br. J. Nutr.* **2009**, *101*, S73–S85. [CrossRef]
18. Ventura, A.K.; Loken, E.; Mitchell, D.C.; Smiciklas-Wright, H.; Birch, L.L. Understanding reporting bias in the dietary recall data of 11-year-old girls. *Obesity* **2006**, *14*, 1073–1084. [CrossRef]
19. Bathalon, G.P.; Tucker, K.L.; Hays, N.P.; Vinken, A.G.; Greenberg, A.S.; McCrory, M.A.; Roberts, S.B. Psychological measures of eating behavior and the accuracy of 3 common dietary assessment methods in healthy postmenopausal women. *Am. J. Clin. Nutr.* **2000**, *71*, 739–745. [CrossRef]
20. Poppitt, S.D.; Swann, D.; Black, A.E.; Prentice, A.M. Assessment of selective under-reporting of food intake by both obese and non-obese women in a metabolic facility. *Int. J. Obes. Relat. Metab. Disord.* **1998**, *22*, 303–311. [CrossRef]
21. Lutomski, J.E.; van den Broeck, J.; Harrington, J.; Shiely, F.; Perry, I.J. Sociodemographic, lifestyle, mental health and dietary factors associated with direction of misreporting of energy intake. *Public Health Nutr.* **2011**, *14*, 532–541. [CrossRef]
22. Derbyshire, E.; Davies, G.J.; Costarelli, V.; Dettmar, P.W. Habitual micronutrient intake during and after pregnancy in Caucasian Londoners. *Matern. Child Nutr.* **2009**, *5*, 1–9. [CrossRef]
23. Horan, M.K.; McGowan, C.A.; Gibney, E.R.; Byrne, J.; Donnelly, J.M.; McAuliffe, F.M. Maternal Nutrition and Glycaemic Index during Pregnancy Impacts on Offspring Adiposity at 6 Months of Age—Analysis from the ROLO Randomised Controlled Trial. *Nutrients* **2016**, *8*, 7. [CrossRef]
24. Winkvist, A.; Persson, V.; Hartini, T.N. Underreporting of energy intake is less common among pregnant women in Indonesia. *Public Health Nutr.* **2002**, *5*, 523–529. [CrossRef]
25. Goldberg, G.R.; Black, A.E.; Jebb, S.A.; Cole, T.J.; Murgatroyd, P.R.; Coward, W.A.; Prentice, A.M. Critical evaluation of energy intake data using fundamental principles of energy physiology: 1. Derivation of cut-off limits to identify under-recording. *Eur. J. Clin. Nutr.* **1991**, *45*, 569–581.
26. Ariens, S.; Ceulemans, E.; Adolf, J.K. Time series analysis of intensive longitudinal data in psychosomatic research: A methodological overview. *J. Psychosom. Res.* **2020**, *137*, 110191. [CrossRef]
27. Moran, L.J.; McNaughton, S.A.; Sui, Z.; Cramp, C.; Deussen, A.R.; Grivell, R.M.; Dodd, J.M. The characterisation of overweight and obese women who are under reporting energy intake during pregnancy. *BMC Pregnancy Childbirth* **2018**, *18*, 204. [CrossRef]
28. Thomas, D.M.; Bredlau, C.; Islam, S.; Armah, K.A.; Kunnipparampil, J.; Patel, K.; Redman, L.M.; Misra, D.; Salafia, C. Relationships between misreported energy intake and pregnancy in the pregnancy, infection and nutrition study: New insights from a dynamic energy balance model. *Obes. Sci. Pract.* **2016**, *2*, 174–179. [CrossRef] [PubMed]
29. Maurer, J.; Taren, D.L.; Teixeira, P.J.; Thomson, C.A.; Lohman, T.G.; Going, S.B.; Houtkooper, L.B. The psychosocial and behavioral characteristics related to energy misreporting. *Nutr. Rev.* **2006**, *64*, 53–66. [CrossRef] [PubMed]
30. Downs, D.S.; Savage, J.S.; Rivera, D.E.; Pauley, A.M.; Leonard, K.S.; Hohman, E.E.; Guo, P.; McNitt, K.M.; Stetter, C.; Kunselman, A. Adaptive, behavioral intervention impact on weight gain, physical activity, energy intake, and motivational determinants: Results of a feasibility trial in pregnant women with overweight/obesity. *J. Behav. Med.* **2021**, *44*, 605–621. [CrossRef] [PubMed]
31. Wilbur, J.; Kolanowski, A.M.; Collins, L.M. Utilizing MOST frameworks and SMART designs for intervention research. *Nurs. Outlook* **2016**, *64*, 287–289. [CrossRef] [PubMed]
32. Symons Downs, D.; Savage, J.S.; Rivera, D.E.; Smyth, J.M.; Rolls, B.J.; Hohman, E.E.; McNitt, K.M.; Kunselman, A.R.; Stetter, C.; Pauley, A.M.; et al. Individually Tailored, Adaptive Intervention to Manage Gestational Weight Gain: Protocol for a Randomized Controlled Trial in Women with Overweight and Obesity. *JMIR Res. Protoc.* **2018**, *7*, e150. [CrossRef]
33. Cappelleri, J.C.; Bushmakin, A.G.; Gerber, R.A.; Leidy, N.K.; Sexton, C.C.; Lowe, M.R.; Karlsson, J. Psychometric analysis of the Three-Factor Eating Questionnaire-R21: Results from a large diverse sample of obese and non-obese participants. *Int. J. Obes.* **2009**, *33*, 611–620. [CrossRef]
34. Harris, P.A.; Taylor, R.; Minor, B.L.; Elliott, V.; Fernandez, M.; O'Neal, L.; McLeod, L.; Delacqua, G.; Delacqua, F.; Kirby, J.; et al. The REDCap consortium: Building an international community of software platform partners. *J. Biomed. Inform.* **2019**, *95*, 103208. [CrossRef]
35. Cohen, S.; Kamarck, T.; Mermelstein, R. A global measure of perceived stress. *J. Health Soc. Behav.* **1983**, *24*, 385–396. [CrossRef]
36. Jimoh, F.; Lund, E.K.; Harvey, L.J.; Frost, C.; Lay, W.J.; Roe, M.A.; Berry, R.; Finglas, P.M. Comparing Diet and Exercise Monitoring Using Smartphone App and Paper Diary: A Two-Phase Intervention Study. *JMIR mHealth uHealth* **2018**, *6*, e17. [CrossRef]
37. Butte, N.F.; Wong, W.W.; Treuth, M.S.; Ellis, K.J.; O'Brian Smith, E. Energy requirements during pregnancy based on total energy expenditure and energy deposition. *Am. J. Clin. Nutr.* **2004**, *79*, 1078–1087. [CrossRef]

38. Guo, P.; Rivera, D.E.; Downs, D.S.; Savage, J.S. Semi-physical Identification and State Estimation of Energy Intake for Interventions to Manage Gestational Weight Gain. In Proceedings of the 2016 American Control Conference (ACC), Boston, MA, USA, 6–8 July 2016; Volume 2016, pp. 1271–1276. [CrossRef]
39. Pauley, A.M.; Hohman, E.; Savage, J.S.; Rivera, D.E.; Guo, P.; Leonard, K.S.; Symons Downs, D. Gestational Weight Gain Intervention Impacts Determinants of Healthy Eating and Exercise in Overweight/Obese Pregnant Women. *J. Obes.* **2018**, *2018*, 6469170. [CrossRef]
40. Ferguson, T.; Rowlands, A.V.; Olds, T.; Maher, C. The validity of consumer-level, activity monitors in healthy adults worn in free-living conditions: A cross-sectional study. *Int. J. Behav. Nutr. Phys. Act.* **2015**, *12*, 42. [CrossRef]
41. Storm, F.A.; Heller, B.W.; Mazzà, C. Step detection and activity recognition accuracy of seven physical activity monitors. *PLoS ONE* **2015**, *10*, e0118723. [CrossRef]
42. Guo, P.; Rivera, D.E.; Pauley, A.M.; Leonard, K.S.; Savage, J.S.; Downs, D.S. A "Model-on-Demand" Methodology for Energy Intake Estimation to Improve Gestational Weight Control Interventions. In Proceedings of the IFAC World Congress. International Federation of Automatic Control World Congress, Stockholm, Sweden, 9–11 July 2018; Volume 51, pp. 144–149. [CrossRef]
43. Black, A.E.; Prentice, A.M.; Goldberg, G.R.; Jebb, S.A.; Bingham, S.A.; Livingstone, M.B.; Coward, W.A. Measurements of total energy expenditure provide insights into the validity of dietary measurements of energy intake. *J. Am. Diet. Assoc.* **1993**, *93*, 572–579. [CrossRef]
44. Cnaan, A.; Laird, N.M.; Slasor, P. Using the general linear mixed model to analyse unbalanced repeated measures and longitudinal data. *Stat. Med.* **1997**, *16*, 2349–2380. [CrossRef]
45. McNeish, D.; Harring, J. Covariance pattern mixture models: Eliminating random effects to improve convergence and performance. *Behav. Res. Methods* **2020**, *52*, 947–979. [CrossRef]
46. Chen, J.; Cade, J.E.; Allman-Farinelli, M. The Most Popular Smartphone Apps for Weight Loss: A Quality Assessment. *JMIR mHealth uHealth* **2015**, *3*, e104. [CrossRef]
47. Rebro, S.M.; Patterson, R.E.; Kristal, A.R.; Cheney, C.L. The effect of keeping food records on eating patterns. *J. Am. Diet. Assoc.* **1998**, *98*, 1163–1165. [CrossRef]
48. Gemming, L.; Utter, J.; Ni Mhurchu, C. Image-assisted dietary assessment: A systematic review of the evidence. *J. Acad. Nutr. Diet.* **2015**, *115*, 64–77. [CrossRef]
49. Lindsay, K.L.; Heneghan, C.; McNulty, B.; Brennan, L.; McAuliffe, F.M. Lifestyle and dietary habits of an obese pregnant cohort. *Matern. Child Health J.* **2015**, *19*, 25–32. [CrossRef]
50. Mullaney, L.; O'Higgins, A.C.; Cawley, S.; Doolan, A.; McCartney, D.; Turner, M.J. An estimation of periconceptional under-reporting of dietary energy intake. *J. Public Health* **2015**, *37*, 728–736. [CrossRef] [PubMed]
51. McGowan, C.A.; McAuliffe, F.M. Maternal nutrient intakes and levels of energy underreporting during early pregnancy. *Eur. J. Clin. Nutr.* **2012**, *66*, 906–913. [CrossRef] [PubMed]
52. Shiraishi, M.; Haruna, M.; Matsuzaki, M.; Murayama, R.; Sasaki, S. Pre-pregnancy BMI, gestational weight gain and body image are associated with dietary under-reporting in pregnant Japanese women. *J. Nutr. Sci.* **2018**, *7*, e12. [CrossRef] [PubMed]
53. Mather, M.; Sutherland, M.R. Arousal-Biased Competition in Perception and Memory. *Perspect. Psychol. Sci.* **2011**, *6*, 114–133. [CrossRef] [PubMed]
54. Vansant, G.; Hulens, M. The assessment of dietary habits in obese women: Influence of eating behavior patterns. *Eat. Disord.* **2006**, *14*, 121–129. [CrossRef]
55. Royal, J.D.; Kurtz, J.L. I ate what?! The effect of stress and dispositional eating style on food intake and behavioral awareness. *Pers. Individ. Dif.* **2010**, *49*, 565–569. [CrossRef]
56. Wallis, D.J.; Hetherington, M.M. Emotions and eating. Self-reported and experimentally induced changes in food intake under stress. *Appetite* **2009**, *52*, 355–362. [CrossRef]
57. Furber, C.M.; Garrod, D.; Maloney, E.; Lovell, K.; McGowan, L. A qualitative study of mild to moderate psychological distress during pregnancy. *Int. J. Nurs. Stud.* **2009**, *46*, 669–677. [CrossRef]
58. Pasquali, R. The hypothalamic-pituitary-adrenal axis and sex hormones in chronic stress and obesity: Pathophysiological and clinical aspects. *Ann. N. Y. Acad. Sci.* **2012**, *1264*, 20–35. [CrossRef]
59. Garden, L.; Clark, H.; Whybrow, S.; Stubbs, R.J. Is misreporting of dietary intake by weighed food records or 24-hour recalls food specific? *Eur. J. Clin. Nutr.* **2018**, *72*, 1026–1034. [CrossRef]
60. Ricciardi, L.; Mostashari, F.; Murphy, J.; Daniel, J.G.; Siminerio, E.P. A national action plan to support consumer engagement via e-health. *Health Aff.* **2013**, *32*, 376–384. [CrossRef]
61. Patel, M.L.; Hopkins, C.M.; Brooks, T.L.; Bennett, G.G. Comparing Self-Monitoring Strategies for Weight Loss in a Smartphone App: Randomized Controlled Trial. *JMIR mHealth uHealth* **2019**, *7*, e12209. [CrossRef]
62. Carroll, R.J.; Midthune, D.; Subar, A.F.; Shumakovich, M.; Freedman, L.S.; Thompson, F.E.; Kipnis, V. Taking advantage of the strengths of 2 different dietary assessment instruments to improve intake estimates for nutritional epidemiology. *Am. J. Epidemiol.* **2012**, *175*, 340–347. [CrossRef]
63. Natamba, B.K.; Sanchez, S.E.; Gelaye, B.; Williams, M.A. Concordance between self-reported pre-pregnancy body mass index (BMI) and BMI measured at the first prenatal study contact. *BMC Pregnancy Childbirth* **2016**, *16*, 187. [CrossRef]

nutrients

MDPI

Article

Association and Interaction Effect of *BHMT* Gene Polymorphisms and Maternal Dietary Habits with Ventricular Septal Defect in Offspring

Manjun Luo [1], Tingting Wang [2,*], Peng Huang [3], Senmao Zhang [1], Xinli Song [1], Mengting Sun [1], Yiping Liu [1], Jianhui Wei [1], Jing Shu [1], Taowei Zhong [1], Qian Chen [1], Ping Zhu [4,*] and Jiabi Qin [1,2,4,5,6,*]

1 Department of Epidemiology and Health Statistics, Xiangya School of Public Health, Central South University, Changsha 410078, China; lmj1990dlh@163.com (M.L.); zsmhncs@163.com (S.Z.); xinlisong@foxmail.com (X.S.); sunmtbeloved@163.com (M.S.); 18843113354@163.com (Y.L.); weijihi@163.com (J.W.); sj1234511@163.com (J.S.); taoweizhong98@163.com (T.Z.); chenqian07172022@163.com (Q.C.)

2 National Health Committee Key Laboratory of Birth Defect for Research and Prevention, Hunan Provincial Maternal and Child Health Care Hospital, Changsha 410028, China

3 Department of Cardiothoracic Surgery, Hunan Children's Hospital, Changsha 410007, China; hpeng1979@163.com

4 Guangdong Cardiovascular Institute, Guangdong Provincial People's Hospital, Guangdong Academy of Medical Sciences, Guangzhou 510080, China

5 Hunan Provincial Key Laboratory of Clinical Epidemiology, Changsha 410078, China

6 Guangdong Provincial Key Laboratory of Pathogenesis, Targeted Prevention and Treatment of Heart Disease, Guangzhou 510640, China

* Correspondence: wangting91123@126.com (T.W.); zhuping6588@163.com (P.Z.); qinjiabi123@163.com (J.Q.)

Abstract: This study attempted to learn the association between maternal betaine-homocysteine methyltransferase (*BHMT*) gene polymorphisms, maternal dietary habits, and their interactions with the risk of ventricular septal defects (VSD) in offspring. A total of 426 mothers of VSD children and 740 control mothers were included in the study. Logistic regression was used to evaluate the level of associations and interaction effects. Our study suggested that mothers reporting excessive intake of smoked foods (aOR = 2.44, 95%CI: 1.89–3.13), barbecued foods (aOR = 1.86, 95%CI: 1.39–2.48), fried foods (aOR = 1.93, 95%CI: 1.51–2.46), and pickled vegetables (aOR = 2.50, 95%CI: 1.92–3.25) were at a significantly higher risk of VSD in offspring, instead, mothers reporting regular intake of fresh fruits (aOR = 0.47, 95%CI: 0.36–0.62), fish and shrimp (aOR = 0.35, 95%CI: 0.28–0.44), fresh eggs, (aOR = 0.56, 95%CI: 0.45–0.71), beans (aOR = 0.68, 95%CI: 0.56–0.83), and milk products (aOR = 0.67, 95%CI: 0.56–0.80) were at a lower risk of VSD in offspring. In addition, maternal *BHMT* gene polymorphisms at rs1316753 (CG vs. CC: aOR = 2.01, 95%CI: 1.43–2.83) and rs1915706 (CT vs. TT: (aOR = 1.81, 95%CI: 1.33–2.46) were significantly associated with increased risk of VSD in offspring. Furthermore, a significant interaction between *BHMT* polymorphisms and maternal bean intake was identified in the study. In conclusion, Maternal *BHMT* polymorphisms at rs1316753 and rs1915706, dietary habits as well as their interaction were observed to be significantly associated with the risk of VSD in offspring.

Keywords: ventricular septal defects; *BHMT* gene plolymorphisms; dietary habits; interaction effects

Citation: Luo, M.; Wang, T.; Huang, P.; Zhang, S.; Song, X.; Sun, M.; Liu, Y.; Wei, J.; Shu, J.; Zhong, T.; et al. Association and Interaction Effect of *BHMT* Gene Polymorphisms and Maternal Dietary Habits with Ventricular Septal Defect in Offspring. *Nutrients* **2022**, *14*, 3094. https://doi.org/10.3390/nu14153094

Academic Editors: Louise Brough, Gail Rees and Jamileh Movassat

Received: 20 May 2022
Accepted: 25 July 2022
Published: 28 July 2022

1. Introduction

Congenital heart disease (CHD) is typically defined as a gross structural abnormality of the heart and/or great vessels that is present at birth [1,2]. It has been reported that the birth prevalence of CHD has increased significantly since the 1930s and reached a maximum of over 9 per 1000 live births since 1995 [1,3]. Ventricular septal defect (VSD) has been recognized as the most common congenital cardiac malformation and accounts for roughly 30–40% of all cardiac anomalies [1,4]. Over the past decades, considerable inherited causes and noninherited modifiable factors have been implicated in the development of CHD and its subgroups [5–8]. Recently, there has been a consensus that genetic factors and environmental factors interact in the etiology of most nonsyndromal forms of CHD [9,10], naturally including VSD.

A recent review showed strong evidence that oral prenatal fortification and supplementation dosing of folic acid (FA) can prevent the incidence of VSD and atrial septal defect (ASD) [11]. Women with a diverse diet during pregnancy (dietary diversity score, DDS $\geq$5) had lower risks of having fetuses with total CHD and VSD [12]. Furthermore, the dietary intake of vitamins and minerals was found to be associated with a reduced risk of CHD in offspring, including B-vitamin, vitamin D, zinc, and selenium [13–15]. Since different nutrients interact with one another in many metabolic pathways, it seems that the association would not remain constant when various nutrients coexist in the same food. In addition, the dietary pattern differs a lot owing to the discrepancy in economics, geographical environment, social culture, race, and so on. Therefore, the first concern we would care to discuss is the association between maternal dietary habits and VSD in offspring.

The human betaine-homocysteine methyltransferase (BHMT) gene maps to 5q13.1–q15, spans about 20 kilobases of DNA and contains eight exons and seven introns [16,17]. The enzyme it encodes, betaine-homocysteine methyltransferase, catalyzes the transfer of a methyl group from betaine to homocysteine (Hcy), forming dimethylglycine and methionine. Generally, the homeostasis of plasma homocysteine benefits from the transulfuration pathway involving cystathionine β synthase (CBS) and the remethylation pathway involving BHMT, BHMT2, and methionine synthase (MS) (Figure 1) [18]. In the latter pathway, the catalytic activity of BHMT2 is absolutely diet-dependent since its substrate, S-methylmethionine, can only be biosynthesized by various plants mainly belonging to the Brassicaceae family rather than mammals [19,20]. Experimental research conducted in mice suggested that BHMT is a predominant enzyme for the elimination of Hcy while the MS has little excess capacity to methylate the Hcy [18]. Therefore, the remethylation reaction catalyzed by BHMT seems to play a vital role in preventing the toxic accumulation of Hcy. In fact, BHMT catalyzes up to 50% of homocysteine metabolism in the human liver, where the enzyme is highly expressed [21,22]. The latest literature revealed that elevated Hcy concentrations acted as a risk factor for multiple congenital anomalies in human production, mainly comprising neural tube defects (NTD), orofacial clefts, and CHD [23–25]. The discovery has been generally accepted that the 677 C$\rightarrow$T mutation in the methylenetetrahydrofolate reductase (MTHFR) gene contributed to elevated tHcy and is a genetic risk factor for diseases associated with hyperhomocysteinaemia [26]. Moreover, this mutation has been applied to antenatal screening for pregnant women in China. The thought naturally emerged that polymorphisms of the BHMT gene exist that reduce BHMT activity and increase plasma Hcy levels and thus increase malformation risk. In fact, research has been dedicated to exploring the association between BHMT gene polymorphisms and CHD, but with fixed results and little involving subgroups of CHD [27–30]. In this study, we focused on the largest subcategory of CHD, namely, VSD, to detect its association with polymorphisms of the maternal BHMT gene.

In addition, betaine, the substrate of BHMT, can be either obtained from food resources or produced from choline endogenously [31]. Likewise, choline can also be produced endogenously via the hepatic phosphatidylethanolamine N-methyltransferase (PEMT) pathway. However, most people must consume this nutrient exogenously to prevent deficiency [32]. Therefore, the BHMT activity, to a certain degree, is diet dependent. Animal studies did observe that pane of nutrition or the supply of some nutrients, including choline and methionine, can alter BHMT activity [33–35]. In addition, it has been reported that women with a high intake of one-carbon cofactors had a lower risk of congenital anomalies in offspring, such as the neural tube defect (NTD) and perimembranous ventricular septal defect (VSD_{pm}) [36,37]. Overall, these valuable clues were collected to put forward a reasonable hypothesis that BHMT gene polymorphisms may interact with maternal dietary habits on congenital anomalies.

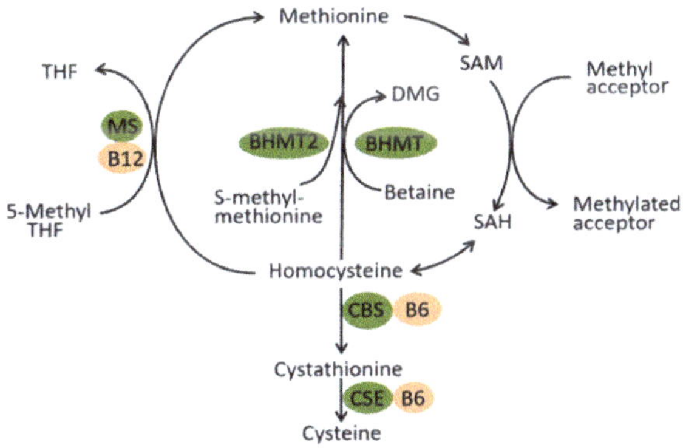

Figure 1. Pathways of homocysteine metabolism. Abbreviation: BHMT Betaine-homocysteine S-methyltransferase; MS methionine synthase; CBS cystathionine β-synthase; CSE cystathionine-γ-lyase; THF tetrahydrofolate; DMG dimethylglycine; SAM S-adenosylmethionine; SAH S-adenosylhomocysteine.

In this study, we determined VSD, the most common subgroup in CHD, as the interested outcome variable, which is relatively more sensitive to maternal nutrient intake. A hospital-based case-control study was carried out in an attempt to learn the following questions: a. the association of maternal dietary habits with risk of VSD in offspring; b. the association of polymorphisms of maternal BHMT gene with risk of VSD in offspring; c. the interaction between BHMT genetic variants and maternal dietary habits on VSD.

2. Materials and Methods

2.1. Design and Participants

This is a hospital-based case-control study that started in February 2018 and was over in March 2020. The cases and controls came from different departments in the same hospital, Hunan children's hospital, which is famous partly for its sophisticated diagnosis and treatment techniques for CHD within the province. Considering the characteristics of the relatively low incidence of VSD compared with other chronic diseases, a convenient sampling method was used in the recruitment of the cases. VSD children, verified by both doppler echocardiography and surgery, were consecutively recruited from the Department of Cardiothoracic Surgery. Children in the control, free of any congenital malformations, were randomly selected from the Department of Child Healthcare. It is worth noting that cases only included VSD children that may or may not be diagnosed with other congenital heart diseases; those coexisting with any other extra-cardiac malformations were excluded from the study. Additionally, informed consent was obtained from all of the participants, and the possible consequences of the study were explained. The exclusion criterions mainly included: minority mothers, mothers conceiving children through in vitro fertilization or other conception methods, adoptive mothers or stepmothers, and mothers suffering from mental disorders or any other physical diseases so that this did not hinder the provision of accurate exposure information and blood samples. Finally, a total of 426 mothers of VSD children and 740 control mothers were included in the study.

The protocol of this study was in accordance with the guidelines of the 1964 Helsinki Declaration, and the Ethics Committee of Xiangya School of Public Health, Central South University, officially approved this study in January 2018. (no. XYGW-2018-36).

2.2. Information Collection

The outcome we focused on in the study was VSD in offspring, which was diagnosed by professional physicians via both doppler echocardiography and surgery. The interested exposures were maternal dietary habits in early pregnancy, which were collected from a self-designed food frequency questionnaire. We consulted The Dietary Guidelines for Chinese Residents and went deep into the local food culture to develop the questionnaire. Eleven main categories were determined, involving smoked foods, barbecued foods, fried foods, pickled vegetables, fresh vegetables, fresh fruits, fresh meat, fish and shrimp, fresh eggs, beans, and milk products. Each category was provided with three choices: a. hardly (less than or equal to two times per week); b. sometimes (three to five times per week); c. often (more than or equal to six times per week). The questionnaire was pre-investigated using eligible mothers (test–retest reliability: $r = 0.826$; internal consistency: $\alpha = 0.769$).

In addition, we also collected various pieces of maternal information that might influence the outcomes of their offspring, mainly including the child-bearing age (<35 years or ≥35 years), pre-pregnancy BMI (calculated with their pre-pregnancy height and weight, <18.5, 18.5–23.9, 24–26.9, or ≥27), education level (less than primary or primary, junior high school, high school or technical secondary school, college or above), consanguineous marriages (yes or no), gestational diabetes mellitus (yes or no), gestational hypertension (yes or no), abnormal pregnancy history before this pregnancy (yes or no), congenital malformations in family members (yes or no), exposure of environmental pollutants (yes or no), antibiotic use in early pregnancy (yes or no), tobacco exposure in early pregnancy (yes or no), alcohol exposure in early pregnancy (yes or no), and periconceptional folate use (yes or no).

An epidemiological survey was conducted by well-trained investigators when participants were waiting for their operation arrangements in the wards or medical check-ups in the Department of Child Health. In China, every expectant mother has a personal Maternal and Child Health Manual, which provides their sociodemographic information, the results of regular medical check-ups, and necessary exposure information. So, in the course of the investigation, we consulted the participants' manual to further confirm the abovementioned information obtained from face-to-face interviews, which enabled us to reduce recall bias to a certain extent.

2.3. Sample Collection and Genotyping

Five milliliters of peripheral venous blood were collected from every single participant after the face-to-face interview. All of the obtained blood samples would be brought back to the laboratory at low temperatures (≤4 °C) within twelve hours and then divided into two layers using a high-speed centrifuge: the blood cell layer and the plasma layer. Both were stored in an ultra-low-temperature freezer until genotyping. The DNA was extracted from the blood cell samples with the QIAamp DNA Blood Mini Kit (Qiagen, Valencia, CA, USA). Genotyping was performed by matrix-assisted laser desorption and ionization time-of-flight mass spectrometry MassARRAY system (Agena iPLEX assay, San Diego, CA, USA). The laboratory technicians who performed SNP detection and recorded the genotype data were blind to whether each sample was from the cases or controls, thereby reducing selection bias to some extent.

Before genotyping, we consulted the NCBI and HapMap databases to determine the major SNP sites of the *BHMT* gene and simultaneously excluded the SNPs whose minor allele frequencies (MAF) were less than 10%. Furthermore, we imposed a minimum SNP genotyping call rate at the level of 50%, which was applied to ensure the data integrity of the individual's genotypes. Moreover, the success rates for the SNPlex assays were >94% for 2 SNPs, from 90 to 94% for 2 SNPs. Finally, these genetic loci (rs3733890, rs1316753, rs567754, and rs1915706) were selected as candidate loci for this study.

2.4. Statistical Analysis

The data for the qualitative variables were expressed as absolute numbers (percentages). The chi-square test was used to assess the differences in qualitative variables across groups. The Hardy–Weinberg equilibrium (HWE) test was used to compare the differences in genotype distribution frequency in the control group (significance level at $p < 0.01$). We utilized a logistic regression model to detect whether the association between maternal dietary habits in early pregnancy, *BHMT* gene polymorphisms, and VSD in offspring existed and the level of the association. Both univariate and multivariate logistic regressions were adopted; the crude odds ratio (cOR) and its 95% confidential intervals (CI) were calculated by the former one without any adjustment; the adjusted odds ratio (aOR) and its 95% confidential intervals (CI) were calculated by the latter one, which adjusted for the significant confounders found using the chi-square test. For the significant SNPs and maternal dietary habits, these originally ternary variables were converted into binary variables. We then introduced all of the potential confounders, genetic factors, environmental factors, and their multiplicative interaction term into the same logistic regression model to determine the presence or absence of gene–environment interaction and assess its significance. When it comes to multiple hypothesis testing, the false discovery rate (FDR) based on the Benjamini–Hochberg method was used to correct for bias. A false discovery rate P value (FDR_P) of <0.1 was considered to be statistically significant. The calculation of FDR_P was completed using R software (version 4.1.3, stats package). Basic analyses were performed using SPSS 26.0 software (SPSS Inc., Chicago, IL, USA). The statistically significant results were those with the two-sided p-value < 0.05, except where otherwise specified.

3. Results

3.1. Comparison of Maternal Baseline Characteristics

In the study, we recruited a total of 426 mothers of VSD children for cases and 740 mothers of non-congenital malformation children for controls. The selection of participants conformed strictly to the pre-made inclusion and exclusion criteria. The median (interquartile range) age of the children the in cases and controls was 8.4 (5.7) months and 7.8 (4.3) months, respectively. The comparisons of the maternal baseline characteristics between cases and controls are summarized in Table 1. There were statistically significant differences between the two groups in the following factors: pre-pregnancy BMI, education level, consanguineous marriages, gestational diabetes mellitus, gestational hypertension, abnormal pregnancy history before this pregnancy, congenital malformations in family members, exposure to environmental pollutants, antibiotic use in early pregnancy, tobacco exposure in early pregnancy, alcohol exposure in early pregnancy, and periconceptional folate use (all p values < 0.05). These abovementioned factors would be adjusted as confounders when evaluating the association of maternal dietary habits, SNPs of the *BHMT* gene, and their interactions with VSD in offspring.

3.2. Maternal Dietary Habits and the Risk of VSD in Offspring

The association of maternal dietary intake in early pregnancy with the risk of VSD in offspring is shown in Table 2. Both univariate and multivariate logistic regression indicated that smoked foods, barbecued foods, fried foods, pickled vegetables, fresh fruits, fish and shrimp, fresh eggs, beans, and milk products were significantly associated with the risk of VSD in offspring. Specifically, children were predisposed to VSD when their mothers reported excessive intake of smoked foods (aOR = 2.44, 95%CI: 1.89–3.13), barbecued foods (aOR = 1.86, 95%CI: 1.39–2.48), fried foods (aOR = 1.93, 95%CI: 1.51–2.46), and pickled vegetables (aOR = 2.50, 95%CI: 1.92–3.25). Instead, a significantly decreased risk of VSD was observed in children whose mothers reported regular intake of fresh fruits (aOR = 0.47, 95%CI: 0.36–0.62), fish and shrimp (aOR = 0.35, 95%CI: 0.28–0.44), fresh eggs, (aOR = 0.56, 95%CI: 0.45–0.71), beans (aOR = 0.68, 95%CI: 0.56–0.83), and milk products (aOR = 0.67, 95%CI: 0.56–0.80).

Table 1. Comparison of maternal baseline characteristics in cases and controls.

Baseline Characteristics	Control Group (n = 740)	Case Group (n = 426)	χ^2	p
Child-bearing age (years)			0.912	0.340
<35	635(85.8%)	374(87.8%)		
≥35	105(14.2%)	52(12.2%)		
Pre-pregnancy BMI [a]				
<18.5	192(25.9%)	77(18.1%)	11.810	**0.008**
18.5–23.9	406(54.9%)	274(64.3%)		
24–26.9	91(12.3%)	47(11.0%)		
≥27	51(6.9%)	28(6.6%)		
Education level			187.573	**<0.001**
Less than primary or primary	9(1.2%)	43(10.1%)		
Junior high school	144(19.5%)	195(45.8%)		
High school or Technical secondary school	246(33.2%)	123(28.9%)		
College or above	341(46.1%)	65(15.3%)		
Consanguineous marriages			13.989	**<0.001**
No	737(99.6%)	413(96.9%)		
Yes	3(0.4%)	13(3.1%)		
Gestational diabetes mellitus			34.302	<0.001
No	717(96.9%)	376(88.3%)		
Yes	23(3.1%)	50(11.7%)		
Gestational hypertension			23.594	**<0.001**
No	723(97.7%)	390(91.5%)		
Yes	17(2.3%)	36(8.5%)		
Abnormal pregnancy history pregnancy			9.363	**0.002**
No	411(55.5%)	197(46.2%)		
Yes	329(44.5%)	229(53.8%)		
Congenital malformations in family members			19.837	**<0.001**
No	733(99.1%)	404(94.8%)		
Yes	7(0.9%)	22(5.2%)		
Exposure to environmental pollutants			43.687	**<0.001**
No	687(92.8%)	340(79.8%)		
Yes	53(7.2%)	86(20.2%)		
Antibiotic use in early pregnancy			7.234	**0.007**
No	729(98.5%)	409(96.0%)		
Yes	11(1.5%)	17(4.0%)		
Tobacco exposure in early pregnancy			78.692	**<0.001**
No	602(81.4%)	244(57.3%)		
Yes	138(18.6%)	182(42.7%)		
Alcohol exposure in early pregnancy			9.461	**0.002**
No	712(96.2%)	392(92.0%)		
Yes	28(3.8%)	34(8.0%)		
Periconceptional folate use			7.026	**0.008**
Yes	687(92.8%)	376(88.3%)		
No	53(7.2%)	50(11.7%)		

Abbreviations: BMI body mass index. [a] Classification according to Chinese standard for obesity BMI.

3.3. Maternal BHMT Gene Polymorphisms and the Risk of VSD in Offspring

Table 3 displays the genotypic distribution of four SNPs between two groups and the results of the HWE test in the controls. All of the SNPs were in accordance with the Hardy–Weinberg equilibrium (all of the p values were <0.05), indicating that the sample was qualified for good group representativeness.

Table 2. Maternal dietary habits and the risk of VSD in offspring.

Maternal Dietary Habits	Control Group	Case Group	Univariate Logistic Regression		Multivariable Logistic Regression [a] Regression	
	(n = 740)	(n = 426)	Cor (95%CI)	*p*	aOR (95%CI)	*p*
Smoked foods			1.81(1.48-2.21)	<0.001	2.44(1.89–3.13)	**<0.001**
Hardly [b]	407(55.0%)	172(40.4%)	1		1	
Sometimes [c]	310(41.9%)	213(50.0%)	1.63(1.27–2.09)	<0.001	2.14(1.57–2.91)	<0.001
Often [d]	23(3.1%)	41(9.6%)	4.22(2.46–7.24)	<0.001	7.98(4.16–15.32)	<0.001
Barbecued foods			1.94(1.53–2.47)	<0.001	1.86(1.39–2.48)	**<0.001**
Hardly	558(75.4%)	260(61.0%)	1		1	
Sometimes	177(23.9%)	153(35.9%)	1.86(1.43–2.41)	<0.001	1.89(1.37–2.60)	<0.001
Often	5(0.7%)	13(3.1%)	5.58(1.97–15.82)	0.001	3.01(0.90–10.07)	0.073
Fried foods			1.55(1.27–1.89)	<0.001	1.93(1.51–2.46)	**<0.001**
Hardly	458(61.9%)	214(50.2%)	1		1	
Sometimes	253(34.2%)	177(41.5%)	1.50(1.16–1.92)	0.002	2.15(1.57–2.94)	<0.001
Often	29(3.9%)	35(8.2%)	2.58(1.54–4.34)	<0.001	3.02(1.62–5.60)	<0.001
Pickled vegetables			1.87(1.51–2.32)	<0.001	2.50(1.92–3.25)	**<0.001**
Hardly	448(60.5%)	184(43.2%)	1		1	
Sometimes	274(37.0%)	220(51.6%)	1.96(1.53–2.50)	<0.001	2.58(1.90–3.52)	<0.001
Often	18(2.4%)	22(5.2%)	2.98(1.56–5.68)	0.001	5.53(2.58–11.82)	<0.001
Fresh vegetables			0.89(0.52–1.52)	0.664	0.86(0.46–1.57)	0.615
Hardly	3(0.4%)	3(0.7%)	1		1	
Sometimes	21(2.8%)	12(2.8%)	0.57(0.10–3.29)	0.531	0.17(0.02–1.11)	0.064
Often	716(96.8%)	411(96.5%)	0.57(0.12–2.86)	0.498	0.24(0.04–1.27)	0.093
Fresh fruits			0.37(0.30–0.47)	<0.001	0.47(0.36–0.62)	**<0.001**
Hardly	14(1.9%)	81(19.0%)	1		1	
Sometimes	41(5.5%)	16(3.8%)	0.07(0.03–0.15)	<0.001	0.06(0.03–0.16)	<0.001
Often	685(92.6%)	329(77.2%)	0.08(0.05–0.15)	<0.001	0.12(0.06–0.24)	<0.001
Fresh meat			0.81(0.61–1.08)	0.155	1.08(0.77–1.54)	0.644
Hardly	21(2.8%)	12(2.8%)	1		1	
Sometimes	38(5.1%)	37(8.7%)	1.70(0.74–3.95)	0.214	1.41(0.52–3.84)	0.498
Often	681(92.0%)	377(88.5%)	0.97(0.47–1.99)	0.931	1.34(0.58–3.08)	0.493
Fish and shrimp			0.27(0.22–0.33)	<0.001	0.35(0.28–0.44)	**<0.001**
Hardly	29(3.9%)	91(21.4%)	1		1	
Sometimes	207(28.0%)	210(49.3%)	0.32(0.20–0.51)	<0.001	0.33(0.20–0.56)	<0.001
Often	504(68.1%)	125(29.3%)	0.08(0.05–0.12)	<0.001	0.12(0.07–0.20)	<0.001
Fresh eggs			0.40(0.33–0.49)	<0.001	0.56(0.45–0.71)	**<0.001**
Hardly	36(4.9%)	58(13.6%)	1		1	
Sometimes	86(11.6%)	127(29.8%)	0.92(0.56–1.51)	0.732	0.76(0.42–1.37)	0.355
Often	618(83.5%)	241(56.6%)	0.24(0.16–0.38)	<0.001	0.37(0.21–0.63)	<0.001
Beans			0.52(0.44–0.61)	<0.001	0.68(0.56–0.83)	**<0.001**
Hardly	107(14.5%)	107(25.1%)	1		1	
Sometimes	216(29.2%)	192(45.1%)	0.89(0.64–1.24)	0.486	1.13(0.76–1.69)	0.544
Often	417(56.4%)	127(29.8%)	0.30(0.22–0.42)	<0.001	0.52(0.35–0.79)	0.002
Milk products			0.51(0.44–0.59)	<0.001	0.67(0.56–0.80)	**<0.001**
Hardly	143(19.3%)	173(40.6%)	1		1	
Sometimes	150(20.3%)	109(25.6%)	0.60(0.43–0.84)	0.003	0.88(0.59–1.31)	0.533
Often	447(60.4%)	144(33.8%)	0.27(0.20–0.36)	<0.001	0.46(0.32–0.65)	<0.001

Abbreviations: VSD ventricular septal defect, cOR crude odds ratio, aOR adjusted odds ratio, CI confidence interval. [a] Adjusted for pre-pregnancy BMI, education level, consanguineous marriages, gestational diabetes mellitus, gestational hypertension, abnormal pregnancy history before this pregnancy, congenital malformations in family members, exposure to environmental pollutants, antibiotic use in early pregnancy, tobacco exposure in early pregnancy, alcohol exposure in early pregnancy, periconceptional folate use. [b] Hardly was defined as less than or equal to two times per week. [c] Sometimes was defined as three to five times per week. [d] Often was defined as more than or equal to six times per week.

Table 3. Genotypic frequencies of maternal *BHMT* polymorphisms and *P* values of HWE test.

SNPs	Location	Major Allele	Minor Allele	MAF	Group	Genotype Frequencies [a]			χ^2	*p*
						AA	AB	BB		
rs3733890	Chr5: 79126136	G	A	0.3250	control	333(45.0%)	333(45.0%)	74(10.0%)	0.4865	0.4855
					case	162(38.0%)	216(50.7%)	48(11.3%)		
rs1316753	Chr5: 79235514	C	G	0.4338	control	248(33.5%)	342(46.2%)	150(20.3%)	2.5913	0.1075
					case	95(22.3%)	247(58.0%)	84(19.7%)		
rs567754	Chr5: 79120593	C	T	0.4628	control	203(27.4%)	389(52.6%)	148(20.0%)	2.4204	0.1198
					case	132(31.0%)	227(53.3%)	67(15.7%)		
rs1915706	Chr5: 79140388	T	C	0.2257	control	442(59.7%)	262(35.4%)	36(4.9%)	0.1261	0.7225
					case	223(52.3%)	176(41.3%)	27(6.3%)		

Abbreviations: *BHMT* betaine-homocysteine methyltransferase, HWE Hardy–Weinberg equilibrium, SNP single nucleotide polymorphism, MAF minimum allele frequency. [a] AA = homozygous wild—type; AB = heterozygous variant type; BB = homozygous variant type.

The association of maternal *BHMT* gene polymorphisms with the risk of VSD in offspring based on logistic regression analysis was summarized in Table 4. After adjusting for potential confounders, statistically significant associations were found between the polymorphisms of the *BHMT* gene at rs1316753, rs1915706, and VSD in offspring. For rs1316753, mothers carrying the CG genotype (aOR = 2.01, 95%CI: 1.43–2.83) were at a significantly higher risk of VSD in offspring compared with those who had the CC genotype. In addition, the dominant model (aOR = 1.88, 95%CI: 1.36–2.61) and the additive model (aOR = 1.30, 95%CI: 1.06–1.60) of rs1316753 were also observed to be significantly associated with increased risk of VSD in offspring. For rs1915706, compared to the TT genotype, mothers with the CT genotype (aOR = 1.81, 95%CI: 1.33–2.46) were more likely to have VSD children. Additionally, the dominant model (aOR = 1.84, 95%CI: 1.37–2.48) and the additive model (aOR = 1.61, 95%CI: 127–2.05) of rs1915706 were significantly associated with an increased risk of VSD in offspring.

Table 4. Polymorphisms of maternal *BHMT* gene associated with risk of VSD in offspring based on logistic regression analysis.

SNPs	Univariate Logistic Reregression		Multivariate Logistic Regression [a]		
	cOR (95%CI)	*p*	aOR (95%CI)	*p*	FDR_P
rs3733890					
GG	1		1		
GA	1.33(1.03–1.72)	0.026	1.28(0.94–1.73)	0.118	0.189
AA	1.33(0.89–2.01)	0.168	1.03(0.61–1.74)	0.918	0.918
Dominant model [b]	1.33(1.04–1.70)	0.021	1.23(0.92–1.65)	0.163	0.217
Recessive model [c]	1.14(0.78–1.68)	0.496	0.90(0.55–1.48)	0.681	0.904
Additive model [d]	1.21(1.01–1.45)	0.038	1.11(0.88–1.39)	0.373	0.373
rs1316753					
CC	1		1		
CG	1.88(1.41–2.51)	<0.001	2.01(1.43–2.83)	<0.001	**<0.001**
GG	1.46(1.02–2.09)	0.037	1.55(1.00–2.40)	0.048	0.096
Dominant model	1.76(1.34–2.31)	<0.001	1.88(1.36–2.61)	<0.001	**<0.001**
Recessive model	0.97(0.72–1.30)	0.821	0.98(0.68–1.41)	0.904	0.904
Additive model	1.25(1.05–1.48)	0.012	1.30(1.06–1.60)	0.014	**0.028**
rs567754					
CC	1		1		
CT	0.90(0.68–1.18)	0.438	0.90(0.65–1.26)	0.555	0.634

Table 4. *Cont.*

SNPs	Univariate Logistic Reregression		Multivariate Logistic Regression [a]		
	cOR (95%CI)	*p*	aOR (95%CI)	*p*	FDR_P
TT	0.70(0.48–1.00)	0.050	0.78(0.51–1.19)	0.249	0.332
Dominant model	0.84(0.65–1.09)	0.197	0.87(0.64–1.20)	0.393	0.393
Recessive model	0.75(0.54–1.02)	0.071	0.83(0.57–1.20)	0.323	0.646
Additive model	0.84(0.71–1.01)	0.058	0.88(0.72–1.09)	0.255	0.340
rs1915706					
TT	1		1		
CT	1.33(1.04–1.71)	0.025	1.81(1.33–2.46)	<0.001	**<0.001**
CC	1.49(0.88–2.51)	0.138	2.05(1.10–3.82)	0.023	0.061
Dominant model	1.35(1.06–1.72)	0.014	1.84(1.37–2.48)	<0.001	**<0.001**
Recessive model	1.32(0.79–2.21)	0.285	1.60(0.88–2.94)	0.124	0.496
Additive model	1.28(1.05–1.56)	0.015	1.61(1.27–2.05)	<0.001	**<0.001**

Abbreviations: *BHMT* betaine-homocysteine methyltransferase, VSD ventricular septal defect, SNP single nucleotide polymorphism, cOR crude odds ratio, aOR adjusted odds ratio, CI confidence interval, FDR_P, false discovery rate P value. [a] Adjusted for pre-pregnancy BMI, education level, consanguineous marriages, gestational diabetes mellitus, gestational hypertension, abnormal pregnancy history before this pregnancy, congenital malformations in family members, exposure of environmental pollutants, antibiotic use in early pregnancy, tobacco exposure in early pregnancy, alcohol exposure in early pregnancy, periconceptional folate use. [b] The dominant model means heterozygote and mutant type homozygote vs. wild type homozygote. [c] The recessive model means mutant type homozygote vs. heterozygote and wild type homozygote. [d] The additive model means mutant type homozygote vs. heterozygote vs. mutant type homozygote.

3.4. Interaction of the Polymorphisms of BHMT Gene and Maternal Dietary Habits on the Risk of VSD in Offspring

Figure 2 shows the level of association between genetic variants of the *BHMT* gene, maternal dietary intake, and VSD in offspring. The interaction of *BHMT* gene polymorphisms and maternal dietary habits in early pregnancy based on multivariate logistic regression analysis is displayed in Table 5. For rs1316753, statistically significant interactions were observed between the variant genotypes (CG + GG) and excessive intake of pickled vegetables (aOR = 0.48, 95%CI: 0.24–0.95) and beans (aOR = 0.40, 95%CI: 0.17–0.95). Nevertheless, this significance vanished from the multiple test corrections based on the Benjamini–Hochberg method (both FDR-p values > 0.1). As for rs1915706, there were significant interactions between the variant genotypes (CT + CC) and a regular intake of beans (aOR = 0.33, 95%CI: 0.15–0.73, FDR-p = 0.035).

The crossover analysis was conducted to further elucidate the interaction between *BHMT* gene polymorphisms at rs1915706 and maternal bean intake on the risk of VSD in offspring (Table 6 and Figure 3). Mothers who had the wild genotype (TT) and meanwhile reported regular intake of beans in early pregnancy were seen as the reference group. After adjustment for potential confounders detected in Table 1, mothers who had the variant genotypes (CT + CC) and meanwhile reported regular intake of beans (aOR = 1.52, 95%CI: 1.09–2.11) and a small intake of beans (aOR = 4.00, 95%CI: 2.17–7.40) were at a significantly higher risk of VSD in offspring compared with those who were in the reference group.

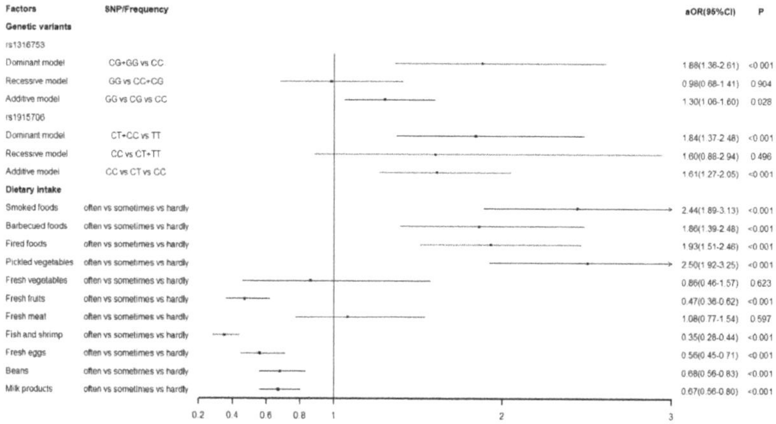

Figure 2. The level of association between genetic variants of *BHMT* gene, maternal dietary intake and VSD in offspring.

Table 5. Interactions of polymorphisms of *BHMT* gene and maternal dietary habits based on multivariate logistic regression.

Dietary Habits [a]	Interaction with rs1316753 [b]			Interaction with rs1915706 [b]		
	aOR (95%CI) [c]	*p*	FDR_P	aOR (95%CI) [c]	*p*	FDR_P
Smoked foods	0.52 (0.26–1.01)	0.055	0.165	0.62 (0.34–1.14)	0.122	0.305
Barbecued foods	1.24 (0.62–2.48)	0.548	0.616	1.33 (0.71–2.49)	0.377	0.610
Fried foods	1.40 (0.72–2.71)	0.316	0.406	1.19 (0.66–2.15)	0.570	0.634
Pickled vegetables	0.48 (0.24–0.95)	**0.034**	0.165	0.66 (0.36–1.19)	0.170	0.340
Fresh fruits	0.30 (0.05–1.68)	0.168	0.360	0.68 (0.18–2.58)	0.571	0.634
Fish and shrimp	0.85 (0.29–2.53)	0.776	0.776	0.66 (0.24–1.84)	0.427	0.610
Fresh eggs	2.37 (0.64–8.83)	0.200	0.360	0.39 (0.13–1.18)	0.095	0.305
Beans	0.40 (0.17–0.95)	**0.038**	0.165	0.33 (0.15–0.73)	**0.006**	**0.035**
Milk products	0.66 (0.32–1.38)	0.273	0.406	1.14 (0.60–2.19)	0.687	0.687

Abbreviations: *BHMT* betaine-homocysteine methyltransferase, aOR adjusted odds ratio, CI confidence interval, FDR_P, false discovery rate *p*-value. [a] Maternal dietary habits were classified as hardly and sometimes/often. [b] Single nucleotide polymorphisms were classified as wild-type and variant genotypes. [c] Adjusted for pre-pregnancy BMI, education level, consanguineous marriages, gestational diabetes mellitus, gestational hypertension, abnormal pregnancy history before this pregnancy, congenital malformations in family members, exposure to environmental pollutants, antibiotic use in early pregnancy, tobacco exposure in early pregnancy, alcohol exposure in early pregnancy, periconceptional folate use.

Table 6. Interaction of rs1915706 and maternal beans intake based on crossover analysis.

rs1915706 [a]	Maternal Beans Intake [b]	Cases	Controls	cOR(95%CI)	aOR(95%CI) [c]
-	-	175 (41.1%)	356 (48.1%)	1	1
-	+	48 (11.3%)	86 (11.6%)	1.14 (0.76–1.69)	0.88 (0.54–1.42)
+	-	144 (33.8%)	277 (37.4%)	1.06 (0.81–1.39)	**1.52 (1.09–2.11)**
+	+	59 (13.8%)	21 (2.8%)	5.72 (3.36–9.71)	**4.00 (2.17–7.40)**

Abbreviations: cOR crude odds ratio, aOR adjusted odds ratio, CI confidence interval. [a] For rs1915706, '-' means wild type, '+' means variant genotype. [b] For maternal beans intake, '–' means regular intake (namely, sometimes/often), '+' means little intake (namely, hardly). [c] Adjusted for pre-pregnancy BMI, education level, consanguineous marriages, gestational diabetes mellitus, gestational hypertension, abnormal pregnancy history before this pregnancy, congenital malformations in family members, exposure to environmental pollutants, antibiotic use in early pregnancy, tobacco exposure in early pregnancy, alcohol exposure in early pregnancy, and periconceptional folate use.

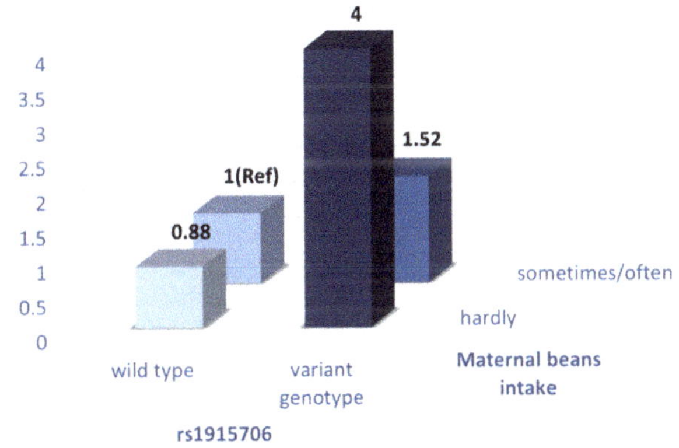

Figure 3. Interaction of rs1915706 and maternal beans intake on the risk of VSD in offspring.

4. Discussion

Research on the causes of CHD has made great strides, and more than 400 genes and important environmental factors have been determined to have substantial evidence in relation to the risk of developing CHD and its subgroups [5–8]. However, the conclusion can be easily drawn from the other hand that a single genetic or environmental factor may impose minimal effects on CHD. Moreover, the interaction of the two factors cannot be overlooked in the occurrence and development of CHD and its subgroups. In this study, we attempted to achieve an insight into the etiology of VSD, the most common subtype of CHD. The main purpose was to decide whether the association and interaction effect of BHMT gene polymorphisms and maternal dietary habits with VSD exists, which is conducive to the achievement of molecular genetic diagnostics and provide diet instruction to expectant mothers in early pregnancy.

Firstly, we explored the association between maternal dietary intake during early pregnancy and the risk of VSD in offspring. The results sent two messages. On the one hand, mothers who reported excessive intake of smoked foods (aOR = 2.44), barbecued foods (aOR = 1.86), fried foods (aOR = 1.93), and pickled vegetables (aOR = 2.50) were more likely to have a VSD-affected child. On the other hand, mothers with an excessive intake of fresh fruits (aOR = 0.47), fish and shrimp (aOR = 0.35), fresh eggs (aOR = 0.56), beans (aOR = 0.68), and milk products (aOR = 0.67) were less likely to have a VSD-affected child. Generally, various harmful chemicals can be generated from improper food processing, and most of them are teratogens and carcinogens, such as nitrites, acrylamide (ACR), polycyclic aromatic hydrocarbons (PAH), and so on. Pickled vegetables have a wide range of nitrite and nitrate contents. Gravidas, who have an excessive intake of pickles, may suffer hypoxemia because increased nitrite can react with hemoglobin, rendering it incapable of carrying oxygen [38]. A recent experimental study established a rodent model and reported that hypoxia was able to cause numerous abnormalities in cardiomyocyte gene expression, the electrophysiologic substrate of the heart, and contractile function, thus delaying cardiac maturation [39]. ACR, identified in food in 2002, is mainly formed via the Maillard reaction, whereby a carbonyl compound reacts with the amino group of asparagine processed at high temperatures (>120 °C, such as barbecuing, frying, and baking) [40,41]. Although no direct evidence manifested its relation to heart defects, a number of animal studies have shown strong neurotoxic, genotoxic, carcinogenic, mutagenic, and teratogenic effects [42]. Food is readily contaminated by PAH during the smoking process involving the combustion of fuel. A recent study reported that greater maternal levels of PAH exposure during pregnancy might be associated with an elevated prevalence of fetal CHD [43]. Moreover, prior experimental research provided strong evidence that PAH exposure can result in abnormal heart looping, an enlarged ventricle with a thinner ventricular wall, and even developmental cardiac defects [44,45]. The protective foods detected in the study, such as fruits, fish and shrimp, eggs, beans, and milk products, are common foods on tables. Furthermore, they are packed with numerous nutrients, such as high-quality protein, vitamins, minerals, and so on, which have been extensively accepted to play a vital role in maintaining the health of gravidas and fetuses.

Moreover, we determined the association between maternal BHMT gene polymorphisms and the risk of VSD in offspring. Four SNPs (rs3733890, rs1316753, rs567754, and rs1915706) were considered in this study, and two SNPs (rs1316753 and rs1915706) were for the first time found to have a statistically significant association with VSD. To date, the BHMT gene remained relatively little studied compared with other folate- and homocysteine-metabolizing genes. The results in our study were only partly in accordance with prior studies. The rs3733890 polymorphism is a well-studied exon of the BHMT gene and undergoes a G-to-A change at nucleotide 716, leading to an arginine-to-glutamine substitution at amino acid 239. Its association with congenital defects has been widely explored but with contradictory results [27,46–48]. In the present study, we did not detect its significance in the occurrence of VSD. Rs567754 is an intronic variant of the BHMT gene, and neither previous data nor our data revealed an association with CHD or VSD in offspring [27]. The interesting thing is that two other SNPs, rs1316753 and rs1915706, were observed to be statistically associated with a remarkably-increased risk of VSD in offspring. To the best of our knowledge, experimental or epidemiological research involving these two polymorphisms remains a nearly unworked area, meaning that their potential functional effects on BHMT are largely unknown. Qiping Feng et al. performed a genotype–phenotype correlation analysis on betaine-homocysteine methyltransferase and found that three introns (rs41272270, rs6875201, and rs7700790) and an intergenic variant (rs16876512) were significantly correlated with both BHMT activity and protein levels [22]. Although this convincing research did not cover the two significant SNPs in our study, the analogy seems to be reasonable that the two intergenic variants, rs1316753 and rs1915706, are also capable of producing potential effects on the expression of the BHMT gene and subsequently influencing plasma hcy concentrations. The correlation between maternal hyperhomocysteinemia and CHD has been extensively studied and reviewed [25,49,50]. Meanwhile, hcy-induced CHDs, such as the transposition of the great arteries (TGA), single ventricle defects (SVD), and VSD, have been found in embryos of different species (mice and chicken) [51]. Therefore, the statistical association between maternal BHMT polymorphisms and VSD in offspring might be explained by the pathway from BHMT activity to elevated hcy levels to multiple congenital anomalies. Nonetheless, more related research is encouraged to provide clearer evidence, thus elucidating the potential mechanism.

Lastly, we also analyzed the gene–environment interaction and observed a significant interaction between genetic variants of the BHMT gene at rs1915706 and maternal bean intake on the risk of VSD in offspring. The expectant mothers who had the variant genotypes (CT + CC) and meanwhile reported a small intake of beans were at a significantly higher risk of VSD in offspring (aOR = 4.00) compared with those with the wild genotype (TT) and reported having a regular intake of beans in early pregnancy. Beans are an excellent source of zinc, choline, and multiple B vitamins (such as folate, thiamin, niacin, riboflavin, and pyridoxine) [52,53]. Notably, BHMT is a zinc-dependent cytosolic enzyme, and its substrate, betaine, is partly derived from dietary choline [31,54]. In addition, a stronger risk reduction in CHD has been found in the maternal folate + B-vitamin supplementation group compared with the maternal folate supplementation group, both setting the non-users as the reference group [14]. Concerning whether a single nutrient can exist in various foods, we speculated that the deficiency of diverse nutrients coexisting in beans coincided with a genetic variant that contributes to the occurrence of VSD. This speculation seemed plausible since similar research had been conducted not long ago. Hartmut Cuny et al. demonstrated that when dietary undersupply during pregnancy was combined with a maternal heterozygous variant in Haao, a gene of the nicotinamide adenine dinucleotide (NAD) synthesis pathway, the incidence of embryo loss and malformations was significantly higher [55]. This is a classical experimental study forcibly indicating a gene-diet interaction. As Gibson G and Berger K commented, the discovery of such interaction suggests that the close monitoring of nutrition in at-risk carrier mothers would be the type of personalized and predictive intervention that advocates of genomic health call for [56]. Regardless, what we found in our study necessitates more convincing experimental research and crowd investigation to confirm it repeatedly.

Furthermore, several limitations in our study should be acknowledged. Firstly, although we perfected the study design and executed it strictly during the whole process as far as possible, the association found in this study, an observational case-control study, was relatively limited compared to a cohort study or an experimental study. So, in other words, well-designed prospective cohorts or reasonable experimental research are needed to validate our findings further. Secondly, the information on food frequency and related exposure in the questionnaire were obtained through retrospective investigation; we cannot rule out the possible limitation of recall bias. Thirdly, this is a hospital-based case-control study, and all of the cases came from the same department in a hospital; though its representativeness in the province for sophisticated diagnosis and treatment techniques, the selection bias still cannot be ignored. Fourthly, several potential confounders were determined and adjusted in the study, but there undoubtedly are other confounding covariates that might also influence the outcomes, such as common genetic polymorphisms and some nutritional biomarkers. The findings would be more convincing if taking these factors into consideration. Last but not least, maternal hcy concentration was not available in our research, which excludes the possibility of verifying the potential explanation that genetic variants of the BHMT gene may cause VSD by elevating maternal hcy levels.

5. Conclusions

In this hospital based case-control study, statistically significant associations were found between the polymorphisms of the *BHMT* gene at rs1316753, rs1915706, and VSD in offspring. Maternal dietary habits were also observed to have a significant impact on the occurrence and development of VSD. A significant interaction between *BHMT* polymorphisms and maternal bean intake was identified in the study. Concerning the limitations of our study, more convincing crowd investigation and experimental research are necessary to repeatedly verify the findings and further elucidate the potential mechanism.

Author Contributions: Conceptualization, T.W., P.Z. and J.Q.; Data curation, M.L.; Formal analysis, M.L.; Funding acquisition, J.Q.; Investigation, X.S., M.S., Y.L., J.W., T.Z. and Q.C.; Methodology, M.L.; Project administration, J.Q.; Resources, P.H.; Software, S.Z. and J.S.; Supervision, T.W.; Visualization, M.L.; Writing—original draft, M.L.; Writing—review & editing, M.L. and T.W. All authors have read and agreed to the published version of the manuscript.

Funding: This research was supported by the Project Funded by National Key Research and Development Project (2018YFE0114500), National Natural Science Foundation Program of China (82073653 and 81803313), China Postdoctoral Science Foundation (2020M682644), Hunan Provincial Science and Technology Talent Support Project (2020TJ-N07), Hunan Provincial Key Research and Development Program (2018SK2063 and 2018SK2064), Natural Science Foundation of Hunan Province (2018JJ2551), Open Project from NHC Key Laboratory of Birth Defect for Research and Prevention (KF2020006), and Science and Technology Planning Project of Guangdong Province (2020A1414010152), Hunan Outstanding Youth Fund Project (2022JJ10087), Natural Science Foundation of Hunan Province of China (2022JJ40207); Changsha Municipal Natural Science Foundation (kq2202470), Postgraduate Scientific Research Innovation Project of Central South University(1053320215987).

Institutional Review Board Statement: The study was conducted in accordance with the Declaration of Helsinki and approved by the Ethics Committee for Clinical Research of Xiangya School of Public Health of Central South University (no. XYGW-2018-36).

Informed Consent Statement: Informed consent was obtained from all subjects involved in the study.

Data Availability Statement: The data presented in this study are available on request from the corresponding author.

Acknowledgments: The department of cardiothoracic surgery in Hunan Children's Hospital lent full support to the research. The staff in the department helped us collect data and blood samples of cases and their busy work provided support for our epidemiological investigation. We want to express our sincere appreciation to all of them.

Conflicts of Interest: The authors declare no conflict of interest.

References

1. Liu, Y.; Chen, S.; Zühlke, L.; Black, G.C.; Choy, M.K.; Li, N.; Keavney, B.D. Global birth prevalence of congenital heart defects 1970–2017: Updated systematic review and meta-analysis of 260 studies. *Int. J. Epidemiol.* **2019**, *48*, 455–463.
2. Mitchell, S.C.; Korones, S.B.; Berendes, H.W. Congenital heart disease in 56, 109 births. *Incidence and natural history. Circulation* **1971**, *43*, 323–332.
3. Van Der Linde, D.; Konings, E.E.; Slager, M.A.; Witsenburg, M.; Helbing, W.A.; Takkenberg, J.J.; Roos-Hesselink, J.W. Birth prevalence of congenital heart disease worldwide: A systematic review and meta-analysis. *J. Am. Coll. Cardiol.* **2011**, *58*, 2241–2247. [CrossRef]
4. Penny, D.J.; Vick, G.W., 3rd. Ventricular septal defect. *Lancet* **2011**, *377*, 1103–1112. [CrossRef]
5. Gelb, B.D.; Chung, W.K. Complex genetics and the etiology of human congenital heart disease. *Cold Spring Harb. Perspect. Med.* **2014**, *4*, a013953. [CrossRef]
6. Zhang, T.N.; Wu, Q.J.; Liu, Y.S.; Lv, J.L.; Sun, H.; Chang, Q.; Liu, C.F.; Zhao, Y.H. Environmental Risk Factors and Congenital Heart Disease: An Umbrella Review of 165 Systematic Reviews and Meta-Analyses with More than 120 Million Participants. *Front. Cardiovasc Med.* **2021**, *8*, 640729. [CrossRef]
7. Morton, S.U.; Quiat, D.; Seidman, J.G.; Seidman, C.E. Genomic frontiers in congenital heart disease. *Nat. Rev. Cardiol.* **2022**, *19*, 26–42.
8. Boyd, R.; McMullen, H.; Beqaj, H.; Kalfa, D. Environmental Exposures and Congenital Heart Disease. *Pediatrics* **2022**, *149*, e2021052151.
9. van der Bom, T.; Zomer, A.C.; Zwinderman, A.H.; Meijboom, F.J.; Bouma, B.J.; Mulder, B.J. The changing epidemiology of congenital heart disease. *Nat. Rev. Cardiol.* **2011**, *8*, 50–60. [CrossRef]
10. Cao, J.; Wu, Q.; Huang, Y.; Wang, L.; Su, Z.; Ye, H. The role of DNA methylation in syndromic and non-syndromic congenital heart disease. *Clin. Epigenetics.* **2021**, *13*, 93. [CrossRef]
11. Wilson, R.D.; O'Connor, D.L. Maternal folic acid and multivitamin supplementation: International clinical evidence with considerations for the prevention of folate-sensitive birth defects. *Prev. Med. Rep.* **2021**, *24*, 101617. [CrossRef] [PubMed]
12. Yang, J.; Cheng, Y.; Zeng, L.; Dang, S.; Yan, H. Maternal dietary diversity during pregnancy and congenital heart defects: A case-control study. *Eur. J. Clin. Nutr.* **2021**, *75*, 355–363. [CrossRef] [PubMed]
13. Yang, J.; Kang, Y.; Chang, Q.; Zhang, B.; Liu, X.; Zeng, L.; Yan, H.; Dang, S. Maternal Zinc, Copper, and Selenium Intakes during Pregnancy and Congenital Heart Defects. *Nutrients* **2022**, *14*, 1055. [CrossRef] [PubMed]
14. Zhang, R.; Guo, L.; Zhao, D.; Qu, P.; Dang, S.; Yan, H. Maternal B-vitamin intake and B-vitamin supplementation during pregnancy in relation to neonatal congenital heart defects: A case-control study with propensity score matching. *Eur. J. Clin. Nutr.* **2021**, *75*, 782–791. [CrossRef]
15. Koster, M.P.; van Duijn, L.; Krul-Poel, Y.H.; Laven, J.S.; Helbing, W.A.; Simsek, S.; Steegers-Theunissen, R.P. A compromised maternal vitamin D status is associated with congenital heart defects in offspring. *Early Hum. Dev.* **2018**, *117*, 50–56. [CrossRef]
16. Sunden, S.L.; Renduchintala, M.S.; Park, E.I.; Miklasz, S.D.; Garrow, T.A. Betaine-homocysteine methyltransferase expression in porcine and human tissues and chromosomal localization of the human gene. *Arch. Biochem. Biophys.* **1997**, *345*, 171–174. [CrossRef] [PubMed]
17. Park, E.I.; Garrow, T.A. Interaction between dietary methionine and methyl donor intake on rat liver betaine-homocysteine methyltransferase gene expression and organization of the human gene. *J. Biol. Chem.* **1999**, *274*, 7816–7824. [CrossRef] [PubMed]
18. Teng, Y.W.; Cerdena, I.; Zeisel, S.H. Homocysteinemia in mice with genetic betaine homocysteine S-methyltransferase deficiency is independent of dietary folate intake. *J. Nutr.* **2012**, *142*, 1964–1967. [CrossRef]
19. Szegedi, S.S.; Castro, C.C.; Koutmos, M.; Garrow, T.A. Betaine-homocysteine S-methyltransferase-2 is an S-methylmethionine-homocysteine methyltransferase. *J. Biol. Chem.* **2008**, *283*, 8939–8945. [CrossRef]
20. Song, J.H.; Lee, H.R.; Shim, S.M. Determination of S-methyl-L-methionine (SMM) from Brassicaceae Family Vegetables and Characterization of the Intestinal Transport of SMM by Caco-2 Cells. *J. Food Sci.* **2017**, *82*, 36–43. [CrossRef]
21. Pérez-Miguelsanz, J.; Vallecillo, N.; Garrido, F.; Reytor, E.; Pérez-Sala, D.; Pajares, M.A. Betaine homocysteine S-methyltransferase emerges as a new player of the nuclear methionine cycle. *Biochim. Biophys. Acta Mol. Cell Res.* **2017**, *1864*, 1165–1182. [CrossRef] [PubMed]

22. Feng, Q.; Kalari, K.; Fridley, B.L.; Jenkins, G.; Ji, Y.; Abo, R.; Hebbring, S.; Zhang, J.; Nye, M.D.; Leeder, J.S.; et al. Betaine-homocysteine methyltransferase: Human liver genotype-phenotype correlation. *Mol. Genet. Metab.* **2011**, *102*, 126–133. [CrossRef]
23. Blanco, R.; Colombo, A.; Pardo, R.; Suazo, J. Maternal biomarkers of methylation status and non-syndromic orofacial cleft risk: A meta-analysis. *Int. J. Oral Maxillofac. Surg.* **2016**, *45*, 1323–1332. [CrossRef]
24. Kucha, W.; Seifu, D.; Tirsit, A.; Yigeremu, M.; Abebe, M.; Hailu, D.; Tsehay, D.; Genet, S. Folate, Vitamin B12, and Homocysteine Levels in Women With Neural Tube Defect-Affected Pregnancy in Addis Ababa, Ethiopia. *Front. Nutr.* **2022**, *9*, 873900. [CrossRef]
25. Dilli, D.; Doğan, N.N.; Örün, U.A.; Koç, M.; Zenciroğlu, A.; Karademir, S.; Akduman, H. Maternal neonatal micronutrient levels in newborns with, C.H.D. *Cardiol. Young* **2018**, *28*, 523–529. [CrossRef]
26. Nelen, W.L. Hyperhomocysteinaemia and human reproduction. *Clin. Chem. Lab. Med.* **2001**, *39*, 758–763. [CrossRef]
27. Shaw, G.M.; Lu, W.; Zhu, H.; Yang, W.; Briggs, F.; Carmichael, S.L.; Barcellos, L.F.; Lammer, E.J.; Finnell, R.H. 118 SNPs of folate-related genes and risks of spina bifida and conotruncal heart defects. *BMC Med. Genet.* **2009**, *10*, 49. [CrossRef]
28. Hobbs, C.A.; Cleves, M.A.; MacLeod, S.L.; Erickson, S.W.; Tang, X.; Li, J.; Li, M.; Nick, T.; Malik, S.; National Birth Defects Prevention Study. Conotruncal heart defects and common variants in maternal and fetal genes in folate, homocysteine, and transsulfuration pathways. *Birth Defects Res. A Clin. Mol. Teratol.* **2014**, *100*, 116–126. [CrossRef] [PubMed]
29. Nembhard, W.N.; Tang, X.; Hu, Z.; MacLeod, S.; Stowe, Z.; Webber, D. Maternal and infant genetic variants, maternal periconceptional use of selective serotonin reuptake inhibitors, and risk of congenital heart defects in offspring: Population based study. *Bmj* **2017**, *356*, j832. [CrossRef] [PubMed]
30. Tang, X.; Cleves, M.A.; Nick, T.G.; Li, M.; MacLeod, S.L.; Erickson, S.W.; Li, J.; Shaw, G.M.; Mosley, B.S.; National Birth Defects Prevention Study. Obstructive heart defects associated with candidate genes, maternal obesity, and folic acid supplementation. *Am. J. Med. Genet. A* **2015**, *167*, 1231–1242. [CrossRef]
31. Ganu, R.S.; Ishida, Y.; Koutmos, M.; Kolokotronis, S.O.; Roca, A.L.; Garrow, T.A.; Schook, L.B. Evolutionary Analyses and Natural Selection of Betaine-Homocysteine S-Methyltransferase (BHMT) and BHMT2 Genes. *PLoS ONE* **2015**, *10*, e0134084. [CrossRef] [PubMed]
32. Wallace, T.C.; Blusztajn, J.K.; Caudill, M.A.; Klatt, K.C.; Zeisel, S.H. Choline: The Neurocognitive Essential Nutrient of Interest to Obstetricians and Gynecologists. *J. Diet Suppl.* **2020**, *17*, 733–752. [CrossRef] [PubMed]
33. Vailati-Riboni, M.; Crookenden, M.; Kay, J.K.; Meier, S.; Mitchell, M.D.; Heiser, A.; Roche, J.R.; Loor, J.J. Hepatic one-carbon metabolism enzyme activities and intermediate metabolites are altered by prepartum body condition score and plane of nutrition in grazing Holstein dairy cows. *J. Dairy Sci.* **2020**, *103*, 2662–2676. [CrossRef] [PubMed]
34. Jacometo, C.B.; Zhou, Z.; Luchini, D.; Corrêa, M.N.; Loor, J.J. Maternal supplementation with rumen-protected methionine increases prepartal plasma methionine concentration and alters hepatic mRNA abundance of 1-carbon, methionine, and transsulfuration pathways in neonatal Holstein calves. *J. Dairy Sci.* **2017**, *100*, 3209–3219. [CrossRef] [PubMed]
35. Coleman, D.N.; Vailati-Riboni, M.; Elolimy, A.A.; Cardoso, F.C.; Rodriguez-Zas, S.L.; Miura, M.; Pan, Y.X.; Loor, J.J. Hepatic betaine-homocysteine methyltransferase and methionine synthase activity and intermediates of the methionine cycle are altered by choline supply during negative energy balance in Holstein cows. *J. Dairy Sci.* **2019**, *102*, 8305–8318. [CrossRef] [PubMed]
36. Petersen, J.M.; Parker, S.E.; Crider, K.S.; Tinker, S.C.; Mitchell, A.A.; Werler, M.M. One-Carbon Cofactor Intake and Risk of Neural Tube Defects Among Women Who Meet Folic Acid Recommendations: A Multicenter Case-Control Study. *Am. J. Epidemiol.* **2019**, *188*, 1136–1143. [CrossRef] [PubMed]
37. Stingone, J.A.; Luben, T.J.; Carmichael, S.L.; Aylsworth, A.S.; Botto, L.D.; Correa, A.; Gilboa, S.M.; Langlois, P.H.; Nembhard, W.N.; Richmond-Bryant, J.; et al. Maternal Exposure to Nitrogen Dioxide, Intake of Methyl Nutrients, and Congenital Heart Defects in Offspring. *Am. J. Epidemiol.* **2017**, *186*, 719–729. [CrossRef] [PubMed]
38. Bedale, W.; Sindelar, J.J.; Milkowski, A.L. Dietary nitrate and nitrite: Benefits, risks, and evolving perceptions. *Meat Sci.* **2016**, *120*, 85–92. [CrossRef]
39. Romanowicz, J.; Guerrelli, D.; Dhari, Z.; Mulvany, C.; Reilly, M.; Swift, L.; Vasandani, N.; Ramadan, M.; Leatherbury, L.; Ishibashi, N.; et al. Chronic perinatal hypoxia delays cardiac maturation in a mouse model for cyanotic congenital heart disease. *Am. J. Physiol. Heart Circ. Physiol.* **2021**, *320*, H1873–H1886. [CrossRef]
40. Friedman, M. Chemistry, biochemistry, and safety of acrylamide. *A review. J. Agric. Food Chem.* **2003**, *51*, 4504–4526. [CrossRef] [PubMed]
41. Tareke, E.; Rydberg, P.; Karlsson, P.; Eriksson, S.; Törnqvist, M. Analysis of acrylamide, a carcinogen formed in heated foodstuffs. *J. Agric. Food Chem.* **2002**, *50*, 4998–5006. [CrossRef] [PubMed]
42. Bušová, M.; Bencko, V.; Veszelits Laktičová, K.; Holcátová, I.; Vargová, M. Risk of exposure to acrylamide. *Cent. Eur. J. Public Health* **2020**, *28*, S43–S46. [CrossRef] [PubMed]
43. Tao, J.; Li, N.; Liu, Z.; Qiu, J.; Deng, Y.; Li, X.; Chen, M.; Yu, J.; Zhu, J.; Yu, P.; et al. Risk of congenital heart diseases associated with NAT2 genetic polymorphisms and maternal polycyclic aromatic hydrocarbons exposure. *Prenat. Diagn.* **2019**, *39*, 968–975. [CrossRef]
44. Sarmah, S.; Marrs, J.A. Zebrafish as a Vertebrate Model System to Evaluate Effects of Environmental Toxicants on Cardiac Development and Function. *Int. J. Mol. Sci.* **2016**, *17*, 2123. [CrossRef]
45. Huang, L.; Wang, C.; Zhang, Y.; Li, J.; Zhong, Y.; Zhou, Y.; Chen, Y.; Zuo, Z. Benzo[a]pyrene exposure influences the cardiac development and the expression of cardiovascular relative genes in zebrafish (Danio rerio) embryos. *Chemosphere* **2012**, *87*, 369–375. [CrossRef]

46. Hobbs, C.A.; Cleves, M.A.; Karim, M.A.; Zhao, W.; MacLeod, S.L. Maternal folate-related gene environment interactions and congenital heart defects. *Obstet Gynecol.* **2010**, *116 Pt 1*, 16–22. [CrossRef]
47. Cao, L.; Wang, Y.; Zhang, R.; Dong, L.; Cui, H.; Fang, Y.; Zhao, L.; Shi, O.; Cai, C. Association of neural tube defects with gene polymorphisms in one-carbon metabolic pathway. *Childs Nerv. Syst.* **2018**, *34*, 277–284. [CrossRef]
48. Imani, M.M.; Lopez-Jornet, P.; López, E.P.; Ghanbari, F.; Sadeghi, M. Association of Betaine-Homocysteine S-Methyl Transferase (rs3797546 and rs3733890) polymorphisms with non-syndromic cleft lip/palate: A meta-analysis. *Int. Orthod.* **2019**, *17*, 643–651. [CrossRef]
49. Kalisch-Smith, J.I.; Ved, N.; Sparrow, D.B. Environmental Risk Factors for Congenital Heart Disease. *Cold Spring Harb. Perspect. Biol.* **2020**, *12*, a037234. [CrossRef]
50. Malik, R.A.; Lone, M.R.; Ahmed, A.; Koul, K.A.; Malla, R.R. Maternal hyperhomocysteinemia and congenital heart defects: A prospective case control study in Indian population. *Indian Heart J.* **2017**, *69*, 17–19. [CrossRef]
51. Mei, X.; Qi, D.; Zhang, T.; Zhao, Y.; Jin, L.; Hou, J.; Wang, J.; Lin, Y.; Xue, Y.; Zhu, P.; et al. Inhibiting MARSs reduces hyperhomocysteinemia-associated neural tube and congenital heart defects. *EMBO Mol. Med.* **2020**, *12*, e9469. [CrossRef] [PubMed]
52. Kumar, S.; Pandey, G. Biofortification of pulses and legumes to enhance nutrition. *Heliyon* **2020**, *6*, e03682. [CrossRef] [PubMed]
53. Wiedeman, A.M.; Barr, S.I.; Green, T.J.; Xu, Z.; Innis, S.M.; Kitts, D.D. Dietary Choline Intake: Current State of Knowledge Across the Life Cycle. *Nutrients* **2018**, *10*, 1513. [CrossRef]
54. Millian, N.S.; Garrow, T.A. Human betaine-homocysteine methyltransferase is a zinc metalloenzyme. *Arch. Biochem. Biophys.* **1998**, *356*, 93–98. [CrossRef] [PubMed]
55. Cuny, H.; Rapadas, M.; Gereis, J.; Martin, E.M.; Kirk, R.B.; Shi, H.; Dunwoodie, S.L. NAD deficiency due to environmental factors or gene-environment interactions causes congenital malformations and miscarriage in mice. *Proc. Natl. Acad. Sci. USA* **2020**, *117*, 3738–3747. [CrossRef]
56. Gibson, G.; Berger, K. Dietary modification, penetrance, and the origins of congenital malformation. *Proc. Natl. Acad. Sci. USA* **2020**, *117*, 5097–5099. [CrossRef]

nutrients

MDPI

Article

Dietary Quality during Pregnancy and Congenital Heart Defects

Jiaomei Yang [1,*], Qianqian Chang [1], Shaonong Dang [1], Xin Liu [1], Lingxia Zeng [1] and Hong Yan [1,2,3]

1 Department of Epidemiology and Health Statistics, School of Public Health, Xi'an Jiaotong University Health Science Center, Xi'an 710061, China
2 Nutrition and Food Safety Engineering Research Center of Shaanxi Province, Xi'an 710061, China
3 Key Laboratory of Environment and Genes Related to Diseases, Xi'an Jiaotong University, Ministry of Education, Xi'an 710061, China
* Correspondence: violetyjm18@xjtu.edu.cn; Tel.: +86-029-8265-5104

Abstract: Limited studies on maternal dietary quality indices and congenital heart defects (CHD) are available. This study aimed to explore the relationship between dietary quality in pregnancy and CHD among the Chinese population. A case-control study was performed in Northwest China, and 474 cases and 948 controls were included. Eligible women waiting for delivery were interviewed to recall diets and other information during pregnancy. Dietary quality was assessed by the Global Diet Quality Score (GDQS) and Mediterranean Diet Score (MDS). Logistic regression models were adopted to evaluate the associations of dietary quality scores with CHD. Pregnant women with higher scores of GDQS and MDS were at a lower risk of fetal CHD, and the adjusted ORs comparing the extreme quartiles were 0.26 (95%CI: 0.16–0.42; $P_{trend} < 0.001$) and 0.53 (95%CI: 0.34–0.83; $P_{trend} = 0.007$), respectively. The inverse associations of GDQS and MDS with CHD appeared to be stronger among women with lower education levels or in rural areas. Maternal GDQS and MDS had good predictive values for fetal CHD, with the areas under the receiver operating characteristic curves close to 0.8. Efforts to improve maternal dietary quality need to be strengthened to decrease the prevalence of CHD among the Chinese population.

Keywords: dietary quality; congenital heart defects; pregnancy; Global Diet Quality Score; Mediterranean Diet Score

Citation: Yang, J.; Chang, Q.; Dang, S.; Liu, X.; Zeng, L.; Yan, H. Dietary Quality during Pregnancy and Congenital Heart Defects. *Nutrients* **2022**, *14*, 3654. https://doi.org/10.3390/nu14173654

Academic Editor: Leanne M. Redman

Received: 22 July 2022
Accepted: 2 September 2022
Published: 4 September 2022

Publisher's Note: MDPI stays neutral with regard to jurisdictional claims in published maps and institutional affiliations.

1. Introduction

Congenital heart defects (CHD) refer to the structural abnormalities of the heart and/or vessels at birth. As the most common congenital anomaly worldwide, the CHD birth prevalence is estimated to be 9.41‰, with millions of newborns diagnosed with CHD each year [1]. In China, the estimated CHD prevalence at live birth is about 9.00‰, with more than 0.15 million incident cases yearly [2]. CHD accounted for over 0.26 million deaths worldwide in 2017, and remained the leading cause of infant morbidity and mortality from congenital abnormalities [3]. Nowadays nearly 20 million people live with CHD globally, causing great burdens on the family and society [3]. Although some environmental and genetic factors have been generally accepted as the risk factors for CHDs, the etiology of CHD remains to be largely unclear [4,5].

Maternal diet in pregnancy, as an important modifiable factor, has been the focus of interventions to improve birth outcomes because of the low cost and low risk. Existing evidence suggests that maternal low intakes of some nutrients including iron, zinc, selenium, folate, and niacin increase the risk of CHD [6–10], while maternal high intake of vitamin E increase the risk of CHD [11]. Previous researches also suggest that mothers with excessive intake of barbecued foods, smoked foods, fried foods, and pickled vegetables are at higher risks of fetal CHD and ventricular septal defects (VSD), while mothers with regular intake of fresh fruits, dairy, and fish and shrimp are at lower risks of fetal CHD and VSD [12–14]. However, most studies on the association between nutrition and CHD to date focus on individual nutrients or foods, which does not fully capture the complex interactions among nutrients and foods. Despite the emphasis of recent dietary recommendations on healthy dietary patterns, limited studies have been published on optimal dietary patterns in pregnancy to reduce the risk of CHD [15–18], especially for the use of dietary quality indices [18]. Dietary quality indices have great potential for use among people because of their easier collection and interpretation, especially in low- and middle-income countries [19,20]. However, the associations between maternal dietary quality indices and CHD have not been investigated in the population except one in America [18].

The Global Diet Quality Score (GDQS) is a novel food group-based dietary score according to the data from 14 countries [21]. The GDQS has the ability to capture nutrient adequacy and diet-related non-communicable disease, and is a promising candidate for global monitoring platforms [21]. The Mediterranean Diet Score (MDS) is developed on the basis of the Mediterranean diet, which is high in fruits, vegetables, whole grains, legumes, fish, and nuts, high in olive oil but low in saturated lipids, low to moderate in dairy, and limited in red meat and wine [22]. Previous studies have shown that the Mediterranean diet in pregnancy benefits maternal and offspring health [19]. To our knowledge, the GDQS has not been assessed for the associations with pregnancy outcomes including CHD. For the MDS, only one study in America has used it to examine the association with CHD [18]. It remains unknown whether maternal MDS during pregnancy could be used to evaluate the association with CHD in Asian countries, where the dietary habits are distinct from those in western countries. The prevalence of CHD (the mild lesions in particular) is higher in Asia than that in other regions, and the increase rate of CHD prevalence (atrial septal defects (ASD) in particular) in Asia is also greater than in other regions [1], which may partly come from the difference in dietary habits. Some studies have described maternal predictors for CHD [23–26], providing a reference for the early prediction of CHD. However, the prediction values for dietary quality indices on CHD have not been explored.

The current study in Northwest China aimed to explore the associations of maternal dietary quality during pregnancy assessed by GDQS and MDS with the risk of CHD, and evaluate the prediction values for dietary quality indices on CHD.

2. Materials and Methods

2.1. Study Design and Participants

We performed a case-control study in six comprehensive hospitals from August 2014 to August 2016 in Xi'an City, Northwest China. These six hospitals were selected according to their qualification to perform the diagnoses of birth defects and their willingness to cooperate. The detailed fetal echocardiography during the 20th–24th month of gestation was in the routine prenatal screening program in the six hospitals, and used as the prenatal diagnosis of CHD. The study design has been published in detail previously [8,15]. Briefly, we recruited participants among the pregnant women waiting for delivery in the cooperated hospitals. Pregnant women whose fetuses had isolated CHD and no genetic abnormalities were included in the case group, and pregnant women whose fetuses had no diagnosed congenital anomalies were included in the control group. Mothers with multiple gestations or diabetes were excluded because of potentially different etiologies. Qualified specialists in the ultrasound, obstetrics, and pediatrics departments strictly enforced the diagnostic standard criteria to finish the diagnoses in cases and controls. We further conducted a telephone follow-up within one year after birth to confirm the diagnosis. All the CHD diagnoses were ascertained by echocardiography and/or cardiac catheterization and/or surgery. We randomly selected controls each month in each hospital, and the ratio of the number of controls to cases included in the same month in the same hospital was 2:1. To detect a significant ($p < 0.05$) OR of 0.75 between groups of good and poor dietary quality with a statistical power of 80%, 443 cases, and 886 controls would be required. Finally, 474 cases and 948 controls with completed questionnaires were included, meeting the requirements of the sample size.

All participants gave written informed consent. The ethics committee of Xi'an Jiaotong University Health Science Center approved this study (No. 2012008).

2.2. Dietary Quality Evaluation

We used a 111-item semi-quantitative food frequency questionnaire (FFQ) to collect maternal diets throughout the entire pregnancy when women were waiting for delivery in the hospital. The median time from the end of the interview to delivery was two days among the cases and controls. Maternal dietary habits tend to be stable across pregnancy [27]; thus, maternal diets during the entire pregnancy are comparable with those in the 3rd–8th week of gestation, the critical period of cardiac development [6,8,15,28]. The FFQ was established according to a validated FFQ designed for pregnant women in Northwest China [29]. Women recalled consumption frequency based on eight predefined categories ranging from never to two or more times per day and reported portion sizes with the help of food portion images [30,31]. The nutrient contents of foods were derived from the Chinese Food Composition Tables [32,33].

The GDQS and MDS were used to assess dietary quality because these priori-defined indices were previously validated and reflected common recommended dietary guidelines. The GDQS consists of 16 healthy food groups (citrus fruits, deep orange fruits, other fruits, dark green leafy vegetables, cruciferous vegetables, deep orange vegetables, other vegetables, legumes, deep orange tubers, nuts and seeds, whole grains, liquid oils, fish and shellfish, poultry and game meat, low-fat dairy, and eggs), 7 unhealthy food groups (processed meat, refined grains, and baked goods, sweets and ice cream, sugar-sweetened beverages, juice, white roots and tubers, and purchased deep fried foods), and 2 food groups regarded as unhealthy in excessive amounts (high-fat dairy, and red meat) [21]. The daily intake of each food group was classified into 3 or 4 categories. For 16 healthy food groups, points from 0 to 4 were given to each intake category, with higher intake receiving more points. For the other 9 food groups, points from 0 to 2 were given according to the intake categories. The GDQS was a sum of all 25 food group scores, with a range of 0 to 49 [21]. The higher the GDQS was, the better the diet quality was. A previously modified version of MDS for pregnant women was used in this study [34], in which 8 components were positively scored (fruits, vegetables, legumes, whole grains, fish, dairy, nuts, monounsaturated-to-saturated fat ratio), and 1 component was negatively scored (red and processed meat). Zero or one points were assigned according to the median intake for each component. The MDS was summed for each component score, and the range was 0 to 9, with higher scores showing better adherence to the Mediterranean diet. Alcohol consumption was excluded from the original MDS because alcohol intake was not recommended during pregnancy and our participants rarely drank alcohol during pregnancy.

2.3. Covariates

We collected the general information about pregnancy face-to-face by a standard questionnaire. The study covariates included (1) socio-demographic characteristics: maternal age (<30 years/$\geq$30 years), work (in employment/without employment), education (junior high school or below/senior high school or above), residence (urban/rural), and parity (0/$\geq$1); (2) maternal health-related factors in early pregnancy: passive smoking (no/yes), anemia (no/yes), medication use (no/yes), and folate/iron supplements use (yes/no). Women with no paid employment outside their homes were regarded as without employment. People exposed to others' tobacco smoke for $\geq$15 min/d was defined as exposure to passive smoking. Women with hemoglobin concentration <110 g/L in early pregnancy were diagnosed with anemia.

2.4. Statistical Analysis

Univariate comparisons between groups were tested by the χ^2 test for categorical variables, and by the Mann-Whitney U test for continuous variables because of the non-normal distributions observed by the Shapiro–Wilk test. Considering the clustering in the design through hospitals, we used mixed logistic regression models to estimate ORs (95%CIs) for total CHDs and CHDs subtypes associated with GDQS and MDS. The GDQS and MDS were divided into four groups according to quartiles of the control distribution. The confounding variables were adjusted in the models if they were reported to be risk factors for CHD [4,5] and changed the estimated by more than 10% [35], which finally included maternal age, work, education, residence, parity, and maternal passive smoking, anemia, medication use, and folate/iron supplement use in early pregnancy. Total energy intake during pregnancy was adjusted in the models to indirectly reflect maternal BMI status that was not collected in the survey. p for trend was calculated by including quartile-specific median value in the model. The risk of CHD associated with per 1 higher score of GDQS and MDS was assessed by mixed logistic regression models. Subgroup analyses were performed by baseline characteristics including maternal age, work, education, residence, parity, and maternal passive smoking, anemia, medication use, and folate/iron supplement use in early pregnancy. The interaction between GDQS or MDS and each of the subgroup factors was tested by the likelihood ratio test comparing regression models with and without an interaction term. The receiver operating characteristic curves (ROC) were constructed to determine the optimal cut-off values of GDQS and MDS in pregnancy for CHD with the maximum Youden index (sensitivity + specificity − 1). The areas under the ROC (AUCs) showed the accuracy of GDQS and MDS as predictive markers for CHD. When the AUC > 0.5, the closer the AUC was to 1, the better the predictive power of the model was, as follows: AUC > 0.9, very good; AUC > 0.8, good; and AUC > 0.7, useful [36].

We used the Stata software (version 15.0; StataCorp, College Station, TX, USA) to conduct the statistical analyses. We set the statistical significance at 0.05 with two-sided.

3. Results

3.1. Baseline Characteristics of the Study Population

Among the 474 CHD babies, 46.8% were diagnosed with VSD, and 46.0% with ASD, followed by atrioventricular septal defects, patent ductus arteriosus, and tetralogy of fallot (Table S1). Women in the cases were less likely to be in employment, have higher education levels, live in an urban area, and be nulliparity when compared with those in the controls (Table 1). Passive smoking, anemia, and medication use in early pregnancy were more common in the cases than in the controls, while folate/iron supplements use in early pregnancy was less common in the cases than in the controls. The proportion of babies with birth weight lower than 2500 g was higher in the cases than in the controls, while no difference in gestational age was found between the two groups. Pregnant women in the cases had lower intakes of energy and most nutrients except carbohydrate in comparison with those in the controls. Women in the cases had significantly lower GDQS and MDS in pregnancy than the controls (both $p < 0.001$).

3.2. The Distribution of Food Components in GDQS and MDS among Cases and Controls

The GDQS scores for all 16 healthy food groups except dark green leafy vegetables, whole grains, and low-fat dairy were significantly lower in the cases than in the controls (all $p < 0.05$) (Table 2). The GDQS scores for juice, purchased deep-fried foods, high-fat dairy, and red meat were also significantly lower in the cases than the controls (all $p < 0.05$), while the GDQS scores for the other five unhealthy food groups were not significantly different between groups (Table 2). The proportions of women consuming fruits, vegetables, legumes, fish, dairy, and nuts above the median intake levels during pregnancy were significantly lower in the cases than in the controls, while the proportion of women consuming red and processed meat above the median intake level during pregnancy was significantly higher in the cases than the controls (Figure 1).

Table 1. Baseline characteristics of the study population.

	Case (N = 474)	Control (N = 948)	p [1]
Sociodemographic characteristics, %			
Maternal age < 30 years	66.5	65.8	0.812
Maternal work, in employment	50.6	78.7	<0.001
Maternal education, senior high school or above	58.9	80.7	<0.001
Urban residence	66.0	71.6	0.030
Nulliparity	57.8	80.3	<0.001
Maternal health-related factors in early pregnancy, %			
Passive smoking	33.5	9.3	<0.001
Anemia	16.9	10.9	0.001
Medication use	41.6	30.4	<0.001
Folate/iron supplements use	76.6	89.2	<0.001
Birth weight < 2500 g, %	9.7	5.3	0.003
Gestational age < 37 weeks, %	6.1	5.1	0.407
Daily nutrients intakes during pregnancy, median (25th percentile, 75th percentile)			
Total energy, kcal	1753.2 (1452.4, 2086.1)	1907.1 (1563.3, 2415.9)	<0.001
Protein, g	44.5 (32.0, 60.5)	56.9 (40.9, 78.9)	<0.001
Fat, g	30.9 (19.0, 47.8)	41.7 (29.0, 59.5)	<0.001
Monounsaturated fatty acid, g	6.9 (3.9, 12.2)	9.7 (6.6, 14.4)	<0.001
Saturated fatty acid, g	13.1 (8.1, 19.3)	17.4 (12.6, 25.0)	<0.001
Carbohydrate, g	185.6 (142.0, 237.7)	190.9 (142.5, 269.8)	0.057
Iron, mg	17.5 (12.6, 23.3)	20.4 (14.3, 28.9)	<0.001
Zinc, mg	4.7 (3.1, 6.8)	6.4 (4.6, 9.1)	<0.001
Selenium, μg	22.7 (15.0, 32.5)	30.8 (21.9, 43.7)	<0.001
Calcium, mg	457.4 (315.8, 643.8)	500.9 (359.8, 707.0)	<0.001
Niacin, mg	9.6 (7.3, 13.2)	12.5 (9.0, 17.3)	<0.001
Folate, μg	195.1 (161.3, 242.9)	220.2 (181.5, 270.5)	<0.001
Vitamin C, mg	63.5 (42.1, 107.0)	77.0 (51.8, 123.2)	<0.001
Dietary quality scores, median (25th percentile, 75th percentile)			
GDQS	27.5 (23.7, 31.0)	31.0 (27.3, 34.3)	<0.001
MDS	4.0 (2.0, 5.0)	5.0 (3.0, 6.0)	<0.001

GDQS, Global Diet Quality Score; MDS, Mediterranean Diet Score; [1] Categorical variables are compared between groups by the χ^2 test, and continuous variables are compared between groups by the Mann–Whitney U test.

Table 2. The distribution of food components in the Global Diet Quality Score among cases and controls.

	Scoring Ranges [1] (Cutoffs, g/d) Low/Middle/High	GDQS Subscores	Case (N = 474)				Control (N = 948)				p [2]
			Low, %	Middle, %	High, %	Score [2]	Low, %	Middle, %	High, %	Score [2]	
Citrus fruits	<24/24–69/>69	0, 1, 2	69.6	17.9	12.4	0.0 (0.0, 1.0)	62.6	26.1	11.4	0.0 (0.0, 1.0)	0.032
Deep orange fruits	<25/25–123/>123	0, 1, 2	96.8	3.2	0	0.0 (0.0, 0.0)	93.4	6.6	0	0.0 (0.0, 0.0)	0.007
Other fruits	<27/27–107/>107	0, 1, 2	0.8	13.7	85.4	2.0 (2.0, 2.0)	0.3	4.4	95.3	2.0 (2.0, 2.0)	<0.001
Dark green leafy vegetables	<13/13–37/>37	0, 2, 4	6.8	42.4	50.8	4.0 (2.0, 4.0)	6.5	39.7	53.8	4.0 (2.0, 4.0)	0.321
Cruciferous vegetables	<13/13–36/>36	0, 0.25, 0.5	7.0	43.7	49.4	0.25 (0.25, 0.5)	2.7	37.8	59.5	0.5 (0.25, 0.5)	<0.001
Deep orange vegetables	<9/9–45/>45	0, 0.25, 0.5	33.3	51.1	15.6	0.25 (0.0, 0.25)	20.8	63.1	16.1	0.25 (0.25, 0.25)	<0.001
Other vegetables	<23/23–114/>114	0, 0.25, 0.5	0.4	25.9	73.6	0.5 (0.25, 0.5)	0.3	15.2	84.5	0.5 (0.5, 0.5)	<0.001
Legumes	<9/9–42/>42	0, 2, 4	14.1	40.1	45.8	2.0 (2.0, 4.0)	1.9	27.8	70.3	4.0 (2.0, 4.0)	<0.001
Deep orange tubers	<12/12–63/>63	0, 0.25, 0.5	74.9	21.7	3.4	0.0 (0.0, 0.25)	57.4	40.4	2.2	0.0 (0.0, 0.25)	<0.001
Nuts and seeds	<7/7–13/>13	0, 2, 4	48.9	14.1	36.9	2.0 (0.0, 4.0)	35.2	18.0	46.7	2.0 (0.0, 4.0)	<0.001
Whole grains	<8/8–13/>13	0, 1, 2	29.1	11.0	59.9	2.0 (0.0, 2.0)	32.0	15.5	52.5	2.0 (0.0, 2.0)	0.082
Liquid oils	<2/2–7.5/>7.5	0, 1, 2	0	33.1	66.9	2.0 (1.0, 2.0)	0	27.4	72.6	2.0 (1.0, 2.0)	0.026
Fish and shellfish	<14/14–71/>71	0, 1, 2	69.0	26.4	4.6	0.0 (0.0, 1.0)	38.1	49.3	12.7	1.0 (0.0, 1.0)	<0.001
Poultry and game meat	<16/16–44/>44	0, 1, 2	93.2	5.1	1.7	0.0 (0.0, 0.0)	81.6	16.6	1.8	0.0 (0.0, 0.0)	<0.001
Low-fat dairy	<33/33–132/>132	0, 1, 2	100.0	0	0	0.0 (0.0, 0.0)	100.0	0	0	0.0 (0.0, 0.0)	1.000
Eggs	<6/6–32/>32	0, 1, 2	27.2	35.0	37.8	1.0 (0.0, 2.0)	8.4	34.9	56.6	2.0 (1.0, 2.0)	<0.001
Processed meat	<9/9–30/>30	2, 1, 0	74.9	19.6	5.5	2.0 (1.0, 2.0)	78.7	18.7	2.6	2.0 (2.0, 2.0)	0.069
Refined grains and baked goods	<7/7–33/>33	2, 1, 0	0	0.6	99.4	0.0 (0.0, 0.0)	0.1	0.2	99.7	0.0 (0.0, 0.0)	0.387
Sweets and ice cream	<13/13–37/>37	2, 1, 0	93.9	3.8	2.3	2.0 (2.0, 2.0)	94.2	4.2	1.6	2.0 (2.0, 2.0)	0.790
Sugar-sweetened beverages	<57/57–180/>180	2, 1, 0	98.3	0.8	0.8	2.0 (2.0, 2.0)	99.4	0.6	0	2.0 (2.0, 2.0)	0.056
Juice	<36/36–144/>144	2, 1, 0	94.9	3.2	1.9	2.0 (2.0, 2.0)	98.5	1.4	0.1	2.0 (2.0, 2.0)	<0.001
White roots and tubers	<27/27–107/>107	2, 1, 0	55.9	39.9	4.2	2.0 (1.0, 2.0)	53.9	44.7	1.4	2.0 (1.0, 2.0)	0.814
Purchased deep-fried foods	<9/9–45/>45	2, 1, 0	87.3	10.1	2.5	2.0 (2.0, 2.0)	90.6	9.1	0.3	2.0 (2.0, 2.0)	0.044
High-fat dairy	<35/35–142/142–734/>734	0, 1, 2, 0	46.0	26.2/27.6	0.2	1.0 (0.0, 2.0)	10.4	41.4/47.9	0.3	1.0 (1.0, 2.0)	<0.001
Red meat	<9/9–46/>46	0, 1, 0	27.4	41.6	31.0	0.0 (0.0, 1.0)	7.2	51.6	41.2	1.0 (0.0, 1.0)	<0.001

GDQS, Global Diet Quality Score. [1] Scoring ranges: the 3 categories here are low, middle, and high separated by a solidus; for high-fat dairy, 4 categories were classified: low, lower middle, high middle, and high (from left to right). [2] Values are present as median (25th percentile, 75th percentile), and compared between groups by Mann–Whitney U test.

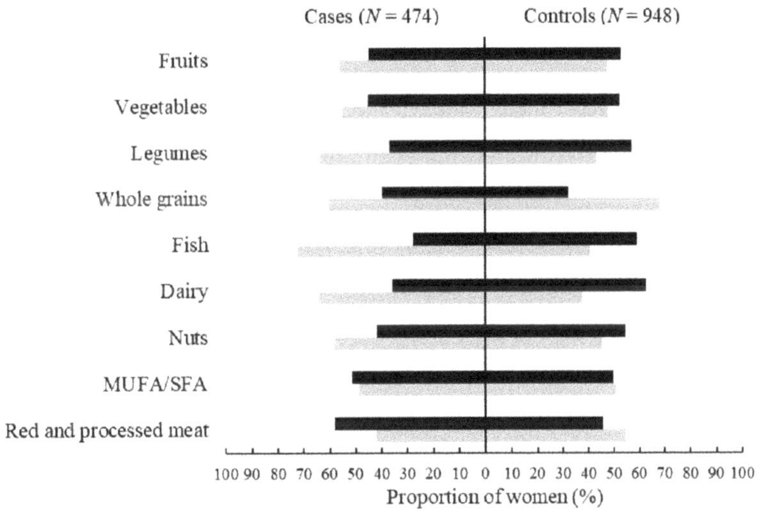

Figure 1. The proportion of women consuming food components in the Mediterranean Diet Score during pregnancy by the median intake levels among cases and controls. MUFA/SFA, monounsaturated-to-saturated fat ratio. Dark shaded bars indicate maternal consumption above the median levels, and light shaded bars indicate maternal consumption equal to or below the median levels. Statistically significant differences were found for the groups of fruits, vegetables, legumes, fish, dairy, nuts, and red and processed meat between cases and controls by the χ^2 test (all $p < 0.05$).

Daily nutrient intakes during pregnancy by GDQS and MDS categories among cases and controls are shown in Tables S2 and S3, respectively. In both cases and controls, daily intakes of energy, macronutrients, and micronutrients were increased with higher scores of GDQS and MDS (all $p < 0.001$).

3.3. Associations of Maternal GDQS and MDS during Pregnancy with CHD

The risk of total CHD was reduced with the increasing quartiles of GDQS and MDS, and the tests for trend were statistically significant (both p for trend <0.05) (Table 3). The fully adjusted ORs comparing the highest with the lowest quartiles of the GDQS and MDS were 0.26 (95%CI: 0.16–0.42) and 0.53 (95%CI: 0.34–0.83), respectively. The risk of total CHD was reduced by 12% (OR: 0.88, 95%CI: 0.85–0.91) and 12% (OR: 0.88, 95%CI: 0.80–0.95) for per 1 higher score of GDQS and MDS, respectively. The fully adjusted models also showed inverse associations of GDQS and MDS with the risks of VSD and ASD (all p for trend <0.05) (Table 3). Per 1 higher score of GDQS and MDS was associated with 12% (OR: 0.88, 95%CI: 0.84–0.92) and 11% (OR: 0.89, 95%CI: 0.81–0.98) lower risk of VSD, respectively. Per 1 higher score of GDQS and MDS was associated with 13% (OR: 0.87, 95%CI: 0.84–0.91) and 10% (OR: 0.90, 95%CI: 0.83–0.98) lower risk of ASD, respectively.

Subgroup analyses showed that the associations of maternal GDQS and MDS during pregnancy with total CHD did not change by maternal age, work, parity, or maternal health-related factors in early pregnancy (passive smoking, anemia, medication use, or folate/iron supplements use) (Figures S1 and S2). However, the inverse association between maternal GDQS and the risk of total CHD appeared to be stronger among women with lower education levels and in rural areas, and the tests for interaction were significant (both $p < 0.05$) (Figure S1). The inverse association between maternal MDS and the risk of total CHD appeared to be stronger among women in rural areas, and the test for interaction was significant ($p = 0.004$) (Figure S2).

Table 3. Associations of maternal GDQS and MDS during pregnancy with congenital heart defects.

		Total Congenital Heart Defects (N_{cases} = 474)		Ventricular Septal Defects (N_{cases} = 222)		Atrial Septal Defects (N_{cases} = 218)	
	$N_{cases}/N_{controls}$	Unadjusted OR (95%CI)	Adjusted OR (95%CI) [1]	Unadjusted OR (95%CI)	Adjusted OR (95%CI) [1]	Unadjusted OR (95%CI)	Adjusted OR (95%CI) [1]
GDQS							
Quartile 1	218/218	1	1	1	1	1	1
Quartile 2	131/241	0.54 (0.41, 0.72)	0.59 (0.42, 0.82)	0.51 (0.35, 0.74)	0.51 (0.32, 0.79)	0.57 (0.39, 0.83)	0.51 (0.34, 0.79)
Quartile 3	75/237	0.32 (0.23, 0.44)	0.36 (0.24, 0.53)	0.35 (0.23, 0.52)	0.38 (0.23, 0.63)	0.39 (0.26, 0.59)	0.35 (0.21, 0.59)
Quartile 4	50/252	0.20 (0.14, 0.28)	0.26 (0.16, 0.42)	0.18 (0.11, 0.29)	0.23 (0.12, 0.44)	0.21 (0.13, 0.34)	0.21 (0.11, 0.41)
p for trend	474/948	<0.001	<0.001	<0.001	<0.001	<0.001	<0.001
Per 1 higher score	474/948	0.87 (0.85, 0.89)	0.88 (0.85, 0.91)	0.87 (0.84, 0.90)	0.88 (0.84, 0.92)	0.88 (0.85, 0.91)	0.87 (0.84, 0.91)
MDS							
Quartile 1	142/164	1	1	1	1	1	1
Quartile 2	159/271	0.67 (0.50, 0.91)	0.76 (0.54, 1.08)	0.68 (0.46, 1.01)	0.87 (0.55, 1.38)	0.80 (0.53, 1.19)	0.83 (0.53, 1.31)
Quartile 3	75/162	0.53 (0.37, 0.76)	0.70 (0.46, 1.08)	0.62 (0.39, 0.98)	0.81 (0.52, 1.26)	0.69 (0.43, 1.11)	0.80 (0.47, 1.36)
Quartile 4	98/351	0.32 (0.23, 0.44)	0.53 (0.34, 0.83)	0.34 (0.22, 0.52)	0.57 (0.34, 0.96)	0.44 (0.28, 0.67)	0.61 (0.38, 0.97)
p for trend	474/948	<0.001	0.007	<0.001	0.010	<0.001	0.016
Per 1 higher score	474/948	0.79 (0.75, 0.84)	0.88 (0.80, 0.95)	0.80 (0.74, 0.87)	0.89 (0.81, 0.98)	0.85 (0.78, 0.91)	0.90 (0.83, 0.98)

GDQS, Global Diet Quality Score; MDS, Mediterranean Diet Score. [1] Adjusted for total energy intake during pregnancy sociodemographic characteristics (maternal age, work, education, residence, and parity), and maternal health-related factors in early pregnancy (passive smoking, anemia, medication use, and folate/iron supplements use).

3.4. The Prediction Values for Maternal GDQS and MDS during Pregnancy on CHD

The ROC suggested that the performances of maternal GDQS during pregnancy were useful in predicting total CHD, VSD, and ASD, with the AUCs being 0.80 (95%CI: 0.78–0.83), 0.80 (95%CI: 0.76–0.83), and 0.78 (95%CI: 0.74–0.81), respectively (Figure 2). The optimal GDQS cut-off scores were 30 for total CHD (sensitivity: 69.6%; specificity: 77.7%), 28 for VSD (sensitivity: 63.5%; specificity: 82.7%), and 30 for ASD (sensitivity: 60.6%; specificity: 84.8%), respectively. The ROC also suggested that the performances of maternal MDS during pregnancy were useful in predicting total CHD, VSD, and ASD, with the AUCs being 0.79 (95%CI: 0.76–0.81), 0.79 (95%CI: 0.76–0.82), and 0.77 (95%CI: 0.74–0.80), respectively (Figure 3). The optimal MDS cut-off scores were 8 for total CHD (sensitivity: 65.2%; specificity: 79.5%), 7 for VSD (sensitivity: 70.7%; specificity: 73.7%), and 7 for ASD (sensitivity: 69.3%; specificity: 73.5%), respectively.

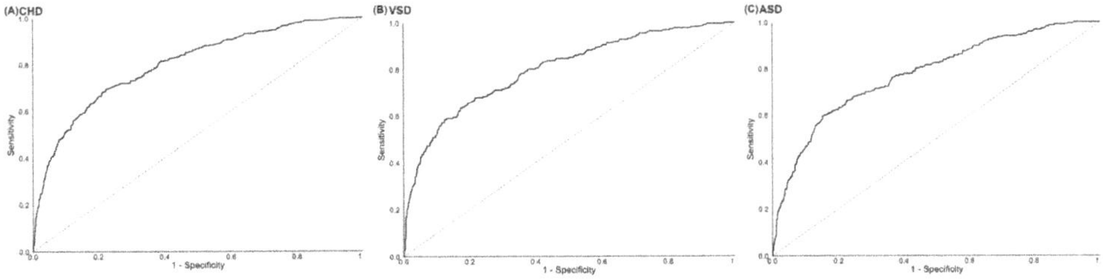

Figure 2. The ROC for the Global Diet Quality Score during pregnancy in the prediction of (**A**) total congenital heart defects, (**B**) ventricular septal defects, and (**C**) atrial septal defects. ASD, atrial septal defects; CHD, congenital heart defects; ROC, receiver operating characteristic curves; VSD, ventricular septal defects. The dotted line refers to the reference line, resulting from random selection.

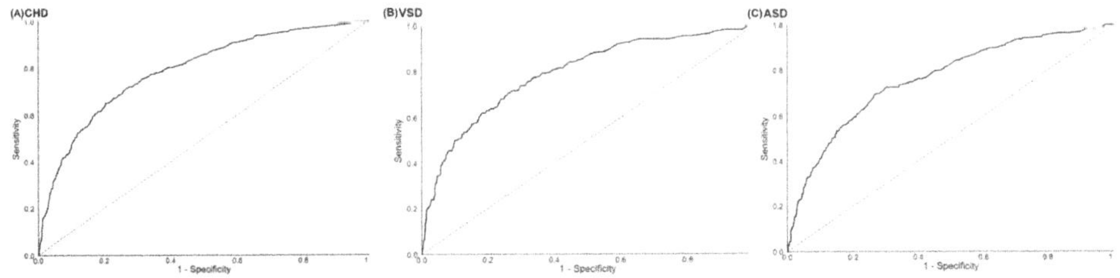

Figure 3. The ROC for the Mediterranean Diet Score during pregnancy in the prediction of (**A**) total congenital heart defects, (**B**) ventricular septal defects, and (**C**) atrial septal defects. ASD, atrial septal defects; CHD, congenital heart defects; ROC, receiver operating characteristic curves; VSD, ventricular septal defects. The dotted line refers to the reference line, resulting from random selection.

4. Discussion

This case-control study suggested that pregnant women with better dietary quality, defined by higher scores of GDQS and MDS, had a reduced risk of having fetuses with total CHD and subtypes. The inverse associations of maternal GDQS and MDS during pregnancy with CHD appeared to be stronger among women with lower education levels or in rural areas. This case-control study also suggested that maternal GDQS and MDS during pregnancy had good predictive values for total CHD and the subtypes in fetuses, with the AUCs close to 0.8.

To date, there was only one study investigating the relationship between maternal dietary quality and CHD [18]. This previous study conducted in America found that better dietary quality, assessed by MDS and Dietary Quality Index for Pregnancy, reduced the risk of CHD, which was consistent with the results in the current study. Some studies evaluated priori dietary quality indices in association with birth defects [37–39], but not CHD. These studies reported significant inverse associations of maternal MDS with the risks of some birth defects (orofacial clefts, neural tube defects, and gastroschisis) [37,38], but not hypospadias [40]. There were three studies examining the risk of CHD in relation to dietary patterns identified by posterior statistical analyses [15–17], rather than the priori indices. A study from America reported that a prudent dietary pattern high in reduced-fat milk, yogurt, fortified cereal, whole-wheat bread, and fish, and low in vegetables and fruits reduced CHD risk [16]. The study in the Netherlands observed that the one-carbon-rich dietary pattern, which was high in fish and seafood, lowered the CHD risk [17]. The study in Shaanxi China found that the prudent dietary pattern, which was high in white meats, red meats, vegetables, legumes, dairy, and snacks, and the dairy and egg pattern, which was high in dairy, nuts, and eggs, and low in beverages, decreased the CHD risk [16]. Although these three studies have identified some posterior dietary patterns associated with CHD, it could hardly be applied in other populations because of the subjective. Our study focused on the priori dietary quality indices, to be more easily reproducible and comparable to prior related studies. The magnitude of the risk for CHD associated with maternal MDS in our study was approximately similar to that observed for CHD in the previous study, with the lowest OR comparing the extreme quartiles being 0.53 (95%CI: 0.34–0.83) and 0.43 (95%CI: 0.25–0.75), respectively [18]. The strength of the inverse association between dietary quality and CHD risk seemed to be stronger for GDQS than MDS in the current study, similar to the stronger association for Dietary Quality Index for Pregnancy than MDS with CHD and other birth defects in the previous studies [18,37]. Since there has been no study investigating health outcomes in relation to maternal GDQS in pregnancy, it is hard for us to compare the results about GDQS in our study with other studies. More studies are needed to explore the relationships between maternal GDQS and health outcomes including CHD and to validate the prediction of maternal GDQS on health outcomes.

Maternal diet is critical to fetal growth and development. Suboptimal diets in pregnancy can cause adverse pregnancy outcomes including congenital abnormalities [28]. Maternal low intakes of zinc, selenium, iron, niacin, and folate have been reported to reduce the risk of CHD [6–8,11]. Maternal diets rich in these nutrients may benefit the development of the cardiovascular system in fetuses. Women with higher scores of GDQS and MDS during pregnancy had higher intakes of these micronutrients in the current study, which may partly explain the protective effect of better dietary quality on CHD. Pregnant women with better dietary quality may have more opportunities to obtain nutrition knowledge and pay more attention to healthy diets, and thus have better nutritional status [15]. In addition, maternal adherence to better dietary quality was reported to decrease maternal oxidative DNA damage and lipid oxidation [39], which may further benefit the normal development of the fetal cardiovascular system [41]. Maternal dietary quality is also likely to be a mediator of metabolic diseases including gestational diabetes mellitus and hypertension in pregnancy, which further influences the fetal cardiovascular system [42]. However, we could not further conduct the mediation analyses because women with diabetes have been excluded and there were only two women with gestational hypertension.

The current study provides valuable evidence for the relationship between maternal dietary quality in pregnancy and the risk of CHD. However, we should acknowledge some limitations. First, due to the limited sample size, the associations of dietary quality with other CHD subtypes could not be separately investigated. Further studies with large sample sizes are needed to explore the association with other CHD subtypes. Second, selection bias cannot be excluded because pregnant women having CHD fetuses tend to choose comprehensive hospitals for delivery. Selection bias may also come from the fact that this study did not recruit CHD fetuses that did not survive. Third, recall bias cannot be excluded because maternal information during pregnancy was retrospectively reported by mothers waiting for delivery. However, previous studies have indicated that diets and events in pregnancy can be recalled well after years [43,44]. To reduce this bias, standard questionnaires and supporting materials such as food portion images and calendars were used to collect information to help participants recall accurately in the survey. Fourth, exposure misclassification may cause because we collected dietary information during the entire pregnancy, rather than in the critical period of heart development in the 3rd–8th week of gestation. However, previous studies have shown that maternal dietary habits tend to be stable throughout pregnancy [27]. Finally, the possibility of residual confounding from unobserved and unknown factors cannot be excluded. For example, we did not collect information on gestational weight gain or BMI, which was reported to be associated with fetal CHD [45]. In fact, the real causal relationship between dietary quality during pregnancy and CHD cannot be revealed in the case-control study. Further intervention studies are needed to examine the influence of maternal dietary quality on fetal CHD.

5. Conclusions

In summary, this case-control study suggested that maternal GDQS and MDS, indicators of dietary quality, were negatively associated with the CHD risk. Moreover, maternal GDQS and MDS during pregnancy had good predictive values for CHD in offspring. These results implied the importance of improving dietary quality in pregnancy to decrease the prevalence of CHD in Northwest China. Further research is warranted to assess the validity of these scoring systems as predictive tools for CHD in other populations.

Supplementary Materials: The following supporting information can be downloaded at: https://www.mdpi.com/article/10.3390/nu14173654/s1, Table S1: The constitution of congenital heart defects subtypes in the cases; Table S2: Daily nutrients intakes during pregnancy by Global Diet Quality Score category among cases and controls; Table S3: Daily nutrients intakes during pregnancy by Mediterranean Diet Score category among cases and controls; Figure S1: Subgroup analyses for the risk of total congenital heart defects associated with per 1 higher score of the Global Diet Quality Score; Figure S2: Subgroup analyses for the risk of congenital heart defects associated with per 1 higher score of the Mediterranean Diet Score.

Author Contributions: Conceptualization, J.Y.; methodology, J.Y., Q.C., X.L., S.D., L.Z. and H.Y.; formal analysis, J.Y., Q.C. and X.L.; investigation, J.Y., Q.C. and X.L.; data curation, L.Z., S.D. and H.Y.; writing—original draft preparation, J.Y. and Q.C.; writing—review and editing, J.Y.; supervision, J.Y., S.D. and H.Y.; project administration, S.D. and L.Z.; funding acquisition, J.Y., S.D. and H.Y. All authors have read and agreed to the published version of the manuscript.

Funding: This research was funded by the National Natural Science Foundation of China (82103852, 81230016), China Postdoctoral Science Foundation (2019M663751), Shaanxi Health and Family Planning Commission (Sxwsjswzfcght2016-013), and National Key R&D Program of China (2017YFC0907200, 2017YFC0907201).

Institutional Review Board Statement: The study was in accordance with the guidelines of the Declaration of Helsinki, and approved by the ethics committee of Xi'an Jiaotong University Health Science Center (No.2012008).

Informed Consent Statement: Informed consent was obtained from all subjects involved in the study.

Data Availability Statement: The data present in this study are available on request from the corresponding authors.

Acknowledgments: The authors are grateful to all medical staff involved in the study for recruiting the participants. The authors are also grateful to all mothers and infants who participated in the study and all investigators who contributed to data collection.

Conflicts of Interest: The authors declare no conflict of interest.

References

1. Liu, Y.; Chen, S.; Zühlke, L.; Black, G.C.; Choy, M.K.; Li, N.; Keavney, B.D. Global birth prevalence of congenital heart defects 1970–2017: Updated systematic review and meta-analysis of 260 studies. *Int. J. Epidemiol.* **2019**, *48*, 455–463. [CrossRef] [PubMed]
2. Zhao, Q.M.; Liu, F.; Wu, L.; Ma, X.J.; Niu, C.; Huang, G.Y. Prevalence of Congenital Heart Disease at Live Birth in China. *J. Pediatr.* **2019**, *204*, 53–58. [CrossRef] [PubMed]

3. Zimmerman, M.S.; Smith, A.G.C.; Sable, C.A.; Echko, M.M.; Wilner, L.B.; Olsen, H.E.; Atalay, H.T.; Awasthi, A.; Bhutta, Z.A.; Boucher, J.L.; et al. Global, regional, and national burden of congenital heart disease, 1990–2017: A systematic analysis for the Global Burden of Disease Study 2017. *Lancet Child Adolesc. Health* **2020**, *4*, 185–200. [CrossRef]
4. Nie, X.; Liu, X.; Wang, C.; Wu, Z.; Sun, Z.; Su, J.; Yan, R.; Peng, Y.; Yang, Y.; Wang, C.; et al. Assessment of evidence on reported non-genetic risk factors of congenital heart defects: The updated umbrella review. *BMC Pregnancy Childbirth* **2022**, *22*, 371. [CrossRef] [PubMed]
5. Zhang, T.N.; Wu, Q.J.; Liu, Y.S.; Lv, J.L.; Sun, H.; Chang, Q.; Liu, C.F.; Zhao, Y.H. Environmental Risk Factors and Congenital Heart Disease: An Umbrella Review of 165 Systematic Reviews and Meta-Analyses with More Than 120 Million Participants. *Front. Cardiovasc. Med.* **2021**, *8*, 640729. [CrossRef] [PubMed]
6. Yang, J.; Kang, Y.; Chang, Q.; Zhang, B.; Liu, X.; Zeng, L.; Yan, H.; Dang, S. Maternal Zinc, Copper, and Selenium Intakes during Pregnancy and Congenital Heart Defects. *Nutrients* **2022**, *14*, 1055. [CrossRef]
7. Zhang, R.; Guo, L.; Zhao, D.; Qu, P.; Dang, S.; Yan, H. Maternal B-vitamin intake and B-vitamin supplementation during pregnancy in relation to neonatal congenital heart defects: A case-control study with propensity score matching. *Eur. J. Clin. Nutr.* **2021**, *75*, 782–791. [CrossRef]
8. Yang, J.; Kang, Y.; Cheng, Y.; Zeng, L.; Shen, Y.; Shi, G.; Liu, Y.; Qu, P.; Zhang, R.; Yan, H.; et al. Iron intake and iron status during pregnancy and risk of congenital heart defects: A case-control study. *Int. J. Cardiol.* **2020**, *301*, 74–79. [CrossRef]
9. Qu, Y.; Lin, S.; Zhuang, J.; Bloom, M.S.; Smith, M.; Nie, Z.; Mai, J.; Ou, Y.; Wu, Y.; Gao, X.; et al. First-Trimester Maternal Folic Acid Supplementation Reduced Risks of Severe and Most Congenital Heart Diseases in Offspring: A Large Case-Control Study. *J. Am. Heart Assoc.* **2020**, *9*, e015652. [CrossRef]
10. Smedts, H.P.; Rakhshandehroo, M.; Verkleij-Hagoort, A.C.; de Vries, J.H.; Ottenkamp, J.; Steegers, E.A.; Steegers-Theunissen, R.P. Maternal intake of fat, riboflavin and nicotinamide and the risk of having offspring with congenital heart defects. *Eur. J. Nutr.* **2008**, *47*, 357–365. [CrossRef]
11. Smedts, H.P.; de Vries, J.H.; Rakhshandehroo, M.; Wildhagen, M.F.; Verkleij-Hagoort, A.C.; Steegers, E.A.; Steegers-Theunissen, R.P. High maternal vitamin E intake by diet or supplements is associated with congenital heart defects in the offspring. *BJOG* **2009**, *116*, 416–423. [CrossRef] [PubMed]
12. Luo, M.; Wang, T.; Huang, P.; Zhang, S.; Song, X.; Sun, M.; Liu, Y.; Wei, J.; Shu, J.; Zhong, T.; et al. Association and Interaction Effect of BHMT Gene Polymorphisms and Maternal Dietary Habits with Ventricular Septal Defect in Offspring. *Nutrients* **2022**, *14*, 3094. [CrossRef] [PubMed]
13. Luo, M.; Wang, T.; Huang, P.; Zhang, S.; Song, X.; Sun, M.; Liu, Y.; Wei, J.; Shu, J.; Zhong, T.; et al. Association of maternal dietary intakes and CBS gene polymorphisms with congenital heart disease in offspring. *Int. J. Cardiol.* **2021**, *322*, 121–128.
14. Zhang, S.; Liu, X.; Yang, T.; Wang, T.; Chen, L.; Qin, J. Association of maternal dietary habits and ADIPOQ gene polymorphisms with the risk of congenital heart defects in offspring: A hospital-based case-control study. *Eur. J. Clin. Nutr.* **2022**, *76*, 373–381. [CrossRef]
15. Yang, J.; Kang, Y.; Cheng, Y.; Zeng, L.; Yan, H.; Dang, S. Maternal Dietary Patterns during Pregnancy and Congenital Heart Defects: A Case-Control Study. *Int. J. Environ. Res. Public Health.* **2019**, *16*, 2957. [CrossRef]
16. Sotres-Alvarez, D.; Siega-Riz, A.M.; Herring, A.H.; Carmichael, S.L.; Feldkamp, M.L.; Hobbs, C.A.; Olshan, A.F. Maternal dietary patterns are associated with risk of neural tube and congenital heart defects. *Am. J. Epidemiol.* **2013**, *177*, 1279–1288. [CrossRef]
17. Obermann-Borst, S.A.; Vujkovic, M.; de Vries, J.H.; Wildhagen, M.F.; Looman, C.W.; de Jonge, R.; Steegers, E.A.; Steegers-Theunissen, R.P. A maternal dietary pattern characterised by fish and seafood in association with the risk of congenital heart defects in the offspring. *BJOG* **2011**, *118*, 1205–1215. [CrossRef]
18. Botto, L.D.; Krikov, S.; Carmichael, S.L.; Munger, R.G.; Shaw, G.M.; Feldkamp, M.L. Lower rate of selected congenital heart defects with better maternal diet quality: A population-based study. *Arch. Dis. Child. Fetal Neonatal Ed.* **2016**, *101*, F43–F49. [CrossRef]
19. Arimond, M.; Wiesmann, D.; Becquey, E.; Carriquiry, A.; Daniels, M.C.; Deitchler, M.; Fanou-Fogny, N.; Joseph, M.L.; Kennedy, G.; Martin-Prevel, Y.; et al. Simple food group diversity indicators predict micronutrient adequacy of women's diets in 5 diverse, resource-poor settings. *J. Nutr.* **2010**, *140*, 2059s–2069s. [CrossRef]
20. Madzorera, I.; Isanaka, S.; Wang, M.; Msamanga, G.I.; Urassa, W.; Hertzmark, E.; Duggan, C.; Fawzi, W.W. Maternal dietary diversity and dietary quality scores in relation to adverse birth outcomes in Tanzanian women. *Am. J. Clin. Nutr.* **2020**, *112*, 695–706. [CrossRef]
21. Bromage, S.; Batis, C.; Bhupathiraju, S.N.; Fawzi, W.W.; Fung, T.T.; Li, Y.; Deitchler, M.; Angulo, E.; Birk, N.; Castellanos-Gutiérrez, A.; et al. Development and Validation of a Novel Food-Based Global Diet Quality Score (GDQS). *J. Nutr.* **2021**, *151*, 75s–92s. [CrossRef] [PubMed]
22. Amati, F.; Hassounah, S.; Swaka, A. The Impact of Mediterranean Dietary Patterns During Pregnancy on Maternal and Offspring Health. *Nutrients* **2019**, *11*, 1098. [CrossRef] [PubMed]
23. Qu, Y.; Deng, X.; Lin, S.; Han, F.; Chang, H.H.; Ou, Y.; Nie, Z.; Mai, J.; Wang, X.; Gao, X.; et al. Using Innovative Machine Learning Methods to Screen and Identify Predictors of Congenital Heart Diseases. *Front. Cardiovasc. Med.* **2021**, *8*, 797002. [CrossRef] [PubMed]
24. Liang, Y.; Li, X.; Hu, X.; Wen, B.; Wang, L.; Wang, C. A predictive model of offspring congenital heart disease based on maternal risk factors during pregnancy: A hospital based case-control study in Nanchong City. *Int. J. Med. Sci.* **2020**, *17*, 3091–3097. [CrossRef] [PubMed]

25. Luo, Y.; Li, Z.; Guo, H.; Cao, H.; Song, C.; Guo, X.; Zhang, Y. Predicting congenital heart defects: A comparison of three data mining methods. *PLoS ONE* **2017**, *12*, e0177811. [CrossRef] [PubMed]
26. Li, H.; Luo, M.; Zheng, J.; Luo, J.; Zeng, R.; Feng, N.; Du, Q.; Fang, J. An artificial neural network prediction model of congenital heart disease based on risk factors: A hospital-based case-control study. *Medicine* **2017**, *96*, e6090. [CrossRef]
27. Crozier, S.R.; Robinson, S.M.; Godfrey, K.M.; Cooper, C.; Inskip, H.M. Women's dietary patterns change little from before to during pregnancy. *J. Nutr.* **2009**, *139*, 1956–1963. [CrossRef]
28. Yang, J.; Cheng, Y.; Zeng, L.; Dang, S.; Yan, H. Maternal dietary diversity during pregnancy and congenital heart defects: A case-control study. *Eur. J. Clin. Nutr.* **2021**, *75*, 355–363. [CrossRef]
29. Cheng, Y.; Yan, H.; Dibley, M.J.; Shen, Y.; Li, Q.; Zeng, L. Validity and reproducibility of a semi-quantitative food frequency questionnaire for use among pregnant women in rural China. *Asia Pac. J. Clin. Nutr.* **2008**, *17*, 166–177.
30. Yang, J.; Dang, S.; Cheng, Y.; Qiu, H.; Mi, B.; Jiang, Y.; Qu, P.; Zeng, L.; Wang, Q.; Li, Q.; et al. Dietary intakes and dietary patterns among pregnant women in Northwest China. *Public Health Nutr.* **2017**, *20*, 282–293. [CrossRef]
31. Yang, J.; Cheng, Y.; Pei, L.; Jiang, Y.; Lei, F.; Zeng, L.; Wang, Q.; Li, Q.; Kang, Y.; Shen, Y.; et al. Maternal iron intake during pregnancy and birth outcomes: A cross-sectional study in Northwest China. *Br. J. Nutr.* **2017**, *117*, 862–871. [CrossRef]
32. Institute of Nutrition and Food Safety, China Center for Disease Control. *China Food Composition Book 2*; Peking University Medical Press: Beijing, China, 2005.
33. Institute of Nutrition and Food Safety, China Center for Disease Control. *China Food Composition Book 1*, 2nd ed.; Peking University Medical Press: Beijing, China, 2009.
34. Mahmassani, H.A.; Switkowski, K.M.; Scott, T.M.; Johnson, E.J.; Rifas-Shiman, S.L.; Oken, E.; Jacques, P.F. Maternal diet quality during pregnancy and child cognition and behavior in a US cohort. *Am. J. Clin. Nutr.* **2022**, *115*, 128–141. [CrossRef] [PubMed]
35. Mickey, R.M.; Greenland, S. The impact of confounder selection criteria on effect estimation. *Am. J. Epidemiol.* **1989**, *129*, 125–137. [CrossRef] [PubMed]
36. Swets, J.A. Measuring the accuracy of diagnostic systems. *Science* **1988**, *240*, 1285–1293. [CrossRef] [PubMed]
37. Carmichael, S.L.; Yang, W.; Feldkamp, M.L.; Munger, R.G.; Siega-Riz, A.M.; Botto, L.D.; Shaw, G. Reduced risks of neural tube defects and orofacial clefts with higher diet quality. *Arch. Pediatr. Adolesc. Med.* **2012**, *166*, 121–126. [CrossRef]
38. Feldkamp, M.L.; Krikov, S.; Botto, L.D.; Shaw, G.M.; Carmichael, S.L. Better diet quality before pregnancy is associated with reduced risk of gastroschisis in Hispanic women. *J. Nutr.* **2014**, *144*, 1781–1786.
39. Morales, E.; García-Serna, A.M.; Larqué, E.; Sánchez-Campillo, M.; Serrano-Munera, A.; Martinez-Graciá, C.; Santaella-Pascual, M.; Suárez-Martínez, C.; Vioque, J.; Noguera-Velasco, J.A.; et al. Dietary Patterns in Pregnancy and Biomarkers of Oxidative Stress in Mothers and Offspring: The NELA Birth Cohort. *Front. Nutr.* **2022**, *9*, 869357. [CrossRef]
40. Carmichael, S.L.; Ma, C.; Feldkamp, M.L.; Munger, R.G.; Olney, R.S.; Botto, L.D.; Shaw, G.M.; Correa, A. Nutritional factors and hypospadias risks. *Paediatr. Perinat. Epidemiol.* **2012**, *26*, 353–360. [CrossRef]
41. Fisher, S.A.; Burggren, W.W. Role of hypoxia in the evolution and development of the cardiovascular system. *Antioxid. Redox Signal.* **2007**, *9*, 1339–1352. [CrossRef]
42. Liu, S.; Joseph, K.S.; Lisonkova, S.; Rouleau, J.; Van den Hof, M.; Sauve, R.; Kramer, M.S.; Canadian Perinatal Surveillance System (Public Health Agency of Canada). Association between maternal chronic conditions and congenital heart defects: A population-based cohort study. *Circulation* **2013**, *128*, 583–589. [CrossRef]
43. Bunin, G.R.; Gyllstrom, M.E.; Brown, J.E.; Kahn, E.B.; Kushi, L.H. Recall of diet during a past pregnancy. *Am. J. Epidemiol.* **2001**, *154*, 1136–1142. [CrossRef] [PubMed]
44. Bosco, J.L.; Tseng, M.; Spector, L.G.; Olshan, A.F.; Bunin, G.R. Reproducibility of reported nutrient intake and supplement use during a past pregnancy: A report from the Children's Oncology Group. *Paediatr. Perinat. Epidemiol.* **2010**, *24*, 93–101. [CrossRef] [PubMed]
45. Zheng, Z.; Yang, T.; Chen, L.; Wang, L.; Zhang, S.; Wang, T.; Zhao, L.; Ye, Z.; Chen, L.; Qin, J. Increased maternal Body Mass Index is associated with congenital heart defects: An updated meta-analysis of observational studies. *Int. J. Cardiol.* **2018**, *273*, 112–120. [CrossRef] [PubMed]

nutrients

Article

Dietary and Nutrient Intake, Eating Habits, and Its Association with Maternal Gestational Weight Gain and Offspring's Birth Weight in Pregnant Adolescents

Reyna Sámano [1,2,*], Hugo Martínez-Rojano [3], Luis Ortiz-Hernández [1,4,*], Oralia Nájera-Medina [1,4], Gabriela Chico-Barba [2,5], Estela Godínez-Martínez [2], Ricardo Gamboa [6] and Estefanía Aguirre-Minutti [7]

1 Programa de Posgrado Doctorado en Ciencias Biológicas y de la Salud, División de Ciencias Biológicas y de la Salud, Universidad Autónoma Metropolitana, Mexico City 04960, Mexico
2 Coordinación de Nutrición y Bioprogramación, Instituto Nacional de Perinatología, Secretaría de Salud, Mexico City 11000, Mexico
3 Sección de Posgrado e Investigación de la Escuela Superior de Medicina del Instituto Politécnico Nacional, Mexico City 11340, Mexico
4 Departamento de Atención a la Salud, CBS, Universidad Autónoma Metropolitana-Xochimilco, Mexico City 04960, Mexico
5 Programa de Maestría y Doctorado en Ciencias Médicas, Odontológicas y de la Salud, Universidad Nacional Autónoma de México, Mexico City 04510, Mexico
6 Departamento de Fisiología, Instituto Nacional de Cardiología, Mexico City 14080, Mexico
7 Licenciatura en Nutrición, Centro Interdisciplinario de Ciencias de la Salud, Unidad Milpa Alta (CICS), Instituto Politécnico Nacional, Mexico City 12000, Mexico
* Correspondence: ssmr0119@yahoo.com.mx (R.S.); lortiz@correo.xoc.uam.mx (L.O.-H.)

Citation: Sámano, R.; Martínez-Rojano, H.; Ortiz-Hernández, L.; Nájera-Medina, O.; Chico-Barba, G.; Godínez-Martínez, E.; Gamboa, R.; Aguirre-Minutti, E. Dietary and Nutrient Intake, Eating Habits, and Its Association with Maternal Gestational Weight Gain and Offspring's Birth Weight in Pregnant Adolescents. *Nutrients* **2022**, *14*, 4545. https://doi.org/10.3390/nu14214545

Academic Editors: Louise Brough and Gail Rees

Received: 16 September 2022
Accepted: 21 October 2022
Published: 28 October 2022

Abstract: Pregnant adolescents' diet and eating habits are inadequate; however, their association with gestational weight gain (GWG) is uncertain. We aimed to analyze whether there is an association between dietary and nutrient intake and eating habits with GWG among pregnant adolescents and their offspring's birth weight. A longitudinal study was performed with 530 participants. We assessed GWG and applied several tools, such as a food frequency questionnaire and 24-h recall, to obtain dietary and nutrient intake and eating habits. The birth weight of adolescents' offspring was registered. Later, we performed crude and adjusted Poisson models. The mean age was 15.8 ± 1.3 years. Of all food groups, the lowest frequency of adequate intake corresponded to vegetables (7%) and legumes (10.2%). Excessive (36.8%) and insufficient (40.9%) GWG were observed. Pregnant adolescents with inadequate legumes intake increased the probability of excessive GWG: (PR 1.86 95% CI 1.00–3.44). Cereals and grains were positively associated with GWG: (PR 1.65, 95% CI 1.18–2.29). Energy, macronutrient intake, and eating habits were not associated with GWG. Offspring's small gestational age (SGA) increased when pregnant adolescents had inadequate sugar-sweetened beverages intake: PR (1.58, 95% CI 1.01–2.49) and when pregnant adolescent watched television (TV). In our sample of Mexican adolescents, dietary and nutrient intake and eating habits were inadequate. Excessive dietary intake from cereals, grains, and animal-sourced foods along with insufficient legumes were associated with excessive GWG. Watching TV while adolescents ate was associated with the birth weight of the offspring.

Keywords: adolescent pregnancy; gestational weight gain; energy intake; food groups; dietary habits; Mexico

1. Introduction

Adolescent pregnancy represents a global public health concern. Nearly 20% of adolescents from low and middle-income countries give birth [1,2]. They have a higher frequency of adverse outcomes such as preterm birth, small-for-gestational-age (SGA), and increased neonatal and maternal mortality risk than pregnant adults [3–5]. Gestational weight gain

(GWG) has been associated with both short-term and long-term consequences, such as anemia and preeclampsia. In the short-term, excessive GWG is associated with adverse newborn outcomes, including preterm birth, large-for-gestational-age, and macrosomia. In the long term, it is associated with significant weight retention after pregnancy and excess body weight later in the mother's life [6]. Therefore, pregnant adolescents need more health services, which are associated with higher costs to provide them with prenatal and postnatal care [7,8]. In addition, although pregnant adolescents have a similar proportion of excessive gestational weight gain (GWG) compared to adults, the former have a higher total GWG in kilograms (kg) [6].

Several countries in sub-Saharan Africa, Latin America, and Asia have moved from low-income to middle-income status, which is accompanied by lifestyle changes, including increased food security, dietary transitions, and reduced physical activity. These changes have led to modifications in maternal diets before and during pregnancy, affecting GWG patterns and the overall pregnancy experience for women in these regions [9–11]. For example, a study from Tanzania reported that, according to Institute of Medicine (IOM) guidelines, 42.0%, 22.0%, and 36.0% of pregnant adults were characterized as having inadequate, adequate, and excessive GWG, respectively [12].

Another problem is that, as pregnant adolescents' linear growth has not reached its peak, their nutrient requirements are higher than adult women [13]. Nevertheless, studies about the dietary patterns of pregnant adolescents are scarce [14]. Pregnant adolescents tend to have low iron intake (28% for Recommended Dietary Allowances-RDA) [15,16]. Moreover, less than 30% have good adherence to folate supplementation [15]. The average intake of calcium in pregnant adolescents from the USA [16], Brazil, and Mexico [15,17,18] ranges from 400 to 900 mg/day, which does not meet the recommended intake of 1000–1300 mg/day [19]. This inadequate nutrient intake in pregnant adolescents can be linked to the low variety of food groups they consume [20,21]. At least 75% of pregnant adolescents who received antenatal care in a public hospital had low intake of vegetables and legumes, around 50% consumed more sweetened beverages than recommended, and 5–25% skipped supper or breakfast [22].

Dietary and nutrient intake and eating habits can potentially affect GWG, as energy and nutrients are necessary for tissue accretion [23]. A few studies have been conducted on adult women to analyze that relationship [24–26]. However, systematic reviews about this topic included only adult women [27–29]. We could not find any studies on the association of dietary and nutrient intake and eating habits with GWG and offspring's birth weight in pregnant adolescents [29]. Nevertheless, evidence derived from Rumanian adult women showed a positive association between a high-fat diet and excessive GWG and a negative association with a high-protein diet [26]. In addition, adult pregnant women who consume foods from the Mediterranean diet (legumes, vegetables, nuts, olive oil, and whole cereals) have high odds of having a lower [24] or adequate GWG [24,25] and a lower risk of having a small-for-gestational-age newborn when eating fruits and vegetables [30–32]. Energy intake has been associated with GWG, while macronutrients have not [28]. This paper aimed to analyze whether there is an association between dietary and nutrient intake and eating habits and GWG among pregnant adolescents and their offspring's birth weight.

2. Materials and Methods

We conducted a longitudinal study with pregnant adolescents aged 11–19 years who received antenatal care at the Instituto Nacional de Perinatología (INPer) in Mexico City. The inclusion criteria were being a woman primigravida with single pregnancy and without chronic diseases. In addition, adolescents with drug addictions, vegans or vegetarians, and those who had a newborn with congenital malformations or stillbirth were excluded.

Six hundred and fifty adolescents were invited to participate in the study. Forty teenagers did not agree to participate, 38 accepted but did not arrive at any assessment, 25 did not deliver at the INPer, 15 cases were incomplete, and two neonates died at birth. There were 530 cases with complete data. During the first visit, we obtained signed consent from adolescents and their parents/guardians as well as sociodemographic data. Anthropometric measurements and dietary assessment were conducted. We obtained maternal and neonatal outcomes from the last consultation from the medical records.

2.1. Dietary and Nutrient Intake, and Eating Habits

We assessed food group consumption to describe dietary intake using a semi-quantitative food frequency questionnaire (FFQ) [33]. Intake of nine food groups was measured. The dietary guidelines for the Mexican population were used as criteria. These guidelines present the following food groups: vegetables; fruits; legumes; cereal and grains; meat, cheese, and eggs (herein, "animal-source foods"); fats and oils; milk and yogurt; table sugar; and sweetened beverages [34]. Participants reported their frequency of intake during the last trimesters. Because it is known that macronutrient intake remains relatively stable during pregnancy [35], one measurement in the second or third trimesters was obtained. The interviewers used food replicas and standard measuring cups, spoons, and glasses to improve serving size estimation. Later, we compared the number of servings consumed with the recommendations for the Mexican population [34]. The number of servings of each food group used as a reference can be reviewed in Appendix A. Adequate consumption was defined when the number of servings was met according to the recommendation. Inadequate consumption (excessive and insufficient) was when the participants ate more or fewer servings than the recommendation range.

Three 24-h dietary recalls were applied. Two were recorded on non-consecutive weekdays and another on weekends. The 24-h recalls were administered by personnel trained in the interview technique. The nutrient and energy intake were estimated using Nutrikcal® software. Later, the mean energy intake in kilocalories (kcal) was calculated. To measure participants' energy intake adequacy, we used the reference of the IOM (2005) [36,37]. We categorized energy intake adequacy as insufficient (<80%), adequate (80–119%), or excessive (>120%). The contribution of carbohydrates, proteins, and lipids to total energy consumption was estimated. The recommendations of the IOM were used as a reference to categorize the distribution of energy contribution of macronutrients [37].

Participants were asked about the following eating habits: their number of meals; frequency of skipping meals (never, 1–3 times, 4–5 times/week); with whom they ate their foods (alone, with family, and friends); where they ate (out of home, home); and what activities they did while eating (doing homework/household chores, watching TV or using a cellphone, or just eating). In addition, we inquired as to whether participants had modified their diet during pregnancy (if it was improving, was worse, or had no change).

2.2. Anthropometric Data and Gestational Weight Gain

In the first interview, the pre-pregnancy self-reported weight was obtained. The self-reported weight is an adequate proxy for pre-pregnancy weight [38,39].

All anthropometric measurements were performed according to Lohman's techniques [40]. Height was measured at the first antenatal visit using a stadiometer (SECA, Hamburg, Germany, model 208, accuracy 0.1 cm). We estimated the pregestational body mass index (pBMI) using the pregestational weight and height. Then, we classified pBMI with AnthroPlus® (World Health Organization, Geneva, Switzerland) according to percentiles: underweight <3rd, normal weight 3–85th, overweight 85–97th, and obesity ≥97th [41].

One or two weeks before delivery, we measured and recorded participants' body weight with a digital scale (TANITA, Tokyo, Japan, model BWB-800, accuracy 0.10 kg). This measure was considered the final gestational weight. The GWG was calculated from the difference between the final gestational weight and the pregestational weight.

The expected weight gain was calculated with the following equation [42]:

Expected weight gain = recommended weight gain for the first trimester + ((gestational age final—13.86 weeks) × (recommended weight gain rate in second and third trimesters)).

The recommendation of GWG rate for the first trimester was according to pBMI: low and normal weight 2 kg, overweight 1 kg, and obesity 0.5 kg. For adolescents in the second and third trimesters, these pBMI figures were low weight 0.51 kg, normal weight 0.42 kg, overweight 0.28 kg, and obesity 0.22 kg/week [43].

The gestational weight gain adequacy percentage was estimated using the recommendations of the US Institute of Medicine [43,44]. Finally, we categorized the GWG percentage as follows: inadequate (<90%), adequate (90 to <125%), and excessive (≥125%).

2.3. Neonatal Outcomes

The sex of the newborn was obtained from the neonatal clinical record. Gestational age was obtained by ultrasound and recorded in weeks and days. If the gestational age was ≤36.6 weeks we classified it as preterm, whereas if the gestational age was between ≥37 and ≤42 weeks this was considered at term.

Standardized personnel measured and recorded birth weight (g) with calibrated equipment (SECA 374, model "Baby and Mommy"; accuracy 0.1 g) and length at birth (cm) (stadiometer SECA 416; accuracy 0.1 cm). SGA was defined when birth weight was <10 percentile, normal birth weight as the neonate being between 10–90 percentile, and large for gestational age (LGA) as >90 percentile, according to the Intergrowth-21s criteria [45].

2.4. Other Variables

In an antenatal visit, trained personnel obtained information on sociodemographic characteristics such as chronological age, marital status, education, occupation, and socioeconomic level. Age was registered at the time of the survey in years and as a dichotomous variable (≤15 or ≥16 to 19 years). In addition, marital status was classified as cohabiting or single.

Education was reported by the pregnant adolescents and was considered as elementary school or less, middle school, and incomplete high school. In addition, we created a school dropout variable according to the school grade and chronological age for adolescents who were more than two years behind in educational training.

Occupation was classified as student or housewife. A questionnaire validated for the Mexican population was used to determine socioeconomic status [46]. In our sample only middle, low–middle, and low were observed.

The initiation of antenatal care and the gestational age at delivery were obtained through ultrasound and reported in weeks. Obstetricians registered maternal adverse outcomes during prenatal visits, and the information from the clinical records was obtained. Complications were identified and recorded in the following categories: gestational diabetes, pregnancy-induced hypertension, eclampsia/pre-eclampsia, and anemia [47,48].

2.5. Statistical Analyses

A descriptive analysis was performed, including percentages for categorical variables. For continuous variables, the Kolmogorov–Smirnov test was used to assess their distribution. The mean was estimated for variables with normal distribution, and the median was obtained for those with a non-normal distribution. Next, we compared the prevalence of outcomes between the categories of nutrition, energy intake, and eating habits. The chi-square test was estimated to assess whether significant differences between categories existed. When the significance of the difference was $p \leq 0.250$, the variable was considered for the next step.

Poisson regression models were calculated to determine the association of outcomes (GWG and offspring's birth weight) with predictors of interest (nutrients, energy intake, and eating habits). We estimated separate models for inadequate and excessive GWG. For this reason, dummy variables were created for the GWG and birth-weight categories. For each outcome, three models were performed: M1, crude M2, adjusted by socioeconomic level, school drop-out, education, gynecological age, chronological age, and antenatal care; and M3, adjusted by the same variables included in M2 plus pBMI. The regression coefficients were transformed to prevalence ratios (PR).

When the cross-tabulation of two eating habits with the outcomes was estimated, the absence of any cases in certain cells was evident. Hence, these variables were not included in the regression analysis.

2.6. Ethical Aspects

This research was approved by the Institutional Ethics, Biosafety, and Research Committees from INPer (registration numbers 212250-49481, 212250-49541, and 2017-2-101, respectively). All adolescents and their guardians were informed of the study's objectives and procedures. Confidentiality was guaranteed by assigning an ID number during each participant's data collection and analysis. Written informed consent was obtained from adolescents and guardians.

3. Results

The mean age of the participants was 15.8 ± 1.3 years. Seventy percent of the adolescents were single, and the rest lived cohabiting with their partners. Most adolescents were homemakers (89%). Their socioeconomic status was low or very low. Three-quarters of the women had elementary education (74.7%). School dropout was experienced by 89.1%.

Gestational weight gain in pregnant adolescents was excessive in 36.6%, adequate in 26%, and insufficient in 37.4%. In addition, it was observed that 20.4% of newborns were SGA (<10th percentile) and 3.8% were LGA (>90th percentile).

The lowest frequency of adequate intake corresponded to vegetables, followed by legumes and animal-source foods (Figure 1). In contrast, the food groups that were eaten most frequently were table sugar, cereals and grains, and dairy foods. None of the nine food groups reached 50% recommended consumption coverage. In addition, 73% of the participants included less than three food groups in their diet.

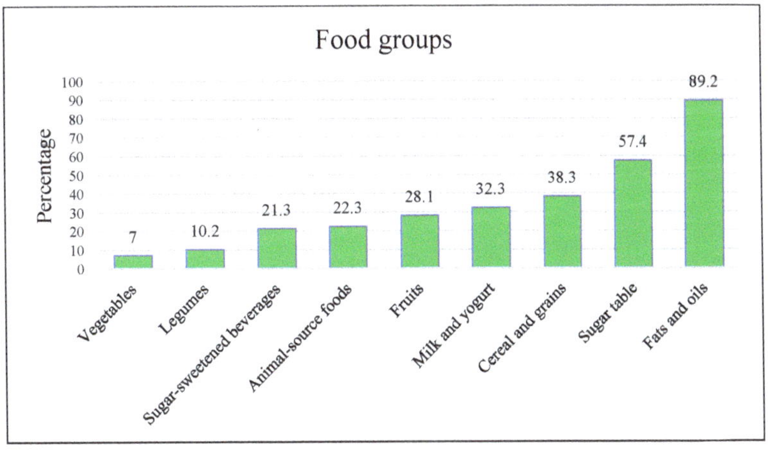

Figure 1. Distribution of adequate intake from different food groups.

One-fifth of the adolescents had two or less meals. Dinner was the most skipped meal. Fifty-six percent skipped meals more than once a week. Fifty-one percent of adolescents watched TV while they ate, and 66% reported that their diet was better during pregnancy than pregestational (Appendix B).

Excessive GWG was more frequent among pregnant adolescents who did not consume legumes than those who consumed them (p = 0.023) (Table 1). The adolescents with high consumption of cereals and grains and animal-source foods had a higher frequency of excessive GWG ($p \leq 0.001$) than those with low or normal consumption. Excessive and insufficient GWG were observed more frequently among pregnant adolescents who excessively consumed sugar-sweetened beverages compared to their counterparts who consumed them adequately ($p = 0.030$). The rate of small for gestational age neonates among mothers who consumed excessive sugar-sweetened beverages was higher than in those with a low intake ($p = 0.066$).

Table 1. Adolescents' gestational weight gain and offspring's birth weight according to dietary intake.

Food Group	Intake	Gestational Weight Gain (%)			Birth Weight (%)		
		Insufficient, n = 205	Excessive, n = 187	*p*-Value	SGA, n = 108	LGA, n = 20	*p*-Value
Vegetables	Adequate, n = 37	32.4	37.8	0.785	27.0	5.4	0.472
	Insufficient, n = 493	37.7	36.5		19.9	3.7	
Fruits	Adequate, n = 149	33.6	36.2	0.335	21.5	3.4	0.891
	Insufficient, n = 381	38.8	36.7		19.9	3.9	
Legumes	Adequate, n = 54	42.6	20.4	0.023	16.7	1.9	0.536
	Insufficient, n = 476	36.8	38.4		20.8	4.0	
Cereal and grains	Adequate, 7-11 n = 203	33.5	36.9	≤0.001	23.6	3.0	0.256
	Insufficient, <7 n = 211	53.1	20.4		20.4	3.3	
	Excessive ≥12 n = 116	15.5	65.5		14.7	6.0	
Animal-	Adequate, n = 118	31.4	39.0	≤0.001	22.0	3.4	0.941
source	Insufficient, n = 368	41.3	32.1		20.1	4.1	
foods	Excessive, n = 44	20.5	68.2		18.2	2.3	
Fats and	Adequate, n = 151	33.1	43.0	0.275	17.9	3.3	0.795
oils	Insufficient, n = 361	39.1	33.5		21.1	3.9	
	Excessive, n = 18	38.9	44.4		27.8	5.6	
Milk and	Adequate, n = 171	38.6	40.9	0.270	20.5	3.5	0.822
yogurt	Insufficient, n = 257	38.1	33.5		20.2	4.7	
	Excessive, n = 102	33.5	37.3		20.6	2.0	
Sugar table	Adequate, n = 226	39.8	33.6	0.442	18.6	4.0	0.671
	Excessive, n = 304	35.5	38.8		21.7	3.6	
Sugar-sweetened	Adequate, n = 171	33.3	33.3	0.030	14.6	4.7	0.066
beverage	Excessive, n = 359	39.3	38.2		23.1	3.3	
Number of	≥4, n = 106	29.2	40.6	0.151	18.9	2.8	0.754
food groups	≤3, n = 424	39.4	35.6		20.8	4.0	

Percentages estimated by rows. SGA: small for gestational age. LGA: large for gestational age. *p*-value determined by Pearson's Chi-Square.

The energy intake of the participants was 2022 ± 657 kcal. The distribution of macronutrients of total energy was as follows: 102 ± 34% energy adequacy, 53 ± 8% carbohydrates, 16 ± 5% proteins, and 31 ± 8% lipids. Table 2 shows that none of the macronutrients and energy intake had statistical significance with respect to the maternal GWG and the birth weight of their offspring.

Table 2. Adolescent's gestational weight gain and offspring's birth weight according to energy and macronutrients intake.

Nutrient Intake	Gestational Weight Gain (%)			Birth Weight (%)		
	Insufficient, n = 205	Excessive, n = 187	*p*-Value	SGA, n = 108	LGA, n = 20	*p*-Value
Adequacy energy						
Adequate (80–120%) n = 248	35.9	38.3	0.577	18.5	3.6	0.736
Low (<80%), n = 147	37.4	32.7		19.7	4.1	
Excessive (>120), n = 135	40.7	37.8		24.4	3.7	
Carbohydrates						
Adequate (45–55%),n = 226	36.7	37.2	0.727	19.0	4.9	0.698
Low (<45%), n = 91	31.9	39.6		18.7	3.3	
Excessive (>55), n = 213	40.4	34.7		22.5	2.8	
Lipids						
Adequate (25–30%), n = 253	38.3	36.4	0.590	24.1	4.0	0.245
Low (<25%), n = 125	41.6	33.6		18.4	2.4	
Excessive (>30%), n = 152	32.2	39.5		15.8	4.6	
Proteins						
Adequate (15–20%), n = 227	38.3	35.2	0.881	24.2	3.5	0.379
Low (<15%), n = 225	35.6	39.1		17.3	4.4	
Excessive (>21%), n = 78	39.7	33.3		17.9	2.6	

Percentages estimated by rows. SGA: small for gestational age. LGA: large for gestational age. p-value determined by Pearson's Chi-Square.

The frequency of GWG and the newborn weight categories did not differ according to eating habits (Table 3).

Table 3. Adolescents' gestational weight gain and offspring's birth weight according to eating habits.

Eating Habits	Gestational Weight Gain (%)			Birth Weight (%)		
	Insufficient, n = 205	Excessive, n = 187	*p*-Value	SGA, n = 108	LGA, n = 20	*p*-Value
Number of meals						
≥3, n = 121	35.5	34.7	0.695	23.1	3.3	0.855
3, n = 300	38.7	35.7		20.3	3.7	
≤2, n = 109	35.8	41.3		17.4	4.6	
Having breakfast						
Yes, n = 505	36.6	36.8	0.263	19.6	4.0	0.099
No, n = 25	52	32.0		36.0	0.0	
Having lunch						
Yes, n = 524	37.8	36.6	0.047	20.6	3.8	0.381
No, n = 6	0.0	33.3		0.0	0.0	
Having dinner-super						
Yes, n = 467	36.8	37.3	0.591	21.2	3.9	0.408
No, n = 63	42.9	31.7		14.3	3.2	
Skipping meals						
Never, n = 245	36.3	37.6	0.157	20.8	3.3	0.819
1–3 times/week, n = 222	40.1	32.0		21.2	4.5	
4–5 times/week, n = 63	31.7	49.2		15.9	3.2	

Table 3. *Cont.*

Eating Habits	Gestational Weight Gain (%)			Birth Weight (%)		
	Insufficient, n = 205	Excessive, n = 187	*p*-Value	SGA, n = 108	LGA, n = 20	*p*-Value
Eating out of home						
Yes, n = 73	32.9	34.2	0.349	20.6	3.7	0.954
No, n = 457	38.1	37.0		19.2	4.1	
Eating alone						
Yes, n = 107	35.5	43.0	0.262	19.6	5.6	0.535
No, n = 423	37.0	35.0		20.6	3.3	
Activities during the meals						
None, n = 205	36.6	34.6	0.793	22.4	1.5	0.190
Watching TV or using a cellphone, n = 270	37.4	38.5		18.5	5.6	
Doing household chores, n = 55	40.0	34.5		21.8	3.6	
Modify their feeding						
Was better, n = 353	36.3	36.5	0.544	19.8	3.4	0.644
Was worse, n = 103	38.8	40.8		23.3	5.8	
No change, n = 74	40.5	31.1		18.9	5.8	

Percentages estimated by rows. SGA: small for gestational age. LGA: large for gestational age. None of the variables was statistically significant. p-value determined by Pearson's Chi-Square.

Pregnant adolescents with insufficient consumption of legumes had a greater probability of excessive GWG than participants with adequate intake (Table 4). Insufficient consumption of cereals and grains was associated with a higher probability of insufficient GWG. In contrast, the excessive consumption of cereals and grains demonstrated a high probability of excessive GWG. In addition, excessive sugar-sweetened beverage consumption was associated with a higher probability of having a small-for-gestational-age newborn.

Table 4. Poisson regression models of adolescents' gestational weight gain and offspring's birth weight as outcome and dietary intake as predictors.

	Gestational Weight Gain				Birth Weight			
	Insufficient		Excessive		SGA		LGA	
	PR	95% CI	PR	95% CI	PR	95% CI	PR	95% CI
Legumes								
M1	1.16	0.75–1.79	**1.89**	**1.03–3.47**	–	–	–	–
M2	0.80	0.51–1.28	**1.95**	**1.05–3.60**	–	–	–	–
M3	0.82	0.52–1.28	**1.86**	**1.00–3.44**	–	–	–	–
Cereal and grains								
<7 servings								
M1	1.59	**1.17–2.14**	0.55	0.38–0.80	–	–	–	–
M2	1.61	**1.19–2.18**	0.55	0.38–0.80	–	–	–	–
M3	1.56	**1.14–2.12**	0.57	0.39–0.83	–	–	–	–
>12 Excessive								
M1	0.46	0.28–0.78	**1.77**	**1.29–2.44**	–	–	–	–
M2	0.47	0.28–0.79	**1.77**	**1.29–2.44**	–	–	–	–
M3	0.49	0.29–0.82	**1.65**	**1.18–2.29**	–	–	–	–

Table 4. *Cont.*

	Gestational Weight Gain				Birth Weight			
	Insufficient		Excessive		SGA		LGA	
	PR	95% CI	PR	95% CI	PR	95% CI	PR	95% CI
Animal–source foods								
Insufficient								
M1	1.32	0.92–1.89	0.82	0.59–1.16	–	–	–	–
M2	1.35	0.94–1.94	0.81	0.57–1.14	–	–	–	–
M3	1.43	0.99–2.05	0.72	0.51–1.02	–	–	–	–
Excessive								
M1	0.65	0.32–1.35	**1.75**	**1.04–2.77**	–	–	–	–
M2	0.70	0.34–1.46	**1.65**	**1.03–2.65**	–	–	–	–
M3	0.80	0.38–1.68	1.33	0.82–2.17	–	–	–	–
Consume sweetened beverages								
M1	1.18	0.87–1.60	1.15	0.84–1.56	1.58	**1.01–2.47**	0.71	0.29–1.75
M2	1.16	0.85–1.59	1.14	0.84–1.56	1.58	**1.00–2.47**	0.77	0.31–1.94
M3	1.19	0.87–1.62	1.14	0.84–1.56	1.58	**1.01–2.49**	0.78	0.31–1.98
≤3 Food groups								
M1	1.40	0.95–2.07	0.88	0.63–1.23	–	–	–	–
M2	1.31	0.89–1.93	0.90	0.64–1.27	–	–	–	–
M3	1.34	0.91–1.98	0.86	0.61–1.21	–	–	–	–

p-value determined by Poisson regression. PR: prevalence ratio; CI: confidence interval; SGA: small for gestational age. LGA: large for gestational age. M stands for Model: M1, crude; M2: adjusted by socioeconomic level, school drop-out, education, gynecological age, chronological age, and antenatal care; M3, adjusted by the same variables included in M2 plus pBMI. In bold are present the significant results.

Lipids intake and eating habits did not have any association with GWG or newborn weight (Table 5).

Table 5. Poisson regression models of adolescents' gestational weight gain and offspring's birth weight as outcome and lipids intake and eating habits as predictors.

	Gestational Gain, %				Birth Weight			
Lipids	Insufficient		Excessive		Small		Large	
	PR	95% CI	PR	95% CI	PR	95% CI	PR	95% CI
Adequate REF								
Insufficient								
M1	–	–	–	–	0.70	0.46–1.08	0.55	0.14–2.21
M2	–	–	–	–	0.74	0.43–1.26	0.35	0.08–1.48
M3	–	–	–	–	0.74	0.44–1.27	0.35	0.08–1.52
Excessive								
M1	–	–	–	–	0.71	0.42–1.20	0.95	0.35–2.56
M2	–	–	–	–	0.73	0.47–1.26	0.86	0.31–1.49
M3	–	–	–	–	0.75	0.49–1.27	0.85	0.31–2.34
Skipping meals								
None REF								

Table 5. *Cont.*

Lipids	Gestational Gain, %				Birth Weight			
	Insufficient		Excessive		Small		Large	
	PR	95% CI	PR	95% CI	PR	95% CI	PR	95% CI
1–3 time/week								
M1	1.10 *	0.82–1.48	0.85	0.63–1.16	–	–	–	–
M2	1.14	0.85–1.53	0.85	0.62–1.16	–	–	–	–
M3	1.15	0.85–1.54	0.82	0.60–1.12	–	–	–	–
4–5 time/week								
M1	0.87	0.54–1.42	1.31	0.87–1.97	–	–	–	–
M2	0.87	0.54–1.42	1.30	0.87–1.97	–	–	–	–
M3	0.92	0.57–1.51	1.17	0.77–1.77	–	–	–	–
Number of meals								
>3 REF								
3								
M1	1.01	0.69–1.47	1.09	0.73–1.62	–	–	–	–
M2	1.03	0.70–1.52	1.12	0.75–1.69	–	–	–	–
M3	1.03	0.70–1.52	1.08	0.72–1.64	–	–	–	–
<2								
M1	1.01	0.66–1.54	1.22	0.79–1.88	–	–	–	–
M2	1.04	0.68–1.59	1.23	0.80–1.90	–	–	–	–
M3	1.08	0.70–1.65	1.09	0.70–1.70	–	–	–	–
Activities during the meals								
Seeing TV								
M1	–	–	–	–	0.83	0.55–1.23	**3.80**	**1.10–13.11**
M2	–	–	–	–	0.84	0.56–1.26	**3.92**	**1.11–13.84**
M3	–	–	–	–	0.87	0.58–1.30	**3.76**	**1.06–13.36**
Doing household chores								
M1	–	–	–	–	0.97	0.52–1.84	2.49	0.42–14.87
M2	–	–	–	–	0.98	0.52–1.87	2.67	0.44–16.45
M3	–	–	–	–	0.98	0.52–1.86	2.89	0.46–18.07

* $p < 0.050$. p-value determined by Poisson regression. PR: prevalence ratio; CI: confidence inter-val; SGA: small for gestational age. LGA: large for gestational age. M stands for model: M1, crude; M2, adjusted by socioeconomic level, school drop-out, education, gynecological age, chronological age, and antenatal care; M3, adjusted by the same variables included in M2 plus pBMI. In bold are present the significant results.

4. Discussion

The results of the present research show that unhealthy eating habits and nutrient intake are frequent in pregnant adolescents. The participants in our study had excessive intake of cereal and grains, animal-source foods, table sugar, and sugar-sweetened beverages, and insufficient consumption of legumes and vegetables. For example, most did not consume the recommended servings of vegetables (93.0%), legumes (89.8%), or sugar-sweetened beverages (79.8%), among other foods, and showed poor eating habits such as skipping meals (56%), eating alone (20.1%), and carrying out activities (61.3%) while they ate.

The present study showed associations between insufficient legumes and excessive cereal and grains consumption and excessive GWG. Meanwhile, sugar-sweetened beverages consumption and using cell phones/watching TV while eating had associations with birth weight.

4.1. Dietary and Nutrients Intake and Eating Habits

Although most of our participants (67%) reported that their diet had improved during the pregnancy, they did not have adequate dietary and nutrient intake or eating habits. Our participants' dietary intake was low in legumes and vegetables and excessive in sweetened-sugar beverage consumption, which is common in most age groups [21,22,49–51]. More than 70% of pregnant adolescents did not eat more than three food groups in their meals. Only fifty percent of Mexican pregnant adolescents in the present study had adequate consumption of energy and macronutrients; similar data has been found in pregnant adults [50]. This dietary pattern could be a risk factor for developing non-transmissible chronic diseases [52,53] and micronutrients deficiencies [54].

More than half of the participants skipped meals, watched TV, or used cell phones while eating. Youth exposed to screens habitually consume ultra-processed foods [55]. Watching TV has been associated with the development of excess weight, obesity, and cardiometabolic risk in the adolescent population [55,56].

4.2. Gestational Weight Gain

Our study reported that excessive gestational weight gain in adolescent pregnant women occurred in 36.6% and was insufficient in 37.4%. This highlights that there is currently a higher probability in pregnant adolescents of not meeting the recommendations GWG of the IOM. This is similar to the findings of Santos et al. in adolescent Brazilians, which showed 37% and 33% insufficient and excessive GWG, respectively [57]. A significant rate of insufficient and excessive GWG was observed in our sample of pregnant adolescents. This population likely experiences nutritional transitions and reduced physical activity [58], which may lead to changes in maternal diets before and during pregnancy, thereby affecting GWG patterns [59].

4.3. Dietary and Nutrient Intake, Eating Habits, and GWG

Insufficient intake of legumes was associated with a higher risk of excessive GWG, even after adjusting for pBMI. Among pregnant adults from Spain and South Africa, the consumption of diets that include legumes [24,60] has been associated with lower GWG. Legumes have nutrient content (high in fiber and antioxidants but low in fat) that can help with keeping a healthy weight [60]. Nevertheless, there is little information on this topic in adolescent pregnant women.

We observed that a higher intake of cereal and grains was associated with excessive GWG. However, with animal-source foods the association was lost when the models were adjusted for pBMI, showing that GWG was affected more by pBMI than by diet in our group of pregnant adolescents. In addition, it has been documented that pBMI is a better predictor of GWG than other variables such as food consumption [61].

Watching TV is a risk factor for developing obesity [56] because it is a sedentary behavior related to higher consumption of ultra-processed foods. Our study found that adolescents who ate while watching TV were associated with LGA neonates. The mechanisms that explain this relationship may be related to maternal consumption of foods with high energy density [62].

We did not find an association between macronutrients and GWG. Our study coincides partially with a previous systematic review that reported macronutrient intake to not be associated with GWG [28]. Hence, it is challenging to estimate macronutrients, which could affect the possible association between GWG and the birth weight of adolescent's offspring. Nevertheless, the scientific evidence establishes that a whole diet and the foods that make it up can be more relevant than individual nutrients to GWG [24,25]. In this sense, in the present study, we observed that legumes, cereals, and grains were associated with GWG. However, not all foods or macronutrients were associated with GWG.

4.4. Dietary Intake, Eating Habits, and Birth Weight

Sugar-sweetened beverages consumption was associated with SGA. There is insufficient evidence to identify possible causal mechanisms to explain the association between maternal consumption of sugar-sweetened beverages and birth weight outcomes [63–65]. Therefore, our findings should be interpreted with caution. However, we believe that an inadequate maternal diet is likely to be associated with the birth weight of their offspring [66].

None of the maternal nutrient intakes were associated with birth weight in our sample, similar to GWG. Data from observational studies indicate that certain dietary habits and patterns during pregnancy have no consistent associations with birth weight. Maternal lack of all foods in their diet is relevant, as it has been demonstrated that the whole diet, beyond individual nutrients, can influence birth weight. However, if most participants do not meet a recommended diet the birth weight effect would likely be attenuated, as reported in pregnant adults [67]. Nonetheless, we did not find scientific evidence to support this hypothesis in the studied group of pregnant adolescents

4.5. Limitations and Strengths

Using the IOM references, we observed a high frequency of excessive and insufficient GWG. However, it is unknown whether the IOM reference is adequate for Mexican pregnant adolescents, which is a public health concern as we currently do not have any official parameters to evaluate GWG in adolescent pregnancy. The number of LGA neonates was small (n = 20). Therefore, certain estimates were imprecise.

Although our sample was for convenience considering the inclusion criteria, we must consider that INPer is a national reference center that provides prenatal control for women from several regions of Mexico. Moreover, our study had a prospective follow-up.

5. Conclusions

To the best of our knowledge, this is the first study to analyze the association between maternal dietary and nutrient intake and eating habits and GWG and birth weight in a sample of pregnant adolescent–baby dyads. Furthermore, we show that when certain elements of the diet are inadequate, optimal maternal and neonatal outcomes can be limited. In addition, all models were adjusted by pBMI in order to control its confounding effect to a certain extent.

Pregnant adolescents need to know the relationship between the components of the diet and GWG to improve their eating habits. Health personnel should promote the consumption of a healthy diet according to the individual requirements of pregnant adolescents and promote avoidance of inappropriate eating habits while considering sociocultural and economic characteristics.

The consumption of adequate amounts of legumes, cereals and grains, animal-sourced foods, and sugar-sweetened beverages is part of the dietary guidelines because their consumption is related to health outcomes such as weight gain and diabetes. However, our study provides evidence of other health outcomes, such as GWG and birth weight in the studied group of pregnant adolescents, which could be affected by eating habits. Our results can inform the development of clinical and nutritional guidelines for antenatal control aimed at preventing complications and promoting healthy pregnancy.

Author Contributions: Conceptualization, R.S. and H.M.-R.; Data curation, R.S., L.O.-H., R.G., E.A.-M. and O.N.-M.; Formal analysis, R.S., L.O.-H. and R.G; Funding acquisition, R.S.; Investigation, H.M.-R., G.C.-B.; E.G.-M., R.G. and E.A.-M.; Methodology, R.S., O.N.-M., G.C.-B., E.G.-M., E.A.-M. and H.M.-R.; Project administration, R.S.; Supervision, R.S. and L.O.-H. and H.M.-R.; Writing—original draft preparation, R.S. and L.O.-H. and H.M.-R. Writing—review and editing, R.S., L.O.-H., G.C.-B., O.N.-M., E.G.-M., H.M.-R., R.G. and E.A.-M. All authors have read and agreed to the published version of the manuscript.

Funding: This study was funded by the Instituto Nacional de Perinatología (registration numbers 212250-49541 and 2017-2-101) and by CONACyT (Registration number A3-S-40575).

Institutional Review Board Statement: The study was approved by the Institute National of Perinatology Ethics Committee (registration number 212250-49481 in October 2008, February 2014, 212250-49541 in February 2014, and 2017-2-101 on 10 April 2019) according to the basic principles of the Declaration of Helsinki.

Informed Consent Statement: Informed consent was obtained from all subjects involved in the study.

Data Availability Statement: The data presented in this study are available from the corresponding author upon reasonable request.

Acknowledgments: We extend profound thanks to all adolescent pregnant women and their parents/guardians for their participation and cooperation in this study.

Conflicts of Interest: The authors declare no conflict of interest.

Appendix A

Recommended intake and number of servings of food groups for adolescent mothers.

Food Group	Recommendation	Real Intake *
Vegetables	>3	0 (0–1)
Fruits	3–4	1.5 (0.5–3)
Grain and cereals	8–11	8 (6–11)
Legumes	2–2.5	0 (0–0)
Animal-source foods	3.5–4	3 (2–4)
Fat and oils	3–5	2 (1–3)
Milk and yogurt	2–2.5	2 (1–2)
Sugar table	<5	1 (0–2)
Sugar sweetened beverages	0	2 (0.5–11)

Academia Nacional de Medicina 2015. México (Fernández-Gaxiola et al. 2015). * Median (p25–75).

Appendix B

GWG of adolescent mother and offspring birth weights according to sociodemographic characteristics (%).

	Gestational Weight Gain %			Birth Weight		
	Insufficient	Excessive	*p*-Value	SGA, n = 108	LGA, n = 20	*p*-Value
Chronological age (years)						
≤15, n = 204	31.9	39.7	0.038	22.5	3.4	0.601
≥16, n = 326	42.9	32.5		19.0	4.0	
Beginning antenatal care						
First, n = 89	37.1	33.7	0.762	15.7	3.4	0.134
Second, n = 338	37.9	37.0		21.0	5.0	
Third, n = 103	42.7	31.1		22.3	0.0	
Marital status						
Single, n = 323	37.8	37.2	0.525	20.4	4.3	0.694
Cohabiting, n = 207	40.1	32.4		20.3	2.9	
Occupation						
Student, n = 57	42.1	36.8	0.655	19.3	1.8	0.668
Housewife, n = 473	38.3	35.1		20.5	4.0	

	Gestational Weight Gain %		p-Value	Birth Weight		p-Value
	Insufficient	Excessive		SGA, n = 108	LGA, n = 20	
Socioeconomic level						
Middle, n = 143	38.5	37.1	0.464	18.9	2.8	0.292
Low, n = 213	34.7	37.1		17.8	3.3	
Very low, n = 174	43.7	31.6		24.7	5.1	
School dropout						
No, n = 193	37.3	38.3	0.526	19.2	3.6	0.858
Yes, n = 337	39.5	33.5		21.1	3.9	
Gestational age						
Term >37, n = 473	40.0	34.7	0.215	19.9	3.6	0.550
Preterm, n = 57	28.1	40.4		26.4	5.3	
Number of prenatal visits						
≤6, n = 437	41.6	33.9	0.459	19.7	3.4	0.877
≥7, n = 93	36.4	36.4		20.9	4.0	

Percentages estimated by rows. SGA: small for gestational age. LGA: large for gestational age. p-value determined by Pearson's Chi-Square.

References

1. Riley, T.; Sully, E.; Ahmed, Z.; Biddlecom, A. Estimates of the Potential Impact of the COVID-19 Pandemic on Sexual and Reproductive Health In Low- and Middle-Income Countries. *Int. Perspect. Sex. Reprod. Health* **2020**, *46*, 73–76. [CrossRef] [PubMed]
2. Murro, R.; Guttmacher Institute; Chawla, R.; Pyne, S.; Venkatesh, S.; Sully, E. *Adding It Up: Investing in the Sexual and Reproductive Health of Adolescents in India*; Guttmacher Institute: New York, NY, USA, 2021.
3. Annan, R.A.; Gyimah, L.A.; Apprey, C.; Asamoah-Boakye, O.; Aduku, L.N.E.; Azanu, W.; Luterodt, H.E.; Edusei, A.K. Predictors of Adverse Birth Outcomes among Pregnant Adolescents in Ashanti Region, Ghana. *J. Nutr. Sci.* **2021**, *10*, e67. [CrossRef] [PubMed]
4. Loredo-Abdalá, A.; Vargas-Campuzano, E.; Casas-Muñoz, A.; González-Corona, J.; Gutiérrez-Leyva, C.J. Adolescent pregnancy: Its causes and repercussions in the dyad. *Rev. Med. Inst. Mex. Seguro Soc.* **2017**, *55*, 223–229. [PubMed]
5. Akseer, N.; Keats, E.C.; Thurairajah, P.; Cousens, S.; Bétran, A.P.; Oaks, B.M.; Osrin, D.; Piwoz, E.; Gomo, E.; Ahmed, F.; et al. Characteristics and Birth Outcomes of Pregnant Adolescents Compared to Older Women: An Analysis of Individual Level Data from 140,000 Mothers from 20 RCTs. *EClinicalMedicine* **2022**, *45*, 101309. [CrossRef] [PubMed]
6. Sámano, R.; Chico-Barba, G.; Flores-Quijano, M.E.; Godínez-Martínez, E.; Martínez-Rojano, H.; Ortiz-Hernandez, L.; Nájera-Medina, O.; Hernández-Trejo, M.; Hurtado-Solache, C. Association of Pregestational BMI and Gestational Weight Gain with Maternal and Neonatal Outcomes in Adolescents and Adults from Mexico City. *Int. J. Environ. Res. Public Health* **2021**, *19*, 280. [CrossRef]
7. Sundaram, A.; Puri, M.; Douglas-Hall, A.; Castle, K.; Wagle, K.; Weissman, E. *Adding It Up: Costs and Benefits of Meeting the Contraceptive and Maternal and Newborn Health Needs of Women in Nepal*; Guttmacher Institute: New York, NY, USA, 2019.
8. Ronen, S.; Lee, J.; Patel, P.; Patel, P. A Comparison of Childbirth Costs for Adolescents and Adults From 2001 to 2010. *J. Adolesc. Health* **2018**, *62*, 59–62. [CrossRef]
9. NCD Risk Factor Collaboration (NCD-RisC). Worldwide Trends in Body-Mass Index, Underweight, Overweight, and Obesity from 1975 to 2016: A Pooled Analysis of 2416 Population-Based Measurement Studies in 128·9 Million Children, Adolescents, and Adults. *Lancet* **2017**, *390*, 2627–2642. [CrossRef]
10. De Amicis, R.; Mambrini, S.P.; Pellizzari, M.; Foppiani, A.; Bertoli, S.; Battezzati, A.; Leone, A. Ultra-Processed Foods and Obesity and Adiposity Parameters among Children and Adolescents: A Systematic Review. *Eur. J. Nutr.* **2022**, *61*, 2297–2311. [CrossRef]
11. Harris, A.; Chilukuri, N.; West, M.; Henderson, J.; Lawson, S.; Polk, S.; Levine, D.; Bennett, W.L. Obesity-Related Dietary Behaviors among Racially and Ethnically Diverse Pregnant and Postpartum Women. *J. Pregnancy* **2016**, *2016*, 9832167. [CrossRef]
12. Yang, J.; Wang, M.; Tobias, D.K.; Rich-Edwards, J.W.; Darling, A.M.; Abioye, A.I.; Pembe, A.B.; Madzorera, I.; Fawzi, W.W. Gestational Weight Gain during the Second and Third Trimesters and Adverse Pregnancy Outcomes, Results from a Prospective Pregnancy Cohort in Urban Tanzania. *Reprod. Health* **2022**, *19*, 140. [CrossRef]
13. Christian, P.; Smith, E.R. Adolescent Undernutrition: Global Burden, Physiology, and Nutritional Risks. *Ann. Nutr. Metab.* **2018**, *72*, 316–328. [CrossRef]

14. Raghavan, R.; Dreibelbis, C.; Kingshipp, B.J.; Wong, Y.P.; Terry, N.; Abrams, B.; Bartholomew, A.; Bodnar, L.M.; Gernand, A.; Rasmussen, K.; et al. *Dietary Patterns before and during Pregnancy and Gestational Age- and Sex-Specific Birth Weight: A Systematic Review*; USDA Nutrition Evidence Systematic Review: Alexandria, VA, Egypt, 2022.
15. Pobocik, R.S.; Benavente, J.C.; Boudreau, N.S.; Spore, C.L. Pregnant Adolescents in Guam Consume Diets Low in Calcium and Other Micronutrients. *J. Am. Diet. Assoc.* **2003**, *103*, 611–614. [CrossRef]
16. Baker, P.N.; Wheeler, S.J.; Sanders, T.A.; Thomas, J.E.; Hutchinson, C.J.; Clarke, K.; Berry, J.L.; Jones, R.L.; Seed, P.T.; Poston, L. A Prospective Study of Micronutrient Status in Adolescent Pregnancy. *Am. J. Clin. Nutr.* **2009**, *89*, 1114–1124. [CrossRef]
17. Pinho-Pompeu, M.; Paulino, D.S.M.; Surita, F.G. Influence of Breakfast and Meal Frequency in Calcium Intake among Pregnant Adolescents. *Matern. Child Nutr.* **2020**, *16*, e13034. [CrossRef]
18. Sámano, R.; Morales, R.M.; Flores-García, A.; Lira, J.; Isoard, F.; de Santiago, S.; Casanueva, E. Las Adolescentes No Pierden Densidad Mineral ósea En El Posparto: Estudio Comparativo Con Adultas. *Salud Pública México* **2011**, *53*, 2–10. [CrossRef]
19. Bourassa, M.W.; Abrams, S.A.; Belizán, J.M.; Boy, E.; Cormick, G.; Quijano, C.D.; Gibson, S.; Gomes, F.; Hofmeyr, G.J.; Humphrey, J.; et al. Interventions to Improve Calcium Intake through Foods in Populations with Low Intake. *Ann. N. Y. Acad. Sci.* **2022**, *1511*, 40–58. [CrossRef]
20. Marvin-Dowle, K.; Burley, V.J.; Soltani, H. Nutrient Intakes and Nutritional Biomarkers in Pregnant Adolescents: A Systematic Review of Studies in Developed Countries. *BMC Pregnancy Childbirth* **2016**, *16*, 268. [CrossRef]
21. Gyimah, L.A.; Annan, R.A.; Apprey, C.; Edusei, A.; Aduku, L.N.E.; Asamoah-Boakye, O.; Azanu, W.; Lutterodt, H. Dietary Diversity and Its Correlates among Pregnant Adolescent Girls in Ghana. *PLoS ONE* **2021**, *16*, e0247979. [CrossRef]
22. Guzmán-Mercado, E.; Vásquez-Garibay, E.M.; Troyo-Sanroman, R.; Romero-Velarde, E. Hábitos de Alimentación En Adolescentes Embarazadas de Acuerdo a Su Estado Civil. *Nutr. Hosp.* **2016**, *33*, 226–231. [CrossRef]
23. Santander Ballestín, S.; Giménez Campos, M.I.; Ballestín Ballestín, J.; Luesma Bartolomé, M.J. Is Supplementation with Micronutrients Still Necessary during Pregnancy? A Review. *Nutrients* **2021**, *13*, 3134. [CrossRef]
24. Cano-Ibáñez, N.; Martínez-Galiano, J.M.; Luque-Fernández, M.A.; Martín-Peláez, S.; Bueno-Cavanillas, A.; Delgado-Rodríguez, M. Maternal Dietary Patterns during Pregnancy and Their Association with Gestational Weight Gain and Nutrient Adequacy. *Int. J. Environ. Res. Public Health* **2020**, *17*, 7908. [CrossRef] [PubMed]
25. Kaiser, L.; Allen, L.H.; American Dietetic Association. Position of the American Dietetic Association: Nutrition and Lifestyle for a Healthy Pregnancy Outcome. *J. Am. Diet. Assoc.* **2008**, *108*, 553–561. [CrossRef] [PubMed]
26. Rugină, C.; Mărginean, C.O.; Meliţ, L.E.; Giga, D.V.; Modi, V.; Mărginean, C. Relationships between Excessive Gestational Weight Gain and Energy and Macronutrient Intake in Pregnant Women. *J. Int. Med. Res.* **2020**, *48*, 300060520933808. [CrossRef] [PubMed]
27. Ferreira, L.B.; Lobo, C.V.; Miranda, A.E.D.S.; Carvalho, B.D.C.; Santos, L.C.D. Dietary Patterns during Pregnancy and Gestational Weight Gain: A Systematic Review. *Rev. Bras. Ginecol. Obstet.* **2022**, *44*, 540–547. [CrossRef] [PubMed]
28. Tielemans, M.J.; Garcia, A.H.; Peralta Santos, A.; Bramer, W.M.; Luksa, N.; Luvizotto, M.J.; Moreira, E.; Topi, G.; de Jonge, E.A.L.; Visser, T.L.; et al. Macronutrient Composition and Gestational Weight Gain: A Systematic Review. *Am. J. Clin. Nutr.* **2016**, *103*, 83–99. [CrossRef]
29. Zou, M.; Northstone, K.; Perry, R.; Johnson, L.; Leary, S. The Association between Later Eating Rhythm and Adiposity in Children and Adolescents: A Systematic Review and Meta-Analysis. *Nutr. Rev.* **2022**, *80*, 1459–1479. [CrossRef]
30. Cano-Ibáñez, N.; Martínez-Galiano, J.M.; Amezcua-Prieto, C.; Olmedo-Requena, R.; Bueno-Cavanillas, A.; Delgado-Rodríguez, M. Maternal Dietary Diversity and Risk of Small for Gestational Age Newborn: Findings from a Case-Control Study. *Clin. Nutr.* **2020**, *39*, 1943–1950. [CrossRef]
31. Martínez-Galiano, J.M.; Amezcua-Prieto, C.; Salcedo-Bellido, I.; González-Mata, G.; Bueno-Cavanillas, A.; Delgado-Rodríguez, M. Maternal Dietary Consumption of Legumes, Vegetables and Fruit during Pregnancy, Does It Protect against Small for Gestational Age? *BMC Pregnancy Childbirth* **2018**, *18*, 486. [CrossRef]
32. Martínez-Galiano, J.M.; Amezcua-Prieto, C.; Cano-Ibañez, N.; Olmedo-Requena, R.; Jiménez-Moleón, J.J.; Bueno-Cavanillas, A.; Delgado-Rodríguez, M. Diet as a Counteracting Agent of the Effect of Some Well-Known Risk Factors for Small for Gestational Age. *Nutrition* **2020**, *72*, 110665. [CrossRef]
33. Mejía-Rodríguez, F.; Orjuela, M.A.; García-Guerra, A.; Quezada-Sanchez, A.D.; Neufeld, L.M. Validation of a Novel Method for Retrospectively Estimating Nutrient Intake during Pregnancy Using a Semi-Quantitative Food Frequency Questionnaire. Matern. *Child Health J.* **2012**, *16*, 1468–1483. [CrossRef]
34. Fernández-Gaxiola, A.C.; Arenas, A.B.; Belausteguigoitia, M.P.; Kaufer-Horwitz, M.; Pérez-Lizaur, A.B.; Dommarco, J.R. *Guías Alimentarias y de Actividad Física: En Contexto de Sobrepeso y Obesidad en la Población Mexicana: Documento de Postura*; Intersistemas: Mexico City, Mexico, 2015; ISBN 9786074435153.
35. Moore, V.M.; Davies, M.J.; Willson, K.J.; Worsley, A.; Robinson, J.S. Dietary Composition of Pregnant Women Is Related to Size of the Baby at Birth. *J. Nutr.* **2004**, *134*, 1820–1826. [CrossRef]
36. Institute of Medicine (US) Panel on the Definition of Dietary Fiber and the Standing Committee on the Scientific Evaluation of Dietary Reference Intakes. *Dietary Reference Intakes Proposed Definition of Dietary Fiber*; National Academies Press: Washington, DC, USA, 2001; ISBN -10.
37. Institute of Medicine; Food and Nutrition Board; Standing Committee on the Scientific Evaluation of Dietary Reference Intakes; Subcommittee on Interpretation and Uses of Dietary Reference Intakes; Subcommittee on Upper Reference Levels of Nutrients;

Panel on the Definition of Dietary Fiber; Panel on Macronutrients. *Dietary Reference Intakes for Energy, Carbohydrate, Fiber, Fat, Fatty Acids, Cholesterol, Protein, and Amino Acids*; National Academies Press: Washington, DC, USA, 2005; ISBN 9780309085250.
38. Carrilho, T.R.B.; Rasmussen, K.; Farias, D.R.; Freitas Costa, N.C.; Araújo Batalha, M.; Reichenheim, M.E.; Ohuma, E.O.; Hutcheon, J.A.; Kac, G. Brazilian Maternal and Child Nutrition Consortium Agreement between Self-Reported Pre-Pregnancy Weight and Measured First-Trimester Weight in Brazilian Women. *BMC Pregnancy Childbirth* **2020**, *20*, 734. [CrossRef]
39. Holland, E.; Moore Simas, T.A.; Doyle Curiale, D.K.; Liao, X.; Waring, M.E. Self-Reported Pre-Pregnancy Weight versus Weight Measured at First Prenatal Visit: Effects on Categorization of Pre-Pregnancy Body Mass Index. Matern. *Child Health J.* **2013**, *17*, 1872–1878. [CrossRef]
40. Lohman, T.J.; Roache, A.F.; Martorell, R. Anthropometric Standardization Reference Manual. *Med. Sci. Sport. Exerc.* **1992**, *24*, 952. [CrossRef]
41. Onis, M. Who Multicentre Growth Reference Study Group WHO Child Growth Standards Based on Length/height, Weight and Age. *Acta Paediatr.* **2007**, *95*, 76–85.
42. Adu-Afarwuah, S.; Lartey, A.; Okronipa, H.; Ashorn, P.; Ashorn, U.; Zeilani, M.; Arimond, M.; Vosti, S.A.; Dewey, K.G. Maternal Supplementation with Small-Quantity Lipid-Based Nutrient Supplements Compared with Multiple Micronutrients, but Not with Iron and Folic Acid, Reduces the Prevalence of Low Gestational Weight Gain in Semi-Urban Ghana: A Randomized Controlled Trial. *J. Nutr.* **2017**, *147*, 697–705. [CrossRef]
43. National Research Council; Institute of Medicine; Board on Children, Youth, and Families; Food and Nutrition Board; Committee to Reexamine. *IOM Pregnancy Weight Guidelines Weight Gain During Pregnancy: Reexamining the Guidelines*; National Academies Press: Washington, DC, USA, 2009; ISBN 9780309149150.
44. Beauchesne, A.R.; Cara, K.C.; Chen, J.; Yao, Q.; Penkert, L.P.; Yang, W.; Chung, M. Effectiveness of Multimodal Nutrition Interventions during Pregnancy to Achieve 2009 Institute of Medicine Gestational Weight Gain Guidelines: A Systematic Review and Meta-Analysis. *Ann. Med.* **2021**, *53*, 1179–1197. [CrossRef]
45. Villar, J.; Cheikh Ismail, L.; Victora, C.G.; Ohuma, E.O.; Bertino, E.; Altman, D.G.; Lambert, A.; Papageorghiou, A.T.; Carvalho, M.; Jaffer, Y.A.; et al. International Standards for Newborn Weight, Length, and Head Circumference by Gestational Age and Sex: The Newborn Cross-Sectional Study of the INTERGROWTH-21st Project. *Lancet* **2014**, *384*, 857–868. [CrossRef]
46. Available online: www.amai.org/NSE/NivelSocioeconomicoAMAI.pdf (accessed on 10 March 2022).
47. Visintin, C.; Mugglestone, M.A.; Almerie, M.Q.; Nherera, L.M.; James, D.; Walkinshaw, S. Guideline Development Group Management of Hypertensive Disorders during Pregnancy: Summary of NICE Guidance. *BMJ* **2010**, *341*, c2207. [CrossRef]
48. Goyal, A.; Gupta, Y.; Singla, R.; Kalra, S.; Tandon, N. American Diabetes Association "Standards of Medical Care-2020 for Gestational Diabetes Mellitus": A Critical Appraisal. *Diabetes Ther.* **2020**, *11*, 1639–1644. [CrossRef]
49. Aburto, T.C.; Batis, C.; Pedroza-Tobías, A.; Pedraza, L.S.; Ramírez-Silva, I.; Rivera, J.A. Dietary Intake of the Mexican Population: Comparing Food Group Contribution to Recommendations, 2012–2016. *Salud Publica Mex.* **2022**, *64*, 267–279. [CrossRef] [PubMed]
50. Slater, K.; Rollo, M.E.; Szewczyk, Z.; Ashton, L.; Schumacher, T.; Collins, C. Do the Dietary Intakes of Pregnant Women Attending Public Hospital Antenatal Clinics Align with Australian Guide to Healthy Eating Recommendations? *Nutrients* **2020**, *12*, 2438. [CrossRef] [PubMed]
51. Appiah, P.K.; Naa Korklu, A.R.; Bonchel, D.A.; Fenu, G.A.; Wadga-Mieza Yankey, F. Nutritional Knowledge and Dietary Intake Habits among Pregnant Adolescents Attending Antenatal Care Clinics in Urban Community in Ghana. *J. Nutr. Metab.* **2021**, *2021*, 8835704. [CrossRef] [PubMed]
52. Rodríguez-Ramírez, S.; Gaona-Pineda, E.B.; Martínez-Tapia, B.; Arango-Angarita, A.; Kim-Herrera, E.Y.; Valdez-Sánchez, A.; Medina-Zacarías, M.C.; Shamah-Levy, T.; Ramírez-Silva, I. Consumo de Grupos de Alimentos Y Su Asociación Con Características Sociodemográficas En Población Mexicana. Ensanut 2018–2019. *Salud Pública México* **2020**, *62*, 693–703. [CrossRef] [PubMed]
53. Vázquez, C.; Escalante, A.; Huerta, J.; Villarreal, M.E. Efectos de La Frecuencia de Consumo de Alimentos Ultraprocesados Y Su Asociación Con Los Indicadores Del Estado Nutricional de Una Población Económicamente Activa En México. *Revista Chilena Nutrición* **2021**, *48*, 852–861. [CrossRef]
54. Quezada-Pinedo, H.G.; Cassel, F.; Duijts, L.; Muckenthaler, M.U.; Gassmann, M.; Jaddoe, V.W.V.; Reiss, I.K.M.; Vermeulen, M.J. Maternal Iron Status in Pregnancy and Child Health Outcomes after Birth: A Systematic Review and Meta-Analysis. *Nutrients* **2021**, *13*, 2221. [CrossRef]
55. O'Brien, W.; Issartel, J.; Belton, S. Relationship between Physical Activity, Screen Time and Weight Status among Young Adolescents. *Sports* **2018**, *6*, 57. [CrossRef]
56. Gamble, A.; Beech, B.M.; Blackshear, C.; Herring, S.J.; Welsch, M.A.; Moore, J.B. Changes in Physical Activity and Television Viewing From Pre-Pregnancy Through Postpartum Among a Socioeconomically Disadvantaged Perinatal Adolescent Population. *J. Pediatr. Adolesc. Gynecol.* **2021**, *34*, 832–838. [CrossRef]
57. Santos, S.F.M.D.; Costa, A.C.C.D.; Araújo, R.G.P.D.S.; Silva, L.A.T.; Gama, S.G.N.D.; Fonseca, V.D.M. Factors associated with the adequacy of gestational weight gain among Brazilian teenagers. *Ciência Saúde Coletiva* **2022**, *27*, 2629–2642. [CrossRef]
58. Jaacks, L.M.; Vandevijvere, S.; Pan, A.; McGowan, C.J.; Wallace, C.; Imamura, F.; Mozaffarian, D.; Swinburn, B.; Ezzati, M. The Obesity Transition: Stages of the Global Epidemic. *Lancet Diabetes Endocrinol.* **2019**, *7*, 231–240. [CrossRef]

59. Goldstein, R.F.; Abell, S.K.; Ranasinha, S.; Misso, M.L.; Boyle, J.A.; Harrison, C.L.; Black, M.H.; Li, N.; Hu, G.; Corrado, F.; et al. Gestational Weight Gain across Continents and Ethnicity: Systematic Review and Meta-Analysis of Maternal and Infant Outcomes in More than One Million Women. *BMC Med.* **2018**, *16*, 153. [CrossRef]
60. Wrottesley, S.V.; Pisa, P.T.; Norris, S.A. The Influence of Maternal Dietary Patterns on Body Mass Index and Gestational Weight Gain in Urban Black South African Women. *Nutrients* **2017**, *9*, 732. [CrossRef] [PubMed]
61. Hung, T.-H.; Hsieh, T.-T. Pregestational Body Mass Index, Gestational Weight Gain, and Risks for Adverse Pregnancy Outcomes among Taiwanese Women: A Retrospective Cohort Study. *Taiwan. J. Obstet. Gynecol.* **2016**, *55*, 575–581. [CrossRef]
62. Sisson, S.B.; Shay, C.M.; Broyles, S.T.; Leyva, M. Television-Viewing Time and Dietary Quality among U.S. Children and Adults. *Am. J. Prev. Med.* **2012**, *43*, 196–200. [CrossRef]
63. Song, Y.; Li, J.; Zhao, Y.; Zhang, Q.; Liu, Z.; Li, J.; Chen, X.; Yang, Z.; Yu, C.; Xiao, X. Severe maternal hyperglycemia exacerbates the development of insulin resistance and fatty liver in the offspring on high fat diet. *Exp. Diabetes Res.* **2012**, *2012*, 254976. [CrossRef]
64. da Mota Santana, J.; de Oliveira Queiroz, V.A.; Pereira, M.; Paixão, E.S.; Brito, S.M.; Dos Santos, D.B.; Oliveira, A.M. Associations between Maternal Dietary Patterns and Infant Birth Weight in the NISAMI Cohort: A Structural Equation Modeling Analysis. *Nutrients* **2021**, *13*, 4054. [CrossRef]
65. Mayer-Davis, E.; Leidy, H.; Mattes, R.; Naimi, T.; Novotny, R.; Schneeman, B.; Kingshipp, B.J.; Spill, M.; Cole, N.C.; Bahnfleth, C.L.; et al. *Beverage Consumption During Pregnancy and Birth Weight: A Systematic Review [Internet]*; USDA Nutrition Evidence Systematic Review: Alexandria, Egypt, 2020.
66. Scholl, T.O.; Hediger, M.L. A review of the epidemiology of nutrition and adolescent pregnancy: Maternal growth during pregnancy and its effect on the fetus. *J. Am. Coll. Nutr.* **1993**, *12*, 101–107. [CrossRef] [PubMed]
67. Chia, A.-R.; Chen, L.-W.; Lai, J.S.; Wong, C.H.; Neelakantan, N.; van Dam, R.M.; Chong, M.F.-F. Maternal Dietary Pat-terns and Birth Outcomes: A Systematic Review and Meta-Analysis. *Adv. Nutr.* **2019**, *10*, 685–695. [CrossRef]

nutrients

MDPI

Article

Inadequate Choline Intake in Pregnant Women in Germany

Merle Roeren †, Anna Kordowski †, Christian Sina and Martin Smollich *

Institute of Nutritional Medicine, University Hospital Schleswig-Holstein, Campus Luebeck, University of Luebeck, 23538 Luebeck, Germany
* Correspondence: martin.smollich@uksh.de
† These authors contributed equally to this work.

Abstract: Choline is an essential nutrient that is involved in various developmental processes during pregnancy. While the general adequate choline intake (AI) for adults has been set at 400 mg/day by the European Food Safety Authority (EFSA), an AI of 480 mg/day has been derived for pregnant women. To date, the choline intake of pregnant women in Germany has not been investigated yet. Therefore, in this survey, the total choline intake from dietary and supplementary sources in pregnant women was estimated using an online questionnaire. A total of 516 pregnant women participated in the survey, of which 283 met the inclusion criteria (13 to 41 weeks of gestational age, 19–45 years). 224 (79%) of the participants followed an omnivorous diet, 59 (21%) were vegetarian or vegan. Median choline intake was 260.4 (±141.4) mg/day, and only 19 women (7%) achieved the adequate choline intake. The median choline intake of omnivores was significantly higher than that of vegetarians/vegans (269.5 ± 141.5 mg/day vs. 205.2 ± 101.2 mg/day; $p < 0.0001$). 5% (13/283) of pregnant women took choline-containing dietary supplements. In these women, dietary supplements provided 19% of the total choline intake. Due to the importance of choline for the developmental processes during pregnancy, the study results prove the urgent need for an improved choline supply for pregnant women.

Keywords: choline; pregnancy; vegan; vegetarian; omnivorous; adequate intake

Citation: Roeren, M.; Kordowski, A.; Sina, C.; Smollich, M. Inadequate Choline Intake in Pregnant Women in Germany. *Nutrients* **2022**, *14*, 4862. https://doi.org/10.3390/nu14224862

Academic Editors: Louise Brough and Gail Rees

Received: 10 October 2022
Accepted: 15 November 2022
Published: 17 November 2022

1. Introduction

Choline is an essential nutrient being involved in many physiological processes in the human body. It is a constituent of the neurotransmitter acetylcholine and it modulates, as a precursor to the cell membrane components phosphatidylcholine and sphingomyelin, membrane integrity, transmembrane signaling, myelination, cell growth, and cell division [1]. Moreover, choline acts as a methyl group donor via the synthesis of s-adenosylmethionine [2], thereby essentially contributing to epigenetic methylation reactions, DNA stability, and cellular metabolism [3–5].

Correspondingly, higher phosphatidylcholine intake is associated with lower risk of incident dementia and better cognitive performance [6], and dietary choline intake has been suggested to play a relevant role in the prevention of cognitive decline [7,8], poststroke cognitive impairment [9], and poststroke depression [10]. Even more, choline has recently been found to be neuroprotective against prenatal alcohol exposure-related brain structure deficits in humans [11,12]. Respective effects of choline may, at least in part, be mediated by a functional interaction with vitamin B12 [13]. Dietary choline can be converted to trimethylamine (TMA) by the colonic microbiota, with TMA being further metabolized to trimethylamine-*N*-oxide (TMAO) in the liver [14]. The role of choline-derived TMAO for cardiovascular health is subject to controversial discussions [15].

A choline deficiency has not been reported at a population level, but has been observed in experimental settings and total parenteral nutrition only [16–18]. However, inadequate choline intake has been linked to non-alcoholic fatty liver disease (NAFLD), skeletal muscle atrophy, neurodegenerative diseases, and several ocular diseases including retinal hemorrhage, glaucoma, and dry eye syndrome [19,20]. Furthermore, a variety of choline-related inherited metabolic diseases has been described [21].

Even though choline, in principle, can be synthesized de novo through the methylation of phosphatidylethanolamine, the endogenous synthesis is not sufficient to meet the physiological choline requirements [22]. Therefore, choline must at least in part be acquired from dietary sources. Choline is mainly found in foods of animal origin such as eggs, poultry, and meat [23,24]. Plant-based foods such as legumes, leafy greens, and nuts, contain only small amounts of choline [25]. For an Australian cohort, it has been shown that eggs, red meat, nuts, legumes, and dairy account for 50% of the choline intake, with eggs alone contributing 17% [26]. In a randomized cross-over trial, the consumption of two eggs significantly increased the plasma choline level of adult [27]. Accordingly, it is difficult to meet the adequate choline intake especially for vegetarians and vegans [28,29].

During pregnancy and lactation, the dietary requirements for choline are substantially higher than for non-pregnant women, since the fetus and the infant accumulate choline at the expense of maternal stores [30,31]. Therefore, the adequate intake (AI) for choline in pregnant women has been set at 480 mg/day by the European Food Safety Authority (EFSA), compared to 400 mg/day for non-pregnant adults [32]. A growing body of evidence strongly suggests that choline plays a crucial role during neuronal fetal development [33], e.g., by contributing to fetal brain and memory development [34], acetylcholine biosynthesis, and neuronal cell signaling [25,35–37]. Accordingly, an increased choline intake during pregnancy probably improves the neurocognitive outcomes in the offspring [4,35,38]. Most recently, a meta-analysis found that a low maternal choline intake is not only associated with impaired child neurocognition and neurodevelopment, but also with an increased risk of neural tube defects [39]. However, substantial evidence from randomized-controlled trials investigating the prenatal effects of choline is still lacking, especially regarding both possible dose response-relationships between maternal choline intake and child neurocognitive outcomes and potential interactive effects of the two methyl-donor nutrients choline and folate [40].

Taking together the major relevance of a sufficient choline intake for the fetal neuronal development, the elevated choline requirements during pregnancy, and the poor choline content of plant-based foods, it can be supposed that pregnant women following a vegetarian or vegan diet have a high risk of not achieving the recommended AI for choline. Moreover, choline is absent in most dietary supplements marketed for pregnant women, with a median daily choline dose of only 25 mg [41,42].

Most surveys during pregnancy suggest that choline intakes are considerably below the AI [23], but the clinical assessment of choline status remains difficult [43]. In Germany, the choline intake of pregnant women has never been assessed systematically before. Therefore, we estimated the dietary and supplementary choline intake of pregnant women in Germany with an online survey. To detect possible subgroup differences, both omnivores and vegetarians/vegans have been included.

2. Materials and Methods

2.1. Study Design and Participants

For this online survey, pregnant women were recruited via social media in November and December 2021, using a questionnaire on the SurveyMonkey platform. The inclusion criteria were a gestational age of 13 weeks or higher, and an age between 19 and 45 years. In total, 516 subjects started the questionnaire, of whom 283 met the inclusion criteria (Figure S1). The sample size calculation was based on epidemiological data: In Germany, the population size is approx. 500,000 pregnant women in the second and third trimester of the pregnancy. With a confidence level set at 90% and a margin of error at 5%, the sample size has been calculated $n = 273$.

The participants were informed about the purpose of the study and their formal consent was collected before they started the questionnaire. Ethical review and approval were not required for the study in accordance with the local legislation and institutional requirements.

2.2. Questionnaire

The study was conducted in Germany and the questionnaire was in German language. It comprised 30 questions that were further divided into four different parts: health and pregnancy; dietary supplement use; a food frequency questionnaire (FFQ) which specified 60 choline-containing food items or groups; and questions about the sociodemographic background of the participants (Figure S2).

The FFQ was based on the National Health and Nutrition Examination Survey (NHANES) questionnaires [44] and the Project Viva FFQ [45], which have been used for the estimation of choline intake before [46]. The questionnaire used in the present study was designed to assess the choline intake from the diet within the previous week. Pictures of hand portion sizes were added to visualize the portion size and to have a standard for the subsequent evaluation. The FFQ focused on choline-containing foods only. To assess the dietary choline intake, we referred to Zeisel's measurements [47]. Using a drop-down list, respondents were able to determine the respective number of foods/food groups consumed during the previous week. Subsequently, the study population was categorized based on their dietary pattern (omnivore vs. vegetarian/vegan).

Finally, participants documented their intake of dietary supplements during the pregnancy (trademark, duration, dosing).

2.3. Data Analysis

The individual dietary choline intake was calculated by multiplying the frequency of consumption per week by consumed amounts of all the assessed food products. The concentration of choline in every respective food item was taken from previous studies [47]. To assess the daily intake, total weekly choline intake of each individual was divided by seven. The median and the interquartile range (IQR) of the entire cohort were calculated. To estimate the daily choline intake from dietary supplements, the participants answered the questions about the frequency and the dosage of the supplements they took.

For all data, statistical analyses were performed using GraphPad Prism. To test for the normal distribution, the Shapiro–Wilk test was applied. Since the normal distribution could not be assumed, non-parametric tests were used to statistically analyze the choline intake. Median values of total choline intake and dietary choline intake were calculated and presented in milligrams per day, with min to max error bars. Choline intake was compared to the adequate choline intake for pregnant women (480 mg/day).

Multivariate analysis for confounding variables was performed by linear regression.

The statistical comparison for the analysis of the different groups (omnivore to vegetarian/vegan to all) was carried out using a Kruskal–Wallis test with Dunn's test for multiple analyses; when only 2 groups were compared, the Mann–Whitney was used. We adjusted for outliers in the whole population referring to the daily intake. Outliers above the 95% percentile and below the 5% percentile were excluded (in total 10 data points, 8 omnivore and 2 vegetarian/vegan).

3. Results

3.1. Study Population

The baseline characteristics of the study population ($n = 283$) are shown in Table 1. Most participants were aged between 26–35 years (234/283), lived with their partner or family (278/283), and had a university degree (144/283). 56 (20%) participants changed their diet due to the pregnancy, and 16 (6%) took choline-containing dietary supplements. Among participants taking choline-containing dietary supplements, only three received a recommendation for it. Referring to health in pregnancy, the mean number of days of feeling nauseous was 50, with 54 (19%) of participants reporting weight loss due to vomiting.

Table 1. Descriptive statistics of the study population. Selected characteristics of the study cohort (n = 283) stratified by dietary patterns. Values are absolute number and percentages unless stated otherwise within diet group according to the categories in the first column.

	Vegetarian/Vegan n **= 59 (21%)**	**Omnivore** n **= 224 (79%)**	**Total** n **= 283 (100%)**
Age (years)			
19–25	6 (10%)	11 (5%)	17 (6%)
26–30	21 (36%)	101 (45%)	122 (43%)
31–35	25 (42%)	87 (39%)	112 (40%)
36–40	6 (10%)	23 (10%)	29 (10%)
41–45	1 (2%)	2 (1%)	3 (1%)
≥46	0	0	0
Living situation			
Living alone	1 (2%)	2 (1%)	3 (1%)
Living with partner	33 (56%)	107 (48%)	140 (49%)
Living with family	24 (41%)	114 (51%)	138 (49%)
Others	1 (2%)	1 (1%)	2 (1%)
Level of education			
Secondary school	1 (2%)	3 (1%)	4 (1%)
Secondary modern school	9 (15%)	47 (21%)	56 (20%)
Grammar school	10 (17%)	64 (29%)	74 (26%)
University	38 (64%)	106 (47%)	144 (51%)
Others	1 (2%)	4 (2%)	5 (2%)
Median (IQR) gestational week	31 (17)	24 (14.75)	25 (15)
Parity			
1	29 (49%)	105 (47%)	134 (47%)
2	17 (29%)	70 (31%)	87 (31%)
≥3	13 (22%)	48 (22%)	62 (22%)
Median (IQR) days feeling nauseous	60 (78)	32 (75)	35 (74)
Weight loss due to vomiting	8 (14%)	46 (21%)	54 (19%)
Changed diet for pregnancy	11 (76%)	45 (20%)	56 (20%)
Choline-containing supplement intake	5 (8%)	11 (5%)	16 (6%)
Choline recommendation by doctor, alternative practitioner, or nutritionist	0 (0%)	3 (1%)	3 (1%)

In the context of qualitative representativeness, our sample is representative for pregnant women in Germany regarding age distribution and living situation. Regarding education, women with a university degree (51%) are overrepresented in our sample.

59 (21%) women followed a vegetarian/vegan diet, while 224 (79%) were omnivorous. These two groups differed across health and sociodemographic characteristics. Vegetarian/vegan women were more likely to be older, more educated, and more likely to take choline-containing dietary supplements (8% vs. 5%). Moreover, they were less likely to lose weight due to vomiting (14% vs. 21%). In contrast, omnivorous women were less likely to change their diet for the pregnancy (20% vs. 76%). No-one in the vegetarian/vegan group received a recommendation to take choline-containing dietary supplements.

3.2. Total Choline Intake

For total choline intake, the estimated choline intake from both diet and dietary supplements were added. Only 7% (19/283) of participants achieved the adequate choline intake of 480 mg/day. The median choline intake was 263.5 ± 147.8 mg/day. 93% of omnivores (208/224) and 95% of vegetarians/vegans (56/59) had an inadequate choline intake when applying the choline AI (median: 274.3 ± 156 mg/day and 209.2 ± 107.7 mg/day, respectively).

After excluding outliers (choline intake > 558.70 mg/day), the median choline intake remained below the AI with 260.4 ± 141.4 mg/day for all, 269.5 ± 141.5 for omnivores, and 205.2 ± 101.2 mg/day for vegetarians/vegans (Figure 1). The difference in daily choline intake between omnivores and vegetarians/vegans was statistically significant ($p < 0.001$) (Figure 1). Calculating the odds ratio (OR), the vegetarian/vegan group had 30% lower odds of meeting the AI than the omnivorous group (95% CI 0.21–2.35, Table 2).

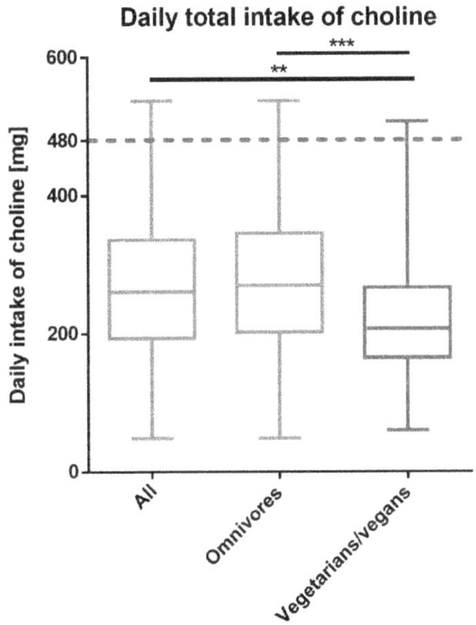

Figure 1. Total (dietary and supplementary) daily choline intake in all (n = 273), omnivorous (n = 217) and vegetarian/vegan (n = 56) participants (outliers excluded). The red dotted line represents the choline AI of 480 mg/day. Data are presented as median with whiskers from 'min to max' and was analyzed with Kruskal–Wallis test following the Dunn's test for multiple comparisons (** adjusted p value < 0.01; *** adjusted p value < 0.001).

Table 2. Participants who met the adequate choline intake (AI) of 480 mg/d.

	All	Omnivores	Vegetarians/Vegans
AI	19 (7%)	16 (7%)	3 (5%)
Total	283	224	59
Odds ratio		1.0	0.70 (0.21–2.35)

As a result of the multivariate analysis for possible confounders (age, education, nauseous days, diet), apart from the diet, the age of 36–40 years was the only confounding factor.

3.3. Dietary Choline Intake

Applying the AI for pregnant women, only 7% of the participants achieved an adequate choline intake. The median dietary choline intake was 267.8 ± 137.7 mg/day for omnivorous women and 204.4 ± 99.5 mg/day for vegetarian/vegan women ($p < 0.0001$) (Figure 2A).

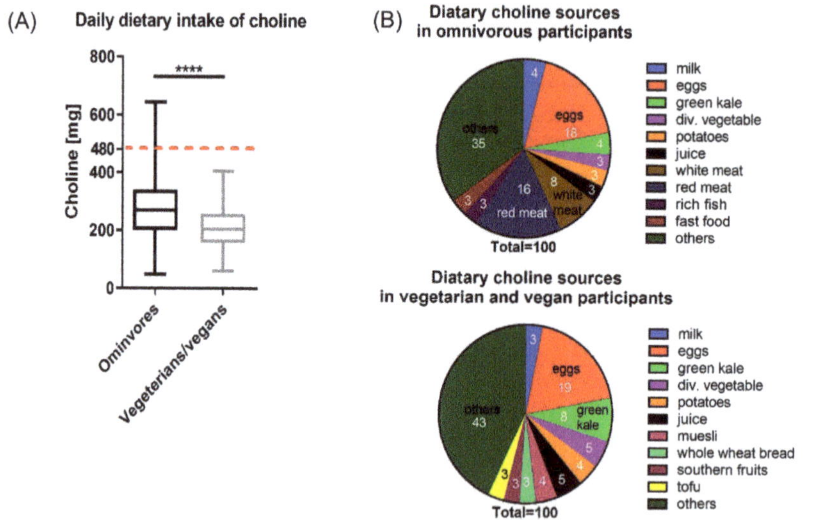

Figure 2. Dietary choline intake. (**A**) Daily dietary choline intake in omnivorous and vegetarian/vegan participants. The AI of 480 mg/day is represented by the red dotted line. Data are presented as median with whiskers from 'min to max' and was analyzed with Mann–Whitney test (**** $p < 0.0001$). (**B**) Dietary choline sources in omnivorous and vegetarian/vegan participants. Data are shown as parts of 100, numbers in the graph indicate the mean contribution of the given food to the total dietary choline intake.

The minimal dietary choline intake was 49 mg per day, being higher among vegetarians/vegans than among omnivores (60.06 mg/day vs. 48.69 mg/day). Diet contributed most to total choline intake in both groups, with differences between omnivores and vegetarians/vegans. The main sources of choline in omnivores were eggs (56.7 mg/day), red meat (48.2 mg/day), and white meat (25.1 mg/day); whereas, in the vegetarians/vegans, eggs, green kale, and fruit juice contributed the most with 42.7 mg/day, 19.1 mg/day, and 11.8 mg/day, respectively (Figure 2B). 3–4% of the total choline intake via food was provided by milk and potatoes in both groups.

3.4. Choline Intake from Dietary Supplements

In total, 13/283 (5%) participants reported to take choline-containing dietary supplements (omnivores: $n = 10$; vegetarians/vegans: $n = 3$, Figure 3A). In these women, dietary supplements accounted for 19% of total choline intake. Differentiating between dietary habits, choline-containing supplements contributed 16% to the total choline intake of omnivores (mean supplementary choline intake: 100.94 mg/day), but 34% (mean supplementary choline intake: 126.67 mg/day) to the total choline intake of vegetarians/vegans (Figure 3B).

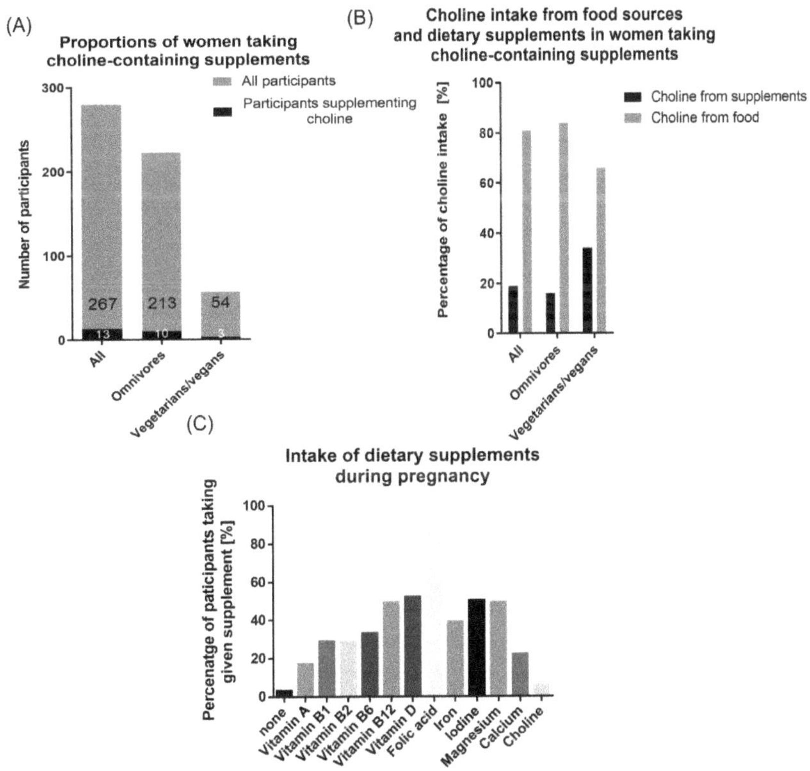

Figure 3. Intake of dietary supplements. (**A**) Proportion of participants taking choline-containing dietary supplements in all (13/267), omnivorous (10/213), and vegetarian/vegan (3/54) participants (**B**) Percentage of choline coming from food sources and dietary supplements in participants supplementing choline (all n = 13; omnivore n = 10, vegetarian/vegan n = 3) (**C**) Intake of dietary supplements during pregnancy. Percentage of participants taking given supplement alone or as a part of a prenatal vitamin complex supplement.

3.5. Dietary Supplement Use

274/283 (97%) participants took any dietary supplement during pregnancy. 90% of the women took folic acid alone or as part of a prenatal vitamin complex (Figure 3C). Vitamin D was supplemented by 52%, iodine by 50%, and magnesium and vitamin B12 by 49% each.

4. Discussion

4.1. Main Finding

Our study was the first to estimate the dietary and supplemental choline intake of pregnant women in Germany, demonstrating that 93% of pregnant women do not meet the adequate choline intake, with vegetarian/vegan women having an even lower chance of achieving the adequate intake. Moreover, taking dietary supplements does not substantially improve the situation.

4.2. Previous Findings on Choline Intake

As early as 1998, choline was recognized as an essential nutrient, and the adequate choline intake has been set for both the general population and pregnant women by the Institute of Medicine (IOM) [48]. In contrast, until now, no respective recommendations have been published by the German Society of Nutrition.

Data on the dietary and supplementary choline intake of healthy adults are only available for North America and few European countries; respective data for Germany are lacking. Most surveys during pregnancy suggest that the AI of choline is met by few women only [23]. Accordingly, the choline intake of healthy, non-pregnant women has recently been estimated at 291 mg/day (France), 285 mg/day (Greece), 334 mg/day (The Netherlands), 294 mg/day (UK), and 362 mg/day (Australia) [26,49]. For Germany, total choline intake estimates have only been published for children and adolescents with an average intake in females ranging from 151–295 mg/day [50]. With the estimated median choline intake in our survey being 260.4 mg/day, our results are consistent with previous findings as they are both close to the estimated choline intake from neighboring countries with similar dietary habits (291–374 mg/day) [49], and very similar to the estimated choline intake of German female adolescents (295 mg/day) [50]. The result of the multivariate analysis indicating that the age of 36–40 years is the only confounding factor (apart from the diet) can be interpreted as a statistical artefact, as it cannot be plausibly explained by physiological/psychological hypotheses and previous studies.

Investigating the choline intake during pregnancy, systematic data for European countries are lacking almost completely. The only data published so far come from a Latvian survey showing an average choline intake among pregnant women of 336 mg/day [51], which too is in line with our results. Moreover, our finding that 93% of pregnant women in Germany do not reach the adequate choline intake is in line with similar data from the US with 91% of the pregnant women not meeting the AI for choline [52].

4.3. *Studies on Choline-Containing Dietary Supplements*

A randomized controlled trial assessed the effect of third trimester maternal choline supplementation (930 mg/day vs. 480 mg/day) on child memory at 7 years of age. Both groups were above the adequate intake levels in Germany [32]. Children of higher supplemented mothers scored better results than children in the control group with lower choline doses. Another study investigating the effect of prenatal choline supplementation (500 mg/day vs. 25 mg/day) on maternal and fetal biomarkers of choline metabolism measured higher plasma concentrations of free choline, betaine, dimethylglycine, phosphatidylcholine, and sphingomyelin among higher supplemented women [53]. Moreover, pregnancy-related metabolic adaptions were supported in this trial. These findings indicate that even the choline AI set for pregnant women by the EFSA may not be sufficient for optimal offspring neurodevelopment. However, in both studies the sample size was relatively small which makes it difficult to draw generalized conclusions. Furthermore, compared to the supplements used in our study, the dietary supplements used in these trials by far exceeded the choline doses used in Germany.

Most women in our study supplemented folic acid (FA) during their pregnancy. Recent studies suggest that imbalances between FA and other methyl-donor nutrients involved in one-carbon metabolism can determine the pregnancy outcomes [54] and metabolic adaptions [55]. Folic acid and choline play critical roles in the production of S-adenosylmethionine (SAM), a key modulator of DNA methylation [56]. However, in contrast to FA, choline is absent in most prenatal dietary supplements in Germany. This aspect is also observed in our study, since most of the women took folic acid-containing dietary supplements while most of these supplements did not contain any choline.

4.4. *Implications*

Our results for the first time demonstrate that the choline intake of pregnant women in Germany generally does not meet the recommendations for an adequate intake, with vegetarian and vegan women having an even lower chance of achieving the AI for choline. Moreover, taking dietary supplements does not improve the situation. Thus, it can be concluded that currently neither the majority of pregnant women, nor health care professionals, nor manufacturers of dietary supplements are aware of choline being a critical nutrient in pregnancy. Furthermore, our results underline the imbalance of folic acid and choline intake in pregnant women in Germany. Several implications arise from our results.

First, obviously, it is very difficult to meet the recommended AI for choline with a regular, omnivorous diet, and it is even more so for pregnant women following a vegetarian or vegan diet. Therefore, it might be suggested to advice pregnant women to change their dietary habits, thereby improving their choline intake. This approach, however, is hardly practicable considering the low success rates of general dietary recommendations. Even more, pregnant women sticking to a vegetarian or vegan diet due to ethical reasons are very unlikely to switch to an omnivorous, egg and meat-containing diet just to increase their choline supply. On the other hand, small dietary changes even of omnivorous women will not be able to substantially increase their choline intake.

Second, the awareness that choline might be an essential nutrient in pregnancy should be raised, both among pregnant women and healthcare professionals, including gynecologists, midwives, general practitioners, and pharmacists. The urgent need for improved choline provision for pregnant women, both through individual counselling and public health interventions, has been emphasized by other authors before [57]. This goal, however, is unlikely to be achieved through general information campaigns, but rather through targeted training and continuing medical education programs. If choline-specific dietary recommendations prove to be insufficient or unsuccessful, the intake of choline-containing dietary supplements might be considered. Particularly, respective supplements may be useful in vegetarian/vegan women and in women suffering from nausea and vomiting during pregnancy. Since vegetarian and vegan diets are increasingly common in pregnant women, there is an increased risk that the maternal choline supply will deteriorate as a result.

Third, the results of our survey suggest that it might be useful to add sufficient amounts of choline to products that are advertised for pregnant women. As shown here, most dietary supplements used do not contain any choline. If they do contain choline, the respective concentrations are too low to substantially improve the choline supply of the pregnant women.

Finally, fourth, more randomized controlled trials are needed to further specify the health benefits for the offspring resulting from an improved maternal choline intake. The adequate choline intake recommendations are not derived from randomized controlled trials but estimated from epidemiological data only. Therefore, it must be kept in mind that not meeting the recommended AI not necessarily means that the respective individual (or her offspring) is insufficient of choline or even suffering from clinically relevant deficiency.

4.5. Strengths and Limitations

It is a particular strength of our study that it makes an important contribution to putting the focus on the choline supply of pregnant women. The results presented here are the first to estimate the total choline intake of pregnant women in Germany, both from dietary and supplementary sources and differentiating between omnivorous and vegetarian/vegan diets. A major strength of our methodology is the semiquantitative questionnaire with hand portion pictures that enabled improved estimation of dietary intakes.

Regarding the limitations, it has to be considered that our data are based on a non-probability convenience sample rather than a representative population-based sample. With this type of sampling, the generalizability of our results is limited to populations that share similar characteristics with our sample. Therefore, it remains questionable whether the results would be similar in a representative sample. Due to the case number calculation, the quantitative representativeness of our results is given. In terms of qualitative representativeness, our sample is representative for pregnant women in Germany regarding age distribution and living situation. However, regarding education, women with a university degree (51%) are overrepresented in our sample, as due to census data only 28% of women < 60 years hold a university degree. Thus, the choline intake of pregnant women without a university degree might differ from the results presented here.

In this context, a selection bias might be relevant, too. Recruitment was done through social media, so pregnant women without appropriate media use were not reached. Women with a heightened interest in nutritional issues and dietary supplements probably preferentially participated in the survey. When interpreting the data, it must be noted that the number of subjects in some subgroups was too small to obtain statistically meaningful results. This problem must be addressed with appropriately powered follow-up studies.

Additionally, the choline content of several foods was unknown since it has never been analyzed and published. As a result, some dietary choline sources were not named so that the final result might be lower. Specifically, the FFQ used in our study did not include vegan and vegetarian meat or dairy alternatives which might have affected the estimated choline intake especially in vegetarians and vegans.

Since the FFQ method is widely used in nutrition surveys, its inherent limitations are well-known and have been discussed in detail elsewhere [58]. Additionally, some participants obviously misread the instructions and filled in the questionnaire not for a week but rather for a whole month. In order to attenuate this error, we excluded outliers as indicated. An alternative approach for food intake assessment might have been repeated dietary recalls or records; however, an FFQ is more achievable in a large cohort and within the given time frame [59], even more, it is less prone to over- or underestimating the food intake than other methods [60].

Of course, the results may not be transferred to other countries without further ado, since not only dietary habits may differ, but also the medical counselling of pregnant women, the market situation of dietary supplements, the health policies and public opinion regarding food fortification, and the women's attitude towards taking dietary supplements.

Finally, any evaluation of choline intake must be done with caution, as intake below the AI not necessarily indicates a health-affecting deficiency [49].

5. Conclusions

Due to the relevance of choline for fetal development, and considering our results that suggest an inadequate choline intake in pregnant women in Germany, efforts to encourage the increased intake of choline-rich foods and/or choline-containing dietary supplements during pregnancy might be useful. This is especially true for pregnant women who follow a vegetarian or vegan diet. Moreover, further research is necessary to define optimal choline requirements in pregnancy.

Supplementary Materials: The following supporting information can be downloaded at: https://www.mdpi.com/article/10.3390/nu14224862/s1, Figure S1: Flow Chart. Figure S2: Original questionnaire in German language with an example of the drop-down list used for the food frequency questionnaire.

Author Contributions: Conceptualization, M.S. and M.R.; methodology, M.R.; formal analysis, M.R. and A.K.; writing—original draft preparation, M.R., A.K. and M.S.; writing—review and editing, C.S. and M.S.; supervision, M.S. All authors have read and agreed to the published version of the manuscript.

Funding: This research received no external funding.

Institutional Review Board Statement: Ethical review and approval were waived for this study due to local legislation and institutional requirements. Approval by the local ethics committee is not required if the study is non-interventional, does not involve biological samples from humans, the data analysis does not lead to a medical guarantee position and the personal data are anonymous and non-traceable.

Informed Consent Statement: Informed consent was obtained from all subjects involved in the study.

Data Availability Statement: Data available upon request from the corresponding author.

Acknowledgments: We would like to thank all the participants for taking part in this study.

Conflicts of Interest: The authors declare no conflict of interest.

References

1. Zeisel, S.H.; Niculescu, M.D. Perinatal Choline Influences Brain Structure and Function. *Nutr. Rev.* **2006**, *64*, 197–203. [CrossRef] [PubMed]
2. Zeisel, S. Choline, Other Methyl-Donors and Epigenetics. *Nutrients* **2017**, *9*, 445. [CrossRef] [PubMed]
3. Jiang, X.; Yan, J.; West, A.A.; Perry, C.A.; Malysheva, O.V.; Devapatla, S.; Pressman, E.; Vermeylen, F.; Caudill, M.A. Maternal choline intake alters the epigenetic state of fetal cortisol-regulating genes in humans. *FASEB J.* **2012**, *26*, 3563–3574. [CrossRef] [PubMed]
4. Blusztajn, J.K.; Mellott, T.J. Choline nutrition programs brain development via DNA and histone methylation. *Central Nerv. Syst. Agents Med. Chem.* **2012**, *12*, 82–94. [CrossRef] [PubMed]
5. Zeisel, S.H. What Choline Metabolism Can Tell Us about the Underlying Mechanisms of Fetal Alcohol Spectrum Disorders. *Mol. Neurobiol.* **2011**, *44*, 185–191. [CrossRef] [PubMed]
6. Ylilauri, M.P.T.; Voutilainen, S.; Lönnroos, E.; Virtanen, H.E.K.; Tuomainen, T.-P.; Salonen, J.T.; Virtanen, J.K. Associations of dietary choline intake with risk of incident dementia and with cognitive performance: The Kuopio Ischaemic Heart Disease Risk Factor Study. *Am. J. Clin. Nutr.* **2019**, *110*, 1416–1423. [CrossRef]
7. Poly, C.; Massaro, J.M.; Seshadri, S.; Wolf, P.A.; Cho, E.; Krall, E.; Jacques, P.F.; Au, R. The relation of dietary choline to cognitive performance and white-matter hyperintensity in the Framingham Offspring Cohort. *Am. J. Clin. Nutr.* **2011**, *94*, 1584–1591. [CrossRef] [PubMed]
8. Vizuete, A.A.; Robles, F.; Rodríguez-Rodríguez, E.; López-Sobaler, A.M.; Ortega, R.M. Association between food and nutrient intakes and cognitive capacity in a group of institutionalized elderly people. *Eur. J. Nutr.* **2009**, *49*, 293–300. [CrossRef]
9. Zhong, C.; Lu, Z.; Che, B.; Qian, S.; Zheng, X.; Wang, A.; Bu, X.; Zhang, J.; Ju, Z.; Xu, T.; et al. Choline Pathway Nutrients and Metabolites and Cognitive Impairment after Acute Ischemic Stroke. *Stroke* **2021**, *52*, 887–895. [CrossRef] [PubMed]
10. Miao, M.; Du, J.; Che, B.; Guo, Y.; Zhang, J.; Ju, Z.; Xu, T.; Zhong, X.; Zhang, Y.; Zhong, C. Circulating choline pathway nutrients and depression after ischemic stroke. *Eur. J. Neurol.* **2021**, *29*, 459–468. [CrossRef]
11. Jacobson, S.W.; Carter, R.C.; Molteno, C.D.; Stanton, M.E.; Herbert, J.S.; Lindinger, N.M.; Lewis, C.E.; Dodge, N.C.; Hoyme, H.E.; Zeisel, S.H.; et al. Efficacy of Maternal Choline Supplementation During Pregnancy in Mitigating Adverse Effects of Prenatal Alcohol Exposure on Growth and Cognitive Function: A Randomized, Double-Blind, Placebo-Controlled Clinical Trial. *Alcohol. Clin. Exp. Res.* **2018**, *42*, 1327–1341. [CrossRef] [PubMed]
12. Warton, F.L.; Molteno, C.D.; Warton, C.M.R.; Wintermark, P.; Lindinger, N.M.; Dodge, N.C.; Zöllei, L.; Kouwe, A.J.; Carter, R.C.; Jacobson, J.L.; et al. Maternal choline supplementation mitigates alcohol exposure effects on neonatal brain volumes. *Alcohol. Clin. Exp. Res.* **2021**, *45*, 1762–1774. [CrossRef] [PubMed]
13. King, J.H.; Kwan, S.T.; Bae, S.; Klatt, K.C.; Yan, J.; Malysheva, O.V.; Jiang, X.; Roberson, M.S.; Caudill, M.A. Maternal choline supplementation alters vitamin B-12 status in human and murine pregnancy. *J. Nutr. Biochem.* **2019**, *72*, 108210. [CrossRef] [PubMed]
14. Wang, Z.; Klipfell, E.; Bennett, B.J.; Koeth, R.; Levison, B.S.; DuGar, B.; Feldstein, A.E.; Britt, E.B.; Fu, X.; Chung, Y.-M.; et al. Gut Flora Metabolism of Phosphatidylcholine Promotes Cardiovascular Disease. *Nature* **2011**, *472*, 57–63. [CrossRef] [PubMed]
15. He, S.; Jiang, H.; Zhuo, C.; Jiang, W. Trimethylamine/Trimethylamine-*N*-Oxide as a Key between Diet and Cardiovascular Diseases. *Cardiovasc. Toxicol.* **2021**, *21*, 593–604. [CrossRef]
16. Chawla, R.K.; Wolf, D.C.; Kutner, M.H.; Bonkovsky, H.L. Choline may be an essential nutrient in malnourished patients with cirrhosis. *Gastroenterology* **1989**, *97*, 1514–1520. [CrossRef]
17. Sheard, N.F.; Tayek, J.A.; Bistrian, B.R.; Blackburn, G.L.; Zeisel, S.H. Plasma choline concentration in humans fed parenterally. *Am. J. Clin. Nutr.* **1986**, *43*, 219–224. [CrossRef]
18. Zeisel, S.H.; da Costa, K.-A. Choline, an essential nutrient for humans. *FASEB J. Off. Publ. Fed. Am. Soc. Exp. Biol.* **1991**, *5*, 2093–2098. [CrossRef]
19. Goh, Y.Q.; Cheam, G.; Wang, Y. Understanding Choline Bioavailability and Utilization: First Step Toward Personalizing Choline Nutrition. *J. Agric. Food Chem.* **2021**, *69*, 10774–10789. [CrossRef]
20. Hwang, J.-S.; Shin, Y.-J. Role of Choline in Ocular Diseases. *Int. J. Mol. Sci.* **2021**, *22*, 4733. [CrossRef]
21. Wortmann, S.B.; Mayr, J.A. Choline-related-inherited metabolic diseases—A mini review. *J. Inherit. Metab. Dis.* **2018**, *42*, 237–242. [CrossRef]
22. Zeisel, S.H.; da Costa, K.-A. Choline: An essential nutrient for public health. *Nutr. Rev.* **2009**, *67*, 615–623. [CrossRef]
23. Derbyshire, E.; Obeid, R.; Schön, C. Habitual Choline Intakes across the Childbearing Years: A Review. *Nutrients* **2021**, *13*, 4390. [CrossRef] [PubMed]
24. Blusztajn, J.K.; Slack, B.E.; Mellott, T.J. Neuroprotective Actions of Dietary Choline. *Nutrients* **2017**, *9*, 815. [CrossRef]
25. Zeisel, S.H.; Klatt, K.C.; Caudill, M.A. Choline. *Adv. Nutr. Int. Rev. J.* **2018**, *9*, 58–60. [CrossRef]
26. Probst, Y.; Sulistyoningrum, D.C.; Netting, M.J.; Gould, J.F.; Wood, S.; Makrides, M.; Best, K.P.; Green, T.J. Estimated Choline Intakes and Dietary Sources of Choline in Pregnant Australian Women. *Nutrients* **2022**, *14*, 3819. [CrossRef]
27. Zhu, C.; Sawrey-Kubicek, L.; Bardagjy, A.S.; Houts, H.; Tang, X.; Sacchi, R.; Randolph, J.M.; Steinberg, F.M.; Zivkovic, A.M. Whole egg consumption increases plasma choline and betaine without affecting TMAO levels or gut microbiome in overweight postmenopausal women. *Nutr. Res.* **2020**, *78*, 36–41. [CrossRef]

28. Wallace, T.C.; Blusztajn, J.K.; Caudill, M.A.; Klatt, K.C.; Natker, E.; Zeisel, S.H.; Zelman, K.M. Choline. *Nutr. Today* **2018**, *53*, 240–253. [CrossRef]
29. Perrin, M.T.; Pawlak, R.; Allen, L.H.; Hampel, D. Total Water-Soluble Choline Concentration Does Not Differ in Milk from Vegan, Vegetarian, and Nonvegetarian Lactating Women. *J. Nutr.* **2019**, *150*, 512–517. [CrossRef]
30. Molloy, A.M.; Mills, J.; Cox, C.; Daly, S.F.; Conley, M.; Brody, L.C.; Kirke, P.N.; Scott, J.M.; Ueland, P.M. Choline and homocysteine interrelations in umbilical cord and maternal plasma at delivery. *Am. J. Clin. Nutr.* **2005**, *82*, 836–842. [CrossRef]
31. Ilcol, Y.O.; Ozbek, R.; Hamurtekin, E.; Ulus, I.H. Choline status in newborns, infants, children, breast-feeding women, breast-fed infants and human breast milk. *J. Nutr. Biochem.* **2005**, *16*, 489–499. [CrossRef] [PubMed]
32. Efsa, N.D.; Panel (EFSA Panel on Dietetic Products, Nutrition and Allergies). Dietary Reference Values for choline. *EFSA J.* **2016**, *14*, 4484. [CrossRef]
33. Cochrane, K.M.; A Williams, B.; Elango, R.; I Barr, S.; Karakochuk, C.D. Pregnancy-induced alterations of 1-carbon metabolism and significance for maternal nutrition requirements. *Nutr. Rev.* **2022**, *80*, 1985–2001. [CrossRef] [PubMed]
34. Jadavji, N.; Deng, L.; Malysheva, O.; Caudill, M.; Rozen, R. MTHFR deficiency or reduced intake of folate or choline in pregnant mice results in impaired short-term memory and increased apoptosis in the hippocampus of wild-type offspring. *Neuroscience* **2015**, *300*, 1–9. [CrossRef]
35. Ross, R.G.; Hunter, S.K.; McCarthy, L.; Beuler, J.; Hutchison, A.K.; Wagner, B.; Leonard, S.; Stevens, K.E.; Freedman, R. Perinatal Choline Effects on Neonatal Pathophysiology Related to Later Schizophrenia Risk. *Am. J. Psychiatry* **2013**, *170*, 290–298. [CrossRef]
36. Wang, Y.; Surzenko, N.; Friday, W.B.; Zeisel, S.H. Maternal dietary intake of choline in mice regulates development of the cerebral cortex in the offspring. *FASEB J.* **2015**, *30*, 1566–1578. [CrossRef]
37. Derbyshire, E.; Obeid, R. Choline, Neurological Development and Brain Function: A Systematic Review Focusing on the First 1000 Days. *Nutrients* **2020**, *12*, 1731. [CrossRef] [PubMed]
38. Caudill, M.A.; Strupp, B.J.; Muscalu, L.; Nevins, J.E.H.; Canfield, R.L. Maternal choline supplementation during the third trimester of pregnancy improves infant information processing speed: A randomized, double-blind, controlled feeding study. *FASEB J.* **2018**, *32*, 2172–2180. [CrossRef]
39. Obeid, R.; Derbyshire, E.; Schön, C. Association between maternal choline, foetal brain development and child neurocognition; systematic review and meta-analysis of human studies. *Adv. Nutr. Int. Rev. J.* **2022**. *online ahead of print*. [CrossRef]
40. Irvine, N.; England-Mason, G.; Field, C.J.; Dewey, D.; Aghajafari, F. Prenatal Folate and Choline Levels and Brain and Cognitive Development in Children: A Critical Narrative Review. *Nutrients* **2022**, *14*, 364. [CrossRef]
41. Wallace, T.C. A Comprehensive Review of Eggs, Choline, and Lutein on Cognition across the Life-span. *J. Am. Coll. Nutr.* **2018**, *37*, 269–285. [CrossRef]
42. Adams, J.B.; Kirby, J.K.; Sorensen, J.C.; Pollard, E.L.; Audhya, T. Evidence based recommendations for an optimal prenatal supplement for women in the US: Vitamins and related nutrients. *Matern. Health Neonatol. Perinatol.* **2022**, *8*, 1–37. [CrossRef]
43. Horita, D.A.; Hwang, S.; Stegall, J.M.; Friday, W.B.; Kirchner, D.R.; Zeisel, S.H. Two methods for assessment of choline status in a randomized crossover study with varying dietary choline intake in people: Isotope dilution MS of plasma and in vivo single-voxel magnetic resonance spectroscopy of liver. *Am. J. Clin. Nutr.* **2021**, *113*, 1670–1678. [CrossRef]
44. NHANES Questionnaires, Datasets, and Related Documentation. Available online: https://wwwn.cdc.gov/nchs/nhanes/default.aspx (accessed on 9 August 2022).
45. Fawzi, W. Calibration of a semi-quantitative food frequency questionnaire in early pregnancy. *Ann. Epidemiol.* **2004**, *14*, 754–762. [CrossRef]
46. Villamor, E.; Rifas-Shiman, S.L.; Gillman, M.W.; Oken, E. Maternal Intake of Methyl-Donor Nutrients and Child Cognition at 3 Years of Age. *Paediatr. Périnat. Epidemiol.* **2012**, *26*, 328–335. [CrossRef]
47. Zeisel, S.H.; Mar, M.-H.; Howe, J.C.; Holden, J.M. Concentrations of Choline-Containing Compounds and Betaine in Common Foods. *J. Nutr.* **2003**, *133*, 1302–1307. [CrossRef]
48. *Institute of Medicine (US) Standing Committee on the Scientific Evaluation of Dietary Reference Intakes and Its Panel on, Choline*; National Academies Press (US): Washington, DC, USA, 1998. Available online: https://www.ncbi.nlm.nih.gov/books/NBK114308/ (accessed on 17 November 2021).
49. Wiedeman, A.M.; Barr, S.I.; Green, T.J.; Xu, Z.; Innis, S.M.; Kitts, D.D. Dietary Choline Intake: Current State of Knowledge Across the Life Cycle. *Nutrients* **2018**, *10*, 1513. [CrossRef] [PubMed]
50. Vennemann, F.B.C.; Ioannidou, S.; Valsta, L.M.; Dumas, C.; Ocké, M.C.; Mensink, G.B.M.; Lindtner, O.; Virtanen, S.M.; Tlustos, C.; D'Addezio, L.; et al. Dietary intake and food sources of choline in European populations. *Br. J. Nutr.* **2015**, *114*, 2046–2055. [CrossRef]
51. Bahnfleth, C.; Canfield, R.; Nevins, J.; Caudill, M.; Strupp, B. Prenatal Choline Supplementation Improves Child Color-location Memory Task Performance at 7 Y of Age (FS05-01-19). *Curr. Dev. Nutr.* **2019**, *3*, 1260–1261. [CrossRef]
52. Wallace, T.C.; Fulgoni, V.L. Usual Choline Intakes Are Associated with Egg and Protein Food Consumption in the United States. *Nutrients* **2017**, *9*, 839. [CrossRef]
53. Taesuwan, S.; McDougall, M.Q.; Malysheva, O.V.; Bender, E.; Nevins, J.E.H.; Devapatla, S.; Vidavalur, R.; Caudill, M.A.; Klatt, K.C. Choline metabolome response to prenatal choline supplementation across pregnancy: A randomized controlled trial. *FASEB J.* **2021**, *35*, e22063. [CrossRef]

54. Imbard, A.; Benoist, J.-F.; Blom, H.J. Neural Tube Defects, Folic Acid and Methylation. *Int. J. Environ. Res. Public Health* **2013**, *10*, 4352–4389. [CrossRef]
55. Hammoud, R.; Pannia, E.; Kubant, R.; Wasek, B.; Bottiglieri, T.; Malysheva, O.V.; Caudill, M.A.; Anderson, G.H. Choline and Folic Acid in Diets Consumed during Pregnancy Interact to Program Food Intake and Metabolic Regulation of Male Wistar Rat Offspring. *J. Nutr.* **2021**, *151*, 857–865. [CrossRef]
56. Radziejewska, A.; Chmurzynska, A. Folate and choline absorption and uptake: Their role in fetal development. *Biochimie* **2018**, *158*, 10–19. [CrossRef]
57. Wallace, T.C.; Blusztajn, J.K.; Caudill, M.A.; Klatt, K.C.; Zeisel, S.H. Choline: The Neurocognitive Essential Nutrient of Interest to Obstetricians and Gynecologists. *J. Diet. Suppl.* **2019**, *17*, 733–752. [CrossRef]
58. Shim, J.-S.; Oh, K.; Kim, H.C. Dietary assessment methods in epidemiologic studies. *Epidemiol. Health* **2014**, *36*, e2014009. [CrossRef]
59. Willemse, J.P.M.M.; Meertens, L.J.E.; Scheepers, H.C.J.; Achten, N.M.J.; Eussen, S.J.; van Dongen, M.C.; Smits, L.J.M. Calcium intake from diet and supplement use during early pregnancy: The Expect study I. *Eur. J. Nutr.* **2019**, *59*, 167–174. [CrossRef]
60. Hjartåker, A.; Andersen, L.F.; Lund, E. Comparison of diet measures from a food-frequency questionnaire with measures from repeated 24-hour dietary recalls. The Norwegian Women and Cancer Study. *Public Health Nutr.* **2007**, *10*, 1094–1103. [CrossRef]

nutrients

MDPI

Article

Dietary Intakes of Folate, Vitamin D and Iodine during the First Trimester of Pregnancy and the Association between Supplement Use and Demographic Characteristics amongst White Caucasian Women Living with Obesity in the UK

Kathy M. Redfern [1], Heidi J. Hollands [2], C. Ross Welch [2], Jonathan H. Pinkney [1] and Gail A. Rees [1,*]

1 Faculty of Health, University of Plymouth, Drake Circus, Plymouth PL4 8AA, UK
2 Department of Fetal Medicine, University Hospitals Plymouth National Health Service Trust, Plymouth PL6 8DH, UK
* Correspondence: gail.rees@plymouth.ac.uk

Abstract: Folate, vitamin D and iodine are key micronutrients in pregnancy, with deficiency associated with poor maternal and infant outcomes. For folate and vitamin D especially, deficiency is more common amongst women with obesity and recommended intakes and guidance on supplementation varies worldwide. The present study aims to investigate dietary and supplementary intakes of these micronutrients amongst a population of pregnant women with obesity in the United Kingdom, alongside key maternal demographic characteristics. Expectant women (n = 75) with a body mass index $\geq$ 30 kg/m^2 at first antenatal appointment were recruited at 12 weeks gestation. Participants were asked about their supplement use preconception and during trimester one in a baseline questionnaire which also asked about demographic characteristics. Women also completed a four day diet diary from which dietary and supplemental intakes of micronutrients intakes were estimated. Folic acid was taken by 96% of women at any point in trimester 1, whilst only 26% of women took the higher 5 mg dose recommended for women with obesity in the UK. For vitamin D and iodine, 56% and 44% of women met the UK RNI, respectively. Maternal age was positively associated with taking supplements of any kind and the 5 mg folic acid supplement, whilst parity was inversely associated with both outcomes. This study strengthens the rationale for further work to be done raising awareness of the need for women with obesity to supplement both with a higher dose of folic acid and vitamin D and to be aware of the role of iodine during pregnancy.

Keywords: pregnancy; maternal obesity; supplementation; folic acid; vitamin D; iodine

Citation: Redfern, K.M.; Hollands, H.J.; Welch, C.R.; Pinkney, J.H.; Rees, G.A. Dietary Intakes of Folate, Vitamin D and Iodine during the First Trimester of Pregnancy and the Association between Supplement Use and Demographic Characteristics amongst White Caucasian Women Living with Obesity in the UK. *Nutrients* **2022**, *14*, 5135. https://doi.org/10.3390/nu14235135

Academic Editor: Annunziata Lapolla

Received: 4 November 2022
Accepted: 28 November 2022
Published: 2 December 2022

1. Introduction

Nutritional status prior to and during pregnancy influences growth and development of the fetus and general maternal health [1]. There is significant interest in the role of maternal under- or over-nutrition on outcomes such as gestational weight gain, infant birth size and other adverse pregnancy outcomes such as gestational diabetes mellitus, pre-eclampsia and pre-term delivery.

The incidence of maternal obesity is increasing worldwide, across Europe and in the United Kingdom (UK; [2,3]). Much of the literature examining diet during pregnancy amongst women with obesity is focused on energy intake, macronutrient intakes and dietary patterns, and studies examining micronutrient intakes during pregnancy have tended to focus on under-nourished women, rather than those with obesity. Women with obesity are often considered to be 'over-nourished' however, a recent observational study conducted in England reported that intakes of iron, vitamin D, iodine and folate were below the reference nutrient intake (RNI) for the majority of women with obesity [4].

Folate and folic acid have been the focus of much micronutrient research in pregnancy due to their role in the prevention of neural tube defects (NTDs). The neural tube closes within 4 weeks of conception, and thus, the Department of Health in the UK recommend that women supplement with 400 µg folic acid daily from pre-conception to 12 weeks gestation [5]. Supplementation has been shown to reduce the risk of NTDs in randomised controlled trials [6]. However, maternal obesity has been shown to be associated with increased risk of NTDs [7] and in the US, despite implementation of the 1998 US folate fortification program of cereal products, increased maternal BMI was associated with lower serum folate status [8]. In the UK, the Royal College of Obstetricians and Gynaecologists (RCOG) recommend that women with obesity, defined as a body mass index (BMI) ≥ 30 kg/m^2, intending to become pregnant or already pregnant should take a higher dose of 5 mg folic acid daily until the end of the first trimester of pregnancy [9], which in the UK, is only available on prescription. A nested cohort study conducted in Dublin, Ireland, observed that women with obesity were significantly less likely to take a pre-pregnancy folic acid supplement than women with a healthy BMI and none reported taking the higher 5 mg dose, although dose was recorded for only 36% of the sample [10].

In addition to folate, vitamin D and iodine are important micronutrients during pregnancy. Iodine has long been known to be important for fetal brain development during pregnancy and a focus for the World Health Organisation (WHO) amongst women of childbearing age in developing countries [11]. However, recent data from the UK has suggested that mild to moderate iodine deficiency exists amongst women of childbearing age in the UK [12]. Recent findings from the Avon Longitudinal Study of Parents and Children (ALSPAC) suggest that mild to moderate iodine deficiency during early pregnancy is associated with impaired cognitive function in offspring [13]. Supplementation with iodine is not currently recommended for women in the UK during pregnancy, although the RNI for the general population of 140 µg/day [14] is present in the majority of pregnancy multivitamin products marketed to women in pregnancy. This is in contrast to advice from WHO/UNICEF who recommend iodine intake is increased from 150 µg to 250 µg/day in pregnancy [15], whilst the European Food Safety Authority (EFSA) recommend 200 µg/day [16]. The UK RNI may therefore be insufficient for pregnant women with a healthy BMI, and it is not known whether women with obesity have higher requirements.

The importance of adequate vitamin D status during pregnancy is important to protect fetal skeletal development and it is widely accepted that maternal vitamin D deficiency should be prevented [17]. In the UK, SACN estimate intakes of 10 µg/day will enable 97.5% of individuals, including pregnant women, to meet or exceed the target of 25-hydroxyvitamin D [25(OH)D] concentrations of 25 nmol/litre [18], whilst the WHO and EFSA recommend 5 µg/day and 15 µg/day, respectively [19,20]. In addition, many European countries at more southerly latitudes than the UK, where sunlight is likely of sufficient strength to trigger the conversion 7-dehydrocholesterol in the skin to cholecalciferol for more months of the year, have higher recommended intakes of vitamin D than the UK of 15–20 µg/day during pregnancy [21]. Obesity is a risk factor for vitamin D deficiency, which may be related to sequestering of vitamin D3 in adipose tissue, and in pregnancy, maternal obesity has been shown to increase the odds of both maternal and neonatal vitamin D deficiency [22]. Vitamin D deficiency has also been shown to be an independent risk factor for pre-eclampsia, a condition which is more frequently observed amongst women with obesity than women with a healthy BMI [23] with supplementation with vitamin D shown to reduce the risk of the reoccurrence of pre-eclampsia [24].

An observational study, conducted in Plymouth, UK, concerned the collection of weight gain, diet, physical activity, sleep and infant data amongst a cohort of pregnant women with obesity. The aim of the present study was to examine the dietary and supplementary intakes of key nutrients of interest in this population: folate, iodine and vitamin D and to investigate for any association between supplement use and key maternal demographic characteristics. We hope that our findings will be of use to health professionals involved in the dietary counselling of women pre-conception and in early pregnancy, and that we will highlight groups of women for whom interventions promoting supplementation may have the most impact.

2. Materials and Methods

Women aged between 18 and 40 years, with a BMI ≥ 30 and <40 kg/m^2 at first hospital booking appointment and pregnant with a singleton pregnancy were eligible to take part in the study. Women meeting inclusion criteria were identified from their antenatal booking notes by a Research Midwife and approached by the researcher at their 12 week dating scan at Derriford Hospital in Plymouth, UK between January 2015 and December 2017. Ethical approval was obtained from the NHS Health Research Authority National Research Ethics Service and local Research and Development (R&D) approval was obtained from University Hospitals Plymouth NHS Trust.

Following recruitment, participants were visited by the researcher who obtained both verbal and written informed consent. The first visit occurred between 12 and 14 weeks gestation at which point participants answered a baseline questionnaire which asked about demographic characteristics as well as preconception supplementation habits. Participants were also given a food diary and asked to record, in as much detail as possible, all food and beverages consumed within a 4 day period following each study visit, giving details about their portion sizes using weights, household measurements, packet sizes and photographs. The 4 day period was chosen in an attempt to maximise compliance with this aspect of data collection, and it was also the same 4 day period that participants were asked to wear an accelerometer for the collection of physical activity data. The 4 day diet diary was adapted from the previously validated UK National Diet and Nutrition Survey in order to maximise validity and reliability of dietary assessment [25]. Subjects were also asked to record any dietary supplements, whether prescribed or self-bought. At the end of the 4-day period, the researcher visited the participant to collect the diary and to clarify portion sizes, the types of foods eaten and supplements taken. The researcher also asked the participant to report whether their dietary intake had been affected by complications such as pregnancy sickness or hyperemesis gravidarum. Dietary assessment data was analysed using DietPlan 7 (Forestfield Software Ltd. 2010, Horsham, UK) to generate nutritional intake data for each participant using data from UK Food Composition Tables [26]. Dietary intakes and supplemental intakes of micronutrients were estimated and reported separately. Food portion sizes were estimated from the photographs, weights given and household measurements using 'Food Portion Sizes' published by the Food Standards Agency in the UK [27]. When foods were missing from the database, nutrient data was obtained from the manufacturer where possible and added manually to the database. For some foods this was not possible, in which case the researcher chose a food with similar nutrient composition from the database.

3. Results

Of the original sample of 75 women, 66 completed at least three days of their diet diary at the end of trimester 1. Table 1 shows descriptive data for these women. Compliance with the diet diary element of the study decreased as pregnancy continued, as did the proportion of women taking a supplement of any kind from decreased from 65% of women at the end of trimester 1, to 46.6% and 46.2% at the end of trimesters 2 and 3, respectively.

Of the 66 women completing a trimester 1 diet diary, 30 (46%) reported taking a supplement containing folic acid pre-conception, while 62 (96%) reported taking a supplement containing folic acid at some point during trimester 1. Table 2 shows the dietary and supplementary intakes of folate/folic acid, vitamin D and iodine reported in diet diaries at the end of trimester 1. At this point, 42 women (64%) report taking a supplement containing folic acid, and all of these women were meeting the UK RNI for folate of 300 µg/day with the addition of supplements. Of the 24 women not reporting supplementation with folic acid at the end of trimester 1, only one woman was achieving the RNI of 300 µg through their dietary intake. There was no statistically significant difference in the dietary intakes of folate between women supplementing (221.5 ± 102.4 µg) and those not taking a supplement (182.5 ± 81.0 µg, p = 0.114).

Table 1. Maternal descriptive data, $n = 66$.

	Mean ± SD (Range)
Maternal age, years	30.1 ± 4.5 (20.0–39.0)
Previous pregnancies, number	0.9 ± 1.0 (0.0–4.0)
Index of Multiple Deprivation, decile	4.3 ± 2.8 (1.0–10.0)
Ethnicity, white Caucasian, *n* (%)	66 (100)
Pregnancy sickness experienced, *n* (%)	53 (80)
Appetite affected due to pregnancy sickness, *n* (%)	52 (79)
Booking BMI, kg/m^2	33.0 ± 1.9 (30.0–37.6)
Energy intake, kcal/day	1766 ± 442.6 (769–2893)
Protein intake, g/day	67.7 ± 20.7 (24.5–144.8)
Fat intake, g/day	67.9 ± 21.1 (24.6–140.4)
Carbohydrate intake, g/day	235.3 ± 64.3 (105.9–408.4)
Women taking a supplement of any kind, trimester 1, *n* (%)	43 (65.2)
Women taking a supplement of any kind, trimester 2, *n* (%) *	27 (46.6)
Women taking a supplement of any kind, trimester 3, *n* (%) **	24 (46.2)

* $n = 58$; ** $n = 52$.

Table 2. Trimester 1 intakes of folate, vitamin D and iodine.

	Total Population	Women Supplementing	Women Not Supplementing	*p*
Folate	$n = 66$	$n = 42$	$n = 24$	
Dietary, μg	207.3 ± 96.4 (54.0–778.5)	221.5 ± 102.4 (100.3–778.5)	182.5 ± 81.0 (54.0–444.8)	0.114
Supplementary, μg	1511.4 ± 2246.8 (0.0–5400.0)	2375.0 ± 2429.4 (350.0–5400)		
Total, μg	1718.7 ± 2257.2 (54.0–5744.8)	2596.5 ± 2429.6 (512.0–5744.8)	182.5 ± 81.0 (54.0–444.8)	<0.001
Women meeting RNI, *n* (%)	43 (65.2)	42 (100)	1 (4.2)	
Vitamin D	$n = 66$	$n = 37$	$n = 29$	
Dietary, μg	1.7 ± 1.1 (0.1–5.0)	2.0 ± 1.1 (0.3–4.6)	1.3 ± 0.9 (0.1–3.5)	0.007
Supplementary, μg	5.8 ± 5.5 (0.0–25.0)	10.4 ± 2.5 (10.0–25.0)		
Total, μg	7.5 ± 5.9 (0.1–26.0)	12.4 ± 2.6 (10.3–26.0)	1.3 ± 0.9 (0.1–3.5)	<0.001
Women meeting RNI, *n* (%)	37 (56.1)	37 (100)	0 (0)	
Iodine	$n = 66$	$n = 28$	$n = 38$	
Dietary, μg	98.8 ± 54.4 (13.7–261.5)	107.4 ± 52.2 (39.9–217.2)	92.5 ± 55.9 (13.7–261.5)	0.082
Supplementary, μg	63.0 ± 74.0 (0.0–150.0)	148.6 ± 3.6 (140.0–150.0)		

Table 2. *Cont.*

	Total Population	Women Supplementing	Women Not Supplementing	*p*
Total, μg	161.8 ± 97.7 (13.7–367.2)	255.9 ± 52.2 (189.9–367.2)	92.5 ± 55.9 (13.7–261.5)	<0.001
Women meeting UK RNI, *n* (%)	34 (51.5)	28 (100)	6 (15.8)	
Women meeting EFSA RNI, *n* (%)	26 (39.4)	24 (85.7)	4 (14.3)	

Mean ± SD. *p* values for the difference between women taking supplements vs. those not taking supplements, independent *t* test.

A total of 37 (56%) and 28 women (42%) reported use of a supplement containing vitamin D and iodine, respectively. With the use of the supplement, these women achieved the UK RNI for vitamin D of 10 μg/day and for iodine of 140 μg/day, although when looking at the EFSA iodine recommendations of 200 μg/day, 4 women who were taking a supplement containing iodine did not meet this target. None of the women not taking a supplement achieved the RNI for vitamin D, while just 6 women (16%) achieved the UK RNI for iodine, which reduced to just 4 women (14%) when considering the EFSA recommendation. Dietary intakes of vitamin D were significantly greater amongst women who were also supplementing (2.0 ± 1.1 μg) than amongst women who did not take a supplement (1.3 ± 0.9 μg, $p = 0.007$). For women taking a supplement containing iodine, dietary intakes were higher (107.4 ± 52.2 μg) than intakes of women not supplementing (92.5 ± 55.9 μg), however, this trend did not reach significance ($p = 0.082$).

A binomial logistic regression was performed to ascertain the effects of maternal age, index of multiple deprivation, booking BMI and previous pregnancies on the likelihood of taking supplements, of any kind, in trimester 1. The logistic regression model was statistically significant, $\chi^2(4) = 16.638$, $p = 0.002$. Of the four predictor variables, increasing maternal age was positively and significantly associated with supplement use, while previous number of pregnancies was inversely and significantly associated with supplement use.

The RCOG recommend that women with obesity supplement with a higher 5 mg dose of folic acid during pregnancy. Table 3 shows that just 17 women (26%) were taking this higher dose at the end of trimester 1, while a further 24 were taking a supplement containing 400 μg. One woman took a supplement containing 25 μg of vitamin D although this particular participant did not consume a folic acid supplement at any point. The remaining women supplementing with vitamin D consumed a supplement containing 10 μg.

Table 3. Breakdown of supplements consumed by women in trimester 1.

	n (% of Total Population)
5 mg folic acid	**17 (26)**
+pregnancy multivitamin	12
+10 μg vitamin D/day	2
No additional supplement	3
400 μg folic acid	**24 (36)**
Within pregnancy multivitamin	19
+10 μg vitamin D/day	3
No additional supplement	2
Vitamin D only	**1**
25 μg/day	1

A second regression analysis was performed to ascertain the effects of the same variables previously examined for supplement use, on the likelihood of taking the recommended 5 mg dose of folic acid. Once again, the model was statistically significant $\chi^2(4) = 16.488$, $p = 0.002$ with maternal age and BMI positively associated with use of the higher 5 mg folic acid dose, and previous number of pregnancies inversely associated. There was no association observed between Multiple Index of Deprivation and higher 5 mg folic acid dose.

4. Discussion

Findings from this observational study demonstrate that whilst 46% and 96% of pregnant women with obesity took a folic acid supplement pre-conception and in the first trimester, respectively, only 26% of women took the higher 5 mg dose recommended by the RCOG. For vitamin D and iodine, 56% and 52% of women met the UK RNI, respectively. For women who did not supplement with these two micronutrients, no women met the RNI for vitamin D and only 16% of women met the RNI for iodine. Maternal age was positively associated with taking supplements of any kind and taking the 5 mg folic acid supplement, whilst parity was inversely associated with both outcomes. The present study is unique in that it focuses on supplementation trends for three key micronutrients of concern amongst pregnant women with obesity.

In terms of folic acid supplementation with the UK recommendation of 400 μg per day, our findings are in keeping with those observed amongst the general pregnant population in the UK. A total of 46% of women in our study supplemented with folic acid pre-conception, which is similar to the rate of 39% observed amongst women with a BMI > 30 kg/m^2 who were actively planning a pregnancy in a prospective cohort conducted in women in the UK [28]. A limitation of the current study is that women were not asked whether their pregnancy was planned or unplanned, although previous studies have suggested higher rates of unplanned pregnancies in women with obesity, due to hormonal contraception failure [29], and unsurprisingly, women planning a pregnancy are more likely to be taking folic acid preconception [30].

The observation in the present study that 96% of women reported taking folic acid at any point in trimester 1 seems to be slightly higher than values reported in the literature from other studies in the UK conducted amongst women of all weights which ranged from 67–85% in three large cohort studies [31–34], but is similar to the rate observed by Cawley et al. of 96.1%, also amongst women of all weights [35]. Of these, 26% of women in the present study were taking the recommended 5 mg folic for women with obesity. Unfortunately, it is not known what proportion of these women took the 5 mg pre-conception, or whether they were prescribed the 5 mg dose once they'd engaged with a healthcare professional during their pregnancy. Therefore, it is not appropriate to compare the findings of the current study directly against those of a recent Irish study, which specifically asked women about pre-conception high dose folic acid compliance and found that no women reported taking this higher dose [10]. Similarly, Cawley et al. [35] report that just 2 of 106 women with obesity reported taking the high dose supplement in their observational study at any time in pregnancy [35].

However, despite a high proportion of women reporting taking a folic acid supplement at any point of trimester 1, by the end of trimester 1, when four-day food records were collected, just 64% of women reported taking a supplement containing folic acid. Of the 24 women not taking a supplement, only one woman met the pregnancy RNI of 300 μg through dietary intakes, leaving 42% of women in the total population with intakes below the RNI. This is concerning as although folate is important preconception for the prevention of NTDs, folate is also essential throughout the rest of pregnancy for the prevention of complications and poor birth outcomes such as anaemia, preterm birth, low birth weight and congenital heart diseases [36]. Although the UK does not recommend to women that they continue a 400 μg/day supplement beyond the end of the first trimester, it is important that women are aware of the need to consume foods rich in folate or fortified with folic acid to meet the RNI in the remainder of their pregnancy, as per NICE guidance [5].

In total, 56% of women reported supplementing with vitamin D at the end of trimester 1, all of whom met the RNI of 10 µg/day. This is considerably higher than the 27% of women meeting vitamin D recommendations in a Finnish observational study conducted amongst women with obesity [37]. Conversely, women who did not report taking a supplement containing vitamin D had mean intakes of 1.4 µg/day, and none of these women met the RNI for vitamin D. These observations are in keeping with those from a recent Irish study, in which only 1% of pregnant women were meeting the RNI for vitamin D from diet alone [38]. These findings suggest that not all women are aware of the recommendation to supplement with 10 µg vitamin D throughout pregnancy, which should be a key feature in public health nutrition campaigns, particularly those aimed at women with obesity, which is a risk factor for maternal and neonatal vitamin D deficiency [22] which in turn is a risk factor for pre-eclampsia [23].

Similarly, when examining iodine intakes in the present study, the 42% of women who reported taking an iodine containing supplement met the UK RNI of 140 µg for iodine. These observations are slightly higher than those observed amongst pregnant women in the US where only 17.8% of women reported taking a supplement containing iodine [39], despite the fact that there is a pregnancy increment in the recommended daily allowance from 150 µg to 220 µg in the USA as per Institute of Medicine recommendations [40] and that the American Thyroid Association recommend a 150 µg/day supplement [41]. Interestingly, although perhaps unsurprisingly, when considering the EFSA iodine recommendations of 200 µg/day in pregnancy, the proportion of supplementing and non-supplementing women meeting the EFSA RNI in the present study decreased compared with the lower UK RNI for which there is not a pregnancy increment. However, it is perhaps not useful to compare iodine intakes in pregnancy to those in other countries, particularly those in which iodised salt is routinely available. For example, iodised salt in the USA and Canada provides approximately 45 µg iodine per gram of salt, whereas in the UK and many other European countries, salt is not iodised. Globally, UNICEF estimate that 89% of the population are consuming iodised salt [42] but it is worth noting that although table salt may be iodised, in many countries the salt added to processed foods, which makes up a large proportion of dietary salt intake, is not iodised. In addition, despite progress towards reducing iodine deficiency globally, there are countries in Northern Europe with iodised salt programmes that are still considered iodine deficient, including Germany, Finland and Norway [43], and a recent study in South Australia suggests that even with mandatory fortification of bread with iodine contributing to iodine sufficiency, it is difficult to achieve urinary iodine concentrations >150 µg/L without additional iodine supplementation [44].

Of the women not supplementing with iodine in the present study, only 6 women (16%) met the RNI from dietary intakes, which gives possible cause for concern as iodine supplements are not currently recommended in the UK, and unlike vitamin D and folic acid, iodine is not included in the NHS Healthy Start vitamins that are available free of charge to low-income women in the UK [45]. The majority of other branded multivitamin products marketed to pregnant women in the UK that are sold in supermarkets and high street pharmacies do contain iodine.

Additionally, it is also well documented that pregnant women in the UK are generally iodine insufficient [12] despite a lack of large good quality studies [46]. In addition, studies have shown even marginal iodine deficiency in pregnancy is associated with impaired cognitive outcomes for offspring [12,47], highlighting the importance of the mineral in future preconception and pregnancy research.

Increasing maternal age was positively associated with supplement use of any kind and taking the 5 mg folic acid dose in the present study, which is in agreement with findings from other studies conducted in the UK [31], Finland [48] and USA [39], and suggests younger women in particular should be targeted for interventions aiming to increase supplement use. In addition, parity was negatively associated with supplement use and taking high dose folic acid, suggesting that women may benefit from a reminder to restart supplement use following a pregnancy when they intend to become pregnant again. It is also possible that some women may not have needed to take the higher dose of folic acid in a previous pregnancy due to their weight being lower, but it is well documented than women are more likely to start subsequent pregnancies at a higher weight and BMI than a previous pregnancy [49]. Therefore, as well as following NICE guidance to achieve a healthy weight between pregnancies [50], women also need to be made aware of the need to take a higher dose of folic acid if they plan to enter a subsequent pregnancy at a higher body weight.

The present study did not observe any associations between supplement use and deprivation, which is in contrast to many studies conducted amongst women of all weights. For example, Brough et al. report that women from higher social groups in the UK were more likely to take a folic acid supplement at any stage of their pregnancy [51]. Similarly, Alwyn et al. report that pregnant women taking a supplement of any kind during pregnancy were less likely to be living in an area with an IMD score in the lowest quartile [31]. It is worth noting that all women in the present study lived in or near Plymouth, in the United Kingdom which as a Local Authority district, has an IMD score in decile 2, placing within the 20% most deprived local authority districts in the country [52]. Although there is variation within the city, this may explain why no association was observed between IMD score and supplementation, as all women live within a city with high deprivation.

A limitation of this study is that women were all of white Caucasian origin, so we were not able to examine whether race or ethnicity predict supplement use in women with obesity. A previous meta-analysis conducted in the United Kingdom demonstrated higher levels of peri-conceptional folic acid use amongst Caucasian women when compared to women of other ethnicities [53]. Future studies should focus on examining supplementation trends for key pregnancy micronutrients in more diverse populations. Although we were able to report parity in the present study, there was no data available for women who may have suffered previous miscarriages, nor did we have information about concomitant medications which may have influenced women taking supplements in early pregnancy. In addition, we acknowledge that based on the mean reported energy intake of 1766 $\pm$ 442.6 kcal/day, it is possible and likely that some women under-reported their dietary intake, which may have led to under-estimations of dietary intakes of micronutrients. However, as this data was collected in the first trimester of pregnancy where pregnancy sickness and changes to appetite are common, we have not excluded any women from analysis.

A strength of this study was that information on dietary intakes and supplement use was recorded using a structured four-day food diary which was distributed, checked and analysed by a single nutrition researcher at each study visit and allowed the researcher to check food and supplement intakes with the women. This reduced the risks of respondent error, recall bias or inter-observer variation. The study is also the first, to the authors' knowledge that specifically examines dietary and supplemental intakes of folate, vitamin D and iodine amongst women with obesity in the UK, with particular focus on preconception intake of the higher folic acid dose and demographic characteristics.

5. Conclusions

In conclusion, findings from the present study suggest that women with obesity in the UK who do not take a pregnancy micronutrient supplement are unlikely to be meeting the RNI for folic acid, vitamin D and iodine, three important micronutrients during pregnancy. Younger women and women who had been pregnant before were less likely to take any micronutrient supplement so it may be particularly important to target interventions and public health information for these women. Particular attention should be paid to folic acid supplementation and ensuring that women with obesity are made aware of the need to take a higher 5 mg dose preconception, alongside 10 μg vitamin D, as advised by the NHS and the RCOG. In the UK, the 5 mg folic acid supplement is only available on prescription, so it is imperative that GPs and midwives are aware of the higher dose recommendations for women with obesity and counsel women prior to conception if possible. This is particularly important for low-income women who may be eligible for free NHS Healthy Start vitamins, which contain the 400 µg folic acid rather than the higher 5 mg dose. Further research is required to investigate iodine status and whether there is potential for iodine supplementation in pregnancy to improve pregnancy and infant outcomes.

Author Contributions: Conceptualization, K.M.R., G.A.R., J.H.P. and C.R.W.; methodology, K.M.R.; G.A.R., J.H.P. and C.R.W.; recruitment, K.M.R. and H.J.H.; formal analysis, K.M.R.; data curation, K.M.R.; writing—original draft preparation, K.M.R.; writing—review and editing, K.M.R., G.A.R., J.H.P., H.J.H. and C.R.W. All authors have read and agreed to the published version of the manuscript.

Funding: This research received no external funding.

Institutional Review Board Statement: The study was conducted in accordance with the Declaration of Helsinki, and approved by the NHS Health Research Authority National Research Ethics Service (London-Central, REC reference number: 14/LO/1660) and local Research and Development (R&D) approval was obtained from University Hospitals Plymouth NHS Trust (R&D reference number: 14/P/134).

Informed Consent Statement: Informed consent was obtained from all subjects involved in the study.

Acknowledgments: This research was supported by the University of Plymouth. The authors would also like to thank University Hospitals Plymouth NHS Trust for hosting the study, as well as all women and their families for participating. Additionally, thank you to Debbie Egan, Tia McDermott and Jackie Bartlett for helping facilitate recruitment in antenatal clinics.

Conflicts of Interest: The authors declare no conflict of interest.

References

1. Institute of Medicine. *Nutrition during Pregnancy: Part I, Weight Gain: Part II, Nutrient Supplements*; National Academy Press: Cambridge, MA, USA, 1990; ISBN 0309041384.
2. Chen, L.-W.; Aris, I.M.; Bernard, J.Y.; Tint, M.-T.; Chia, A.; Colega, M.; Gluckman, P.D.; Shek, L.P.-C.; Saw, S.-M.; Chong, Y.-S.; et al. Associations of Maternal Dietary Patterns during Pregnancy with Offspring Adiposity from Birth Until 54 Months of Age. *Nutrients* **2017**, *9*, 2. [CrossRef] [PubMed]
3. Euro-Peristat Characteristics of Childbearing Women. In *The European Perinatal Health Report 2015*; 2015; pp. 35–66. Available online: https://www.europeristat.com/images/EPHR2015_Characteristics_of_childbearing_women.pdf (accessed on 15 February 2020).
4. Charnley, M.; Newson, L.; Weeks, A.; Abayomi, J. Pregnant Women Living with Obesity: A Cross-Sectional Observational Study of Dietary Quality and Pregnancy Outcomes. *Nutrients* **2021**, *13*, 1652. [CrossRef] [PubMed]
5. National Institute for Health and Care Excellence. Recommendations: Folic Acid. In *Maternal and Child Nutrition: Public Health Guideline (PH11)*; NICE: London, UK, 2014. Available online: https://www.nice.org.uk/guidance/ph11 (accessed on 15 September 2022).
6. Lumley, J.; Watson, L.; Watson, M.; Bower, C. Periconceptional Supplementation with Folate and/or Multivitamins for Preventing Neural Tube Defects. In *Cochrane Database of Systematic Reviews*; Lumley, J., Ed.; John Wiley & Sons, Ltd.: Chichester, UK, 2001; p. CD001056.
7. Rasmussen, S.A.; Chu, S.Y.; Kim, S.Y.; Schmid, C.H.; Lau, J. Maternal Obesity and Risk of Neural Tube Defects: A Metaanalysis. *Am. J. Obstet. Gynecol.* **2008**, *198*, 611–619. [CrossRef] [PubMed]
8. Mojtabai, R. Body Mass Index and Serum Folate in Childbearing Age Women. *Eur. J. Epidemiol.* **2004**, *19*, 1029–1036. [CrossRef] [PubMed]
9. Denison, F.; Aedla, N.; Keag, O.; Hor, K.; Reynolds, R.; Milne, A.; Diamond, A. Care of Women with Obesity in Pregnancy. *BJOG An Int. J. Obstet. Gynaecol.* **2019**, *126*, e62–e106. [CrossRef]
10. Farah, N.; Kennedy, C.; Turner, C.; O'dwyer, V.; Kennelly, M.M.; Turner, M.J. Maternal Obesity and Pre-Pregnancy Folic Acid Supplementation. *Obes. Facts* **2013**, *6*, 211–215. [CrossRef]
11. World Health Organisation. *Reaching Optimal Iodine Nutrition in Pregnant and Lactating Women and Young Children*; World Health Organisation: Geneva, Switzerland, 2007.
12. Bath, S.C.; Walter, A.; Taylor, A.; Wright, J.; Rayman, M.P. Iodine Deficiency in Pregnant Women Living in the South East of the UK: The Influence of Diet and Nutritional Supplements on Iodine Status. *Br. J. Nutr.* **2014**, *111*, 1622–1631. [CrossRef]
13. Bath, S.C.; Steer, C.D.; Golding, J.; Emmett, P.; Rayman, M.P. Effect of Inadequate Iodine Status in UK Pregnant Women on Cognitive Outcomes in Their Children: Results from the Avon Longitudinal Study of Parents and Children (ALSPAC). *Lancet* **2013**, *382*, 331–337. [CrossRef]

14. Scientific Advisory Committee on Nutrition. SACN Statement on Iodine and Health. 2014. Available online: https://www.gov.uk/government/publications/sacn-statement-on-iodine-and-health-2014 (accessed on 15 September 2022).
15. World Health Organisation. *Assessment of Iodine Deficiency Disorders and Monitoring Their Elimination: A Guide for Programme Managers*, 3rd ed.; World Health Organisation: Geneva, Switzerland, 2007.
16. EFSA Panel on Dietetic Products, N. and A. (NDA) Scientific Opinion on Dietary Reference Values for Iodine. *EFSA J.* **2014**, *12*, 3660. [CrossRef]
17. Fiscaletti, M.; Stewart, P.; Munns, C.F. The Importance of Vitamin D in Maternal and Child Health: A Global Perspective. *Public Health Rev.* **2017**, *38*, 19. [CrossRef]
18. Scientific Advisory Committee on Nutrition. Vitamin D and Health. 2016. Available online: https://www.gov.uk/government/publications/sacn-statement-on-iodine-and-health- (accessed on 15 September 2022).
19. WHO/FAO. *Vitamin and Mineral Requirements in Human Nutrition*, 2nd ed.; World Health Organisation: Geneva, Switzerland, 2004.
20. EFSA Panel on Dietetic Products, N. and A. (NDA) Dietary Reference Values for Vitamin D. *EFSA J.* **2016**, *14*, e04547. [CrossRef]
21. Spiro, A.; Buttriss, J.L. Vitamin D: An Overview of Vitamin D Status and Intake in Europe. *Nutr. Bull.* **2014**, *39*, 322–350. [CrossRef] [PubMed]
22. Bodnar, L.M.; Catov, J.M.; Roberts, J.M.; Simhan, H.N. Prepregnancy Obesity Predicts Poor Vitamin D Status in Mothers and Their Neonates. *J. Nutr.* **2007**, *137*, 2437–2442. [CrossRef] [PubMed]
23. Bodnar, L.M.; Catov, J.M.; Simhan, H.N.; Holick, M.F.; Powers, R.W.; Roberts, J.M. Maternal Vitamin D Deficiency Increases the Risk of Preeclampsia. *J. Clin. Endocrinol. Metab.* **2007**, *92*, 3517–3522. [CrossRef]
24. Behjat Sasan, S.; Zandvakili, F.; Soufizadeh, N.; Baybordi, E. The Effects of Vitamin D Supplement on Prevention of Recurrence of Preeclampsia in Pregnant Women with a History of Preeclampsia. *Obstet. Gynecol. Int.* **2017**, *2017*, 8249264. [CrossRef]
25. Whitton, C.; Nicholson, S.K.; Roberts, C.; Prynne, C.J.; Pot, G.K.; Olson, A.; Fitt, E.; Cole, D.; Teucher, B.; Bates, B.; et al. National Diet and Nutrition Survey: UK Food Consumption and Nutrient Intakes from the First Year of the Rolling Programme and Comparisons with Previous Surveys. *Br. J. Nutr.* **2011**, *106*, 1899–1914. [CrossRef] [PubMed]
26. Finglas, P.M.; Roe, M.A.; Pinchen, H.; Berry, R.; Chirvh, S.; Dodhia, S.; Farron-Wilson, M.; Swan, G. *McCance and Widdowson's the Composition of Foods*; The Royal Society of Chemistry: London, UK, 2015; ISBN 978-1-84973-636-7.
27. Food Standards Agency. *Food Portion Sizes*, 3rd ed.; Mills, A., Patel, S., Eds.; H.M.S.O.: London, UK, 2012.
28. McDougall, B.; Kavanagh, K.; Stephenson, J.; Poston, L.; Flynn, A.C.; White, S.L. Health Behaviours in 131,182 UK Women Planning Pregnancy. *BMC Pregnancy Childbirth* **2021**, *21*, 530. [CrossRef]
29. Holt, V.L.; Scholes, D.; Wicklund, K.G.; Cushing-Haugen, K.L.; Daling, J.R. Body Mass Index, Weight, and Oral Contraceptive Failure Risk. *Obstet. Gynecol.* **2005**, *105*, 46–52. [CrossRef]
30. Rosenberg, K.D.; Gelow, J.M.; Sandoval, A.P. Pregnancy Intendedness and the Use of Periconceptional Folic Acid. *Pediatrics* **2003**, *111*, 1142–1145. [CrossRef]
31. Alwan, N.A.; Greenwood, D.C.; Simpson, N.A.B.; McArdle, H.J.; Cade, J.E. The Relationship between Dietary Supplement Use in Late Pregnancy and Birth Outcomes: A Cohort Study in British Women. *BJOG Int. J. Obstet. Gynaecol.* **2010**, *117*, 821–829. [CrossRef]
32. Hodgetts, V.A.; Morris, R.K.; Francis, A.; Gardosi, J.; Ismail, K.M. Effectiveness of Folic Acid Supplementation in Pregnancy on Reducing the Risk of Small-for-Gestational Age Neonates: A Population Study, Systematic Review and Meta-Analysis. *BJOG Int. J. Obstet. Gynaecol.* **2015**, *122*, 478–490. [CrossRef] [PubMed]
33. Petry, C.J.; Ong, K.K.; Hughes, I.A.; Dunger, D.B. Folic Acid Supplementation during Pregnancy and Associations with Offspring Size at Birth and Adiposity: A Cohort Study. *BMC Res. Notes* **2021**, *14*, 160. [CrossRef] [PubMed]
34. Langley-Evans, S.C.; Langley-Evans, A.J. Use of Folic Acid Supplements in the First Trimester of Pregnancy. *J. R. Soc. Promot. Health* **2002**, *122*, 181–186. [CrossRef] [PubMed]
35. Cawley, S.; Mullaney, L.; McKeating, A.; Farren, M.; McCartney, D.; Turner, M.J. An Analysis of Folic Acid Supplementation in Women Presenting for Antenatal Care. *J. Public Health* **2016**, *38*, 122–129. [CrossRef] [PubMed]
36. Obeid, R.; Oexle, K.; Rißmann, A.; Pietrzik, K.; Koletzko, B. Folate Status and Health: Challenges and Opportunities. *J. Perinat. Med.* **2016**, *44*, 261–268. [CrossRef]
37. Garnæs, K.K.; Elvebakk, T.; Salvesen, Ø.; Stafne, S.N.; Mørkved, S.; Salvesen, K.Å.; Moholdt, T. Dietary Intake in Early Pregnancy and Glycemia in Late Pregnancy among Women with Obesity. *Nutrients* **2022**, *14*, 105. [CrossRef]
38. Mullaney, L.; Cawley, S.; Kennedy, R.; O'Higgins, A.C.; McCartney, D.; Turner, M.J. Maternal Nutrient Intakes from Food and Drinks Consumed in Early Pregnancy in Ireland. *J. Public Health* **2017**, *39*, 754–762. [CrossRef]
39. Gupta, P.M.; Gahche, J.J.; Herrick, K.A.; Ershow, A.G.; Potischman, N.; Perrine, C.G. Use of Iodine-Containing Dietary Supplements Remains Low among Women of Reproductive Age in the United States: NHANES 2011–2014. *Nutrients* **2018**, *10*, 422. [CrossRef]
40. Institute of Medicine (US) Panel on Micronutrients. *Dietary Reference Intakes for Vitamin A, Vitamin K, Arsenic, Boron, Chromium, Copper, Iodine, Iron, Manganese, Molybdenum, Nickel, Silicon, Vanadium, and Zinc*; National Academies Press (US): Washington, DC, USA, 2001.
41. The Public Health Committee of the American Thyroid Association. Iodine Supplementation for Pregnancy and Lactation—United States and Canada: Recommendations of the American Thyroid Association. *Thyroid* **2006**, *16*, 949–951. [CrossRef]

42. UNICEF Iodized Salt Consumption. Available online: https://data.unicef.org/resources/dataset/iodized-salt-consumption/ (accessed on 23 August 2022).
43. Iodine Global Network. *Global Scorecard of Iodine Nutrition in 2021*; Iodine Global Network: Ottawa, ON, Canada, 2021.
44. Condo, D.; Huyhn, D.; Anderson, A.J.; Skeaff, S.; Ryan, P.; Makrides, M.; Mühlhaüsler, B.S.; Zhou, S.J. Iodine Status of Pregnant Women in South Australia after Mandatory Iodine Fortification of Bread and the Recommendation for Iodine Supplementation. *Matern. Child Nutr.* **2017**, *13*, e12410. [CrossRef]
45. NHS Business Services Authority. Healthy Start. Information for Health Professionals, Local Authorities and Supporting Organisations. 2021. Available online: https://media.nhsbsa.nhs.uk/resources/f/nhs-healthy-start-scheme (accessed on 23 November 2022).
46. Jiang, H.; Powers, H.J.; Rossetto, G.S. A Systematic Review of Iodine Deficiency among Women in the UK. *Public Health Nutr.* **2019**, *22*, 1138–1147. [CrossRef] [PubMed]
47. Robinson, S.M.; Crozier, S.R.; Miles, E.A.; Gale, C.R.; Calder, P.C.; Cooper, C.; Inskip, H.M.; Godfrey, K.M. Preconception Maternal Iodine Status Is Positively Associated with IQ but Not with Measures of Executive Function in Childhood. *J. Nutr.* **2018**, *148*, 959–966. [CrossRef] [PubMed]
48. Arkkola, T.; Uusitalo, U.; Pietikäinen, M.; Metsälä, J.; Kronberg-Kippilä, C.; Erkkola, M.; Veijola, R.; Knip, M.; Virtanen, S.M.; Ovaskainen, M.-L. Dietary Intake and Use of Dietary Supplements in Relation to Demographic Variables among Pregnant Finnish Women. *Br. J. Nutr.* **2006**, *96*, 913–920. [CrossRef] [PubMed]
49. Ziauddeen, N.; Roderick, P.J.; Macklon, N.S.; Alwan, N.A. The Duration of the Interpregnancy Interval in Multiparous Women and Maternal Weight Gain between Pregnancies: Findings from a UK Population-Based Cohort. *Sci. Rep.* **2019**, *9*, 9175. [CrossRef] [PubMed]
50. National Institute for Health and Care Excellence. Weight Management before, during and after Pregnancy. 2010. Available online: https://www.nice.org.uk/guidance/ph27/resources/weight-management-before-during-and-after-pregn (accessed on 12 September 2022).
51. Brough, L.; Rees, G.A.; Crawford, M.A.; Dorman, E.K. Social and Ethnic Differences in Folic Acid Use Preconception and during Early Pregnancy in the UK: Effect on Maternal Folate Status. *J. Hum. Nutr. Diet. Off. J. Br. Diet. Assoc.* **2009**, *22*, 100–107. [CrossRef]
52. Plymouth City Council Index of Multiple Deprivation (IMD) 2019. Plymouth Summary Analysis. Available online: https://www.plymouth.gov.uk/sites/default/files/IMD%202019%20report%20Final%200.1.pdf (accessed on 15 February 2020).
53. Peake, J.N.; Copp, A.J.; Shawe, J. Knowledge and Periconceptional Use of Folic Acid for the Prevention of Neural Tube Defects in Ethnic Communities in the United Kingdom: Systematic Review and Meta-Analysis. *Birth Defects Res. Part A Clin. Mol. Teratol.* **2013**, *97*, 444–451. [CrossRef]

nutrients

MDPI

Article

Effects of Climate, Sun Exposure, and Dietary Intake on Vitamin D Concentrations in Pregnant Women: A Population-Based Study

Ya-Li Huang [1,2], Thu T. M. Pham [2,3], Yi-Chun Chen [4], Jung-Su Chang [4,5,6,7], Jane C.-J. Chao [4,5,8] and Chyi-Huey Bai [1,2,5,*]

1 Department of Public Health, School of Medicine, College of Medicine, Taipei Medical University, Taipei 110-31, Taiwan
2 School of Public Health, College of Public Health, Taipei Medical University, Taipei 110-31, Taiwan
3 Faculty of Public Health, Hai Phong University of Medicine and Pharmacy, Hai Phong 042-12, Vietnam
4 School of Nutrition and Health Sciences, Taipei Medical University, Taipei 110-31, Taiwan
5 Nutrition Research Center, Taipei Medical University Hospital, Taipei 110-31, Taiwan
6 Graduate Institute of Metabolism and Obesity Sciences, College of Nutrition, Taipei Medical University, Taipei 110-31, Taiwan
7 Chinese Taipei Society for the Study of Obesity, Taipei 110-31, Taiwan
8 Master Program in Global Health and Development, College of Public Health, Taipei Medical University, Taipei 110-31, Taiwan
* Correspondence: baich@tmu.edu.tw

Abstract: Background: Vitamin D deficiency (VDD) is a global micronutrient issue that commonly occurs in pregnant women, leading to adverse health outcomes. We examined the role of sunlight-related factors and dietary vitamin D intake on vitamin D concentrations among pregnant women in different climate zones. Methods: We conducted a nationwide cross-sectional survey in Taiwan between June 2017 and February 2019. The data of 1502 pregnant women were collected, including sociodemographic information and characteristics related to pregnancy, diet, and sun exposure. Serum 25-hydroxyvitamin D concentrations were measured, and VDD was assessed as a concentration of less than 20 ng/mL. Logistic regression analyses were used to explore the factors associated with VDD. Furthermore, the area under the receiver operating characteristic (AUROC) curve was used to analyze the contribution of sunlight-related factors and dietary vitamin D intake to vitamin D status stratified by climate zones. Results: The prevalence of VDD was 30.1% and was the highest in the north. Sufficient intake of red meat (odds ratio (OR): 0.50, 95% confidence interval (CI): 0.32–0.75; $p = 0.002$), vitamin D and/or calcium supplements (OR: 0.51, 95% CI: 0.39–0.66; $p < 0.001$), sun exposure (OR: 0.75, 95% CI: 0.57–0.98; $p = 0.034$), and blood draw during sunny months (OR: 0.59, 95% CI: 0.46–0.77; $p < 0.001$) were associated with a lower likelihood of VDD. Additionally, in northern Taiwan, which is characterized by a subtropical climate, dietary vitamin D intake (AUROC: 0.580, 95% CI: 0.528–0.633) had a greater influence on vitamin D status than did sunlight-related factors (AUROC: 0.536, 95% CI: 0.508–0.589) with a z value = 51.98, $p < 0.001$. By contrast, sunlight-related factors (AUROC: 0.659, 95% CI: 0.618–0.700) were more important than dietary vitamin D intake (AUROC: 0.617, 95% CI, 0.575–0.660) among women living in tropical areas of Taiwan (z value = 54.02, $p < 0.001$). Conclusions: Dietary vitamin D intake was essential to alleviate VDD in the tropical region, whereas sunlight-related factors played a greater role in subtropical areas. Safe sunlight exposure and adequate dietary vitamin D intake should be promoted appropriately as a strategic healthcare program.

Keywords: 25-hydroxyvitamin D [25(OH)D] concentration; diet; pregnant women; sunlight; Taiwan; vitamin D deficiency

Citation: Huang, Y.-L.; Pham, T.T.M.; Chen, Y.-C.; Chang, J.-S.; Chao, J.C.-J.; Bai, C.-H. Effects of Climate, Sun Exposure, and Dietary Intake on Vitamin D Concentrations in Pregnant Women: A Population-Based Study. *Nutrients* **2023**, *15*, 1182. https://doi.org/10.3390/nu15051182

Academic Editors: Louise Brough and Gail Rees

Received: 1 February 2023
Revised: 23 February 2023
Accepted: 24 February 2023
Published: 27 February 2023

1. Introduction

Vitamin D deficiency (VDD) has become an urgent micronutrient issue globally [1] because of its high prevalence [2], and it has become a potential cause of non-communicable [3,4] and infectious [5,6] diseases. Although VDD has been addressed as a global public health problem in all age groups, the population-representative data regarding vitamin D were limited to several risky groups [7]. Pregnant women are a vulnerable population affected by VDD [1], which can lead to adverse pregnancy outcomes [8,9]. Moreover, VDD may result in health disparities [10], which leads to the increment of stillbirths and pregnancy-related deaths [11]. Hence, improving vitamin D status is necessary to upgrade the reproductive health and well-being of mothers and their infants.

The major factors for VDD are sun exposure and dietary vitamin D intake [12]. However, obtaining vitamin D through sun exposure can be inefficient or unsafe because of the skin cancer risk from ultraviolet radiation [13]. Additionally, the dermal synthesis of vitamin D was suggested to be influenced in different climate zones using an in vitro model [14]. The adequate achievement of vitamin D intake from diet alone is hard [15]. Therefore, vitamin D supplementation is a crucial nutritional priority recommended by many physicians to achieve optimal serum concentration [16] that could prevent short and long-term maternal and infant health complications [17].

Vitamin D status has been explored in the literature. However, population-based research on pregnant women in East Asia is still limited. To our best knowledge, relevant information regarding the potential effect of the climatic zone has not been explored. Taiwan is an East Asian island characterized by two climatic zones [18]. Based on this unique advantage, Taiwan has the opportunity to assess whether sunlight-related factors and dietary vitamin intake contribute differently to vitamin D levels among people living in different parts of the country. Exploring the prevalence of VDD and its potential risk factors among pregnant women in Taiwan is an important task to address the research gap and for future policy planning. This study aimed to assess the determinants of VDD and to examine the contribution of sunlight-related factors and dietary vitamin D intake to vitamin D status in different regions of Taiwan using a nationally representative survey.

2. Materials and Methods

Study Population

A national cross-sectional nutritional survey of pregnant women was conducted from June 2017 to February 2019 across Taiwan. A multiple-stage cluster sampling approach was used, including (1) the selection of eight layers according to geographical location (northern, central, southern, and eastern Taiwan) and (2) the random selection of hospitals (large and small sizes) from the list based on the number of women availing pregnancy-related services per year and the probability proportional to size in each layer and (3) the whole selection of participants arriving in the selected hospitals for antenatal examination with the expectation of 150–300 women from one or two hospitals in each layer enrolled based on the potential number of annual outpatients in each hospital [19]. The distribution of eleven selected hospitals across Taiwan was in Figure 1.

We calculated a sample size of 1062 based on 200,000 deliveries by pregnant women during the study period, with a 3% margin of error and a 95% confidence interval (CI). We recruited participants aged ≥15 years who were legal residents of Taiwan and who underwent antenatal examinations at the selected hospitals. A satisfactory sample of 1502 pregnant women was included in the final analysis after the exclusion of nonsingleton pregnancies, participants unable to understand and speak Mandarin, and incomplete questionnaires. All participants provided written informed consent before taking the survey.

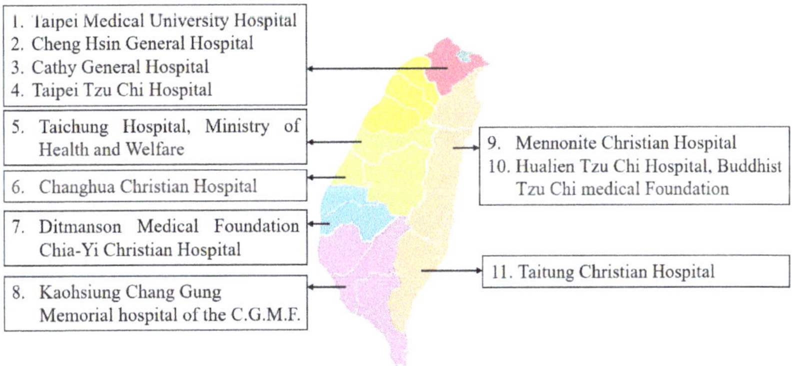

Figure 1. The distribution of eleven selected hospitals across Taiwan.

3. Data Collection

During study periods, all pregnant women making an antenatal visit were enrolled consecutively. At recruitment, collection of questionnaires, physical examination and blood sample were performed. Information was obtained from standardized face-to-face interviews by trained interviewers using the structured questionnaires. Variables regarding participants' sociodemographic status, histories of diseases before and during pregnancy, pregnancy-related factors, and intake histories of prenatal and natal dietary supplements were collected by the self-reported baseline questionnaire. The dosage of supplements during pregnancy was asked and recorded in brand, exact dosage and frequency per week. Food frequency questionnaires was also used to record the intake frequency during past 3 months in 66 items of foods including egg, milk, meat, fish and vegetables. After interview of questionnaires, a 24 h dietary recall was recorded by trained dietitians. Food models were used to assist participants in recalling the food portion sizes and details of the dietary information. Then, we estimated participants' energy intake and nutrient intake from foods. The intakes of several nutrients (e.g., vitamin D) were labeled the sources of foods or supplements respectively. We used the online software Cofit Pro (Cofit Health Care, Taipei, Taiwan) to analyze participants' nutrient intake using the 2015 version of the Taiwan Food and Nutrient Database.

At the time of recruitment, pre-pregnancy body weight was self-reported by pregnant women, and their current body height and weight were measured. Blood samples were drawn, centrifuged, then froze (−80 °C) and analyzed in batches.

3.1. Sociodemographic and Pregnancy-Related Characteristics

Pregnant women were queried regarding their age (years); residential area; education level; household monthly income; religion; gravidity; parity; number of fetuses in the current pregnancy; gestational age; and body height (cm) and weight (kg) before pregnancy, which were used to calculate pre-pregnancy body mass index (BMI, kg/m^2). Additional information related to pregnancy was extracted from the prenatal visit records of participants. The residence was categorized as living in Taiwan's northern, central, southern, or eastern regions.

3.2. Dietary Characteristics

Pregnant women were asked whether they consumed sufficient amounts of the four groups of the following food items: (1) dairy products (e.g., fresh milk, yogurt, cheese, cream cheese, and powdered milk); (2) eggs; (3) red meat (e.g., pork, beef, and mutton); and (4) nut fruits (e.g., stone fruit, nuts, pistachios, and almonds). Women also reported their frequency of using vitamin D and/or calcium supplements during pregnancy as "never", "less than 1 day per week", "2–5 days/week", and "almost daily". Then, this factor was recoded into two categories of usage, "yes" or "no", due to the small sample size. The 24 h dietary intake was recorded to assess the intake of total energy (kcal), raw protein (g), raw fat (g), total carbohydrates (g), and vitamin D content (mg) and the use of vitamin supplements. The percentages of calories from protein, fat, and carbohydrates were also calculated [19].

The dosages of supplements were calculated if participants provided the exact dosage. However, these parameters were frequently missing, as were the brands and models of vitamins. Therefore, in the present study, we only analyzed the usage frequency of vitamin D-only or D-based supplements.

3.3. *Sunshine-Related Factors*

Sun exposure was estimated using the question, "Were you exposed to outdoor sunlight last month?" and the answers were categorized as "no" if exposed to sunlight for less than 10 min per day and "yes" if exposed to sunlight for more than 10 min per day. The seasons of blood draw were categorized according to the month of blood sample collection, as follows: sunny months (June to November) and rainy months (December to May) established according to the rainfall report of the Central Weather Bureau, Taiwan. Participants also reported whether they had to stay indoors (e.g., bedridden) for any reason during their pregnancy ("yes" or "no" response) and the number of methods used for sun protection (e.g., sunscreen, parasols, hats and outerwear with UV-block) and how often they are used.

3.4. *Vitamin D Deficiency Assessment*

As 25-hydroxyvitamin D [25(OH)D] has the long half-life (15 days) and relative stability of concentration in the blood [20], the circulating 25(OH)D is the useful biomarker of vitamin D in the human body [21]. The plasma 25-hydroxyvitamin D [25(OH)D] concentration was measured using an electrochemiluminescence immunoassay, as described previously [19]. Although there is no consensus in the definition of the suboptimal vitamin D level, VDD was defined as a 25(OH)D level of <20 ng/mL, which is a common threshold for people in at-risk groups, including pregnant women [22–24]. The cutoff point of less than 20 ng/mL was also recommended for use for VDD by Institution of Medicine, Academy of Medicine and American Academy of Pediatrics.

4. Ethical Consideration

This study was funded by the Health Promotion Administration, Ministry of Health and Welfare in Taiwan (C1050912) and was approved by the institutional review board of the government and selected hospitals (IRB number: N201707039).

5. Statistical Analysis

First, descriptive analysis was performed to explore the distribution of independent variables. We performed chi-square tests (for categorical variables) and *t* tests or Mann–Whitney tests (for continuous variables) to compare the distribution of independent variables between pregnant women with and without VDD. Second, logistic regression analysis was used to determine the factors associated with VDD. Two models were constructed. Model 1 comprised variables associated with VDD that had $p < 0.1$ in bivariate analysis, including age, residential area, parity, gestational age, pre-pregnancy BMI, egg intake, red meat intake, fat, vitamin D content, vitamin supplements, sun exposure, remaining indoors during pregnancy, and the season of blood draw. Gravidity and carbohydrate intake were removed from model 1 because they were highly correlated with parity ($rho = 0.82$) and fat intake ($rho = -0.89$), respectively (Table S1). Model 2 comprised factors associated with VDD that had $p < 0.1$ in model 1, including age, residential area, gestational age, red meat intake, vitamin D content, vitamin supplements, sun exposure, remaining indoors during pregnancy, and the season of blood draw. Odds ratios (ORs) and 95% CIs were reported, and $p < 0.05$ was considered statistically significant.

Further sensitivity analysis was performed and stratified by residential area (north vs. south and other regions) to examine the contribution of modifiable factors to vitamin D status. Two models were constructed for each layer, including one model adjusted for sunlight-related factors (season of blood draw and sun exposure) and one model adjusted for dietary vitamin D intake (red meat and supplements). The area under the receiver operating characteristic (AUROC) curve was computed to compare the models. It is favored due to the characteristics of invariant and independent from the prevalence of the condition. All analyses were performed using R software (version 4.1.3; R Foundation for Statistical Computing, Vienna, Austria).

6. Results

6.1. Characteristics of Study Participants

The data contained several missing values, but the distribution of variables before and after removing the missing information was the same. Therefore, the entire data of the 1502 pregnant women were used for analysis. Overall, the mean 25(OH)D concentration was 25.5 ± 8.9 ng/mL, and the prevalence of VDD was 30.1% (weighted). Compared with women without VDD, those with VDD were younger (p = 0.017); lived in the north (p < 0.001); had uniparity (p = 0.01); were in the first trimester of gestation (p < 0.001); consumed high quantities of carbohydrates (p = 0.013) but insufficient eggs (p = 0.034), red meat (p < 0.001), fat (p = 0.023), and vitamin D and/or calcium supplements (p < 0.001); had little sun exposure (p = 0.001); remained indoors during pregnancy (p = 0.018); and had blood drawn during the rainy months (p = 0.004). These data are displayed in (Table 1).

Table 1. Characteristics of study participants according to vitamin D status (n = 1502).

Variables	Total	Non-VDD (1095, 72.9%)	VDD (407, 27.1%)	p
	n (%)	n (%)	n (%)	
Maternal age (years) (mean ± SD)	32.5 ± 4.8	32.7 ± 4.8	32.1 ± 4.8	0.017
Residential area				<0.001
North	501 (33.4)	312 (28.5)	189 (46.4)	
Central	371 (24.7)	260 (23.7)	111 (27.3)	
South and east	291 (19.4)	254 (23.2)	37 (9.1)	
Eastern and outlying islands	339 (22.6)	269 (24.6)	70 (17.2)	
Education level *				0.291
High school and below	237 (15.9)	182 (16.8)	55 (13.5)	
College, university	1025 (68.7)	740 (68.1)	285 (70.0)	
Postgraduate studies	231 (15.5)	164 (15.1)	67 (16.5)	
Household monthly income				0.465
Less than NT$30,000	212 (14.4)	162 (15.1)	50 (12.5)	
NT$30,000–59,999	634 (43.0)	464 (43.2)	170 (42.4)	
NT$60,000–99,999	443 (30.1)	318 (29.6)	125 (31.2)	
More than NT$100,000	185 (12.6)	129 (12.0)	56 (14.0)	
Religion				0.242
None	689 (45.9)	488 (44.6)	201 (49.4)	
Buddhism	281 (18.7)	205 (18.7)	76 (18.7)	
Taoism	345 (23.0)	265 (24.2)	80 (19.7)	
Other (Yiguandao, Christian, Catholic, Muslim)	187 (12.5)	137 (12.5)	50 (12.3)	
Gravidity *				0.061
1	694 (46.3)	487 (44.6)	207 (51.0)	
2	498 (33.2)	366 (33.6)	132 (32.5)	
3	199 (13.3)	158 (14.5)	41 (10.1)	
≥4	107 (7.1)	81 (7.4)	26 (6.4)	
The ordinal of current pregnancy (parity) *				0.010
1st child	824 (55.0)	577 (52.9)	247 (60.7)	
2nd child	527 (35.2)	395 (36.2)	132 (32.4)	
≥3rd child	146 (9.8)	118 (10.8)	28 (6.9)	

Table 1. *Cont.*

Variables	Total	Non-VDD (1095, 72.9%)	VDD (407, 27.1%)	*p*
	n (%)	*n* (%)	*n* (%)	
Number of fetuses in this pregnancy				0.972
≥2	33 (2.2)	24 (2.2)	9 (2.2)	
Gestational age				<0.001
1st trimester (less than 17 weeks)	375 (25.0)	235 (21.5)	140 (34.4)	
2nd trimester (17 weeks to less than 29 weeks)	485 (32.3)	357 (32.6)	128 (31.4)	
3rd trimester (more than 29 weeks)	642 (42.7)	503 (45.9)	139 (34.2)	
Pre-pregnancy BMI *				0.098
Normal (18.5 ≤ BMI < 25.0)	141 (9.4)	99 (9.1)	42 (10.3)	
Underweight (<18.5)	1018 (68.1)	730 (67.0)	288 (70.9)	
Overweight/obese (≥25.0)	336 (22.5)	260 (23.9)	76 (18.7)	
Dairy products *				0.546
Enough	1213 (81.2)	888 (81.6)	325 (80.2)	
Egg *				0.034
Enough	1397 (93.6)	1027 (94.4)	370 (91.4)	
Red meat *				<0.001
Enough	1390 (93.1)	1029 (94.6)	361 (89.1)	
Nut fruits *				0.514
Enough	875 (58.6)	643 (59.2)	232 (57.3)	
Fat (%) (mean ± SD)	35.8 ± 9.0	36.1 ± 9.1	34.9 ± 8.9	0.023
Protein (%) (mean ± SD)	15.3 ± 3.7	15.3 ± 3.7	15.0 ± 3.7	0.147
Carbohydrate (%) (mean ± SD)	49.8 ± 9.8	49.4 ± 9.9	50.8 ± 9.5	0.013
Vitamin D content (g) (median, IQR)	2.8 (7.7)	2.8 (9.6)	2.5 (4.8)	0.031
Vitamin supplements *				<0.001
Vitamin D and/or Calcium	698 (47.7)	560 (52.3)	138 (35.0)	
Sun exposure				0.001
Yes	1046 (69.6)	789 (72.1)	257 (63.1)	
Protective methods for sunshine (mean ± SD)	1.6 ± 1.3	1.6 ± 1.3	1.6 ± 1.3	0.504
Remained indoors during pregnancy				0.018
Yes	228 (15.3)	152 (14.0)	76 (19.0)	
Season of blood draw				0.004
Sunny months	927 (61.7)	700 (63.9)	227 (55.8)	

Abbreviations: BMI, body mass index; IQR, interquartile range; NT$, New Taiwan dollar; SD, standard deviation; VDD, vitamin D deficiency. * Variables containing missingness of ≤0.6%, with the exception of remaining indoors during pregnancy, number of fetuses in this pregnancy, household monthly income, and vitamin supplements, which have 0.9%, 1.1%, 1.9%, and 2.5% missingness, respectively.

6.2. Associated Factors of Vitamin D Deficiency

As displayed in Table 2, the likelihood of VDD was significantly lower in pregnant women who were older (OR: 0.95, $p < 0.001$); lived in central (OR: 0.66, $p = 0.010$), southern, or eastern Taiwan (OR: 0.20, $p < 0.001$) or in the eastern and outlying islands (OR: 0.33, $p < 0.001$); were in the second trimester (OR: 0.72, $p = 0.046$) or the third trimester (OR: 0.60, $p = 0.002$); consumed sufficient red meat (OR: 0.50, $p = 0.002$); took vitamin D and/or calcium supplements (OR: 0.51, $p < 0.001$); received sun exposure (OR: 0.75, $p = 0.034$); and had blood drawn during the sunny months (OR: 0.59, $p < 0.001$).

In the sensitivity analysis, among participants living in northern Taiwan, dietary vitamin D intake (AUROC: 0.580, 95% CI: 0.528–0.633) had a greater influence on vitamin D status than did sunlight-related factors (AUROC: 0.536, 95% CI: 0.508–0.589). By contrast, among participants living in the south and other parts of Taiwan, sunlight-related factors (AUROC: 0.659, 95% CI: 0.618–0.700) were more influential than dietary vitamin D intake (AUROC: 0.617, 95% CI: 0.575–0.660). The differences in regional models were significant, with z value = 51.98, $p < 0.001$ for northern Taiwan and z value = 54.02, $p < 0.001$ for the remaining regions. These results are visualized in Figure 2.

Table 2. Factors associated with vitamin D deficiency via multiple logistic regression analysis models (n= 1502).

Variables	Model 1			Model 2		
	OR	95% CI	p	OR	95% CI	p
Age	0.96	0.93–0.98	0.005	0.95	0.93–0.98	<0.001
Residential area						
North	1.00					
Central	0.68	0.50–0.94	0.021	0.66	0.48–0.90	0.010
South and east	0.22	0.14–0.33	<0.001	0.20	0.13–0.31	<0.001
Eastern and outlying Islands	0.36	0.25–0.52	<0.001	0.33	0.23–0.47	<0.001
The ordinal of current pregnancy (parity)						
1st child	1.00					
2nd child	0.83	0.62–1.10	0.203			
≥3rd child	0.69	0.42–1.12	0.141			
Gestational age						
1st trimester (less than 17 weeks)	1.00			1.00		
2nd trimester (17 weeks to less than 29 weeks)	0.73	0.52–1.01	0.054	0.72	0.52–0.99	0.046
3rd trimester (more than 29 weeks)	0.61	0.44–0.84	0.002	0.60	0.44–0.83	0.002
Pre-pregnancy BMI						
Normal (18.5 ≤ BMI < 25.0)	1.00					
Underweight (<18.5)	1.04	0.67–1.59	0.850			
Overweight/obese (≥25.0)	0.87	0.63–1.20	0.397			
Egg intake						
Not enough	1.00					
Enough	0.72	0.43–1.23	0.236			
Red meat intake						
Not enough	1.00			1.00		
Enough	0.54	0.34–0.86	0.010	0.50	0.32–0.78	0.002
Fat (%)	0.99	0.98–1.01	0.711			
Vitamin D content						
≤median	1.00			1.00		
>median	0.80	0.62–1.03	0.091	0.78	0.60–1.00	0.057
Vitamin supplements						
No relevant supplements	1.00			1.00		
Vitamin D and/or calcium	0.47	0.36–0.62	<0.001	0.51	0.39–0.66	<0.001
Sun exposure						
No	1.00			1.00		
Yes	0.77	0.59–1.01	0.064	0.75	0.57–0.98	0.034
Remained indoors during pregnancy						
No	1.00			1.00		
Yes	1.33	0.95–1.87	0.089	1.35	0.97–1.88	0.071
Season of blood draw						
Rainy months	1.00					
Sunny months	0.57	0.44–0.75	<0.001	0.59	0.46–0.77	<0.001

Abbreviations: BMI, body mass index; CI, confidence interval; NT$, New Taiwan dollar; OR, odds ratio.

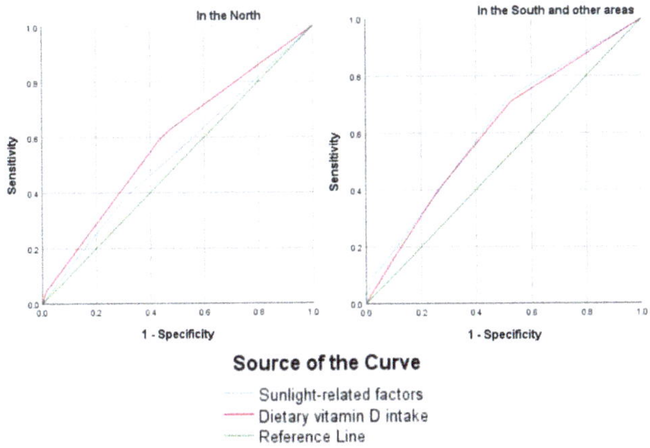

Figure 2. Contribution of sunlight-related factors and dietary vitamin D intake to vitamin D status in different regions of Taiwan.

7. Discussion

In the present study, the prevalence of 25(OH)D level < 20 ng/mL among pregnant women in Taiwan was 30.1% (weighted). The determinants of VDD included age, gestational age, red meat intake, vitamin D and/or calcium supplements, residential area, sun exposure, and the season of blood draw.

The occurrence of VDD [25(OH)D < 20 ng/mL] is common in pregnant women, although the rates vary in different Asian countries, ranging from 7% to 40.7% [25,26]. The present study found that VDD occurred more frequently in pregnant women living in northern Taiwan than in those living in southern Taiwan. A nationwide report on VDD among older adults (a risk group of VDD) had similar findings, reporting that VDD occurrence was higher in the north than in the south [27]. This phenomenon has several possible explanations. First, northern Taiwan has a higher latitude than other regions [28], and vitamin D status decrease with increasing latitudes [29]. Second, northern Taiwan has a humid subtropical climate, and sunlight may be of lower intensity than that in southern Taiwan and other regions characterized by a tropical monsoon climate. The association between age and VDD was found in the previous studies with the controversial findings. The former authors showed that age over thirty was the risk factor for VDD among pregnant women [26]. However, the current study indicated that younger age was a contributing factor for VDD, which was in line with other studies [30,31]. Our findings could be due to the habits of avoiding sunlight among almost youngers that they were likely to apply sun protection (e.g., using sunscreen, wearing long-sleeved clothes, preferring indoor activities). Thus, our findings indicate that it is worth planning VDD prevention, such as educating health literacy related to VDD and lifestyle changes in younger women, and such methods should be promoted integrating with efficient intervention strategies.

Regarding the impact of gestational age on maternal VDD, the findings are inconsistent across studies. Although several studies have reported that vitamin D status decreased during advanced gestation [32], our results are in line with those of studies reporting that the likelihood of VDD was reduced during the second and third trimesters. For example, Perreault et al. indicated that serum 25(OH)D concentrations were significantly greater in the last trimester compared to the first trimester [33]. Similarly, Savard et al. found that serum 25(OH)D levels significantly increased across trimesters [34]. In addition, Shen et al. noted a positive relationship between the increased vitamin D concentration and later gestational week [35].

It has been well established that sunlight is the main source of vitamin D. Hence, sun exposure and the summer season are the most important contributing factors to the vitamin D concentration. Nevertheless, if sun exposure cannot provide sufficient vitamin D because of factors such as sunlight intensity, time of exposure, and application of sun protection, the vitamin D status in the human body can be adjusted through nutrition and dietary intake. In the literature, the natural vitamin D content in foodstuffs is usually limited to vitamin D3 from animal products [36]. Our findings indicated that the consumption of red meat was associated with lower VDD rates. Moreover, the present study demonstrated that vitamin D and/or calcium supplements could reduce the likelihood of VDD.

In our sensitivity analysis, the effects of sunlight-related factors and dietary vitamin D intake on 25(OH)D levels varied by region. In northern Taiwan, dietary vitamin D intake was more important than sunlight-related factors for improving maternal vitamin D status; however, sunlight-related factors were the main sources of vitamin D for pregnant women living in the south and other parts of Taiwan, and vitamin D intake played a minor role. These variations in effectiveness corresponded to the variations in climate across Taiwan. These findings can assist health policymakers in designing regional strategies for the prevention of prenatal VDD.

To date, suboptimal vitamin D levels is mostly indicated for bone health but remain controversial across populations and countries. For some investigators, deficiency was defined as specific to bone; however, insufficiency was defined relating to other health outcomes. For others, deficiency covered diseased population and insufficiency covered at-risk population. One of the most commonly used definitions comes from the Endocrine Society Clinical Practice Guidelines [24]; vitamin D deficiency was defined as 25(OH)D values below 20 ng/mL (50 nmol/L), and vitamin D insufficiency was defined as 25(OH)D of 21–29 ng/mL (52.5–72.5 nmol/L). This guideline was accepted and used widely by the International Osteoporosis Foundation, American Association for Clinical Endocrinologists, Institute of Medicine, American Academy of Pediatrics, and government of Australia, New Zealand, Germany, Austria and Switzerland as well as in Taiwan. In any case, cut point is very important when looking at the results in 25(OH)D level.

Particularly in older adults, having a higher BMI or body fat percentage are significant subject-specific characteristics that negatively affect vitamin D metabolism [37]. Normal-weight women reached the higher 25(OH)d level after vitamin D supplementation faster than women with obesity [38]. However, in pregnant women, the association between BMI and VDD was not consistent across the studies. While several studies showed that high BMI was associated with VDD, others showed that BMI was not statistically significantly associated with VDD [39,40]. Obesity is strongly associated with insufficient dietary vitamin D intake and low sun exposure. Pre-pregnancy obesity predicts poor vitamin D status in mothers [41]. In our study, pre-pregnancy BMI (as a continuous variable) was significantly different in two groups of VDD and non-VDD, but in logistic regression, after adjusting for confounders, pre-pregnancy BMI was not significantly associated with VDD. The findings for BMI (as a categorical variable) were also insignificant in multiple logistic regression. Obesity is not associated with 25(OH)D levels in our study.

The present study is the first national report on vitamin D status among pregnant women in Taiwan. Our findings demonstrated specific differences in the effects of sunlight-related factors and vitamin D intake on vitamin D concentrations in distinct regions of Taiwan. However, several limitations should be considered. First, because this was a cross-sectional study, we can only note associations; we cannot determine the causal relationship. Second, several factors influencing vitamin D status were not assessed in our study, such as occupation and the brand and dose of supplements. Third, we used a self-report questionnaire, which may introduce assessment bias because of subjective responses. Fourth, although the present study highlights the critical role of dietary vitamin D intake, the data on nutrient quantitation per serving are unavailable.

8. Conclusions

VDD was prevalent in pregnant women in Taiwan. On the basis of our findings, we recommend the promotion of a robust health policy regarding safe sunlight exposure and effective dietary vitamin D intake, with adjustments according to the characteristics of various climate zones. In doing so, clinicians can enhance maternal vitamin D status, reduce the VDD-induced burden, and improve health and well-being.

Supplementary Materials: The following supporting information can be downloaded at: https://www.mdpi.com/article/10.3390/nu15051182/s1, Table S1: Spearman's correlations among the studied variables (n = 1502).

Author Contributions: Y.-L.H., T.T.M.P., Y.-C.C., J.-S.C., J.C.-J.C. and C.-H.B.: conceptualization, methodology, validation, investigation, data curation, and writing review and editing draft. Y.-L.H., T.T.M.P. and C.-H.B.: formal analysis and writing—original draft. Y.-L.H., J.C.-J.C. and C.-H.B.: project administration. C.-H.B.: supervision and funding acquisition. All authors have read and agreed to the published version of the manuscript.

Funding: This research was funded by the Health Promotion Administration, Ministry of Health and Welfare in Taiwan (grant number MOHW107-HPA-H-124-133204) and was partially supported by a grant from the Collaborative Research Project of College of Medicine, Taipei Medical University, Taiwan. The content of this research may not represent the opinions of the Health Promotion Administration, Ministry of Health and Welfare, Taiwan.

Institutional Review Board Statement: The study was conducted in accordance with the Declaration of Helsinki, and approved by the Institutional Review Board of the government and selected hospitals (IRB number: N201707039).

Informed Consent Statement: Informed consent was obtained from all subjects involved in the study.

Data Availability Statement: Not applicable.

Acknowledgments: The authors acknowledge all the participants and institutions for their contributions to the Nutritional Survey of Pregnant women in Taiwan.

Conflicts of Interest: The authors declare that the research was conducted in the absence of any commercial or financial relationships that could be construed as a potential conflict of interest.

References

1. Kiely, M.E.; McCarthy, E.K.; Hennessy, Á. Iron, iodine and vitamin D deficiencies during pregnancy: Epidemiology, risk factors and developmental impacts. *Proc. Nutr. Soc.* **2021**, *80*, 290–302. [CrossRef] [PubMed]
2. Roth, D.E.; Abrams, S.A.; Aloia, J.; Bergeron, G.; Bourassa, M.W.; Brown, K.H.; Calvo, M.S.; Cashman, K.D.; Combs, G.; De-Regil, L.M.; et al. Global prevalence and disease burden of vitamin D deficiency: A roadmap for action in low- and middle-income countries. *Ann. N. Y. Acad. Sci.* **2018**, *1430*, 44–79. [CrossRef] [PubMed]
3. Föcker, M.; Antel, J.; Grasemann, C.; Führer, D.; Timmesfeld, N.; Öztürk, D.; Peters, T.; Hinney, A.; Hebebrand, J.; Libuda, L. Effect of an vitamin D deficiency on depressive symptoms in child and adolescent psychiatric patients—A randomized controlled trial: Study protocol. *BMC Psychiatry* **2018**, *18*, 57. [CrossRef] [PubMed]
4. Woon, F.C.; Chin, Y.S.; Ismail, I.H.; Abdul Latiff, A.H.; Batterham, M.; Chan, Y.M.; On Behalf Of The Micos Research Group. Maternal Vitamin D Levels during Late Pregnancy and Risk of Allergic Diseases and Sensitization during the First Year of Life-A Birth Cohort Study. *Nutrients* **2020**, *12*, 2418. [CrossRef]
5. Balcells, M.E.; García, P.; Tiznado, C.; Villarroel, L.; Scioscia, N.; Carvajal, C.; Zegna-Ratá, F.; Hernández, M.; Meza, P.; González, L.F.; et al. Association of vitamin D deficiency, season of the year, and latent tuberculosis infection among household contacts. *PLoS ONE* **2017**, *12*, e0175400. [CrossRef]
6. Ghasemian, R.; Shamshirian, A.; Heydari, K.; Malekan, M.; Alizadeh-Navaei, R.; Ebrahimzadeh, M.A.; Ebrahimi Warkiani, M.; Jafarpour, H.; Razavi Bazaz, S.; Rezaei Shahmirzadi, A.; et al. The role of vitamin D in the age of COVID-19: A systematic review and meta-analysis. *Int. J. Clin. Pract.* **2021**, *75*, e14675. [CrossRef]
7. Palacios, C.; Gonzalez, L. Is vitamin D deficiency a major global public health problem? *J. Steroid Biochem. Mol. Biol.* **2014**, *144 Pt A*, 138–145. [CrossRef]
8. Heyden, E.L.; Wimalawansa, S.J. Vitamin D: Effects on human reproduction, pregnancy, and fetal well-being. *J. Steroid Biochem. Mol. Biol.* **2018**, *180*, 41–50. [CrossRef]
9. Van der Pligt, P.; Willcox, J.; Szymlek-Gay, E.A.; Murray, E.; Worsley, A.; Daly, R.M. Associations of Maternal Vitamin D Deficiency with Pregnancy and Neonatal Complications in Developing Countries: A Systematic Review. *Nutrients* **2018**, *10*, 640. [CrossRef]
10. Ames, B.N.; Grant, W.B.; Willett, W.C. Does the High Prevalence of Vitamin D Deficiency in African Americans Contribute to Health Disparities? *Nutrients* **2021**, *13*, 499. [CrossRef]
11. Women's Health. By the Numbers: Health Disparities in Pregnancy. Available online: https://magazine.medlineplus.gov/article/by-the-numbers-health-disparities-in-pregnancy (accessed on 15 January 2023).
12. Cashman, K.D. Vitamin D Deficiency: Defining, Prevalence, Causes, and Strategies of Addressing. *Calcif. Tissue Int.* **2020**, *106*, 14–29. [CrossRef]
13. Powers, J.M.; Murphy, J.E.J. Sunlight radiation as a villain and hero: 60 years of illuminating research. *Int. J. Radiat. Biol.* **2019**, *95*, 1043–1049. [CrossRef]
14. Leal, A.; Corrêa, M.P.; Holick, M.F.; Melo, E.V.; Lazaretti-Castro, M. Sun-induced production of vitamin D(3) throughout 1 year in tropical and subtropical regions: Relationship with latitude, cloudiness, UV-B exposure and solar zenith angle. *Photochem. Photobiol. Sci* **2021**, *20*, 265–274. [CrossRef]
15. Benedik, E. Sources of vitamin D for humans. *Int. J. Vitam. Nutr. Res.* **2022**, *92*, 118–125. [CrossRef] [PubMed]
16. Grant, W.B.; Al Anouti, F.; Moukayed, M. Targeted 25-hydroxyvitamin D concentration measurements and vitamin D3 supplementation can have important patient and public health benefits. *Eur. J. Clin. Nutr.* **2020**, *74*, 366–376. [CrossRef]
17. Pérez-López, F.R.; Pilz, S.; Chedraui, P. Vitamin D supplementation during pregnancy: An overview. *Curr. Opin. Obstet. Gynecol.* **2020**, *32*, 316–321. [CrossRef]
18. Geography of Taiwan. Available online: https://en.wikipedia.org/wiki/Geography_of_Taiwan#Climate (accessed on 18 May 2022).
19. Pham, T.T.M.; Huang, Y.L.; Chao, J.C.; Chang, J.S.; Chen, Y.C.; Wang, F.F.; Bai, C.H. Plasma 25(OH)D Concentrations and Gestational Diabetes Mellitus among Pregnant Women in Taiwan. *Nutrients* **2021**, *13*, 2538. [CrossRef] [PubMed]
20. Seamans, K.M.; Cashman, K.D. Existing and potentially novel functional markers of vitamin D status: A systematic review. *Am. J. Clin. Nutr.* **2009**, *89*, 1997S–2008S. [CrossRef]

21. Cashman, K.D.; van den Heuvel, E.G.; Schoemaker, R.J.; Prévéraud, D.P.; Macdonald, H.M.; Arcot, J. 25-Hydroxyvitamin D as a Biomarker of Vitamin D Status and Its Modeling to Inform Strategies for Prevention of Vitamin D Deficiency within the Population. *Adv. Nutr.* **2017**, *8*, 947–957. [CrossRef] [PubMed]
22. Ross, A.C.; Manson, J.E.; Abrams, S.A.; Aloia, J.F.; Brannon, P.M.; Clinton, S.K.; Durazo-Arvizu, R.A.; Gallagher, J.C.; Gallo, R.L.; Jones, G.; et al. The 2011 report on dietary reference intakes for calcium and vitamin D from the Institute of Medicine: What clinicians need to know. *J. Clin. Endocrinol. Metab.* **2011**, *96*, 53–58. [CrossRef]
23. Sempos, C.T.; Binkley, N. 25-Hydroxyvitamin D assay standardisation and vitamin D guidelines paralysis. *Public Health Nutr.* **2020**, *23*, 1153–1164. [CrossRef]
24. Holick, M.F.; Binkley, N.C.; Bischoff-Ferrari, H.A.; Gordon, C.M.; Hanley, D.A.; Heaney, R.P.; Murad, M.H.; Weaver, C.M.; Endocrine, S. Evaluation, treatment, and prevention of vitamin D deficiency: An Endocrine Society clinical practice guideline. *J. Clin. Endocrinol. Metab.* **2011**, *96*, 1911–1930. [CrossRef]
25. Hien, V.T.; Lam, N.T.; Skeaff, C.M.; Todd, J.; McLean, J.M.; Green, T.J. Vitamin D status of pregnant and non-pregnant women of reproductive age living in Hanoi City and the Hai Duong province of Vietnam. *Matern. Child Nutr.* **2012**, *8*, 533–539. [CrossRef] [PubMed]
26. Yang, C.; Jing, W.; Ge, S.; Sun, W. Vitamin D status and vitamin D deficiency risk factors among pregnancy of Shanghai in China. *BMC Pregnancy Childbirth* **2021**, *21*, 431. [CrossRef] [PubMed]
27. Chuang, S.C.; Chen, H.L.; Tseng, W.T.; Wu, I.C.; Hsu, C.C.; Chang, H.Y.; Chen, Y.I.; Lee, M.M.; Liu, K.; Hsiung, C.A. Circulating 25-hydroxyvitamin D and physical performance in older adults: A nationwide study in Taiwan. *Am. J. Clin. Nutr.* **2016**, *104*, 1334–1344. [CrossRef]
28. Taiwan Geographic Coordinates. Available online: https://www.geodatos.net/en/coordinates/taiwan (accessed on 18 May 2022).
29. Leary, P.F.; Zamfirova, I.; Au, J.; McCracken, W.H. Effect of Latitude on Vitamin D Levels. *J. Am. Osteopath Assoc.* **2017**, *117*, 433–439. [CrossRef]
30. Al Zarooni, A.A.R.; Nagelkerke, N.; Al Marzouqi, F.I.; Al Darmaki, S.H. Risk factors for vitamin D deficiency in Abu Dhabi Emirati population. *PLoS ONE* **2022**, *17*, e0264064. [CrossRef]
31. AlFaris, N.A.; AlKehayez, N.M.; AlMushawah, F.I.; AlNaeem, A.N.; AlAmri, N.D.; AlMudawah, E.S. Vitamin D Deficiency and Associated Risk Factors in Women from Riyadh, Saudi Arabia. *Sci. Rep.* **2019**, *9*, 20371. [CrossRef]
32. Takaoka, N.; Nishida, K.; Sairenchi, T.; Umesawa, M.; Noguchi, R.; Someya, K.; Kobashi, G. Changes in vitamin D status considering hemodilution factors in Japanese pregnant women according to trimester: A longitudinal survey. *PLoS ONE* **2020**, *15*, e0239954. [CrossRef]
33. Perreault, M.; Atkinson, S.A.; Meyre, D.; Fusch, G.; Mottola, M.F. Summer Season and Recommended Vitamin D Intake Support Adequate Vitamin D Status throughout Pregnancy in Healthy Canadian Women and Their Newborns. *J. Nutr.* **2020**, *150*, 739–746. [CrossRef] [PubMed]
34. Savard, C.; Bielecki, A.; Plante, A.S.; Lemieux, S.; Gagnon, C.; Weiler, H.A.; Morisset, A.S. Longitudinal Assessment of Vitamin D Status across Trimesters of Pregnancy. *J. Nutr.* **2021**, *151*, 1937–1946. [CrossRef]
35. Shen, Y.; Pu, L.; Si, S.; Xin, X.; Mo, M.; Shao, B.; Wu, J.; Huang, M.; Wang, S.; Muyiduli, X.; et al. Vitamin D nutrient status during pregnancy and its influencing factors. *Clin. Nutr.* **2020**, *39*, 1432–1439. [CrossRef] [PubMed]
36. Schmid, A.; Walther, B. Natural Vitamin D Content in Animal Products. *Adv. Nutr.* **2013**, *4*, 453–462. [CrossRef] [PubMed]
37. Di Filippo, L.; De Lorenzo, R.; Giustina, A.; Rovere-Querini, P.; Conte, C. Vitamin D in Osteosarcopenic Obesity. *Nutrients* **2022**, *14*, 1816. [CrossRef]
38. Gallagher, J.C.; Yalamanchili, V.; Smith, L.M. The effect of vitamin D supplementation on serum 25OHD in thin and obese women. *J. Steroid Biochem. Mol. Biol.* **2013**, *136*, 195–200. [CrossRef]
39. Savastano, S.; Barrea, L.; Savanelli, M.C.; Nappi, F.; Di Somma, C.; Orio, F.; Colao, A. Low vitamin D status and obesity: Role of nutritionist. *Rev. Endocr. Metab. Disord.* **2017**, *18*, 215–225. [CrossRef]
40. Yang, Y.; Cai, Z.; Zhang, J. The effect of prepregnancy body mass index on maternal micronutrient status: A meta-analysis. *Sci. Rep.* **2021**, *11*, 18100. [CrossRef] [PubMed]
41. Bodnar, L.M.; Catov, J.M.; Roberts, J.M.; Simhan, H.N. Prepregnancy obesity predicts poor vitamin D status in mothers and their neonates. *J. Nutr.* **2007**, *137*, 2437–2442. [CrossRef]

nutrients

MDPI

Article

Self-Reported Intake and Circulating EPA and DHA Concentrations in US Pregnant Women

Keri Lanier [1], Breanna Wisseman [2], Cody Strom [3], Carol A. Johnston [4], Christy Isler [5], James DeVente [5], Edward Newton [5], Roman Pawlak [6], Brittany R. Allman-Tucker [7], Samantha McDonald [8] and Linda E. May [2,5,9,*]

1 School of Osteopathic Medicine, Campbell University, Lillington, NC 27546, USA
2 Department of Kinesiology, East Carolina University (ECU), Greenville, NC 27858, USA
3 Department of Kinesiology and Sport, University of Southern Indiana, Evansville, IN 47712, USA
4 Department of Human Development and Family Science, East Carolina University (ECU), Greenville, NC 27858, USA
5 Department of Obstetrics and Gynecology, East Carolina University (ECU), Greenville, NC 27858, USA
6 Department of Nutrition, East Carolina University (ECU), Greenville, NC 27858, USA
7 Department of Sport and Exercise Science, University of Central Arkansas, Conway, AR 72035, USA
8 Kinesiology and Recreation, Illinois State University, Normal, IL 61790, USA
9 East Carolina Diabetes and Obesity Institute, East Carolina University (ECU), Greenville, NC 27858, USA
* Correspondence: mayl@ecu.edu; Tel.: +1-(252)-737-7072; Fax: +1-(252)-737-7368

Abstract: In the United States, pregnant women have low concentrations of docosahexaenoic acid (DHA) and eicosapentaenoic acid (EPA), which are essential for fetal development. Although maternal blood provides accurate polyunsaturated fatty acid (PUFA) concentrations, venipuncture is expensive and not always accessible. PUFA-containing foods consumption, both omega-3 ad omega-6 is supposed to reflect in the status (plasma, RBC, adipose tissue) of docosahexaenoic acid (DHA) and eicosapentaenoic acid (EPA). De novo synthesis of DHA and EPA during pregnancy is supposed to be higher compared to pre and/or post-pregnancy periods. Thus, this study aimed to determine the association between maternal self-reported dietary intake of foods high in DHA and EPA, along with vegetable oils as a source of omega-6 fatty acids, with maternal blood DHA and EPA concentrations. Pregnant women (13–16 weeks gestation) were recruited and asked to complete a food-frequency questionnaire (FFQ) and blood draw at enrollment and 36 weeks. Circulating concentrations of DHA and EPA were quantified and change scores were calculated. Correlations were done to determine associations between FFQ results and EPA/DHA maternal blood concentrations. Regression analyses were run to examine significant predictors of the main outcomes. Overall, PUFA-food consumption and RBC's DHA levels decreased from early to late pregnancy; self-reported PUFA-rich food consumption positively correlated with DHA and EPA levels. DHA concentration was predicted by self-reported PUFA-rich oils (sunflower/soy/corn/olive) consumption, but EPA concentration was predicted by maternal BMI. These findings suggest that EPA and DHA consumption decreased across pregnancy and the FFQ can be utilized as an effective method for estimating PUFA blood concentration during pregnancy.

Keywords: dietary assessment; food intake; polyunsaturated fatty acid; DHA; EPA; pregnancy

Citation: Lanier, K.; Wisseman, B.; Strom, C.; Johnston, C.A.; Isler, C.; DeVente, J.; Newton, E.; Pawlak, R.; Allman-Tucker, B.R.; McDonald, S.; et al. Self-Reported Intake and Circulating EPA and DHA Concentrations in US Pregnant Women. *Nutrients* **2023**, *15*, 1753. https://doi.org/10.3390/nu15071753

Academic Editors: Leanne M. Redman, Louise Brough and Gail Rees

Received: 28 January 2023
Revised: 30 March 2023
Accepted: 3 April 2023
Published: 4 April 2023

1. Introduction

In the United States (US), pregnant women usually have low ratios of omega-3 fatty acids to omega-6 fatty acids, due to a Western diet that prioritizes red meats, chicken, and corn oil, which exceeds the suggested omega-3s to omega-6s ratio of 1:4 up to 1:15 [1–3]. A diet high in cold-water fish, algae, and low intake of omega-6 fatty acids can help maintain the minimum suggested ratio, i.e., 1:4, of polyunsaturated fatty acids (PUFAs). This type of diet, high in omega-3 fatty acids, such as docosahexaenoic acid (DHA) and eicosapentaenoic acid (EPA), is important for the nervous system and health [4,5]. DHA and EPA play a critical role in fetal development, especially the fetal nervous system [4]. These PUFAs influence fetal brain development as well as inflammatory properties throughout the body [4]. DHA, in particular, is important for developing neuronal connections, neurogenesis, and protection from oxidative stress in utero [4]. For this reason, it is important to be able to accurately measure whole-body PUFA levels in pregnant women.

Previously, food-frequency questionnaires (FFQs) have been validated in Chinese men and women as well as in Australian women in late pregnancy [6,7]. Similarly, in Japan, there has been some utility established for assessing self-reported DHA and EPA via questionnaire, in early and late pregnancy [8]. However, these studies utilized only red blood cells (RBCs) in their analyses, which can only provide an assessment of long-term PUFA consumption habits [9,10]; whereas plasma levels provide a short-term assessment of PUFA levels and may more closely mimic PUFA food intake. However, this assessment has not been done previously in US women. Furthermore, studies in other countries varied in timepoints of assessments during pregnancy; and/or utilized a FFQ that was not inclusive of PUFA-containing foods. Foods such as fish, sunflower/soy/corn/olive oils, and almond/cashew milk contribute to PUFA consumption [11,12]. DHA and EPA are important fatty acids that play an integral role in fetal neurological development; therefore, it is imperative that healthcare providers are aware of maternal PUFA intake. While venipuncture sampling is a practical method for assessing maternal DHA and EPA blood concentrations, this process is invasive, costly, and time-consuming. With fetal brain development beginning in early pregnancy, it is important to have a rapid method for estimating maternal PUFAs, allowing for early intervention if levels are too low [13]. FFQs are non-invasive, easy to distribute and understand, and provide a rapid assessment of maternal food intake, thus, making them a low-cost, clinic- and patient-friendly alternative to venipuncture blood sampling. While previous research has been done in other populations, there is no literature validating a FFQ with DHA and EPA levels in the United States during early and late pregnancy. Therefore, the purpose of the present study was twofold: (1) to measure DHA and EPA levels in RBC and plasma in early and late pregnancy, and (2) to determine the association, and possible predictors, between self-reported consumption of PUFA-containing foods with DHA and EPA concentrations in maternal RBC and plasma in early and late pregnancy. We hypothesize that: (1) PUFA-rich foods, DHA, and EPA levels in plasma and RBCs will be similar in early and late pregnancy, and (2) there will be a positive correlation, and possible predictors, between self-reported PUFA-rich food consumption and circulating PUFA plasma, but not necessarily RBC, concentrations.

2. Methods

2.1. Study Design and Participants

The present study was a post hoc secondary analysis of a larger prospective randomized controlled trial designed to examine the influence of maternal exercise during pregnancy on fetal and infant health outcomes [14]. Participants were enrolled if they were 18–40 years old, able to communicate in English, $\leq$16 weeks pregnant, had a pre-pregnancy BMI of 18.5–39.9 kg/m^2, and had a singleton pregnancy. All women were required to receive written clearance from an obstetric provider to participate in the study. Participants were excluded from the study if they had pre-existing diabetes mellitus, hypertension, cardiovascular disease, co-morbidities known to affect fetal growth and well-being (e.g., systemic lupus erythematosus), or used tobacco, alcohol, and illicit drugs. All protocols were approved by the East Carolina University Institutional Review Board. Clinical Trial Registry is #NCT03517293. Written informed consent was obtained from each participant.

Pre-screening eligibility questionnaires and neonatal electronic health records were used to determine maternal age, gravida, parity, pre-pregnancy weight and height, education level, gestational weight gain (GWG), and gestational age (weeks). Height was measured using a stadiometer and weight was collected using a standard scale at 16 and 36 weeks gestation. Pregnancy weight was assessed at the same time points using a calibrated digital scale. Pre-pregnancy weight was self-reported at enrollment (≤16 weeks). A standardized equation was used to calculate BMI at each time point [15]: $BMI = ((\text{weight (kg)}) \div ([\text{height } (m^2)]))$; BMI classification used standard cutoffs: normal weight: 18.5–24.9 kg/m^2; overweight 25–29.99 kg/m^2; obese ≥ 30 kg/m^2.

2.2. Maternal Food-Frequency Questionnaire

Participants (N = 47) were asked to complete a food-frequency questionnaire (FFQ) at enrollment (13–16 weeks) and 36 weeks gestation to obtain self-reported PUFA levels. The FFQ asked women to specifically report foods, such as PUFA-rich foods, consumed during pregnancy [16]. The women were asked to report the frequency of consumption of foods based on the scale: 1—rarely or never eat the food, 2—eat the food once every 2 weeks, 3—eat the food 1–3 times/week, 4—eat the food 4–7 times/week, or 5—eat the food more than once per day. The individual PUFA-rich foods (white-flesh fish, other fish (e.g., salmon), almonds) were rated on the 5-point Likert scale [11,12]. Both the polyunsaturated margarines and sunflower/soy/corn/olive oils were rated on "Yes, you consume" or "No"; these two dichotomous measures were converted to No = 0 and Yes = 1 for analysis. All individual PUFA-rich food column numerical values were then summed for a PUFA summary score for each participant during pregnancy.

2.3. Maternal Plasma and RBC Collection and Analysis

A fasting venous blood sample was collected from women at enrollment (13–16 weeks) and 36 weeks gestation. All samples were completed following a ≥8 h fast and collected between 6–9 a.m. Blood was centrifuged and stored using standard procedures as described previously [14]. Both blood plasma and RBCs were utilized for analysis as plasma provides a representation of recent concentrations and RBCs provide longer term (~120 days) concentrations [9,10].

2.4. Maternal DHA and EPA

Chemicals and reagents: Optima grade acetonitrile, water, formic acid, methanol, and isopropanol were purchased from Fisher Scientific (Hampton, NH, USA).

Preparation of calibration and quality control standards: Working stock solutions were prepared for calibrators. Samples were screened for quality control (QC). Calibration curves were generated from 0.01–7.5 mg/mL. A positive cutoff limit was established at 10 mg/mL. Low and high QC samples were prepared by the addition of 10 or 500 ng/mL and were fortified as a QC solution.

Targeted LC/MS: An Agilent Poroshell (Agilent Technologies, Santa Clara, CA, USA) 120 EC-C8, 3 × 100 mm 2.7 μm column was used for separation of the analytes on an Exion HPLC. The column temperature was maintained at 32 °C. A gradient was used to separate the compounds using mobile phase A: 95:5 water with 0.1% formic acid:acetonitrile and mobile phase B: acetonitrile. A linear gradient was performed as follows: 0% B for 2 min, 90% B for 9 min, 90% B for 1 min, 0% B for 1 min, hold at 0% B for 5 min for a total run time of 18 min. The flow rate was 0.3 mL/min and 5 μL of sample was injected. MS-MS analysis was conducted using an AB SCIEX 3200 (Danaher Corporation, Toronto, ON, Canada) triple quadrupole mass spectrometer. The mass spectrometer was in negative ionization mode and analysis was conducted using multiple reaction monitoring (MRM). The source parameters were set to a curtain gas 50 psi, heater gas 50 psi, ion spray voltage 5500 V, and source temperature 500 °C. The instrument parameters were optimized using direct infusion of each analyte using a split tee injection with the LC flow. SCIEX Analyst software (v.1.6.2—Sciex Applied Biosystems, Framingham, MA, USA) was used for instrument control. Confirmation analysis was performed using MultiQuant where the calibrators and quality controls were carried through the same processes as the specimens being tested. Least squared regression with 1/x weighing was used to evaluate the linearity with adequate compensation for heteroscedasticity during all experiments.

2.4.1. Solid Phase Extraction (SPE)

DHA and EPA were extracted from RBCs [17,18]. Plasma samples were prepared following a similar method. Plasma samples were prepared utilizing a 3.9:1 Optima grade H_2O (Fisher Scientific, Hampton, NH, USA) to plasma solution, were vortexed, and homogenized. Aliquots of 490 mL of plasma solution were diluted to a 1 mL solution with 500 mL of methanol (MeOH) and 10 mL deuterated DHA (DHA-d5) and EPA (EPA-d5) internal standard solution. Immediately following solution preparation, both the RBC and plasma solutions were centrifuged at 13.2 rpm for 20 min. Strata-X reversed-phase SPE columns (Phenomenex, Torrance, CA, USA) and positive pressures (1 to 25 psi) were used to extract the supernatants on a Biotage Pressure+ manifold (Biotage, Charlotte, NC, USA). Columns were conditioned with 1 mL of MeOH and equilibrated with 2 mL of H_2O. Supernatants were loaded onto the conditioned columns and were washed with 1 mL of 10:90 MeOH:H_2O. The organic fraction of metabolites was collected by loading 1 mL of MeOH and 1 mL of 60:20:20 Acetonitrile(ACN):MeOH:IPA in duplicate, then evaporated using a steady flow of nitrogen gas and heat of 40 °C. Samples were reconstituted in 100 mL of 50:50:0.01 H_2O:MeOH:formic acid and the solution was transferred into 100 μL autosampler vials for analysis on an AB SCIEX 3200 triple quadrupole mass spectrometer. A processed blank was extracted using the same method. All samples were stored and run in batches.

2.4.2. Calibration Curve

A calibration curve was used to quantify the analytes. Stock solutions were prepared in ethanol with DHA and EPA standards, each at a concentration of 25 mg/mL. DHA and EPA standard solutions were prepared by serial dilution of the stock solutions in ACN to create primary standards at 0.01, 0.05, 0.1, 0.5, 1, 2.5, 5.0, and 7.5 mg/mL. Deuterated DHA and EPA were used as internal standards prepared at 0.5 mg/mL in ethanol. The deuterated DHA and EPA solution controlled for extraction recovery, injection of the mass spectrometer, and ionization variability. The stock solutions were processed and extracted using the same method of the plasma solution.

2.4.3. Liquid Chromatography/Mass Spectrometry (LC/MS/MS)

Extracted samples were run on an AB SCIEX 3200 triple quadrupole mass spectrometer in negative ionization mode using previously published methods [17–19]. Change values for DHA and EPA were calculated between timepoints by subtracting 16-week concentrations from 36-week concentrations.

2.5. Statistical Analyses

Summary statistics were run for maternal descriptors, PUFA-rich foods from the FFQ, as well as levels from maternal blood. For FFQ, data was converted into the average number of times consumed per week as such: rarely or never eat the food = 0, eat the food once every 2 weeks = 0.5 times per week, eat the food 1–3 times/week = 2 times per week, eat the food 4–7 times/week = 5.5 times per week, or eat the food more than once per day = 7 times per week. Both the polyunsaturated margarines and sunflower/soy/corn/olive oils were rated on for whether they were used with foods (i.e., breads, vegetables) and with cooking. For both margarine and oil responses: Yes = 7 per week, No consumption = 0 per week; thus, the potential score for margarine and oils ranged from 0 to 14 considering use with food and with cooking to both questions. The summation of these columns provided the PUFA summary score for each participant during pregnancy. Data are reported as mean ± standard deviation (SD) unless data was not non-normally distributed then median (minimum, maximum) were reported. Difference values were determined by subtracting the 16-week value from the 36-week value for maternal lipid levels. Based on difference values (16 to 36-week change scores), all participants were coded as improved (increased score), no change, or decreased score for all DHA, EPA, and FFQ summary data. Participants that had a decreased DHA or EPA blood value and decreased FFQ value were coded as non-responders, while those with increased DHA or EPA blood values with increased FFQ values were coded as responders. Thus t-tests were completed to compare non-responders with responders. Spearman's rank correlation tests were performed to determine relationships between maternal self-reported consumption of PUFA-rich foods with measured values from blood. Linear regressions were done to determine if self-reported values were predictors of maternal blood levels. Significance level was set a priori at 0.05 and SPSS was used for all analyses (SPSS 25.0 Chicago, IL, USA).

3. Results

Study Population. For this analysis, 156 pregnant women expressed interest; of these women, 145 were qualified and consented. Throughout the study, 38 participants were lost-to-follow-up with participant refusal (n = 6), moved, no time or lost interest (n = 29), discontinued due to drug use (n = 1), discontinued due to bed rest (n = 1), or miscarried (n = 1). Of the remaining 107 participants, 60 were excluded due to missing data for plasma, RBCs, and/or incomplete questionnaire data. Thus, a final sample of 47 pregnant women completed 16-week and 36-week FFQs and venipunctures for this post hoc analysis. On average, participants were 31 years old, had a mean BMI in a healthy range, with appropriate GWG, and delivered full-term healthy babies free from congenital issues (Table 1). The median response from the FFQ was that most women did not consume white fish, other fish, almond/cashew milk, or use polyunsaturated margarine on a regular weekly basis at 16 and 36 weeks gestation; at 16 and 36 weeks, participants reported using oil on foods and for cooking (Table 2). Overall, the PUFA summary decreased from 16 to 36 weeks gestation (Table 2).

Table 1. Maternal descriptors.

	Mean ± SD
Age (years)	30.56 ± 2.63
Gravida [a]	2 (1, 4)
Parity [a]	0 (0, 2)
Pre-pregnancy BMI (kg/m^2) [a]	23.47 (20.5, 42.5)
16-week BMI (kg/m^2) [a]	24.4 (21.5, 43.9)
36-week BMI (kg/m^2) [a]	28.1 (24.76, 43.3)
Education (years) [a]	19 (13, 23)
Gestational weight gain (kg)	12.35 ± 6.42
Gestational age (weeks)	39.83 ± 1.05

All values reported as mean ± SD. [a] Values reported as median (minimum, maximum) and used a Mann–Whitney U test due to non-normal distribution. BMI: body mass index.

Table 2. Self-reported frequency of food consumption per week at 16 and 36 weeks gestation.

Food Intake Categories	16 Weeks	36 Weeks
White fish (servings/wk)	0 (0, 2)	0 (0, 0.5)
Other fish (servings/wk)	0 (0, 0.5)	0 (0, 0.5)
Milk (almond or cashew) (servings/wk)	0 (0, 8)	0 (0, 8)
Polyunsaturated margarine (servings/wk)	0 (0, 0)	0 (0, 0)
Oil number (servings/wk)	7 (0, 14)	7 (0, 14)
PUFA summary [a] (servings/wk)	9.25 ± 7.4	7.8 ± 7.11

All values reported as median (minimum, maximum) and used a Mann–Whitney U test due to non-normal distribution. [a] Values reported as mean ± SD. PUFA: polyunsaturated fatty acid.

3.1. EPA and DHA Status

Both maternal RBC DHA concentration and plasma DHA concentration decreased from 16 to 36 weeks. In contrast, maternal RBC EPA concentration increased from 16 to 36 weeks (Table 3). When comparing participants with overall decreased DHA or EPA blood values and decreased FFQ values (non-responders) to those participants with overall increased DHA or EPA blood values and increased FFQ values (responders), participants that have overall decreased DHA and EPA blood values have significantly increased GWG ($p = 0.02$) with no differences in maternal age, gravida, and pre-pregnancy BMI.

Table 3. Maternal blood EPA and DHA concentrations at 16 and 36 weeks gestation and the difference from early to late pregnancy.

	16 Weeks	36 Weeks	Difference
RBC DHA (ng/dL)	1279.56 ± 631.08	1187.0 (450.2, 6012.0) [a]	−42.2 (−2006.0, 5501.8) [a]
Plasma DHA (ng/dL)	448.02 ± 186.03	415.7 ± 193.89	−32.32 ± 276.17
RBC EPA (ng/dL)	715.18 ± 426.76	930.8 (165.1, 4656.0) [a]	10.95 (−395, 3867) [a]

All values reported as mean ± SD. [a] Values reported as median (minimum, maximum) and used a Mann–Whitney U test due to non-normal distribution. RBC: Red Blood Cell, DHA: docosahexaenoic acid, EPA: eicosapentaenoic acid.

3.2. Correlation Analysis

There were no correlations between maternal DHA or EPA in blood compared to self-reported fish consumption. There were moderate positive correlations between self-reported almond/cashew milk consumption at 36 weeks gestation with 36-week plasma concentration of DHA ($p = 0.01$, r = 0.582) as well as with the change value of plasma DHA ($p = 0.041$, r = 0.473) from 16 to 36 weeks (Table 4). Similarly, self-reported 36-week DHA- and EPA-rich oil consumption (sunflower/soy/corn/olive) moderately correlates with 16-week EPA on RBCs ($p = 0.04$, r = −0.306), 36-week plasma DHA ($p = 0.046$, r = 0.464), and the change in plasma DHA ($p = 0.02$, r = 0.519) from 16 to 36 weeks (Table 4). Lastly, self-reported 36-week PUFA-rich summary score moderately correlates with 36-week plasma DHA ($p = 0.01$, r = 0.566), and the change in plasma DHA ($p = 0.01$, r = 0.567) from 16 to 36 weeks gestation (Table 4).

Table 4. Correlation between self-reported PUFA-rich food consumption and maternal blood and plasma DHA or EPA concentrations.

Measure	*p*-Value	Pearson Correlation
16-week PUFA-rich foods summary		
RBC EPA difference	0.055	0.282
36-week milk (almond or cashew) consumption		
36-week plasma DHA	0.009	0.582
Difference plasma DHA	0.041	0.473
36-week PUFA oil consumption		
36-week plasma DHA	0.046	0.464
Difference plasma DHA	0.023	0.519
16-week RBC EPA	0.037	−0.306
36-week PUFA-rich foods summary		
36-week plasma DHA	0.012	0.566
Difference plasma DHA	0.011	0.567

3.3. Regression Analysis

We found predictive models for plasma and RBC concentrations of EPA and DHA (Table 5). Controlling for gravida and 16-week self-reported PUFA-rich food summary, 16-week maternal BMI ($p = 0.01$) predicted 16-week maternal EPA on RBCs (Table 5); this suggests that changes in 1 unit of BMI correlates with about 2 ng/dL of maternal EPA, which may not be clinically meaningful. When controlling for gravida and GWG, 36-week self-reported PUFA oil consumption ($p = 0.02$) significantly predicted 36-week plasma DHA (Table 5); this suggests that if women added 2–3 servings/day of PUFA oil, this could increase plasma DHA by 10 ng/dL, which could result in clinically meaningful differences. Other models that approached significance or did not have any significant individual predictors are not shown.

Table 5. Regression models to predict DHA and EPA levels in maternal blood.

	p-Value	95% CI Lower Bound	95% CI Upper Bound	Beta Value	STD Error
16-week RBC EPA (Model 1)		**p-value = 0.045 * Adjusted R^2 = 0.111**			
16-week PUFA-rich food summary	0.65	−30.641	19.232	−0.069	12.365
16-week BMI	0.01 *	−53.157	−6.463	−0.368	11.577
Difference in RBC EPA (Model 2)		**p-value = 0.046 * Adjusted R^2 = 0.154**			
Age	0.08	−150.318	9.005	−0.27	39.316
Education	0.08	−358.107	22.805	−0.321	93.997
16-week PUFA-rich food summary	0.23	−25.153	99.696	0.189	30.809
36-week plasma DHA (Model 3)		**p-value= 0.044 * Adjusted R^2 = 0.333**			
Gestational weight gain	0.09	−0.878	11.674	0.393	2.926
36-week other fish consumption	0.051	−1.07	758.032	0.443	176.964
36-week PUFA oil consumption	0.02 *	2.956	35.063	0.548	7.485

BMI: body mass index; PUFA: polyunsaturated fatty acid. Bolded headers indicate significant models. * $p < 0.05$. Non-significant measures in each regression model includes: Model 1: gravida; Model 2: gravida, 16-week BMI; Model 3: gravida.

4. Discussion

The purpose of the study was: (1) to measure DHA and EPA levels from maternal blood in early and late pregnancy, and (2) to determine the association, and possible predictors, between self-reported consumption of PUFA-containing foods with DHA and EPA concentrations in maternal blood in early and late pregnancy. We hypothesized that: (1) PUFA-rich foods, DHA, and EPA levels will be similar in early and late pregnancy, and (2) there will be a positive correlation, and possible predictors, between self-reported PUFA-rich food consumption and circulating PUFA concentrations which was consistent with our findings. Our main findings were as follows: (1) DHA levels in maternal blood, and self-reported PUFA-food average weekly consumption, decreased from 16 to 36 weeks gestation; (2) self-reported PUFA-rich food average weekly consumption positively correlates with measured DHA and EPA levels in blood; and (3) DHA, but not EPA, concentration in blood was predicted by self-reported PUFA oils consumption.

We found both self-reported PUFA-food weekly consumption and measured DHA levels decreased from early to late pregnancy, which was different than expected. This suggests that there is decreased maternal consumption of PUFA-rich oils as pregnancy progresses. Previous literature on this topic reports conflicting results. One study notes that serum fatty acid concentrations of DHA, EPA, and total omega-3 PUFA's increase from the first to second trimester, with a slight, but continued, increase from the second to third trimester, which was attributed to an increase in lipids transported across the placenta after 20 weeks gestation [20]; however, our study was of US women with MS technology and the previous findings were in Brazilian women and LC technology, possibly explaining the difference in findings. Similar to our findings, another study reported decreasing levels of maternal plasma levels of DHA from 27 weeks gestation until delivery [21]. One further longitudinal study from Spain found an increase of total omega-6 PUFA's, a decrease of EPA, and no significant change of DHA, from the first to the third trimester of maternal plasma [22]. In the present study, decreasing concentrations of DHA on RBCs and in plasma were found from early and late pregnancy. The decreasing levels of DHA may be explained by a decrease in consumption of DHA and EPA-containing oils throughout the pregnancy. Previous studies have focused on the intake of fish throughout pregnancy [8]; whereas the present study suggests a potential recommendation of increasing maternal PUFA-rich oil intake during pregnancy. Since those with generally decreased DHA or EPA in blood and on the questionnaire have significantly increased GWG, further research is needed to determine why these women may have an overall decrement in nutrition quality as pregnancy progresses.

As we hypothesized, we found self-reported 36-week PUFA-rich average weekly food consumption positively correlates with DHA and EPA levels at 36 weeks. Similar to the present study, previous research by Kobayashi et al. found a correlation between food intake and serum levels of EPA ($R = 0.37$) and DHA ($R = 0.27$) during pregnancy [8]. This study utilized a FFQ which had users rate foods such as fish, shellfish, and other fish products based on consumption and portion size during early (8–14 weeks) and late (26–35 weeks) gestation in Japan [8]. This differed from the current study in which correlations were analyzed for specific foods, allowing further assessment of which food items correlate best with the blood sample findings. Furthermore, the FFQ utilized in the Kobayashi et al. study has limited accuracy in measuring cooking oil as a possible source of PUFA intake; this is a limitation that our study was able to address [8]. Other research evaluated the validation of a FFQ measuring PUFA status in non-pregnant adults [7]. This study found a positive correlation between self-reported dietary DHA intake, specifically fish, with plasma DHA, but no correlation between plasma EPA [7]. The discrepancy between these findings and our findings of a positive correlation with both plasma DHA and EPA could be due to the type of FFQ used. The FFQ utilized in the previously mentioned research emphasized PUFA status from fish consumption, whereas the questionnaire utilized in the present study emphasized PUFA-rich foods, such as fish, oils, and margarine. These details provide validation regarding the participant's diet relative to a sensitive measure of EPA and DHA intake, thus accounting for the difference in results.

Finally, we found that 36-week DHA concentration was predicted by 36-week self-reported PUFA oil consumption, but EPA concentrations were predicted by maternal BMI. These findings suggest that maternal DHA levels could potentially be estimated by FFQ self-reported PUFA oil levels during pregnancy. This would provide a non-invasive method of assessing late pregnancy PUFA status, to ensure recommended levels are met, as an essential part of proper fetal development. Interestingly, maternal EPA concentrations were predicted with a negative association with maternal BMI. Similar to our findings, a study by Young et al. reported a negative association between BMI of non-pregnant women and omega-3 index [22]. The negative association was proposed to be due to altered metabolic pathways in the absorption and utilization of omega-3 fatty acids in women with obesity compared to healthy BMI [22]. The similar findings between our study and that of Young et al. suggests that the utilization of EPA is similar in non-gravid and gravid women. Further research is needed to accurately define the role of maternal BMI, most likely adiposity status, in pregnant women and EPA concentrations.

The strengths of our study include the unique comparison of early and late pregnant women with blood samples and questionnaire data. While our study provides valuable insights, this research is not without its limitations. First, the small sample and non-normally distributed variables, may influence linear regression analysis; however, the uniqueness of the data argue for further investigation with a larger sample to enable the accuracy and efficiency of linear regression estimates. With more data, the type 2 error in the study would be reduced, leading to a higher sensitivity and greater generalizability of the outcomes. Furthermore, as with any self-report method for assessment, there is a potential for self-reported bias when responding. Women may feel compelled to alter their answers based on what they think they should be consuming, not what they consumed. It is important to note that some of the foods contained in the FFQ contained omega-3 and omega-6 fats; therefore, further research needs to explore how women's self-reported response relates to blood levels of both types of unsaturated fats. However, given the correlation between the self-reported data and the direct measurement of blood variables and the low-cost, patient- and clinic-friendly use of FFQ relative to the use of venipuncture, this warrants further investigation.

Future research should expand upon the current study by assessing neonatal outcomes according to self-reported PUFA status. Furthermore, more research can be done to optimize the use of the FFQ and address a larger, more diverse pregnant population. The FFQ from the present study can be implemented in OB/GYN clinics with the goal of providing patient knowledge on PUFA-containing foods and creating obtainable goals for patients on the amount of those foods to consume. Further research should focus on overall nutrition quality in those women who have trends of increased GWG. This may create more education for patients and create better outcomes for neonates.

5. Conclusions

In conclusion, the present study found that average weekly PUFA consumption and blood levels seem to decrease throughout pregnancy. Importantly, the Sheffield FFQ seems to be an effective method for estimating late pregnancy DHA and EPA blood levels. This research allows for a compelling and non-invasive method for estimating DHA and EPA concentration in pregnant women, especially the third trimester. Furthermore, by utilizing a FFQ, women can be aware of their DHA and EPA status, thus, allowing a simpler approach for patients and clinical professionals to track PUFA intake throughout pregnancy. The present study provides insight into an easy, cost-effective method for estimating DHA and EPA status in pregnant women but warrants further nutrition analysis. Overall, the Sheffield FFQ might provide a noninvasive, low-cost method to estimate DHA and EPA status, especially in late pregnancy; however, further investigation with a larger sample is warranted.

Author Contributions: K.L. assisted writing the manuscript, formatted data in the tables, and performed literature review; B.W. assisted writing the manuscript, sample collection, formatted data; C.S. assisted writing the manuscript, preparing and cleaning data, sample collection, and running the DHA and EPA serum analysis; C.A.J. assisted with the data analysis; C.I., J.D. and E.N. assisted with the recruitment, retention of participants as well as review of the manuscript; R.P., B.R.A.-T. and S.M. assisted with the data interpretation, and review of the manuscript; L.E.M. completed study design, recruitment, oversaw all aspects of project, obtained funding, oversaw sample collection and processing, oversaw data cleaning and analysis, led/assisted/the writing process. All authors have read and agreed to the published version of the manuscript.

Funding: American Heart Association (AHA grant #15GRNT24470029; #18IPA34150006) and by ECU Internal Funds.

Institutional Review Board Statement: The study was conducted in accordance with the Declaration of Helsinki and approved by the Institutional Review Board of East Carolina University (protocol code IRB # 12-002524 and approved on 30 September 2021.

Informed Consent Statement: Written informed consent was obtained from the participants prior to publishing results.

Data Availability Statement: De-identified data can be shared upon request to the corresponding author.

Conflicts of Interest: The authors report no conflict of interest.

References

1. Greenberg, J.A.; Bell, S.J.; Ausdal, W.V. Omega-3 Fatty Acid supplementation during pregnancy. *Rev. Obstet. Gynecol.* **2008**, *1*, 162–169. [PubMed]
2. Denomme, J.; Stark, K.D.; Holub, B.J. Directly quantitated dietary (n − 3) fatty acid intakes of pregnant Canadian women are lower than current dietary recommendations. *J. Nutr.* **2005**, *135*, 206–211. [CrossRef] [PubMed]
3. Casado-Díaz, A.; Santiago-Mora, R.; Dorado, G.; Quesada-Gómez, J.M. The omega-6 arachidonic fatty acid, but not the omega-3 fatty acids, inhibits osteoblastogenesis and induces adipogenesis of human mesenchymal stem cells: Potential implication in osteoporosis. *Osteoporos. Int.* **2013**, *24*, 1647–1661. [CrossRef] [PubMed]
4. Innis, S.M. Dietary (n − 3) fatty acids and brain development. *J. Nutr.* **2007**, *137*, 855–859. [CrossRef]

Control and Prevention (CDC) suggests that gestational anemia can be indicated by an Hb level of <6.83 mmol/L (<11 g/dL) in the first and third trimesters and that of <6.52 mmol/L (<10.5 g/dL) in the second trimester [4].

Gestational anemia increases the incidence rates of perinatal mortality, stillbirth, abnormal or retarded brain growth, and fetal morbidity [5,6]. Iron deficiency anemia is the most common type of gestational anemia and indicated by a serum ferritin level of <0.034 nmol/L (<15 μg/L) [7]. Other common causes of gestational anemia include folate (megaloblastic anemia) or vitamin B_{12} (pernicious anemia) deficiency, which contributes to maternal morbidities [8,9]. Fetal nutrient deficiencies may result from congenital abnormality, low birth weight, and preterm delivery [10,11]. Iron is a key micronutrient essential for tissue oxygenation and erythropoiesis. Blood loss, decreased iron intake, and impaired iron absorption could contribute to iron deficiency [12]. Gestational iron storage and the absorption of dietary iron are important for the maintenance of iron homeostasis. Ferritin is a protein form which stores iron and serves as a preliminary predictor of lower hemoglobin and anemia [13,14]. Hence, in the present study, the major variables related to anemia were ferritin followed by hemoglobin and serum iron levels. In a study that took place in the UK and Australia, a serum ferritin test in the first trimester was suggested to verify whether pregnant women needed to be referred for iron therapy, and serum ferritin levels were considered to be assessed in the first antenatal visit for women from areas with a high prevalence of iron-deficiency anemia, along with a full blood count test in early pregnancy for women at high risk of iron-deficiency anemia [15]. Additionally, a prospective cohort study of maternal and infant health and nutrition surveillance in Bangladesh determined maternal plasma ferritin levels at gestational weeks 14 and 30 and found that plasma ferritin levels in the late gestation of pregnancy were negatively correlated with infant birth weight [16], indicating the crucial role of ferritin as a form of iron storage in fetal growth outcome.

Several dietary nutrients affect iron balance, and the antioxidant vitamin C, as an acidic substance, promotes iron absorption [17]. Most earlier studies have focused on the role of vitamin C in dietary iron absorption [18,19]. However, few studies have explored the association between dietary patterns (DPs) and vitamin D levels in women with gestational anemia. Iron absorption was reportedly enhanced by vitamin D through reducing the levels of hepcidin and proinflammatory cytokines [20,21]. However, the role of vitamin D in anemia prevention and iron absorption remains controversial [22]. In animal- and population-based pregnancy studies, Qiu et al. [23] and Si et al. [24] both reported a positive association between blood vitamin D levels and iron status. A cross-sectional study conducted by Mayasari et al. revealed an association between dietary intake and serum hepcidin levels during pregnancy [25]. Furthermore, an evidence-based study conducted by Michalski et al. among Vietnamese women of reproductive age reported a positive association between serum, instead of dietary, vitamin D and Hb levels [26]. Additionally, Wong et al. found that serum vitamin D levels were positively associated with serum ferritin levels in Chinese pregnant women [27]. However, the aforementioned studies did not explore any other iron-related biomarkers. Our knowledge regarding DPs, vitamin D levels, and iron status remains limited. In the present study, DP was used as a supportive approach to investigate the association between overall dietary factors and disease outcomes [28]. Thus, we investigated the association of DPs with vitamin D levels and other iron-related biomarkers in pregnant women.

2. Materials and Methods

2.1. Study Design and Population Demographics

This population-based cross-sectional study was conducted using a database associated with the Nationwide Nutrition and Health Survey in Pregnant Women in Taiwan (2017–2019; Pregnant NAHSIT 2017–2019). Relevant data were collected from a total of 11 recognized hospitals in Taiwan. The inclusion criteria were as follows: being aged >15 years; receiving a maternal handbook; using an obstetric inspection service more than once; being able to communicate in Mandarin, Taiwanese, and other languages; and being willing to participate in our study and provide consent. The exclusion criteria included having multiparity (>3) and being nonresponsive.

The data of 1502 pregnant women were used in the present study. After the participants signed the consent form, the researchers assigned the date for collecting data during their prenatal visits. The collected data were classified into the following four categories: sociodemographic, anthropometric, biochemical, and dietary (including supplements, such as milk powder, multivitamin/multimineral, iron, vitamin B complex, folate, vitamin D, and calcium, and dietary assessment) data. Sociodemographic and anthropometric data were obtained using a self-reported questionnaire, whereas dietary data were collected by well-trained registered dieticians during face-to-face interviews with the women. The data collection from all the questionnaires took 60–90 min. Biochemical analyses were performed using blood samples collected during prenatal visits. This study was approved by the Joint Institutional Review Board of Taipei Medical University, Taiwan (approval number: TMU-JIRB N201707039) and conducted in accordance with the ethical principles of the Declaration of Helsinki.

2.2. Dietary Assessment

Dietary assessment was performed using a 24 h dietary recall method and a validated semiquantitative food frequency questionnaire (FFQ) modified from the NAHSIT FFQ [25]. Food pictures and measurement cups or spoons were used when 24 h dietary recall was conducted by registered dieticians. The FFQ is the most commonly used, reliable, and cost-effective tool for nutrition surveys and has high reproducibility [29]. A total of 59 food items were identified using the FFQ. For the present study, a total of 32 food groups were developed based on the categories and nutrient contents of the aforementioned food items [25]. Food items having similar nutrient characteristics were categorized under the same group (Supplementary Table S1).

The daily, weekly, or monthly frequencies of food intake were recorded in the FFQ. The total monthly frequency of a particular food group was calculated. According to the 24 h dietary recall data, nutrient intake was calculated using Cofit Pro (Cofit Healthcare, Taipei, Taiwan), an online software available on the Taiwan Food Nutrient Database.

DPs can be determined using two approaches: a priori (a hypothesis-derived prospective study) and a posteriori (a data-driven, frequency-based retrospective study) methods [30]. Principal component analysis (PCA) was performed in the present study to determine the DPs of the women, because PCA (an a posteriori method) offered the highest interpretability with minimal information loss and reduced dataset dimensionality [31].

2.3. Anthropometric and Biochemical Data Collection

Pre-pregnancy body mass index (BMI) was calculated using body weight (kg) divided by height (m^2). Both body weight and height before pregnancy were self-reported and collected in the questionnaire. Blood was drawn from the median cubital and cephalic veins. Serum hemoglobin (Hb) levels were measured using a hematology analyzer (Sysmex Corp., Kobe, Japan). Serum iron levels (μmol/L) were determined spectrophotometrically using a Beckman Coulter Unicel DxC 800 (Beckman Coulter, Brea, CA, USA) after iron was released by acetic acid from transferrin and reduced to ferrous iron by hydroxylamine and thioglycolate [25]. Serum ferritin levels were assessed by an enzyme-linked immunosorbent assay using the Beckman Coulter Unicel DxC 800 (Beckman Coulter, Brea, CA, USA) [25]. The total iron-binding capacity (TIBC, μmol/L) was evaluated by the colorimetric immunoassay method using the Beckman Coulter Unicel DxC 800 (Beckman Coulter, Brea, CA, USA) [32]. Transferrin saturation (%) was calculated by the percentage of serum iron levels divided by the TIBC value [33]. The serum levels of folate [34] and vitamin B_{12} [35] were measured using SimulTRAC-SNB radioimmunoassay kits (MP Biomedicals, Santa Ana, CA, USA) with ^{125}I or ^{57}Co as the tracer, respectively. Serum 25(OH) vitamin D levels were determined by an electrochemiluminescence immunoassay using an Elecsys vitamin

D total reagent kit with ruthenium-labeled vitamin-D-binding protein (Roche Diagnostics Ltd., Taipei, Taiwan) [36].

2.4. *Anthropometric and Biochemical Parameters in Gestational Anemia*

The Ministry of Health and Welfare, Taiwan, has recommended the following BMI-based classification of adults: underweight (<18.5 kg/m^2), normal weight (18.5 to <24 kg/m^2), overweight (24 to <27 kg/m^2), and obesity (>27 kg/m^2) [37]. Gestational anemia was defined according to the criteria outlined by the WHO and CDC. The normal cutoff values of serum iron and TIBC in women without anemia are 10.7 µmol/L (60 µg/dL) [38] and 42.96–80.55 µmol/L (240–450 µg/dL) [39]. The WHO recommends the following cutoff values for gestational anemia: serum ferritin level <0.034 nmol/L (<15 µg/L) [40] and transferrin saturation <16% [41]. The reference levels of serum folate for all age populations are 13.6–45.3 nmol/L (6–20 ng/mL) [42]. The Endocrine Society has defined vitamin D insufficiency as a vitamin D level of <75 nmol/L (<30 ng/mL) [43].

2.5. *Statistical Analysis*

Statistical analysis was performed using SPSS (version 22.0, IBM Corp., Armonk, NY, USA) and SAS (version 9.4, SAS Institute Inc., Chicago, IL, USA). A one-way analysis of variance was used for continuous variables expressed as mean ± standard deviation, whereas the chi-square test was used for categorical variables expressed as number and percentage. Tukey's post hoc multiple comparisons were performed to determine significant within-group differences among continuous variables. We identified DPs by PCA using SAS. A total of four DPs were identified through orthogonal varimax rotation with a mean eigenvalue of 1.0 and a factor loading of >0.30 [44]. Factor loadings of <0.30 were omitted for simplification. A high factor loading indicates a strong association between food groups and disease. For each DP, DP scores were calculated by total food intake (frequency/month) times factor loading. We used the following three models to verify the association between DPs and blood biomarker levels: model 1 (crude model), model 2 (adjusted for age, region of residence, parity, and trimester), and model 3 (adjusting factors in model 2 plus daily dietary intake). A simple linear regression analysis was conducted using the independent (DP) and dependent (biochemical biomarkers) variables to identify the trend (positive or negative) of association. Data are presented in terms of the regression of coefficient (β) and 95% confidence intervals (CIs). For further confirmation, each DP was categorized into tertiles. Tertiles 1 (T1), 2 (T2), and 3 (T3) represent the lowest, mid, and highest DP scores, respectively. Furthermore, a binomial logistic regression analysis was performed to identify the disease trend across the tertiles of each DP and biochemical biomarkers, and the odds ratios (ORs) of T2 and T3 were compared with the reference group (T1). Data are presented in terms of odds ratios and 95% CIs. The OR value of >1 or <1 with statistical significance indicates increased or decreased disease risk, whereas OR = 1 represents nonsignificant effects [45]. Statistical significance was set at $p \leq 0.05$.

3. Results

3.1. *Sociodemographic and Anthropometric Characteristics of the Women*

Pregnant women in T3 of serum vitamin D were older (32.9 ± 4.9 vs. 32.0 ± 4.7 years) than those in T1 of serum vitamin D (Table 1). Most pregnant women in T3 of serum vitamin D lived in the southern part of Taiwan (32%), were primiparous (49.3%), and were in the third trimester of pregnancy (53%). The women across the vitamin D tertiles did not differ significantly in terms of education level, family monthly income, duration of sun exposure, or BMI.

Table 1. Sociodemographic and anthropometric characteristics of the women across the tertiles of serum vitamin D (n = 1502) [1].

Variables	Total (n)	Tertiles of Serum Vitamin D [2]			p-Value [3]
		T1 (n = 505)	T2 (n = 486)	T3 (n = 511)	
Sociodemographic Data					
Age (years)	1502	32.0 ± 4.7 [a]	32.7 ± 4.7 [ab]	32.9 ± 4.9 [b]	0.008
Region of residence	1499				0.000
Northern		231 (45.8)	153 (31.5)	117 (23.0)	
Central		130 (25.8)	124 (25.5)	117 (23.0)	
Southern		51 (10.1)	77 (15.8)	163 (32.0)	
Eastern and other		92 (18.3)	132 (27.2)	112 (22.0)	
Parity	1497				0.002
1		306 (60.7)	267 (55.2)	251 (49.3)	
2		164 (32.5)	170 (35.1)	193 (37.9)	
≥3		34 (6.8)	47 (9.7)	65 (12.8)	
Trimester	1502				0.000
First, weeks 0–12		172 (34.1)	125 (25.7)	78 (15.3)	
Second, weeks 13–26		164 (32.5)	159 (32.7)	162 (31.7)	
Third, weeks 27–40		169 (33.4)	202 (41.6)	271 (53.0)	
Education	1493				0.165
≤Junior high school		68 (13.5)	72 (15.0)	97 (19.1)	
College or university		355 (70.3)	330 (68.8)	340 (66.9)	
Graduate school		82 (16.2)	78 (16.2)	71 (14.0)	
Monthly income (NTD)	1474				0.117
<30,000		63 (12.6)	69 (14.8)	80 (15.8)	
30,000–59,999		209 (41.7)	187 (40.1)	238 (46.9)	
60,000–99,999		162 (32.3)	150 (32.2)	131 (25.8)	
≥100,000		67 (13.4)	60 (12.9)	58 (11.5)	
Sun exposure (min/d)					
<10		158 (31.3)	147 (30.4)	155 (30.5)	
10 to <20	1498	155 (30.7)	150 (31.0)	144 (28.2)	0.676
20 to <60		172 (34.0)	158 (32.6)	179 (35.2)	
≥60		20 (4.0)	29 (6.0)	31 (6.1)	
Anthropometric Data					
Pre-pregnant BMI (kg/m^2)	1479	22.4 ± 3.9	22.9 ± 4.2	22.8 ± 4.0	0.082
<18.5		52 (10.5)	45 (9.4)	44 (8.7)	0.739
18.5 to <24.0		312 (62.9)	285 (59.6)	309 (61.2)	
24.0 to <27.0		71 (14.3)	76 (15.9)	84 (16.6)	
≥27		61 (12.3)	72 (15.1)	68 (13.5)	

[1] Continuous data are presented as the mean ± standard deviation, whereas categorical data are presented as the number and percentage in the parentheses. Different superscript letters for continuous variables indicate significantly different ($p \leq 0.05$) using Turkey's post hoc test. [2] Tertiles of serum vitamin D levels: T1: 20 to >53 nmol/L, T2: 54 to >71 nmol/L, and T3: 72 to 154 nmol/L. [3] The p-value was determined using one-way analysis of variance test for continuous variables and chi-square test for categorical variables. BMI, body mass index.

3.2. Biochemical Characteristics of the Women

Pregnant women in T3 of serum vitamin D had higher levels of serum Hb (7.4 ± 1.3 mmol/L), iron (13.9 ± 7.8 μmol/L), TIBC (85.6 ± 17.1 μmol/L), folate (32.3 ± 17.0 nmol/L), and vitamin B_{12} (249.0 ± 169.8 pmol/L), but lower serum ferritin levels (0.05 ± 0.05 nmol/L) than those in T1 of serum vitamin D did (Table 2). Categorical classification revealed that the levels of serum Hb and folate were >6.76 mmol/L and ≥13.5 nmol/L, respectively, in most women in T3 of serum vitamin D. The number of individuals with anemia defined as Hb <6.83 mmol/L (<11 g/dL) in trimesters 1 and 3 or Hb <6.52 mmol/L (10.5 g/dL) in trimester 2 was 322 (21.4%), and we did not further analyze the data based on the pregnant women with or without anemia due to there being much fewer women with anemia compared with those without anemia.

Table 2. Biochemical characteristics of the women across the tertiles of serum vitamin D (n = 1502) [1].

Serum Variables	Tertiles of Serum Vitamin D [2]			
	T1 (n = 505)	T2 (n = 486)	T3 (n = 511)	p-Value [3]
Hemoglobin (mmol/L)	7.2 ± 1.1 [a]	7.3 ± 1.2 [ab]	7.4 ± 1.3 [b]	0.038
<4.34	4 (0.8)	5 (1.0)	1 (0.2)	0.051
4.34–6.14	38 (7.5)	43 (8.9)	42 (8.2)	
6.15–6.76	80 (15.8)	50 (10.3)	59 (11.5)	
6.77–8.69	364 (72.1)	369 (75.9)	376 (73.6)	
>8.69	19 (3.8)	19 (3.9)	33 (6.5)	
Iron (µmol/L)	12.0 ± 6.8 [a]	12.8 ± 6.6 [a]	13.9 ± 7.8 [b]	0.000
Ferritin (nmol/L)	0.06± 0.15 [a]	0.05 ± 0.06 [ab]	0.05 ± 0.05 [b]	0.028
TIBC (µmol/L)	81.5 ± 19.9 [a]	83.2 ± 17.2 [ab]	85.6 ± 17.1 [b]	0.001
Transferrin saturation (%)	16.2 ± 9.4	16.6 ± 10.1	16.7 ± 10.2	0.779
Folate (nmol/L)	25.5 ± 15.6 [a]	29.2 ± 16.6 [b]	32.3 ± 17.0 [c]	0.000
<6.8	13 (2.6)	10 (2.0)	10 (2.0)	0.000
6.8–13.4	101 (20.0)	65 (13.4)	54 (10.6)	
13.5–45.3	342 (67.7)	346 (71.2)	349 (68.3)	
>45.3	49 (9.7)	65 (13.4)	98 (19.2)	
Vitamin B_{12} (pmol/L)	215.1 ± 154.9 [a]	232.1 ± 108.9 [ab]	249.0 ± 169.8 [b]	0.001
Vitamin D (nmol/L)	42.4 ± 8.0 [a]	62.3 ± 5.2 [b]	89.1 ± 15.1 [c]	0.000

[1] Continuous data are presented as the mean ± standard deviation, whereas categorical data are presented as the number and percentage in the parentheses. Different superscript letters for continuous variables indicate significant difference ($p \leq 0.05$) using Turkey's post hoc test. [2] Tertiles of serum vitamin D levels: T1: 20 to >53 nmol/L, T2: 54 to >71 nmol/L, and T3: 72 to 154 nmol/L. [3] The p-value was determined using one-way analysis of variance test for continuous variables and chi-square test for categorical variables. TIBC, total iron-binding capacity.

3.3. Dietary Intake of the Women

Daily dietary intakes of energy, macronutrients, iron, folate, vitamin B_{12}, and vitamin D were determined using 24 h dietary recall data. Pregnant women in T3 of serum vitamin D had higher intakes of protein (g), fat (g and % of energy), iron, folate, and vitamin D, but lower intakes of carbohydrates (% of energy) than those in T1 of serum vitamin D did (Supplementary Table S2). No significant differences were found in pregnant women across the tertiles of serum vitamin D in terms of energy or vitamin B_{12} intake.

Pregnant women in T3 of serum vitamin D had higher monthly intake frequencies for supplements of multivitamin/multimineral, folate, and calcium than those in T1 of serum vitamin D did (Supplementary Table S2). Other dietary supplements such as milk powder (17.6%), iron (11.2%), vitamin B complex (18.0%), and vitamin D (11.1%) were not assessed for the monthly intake frequency because a lower proportion (<20%) of the women took these supplements.

3.4. Dietary Patterns

The PCA revealed a total of four DPs (Figure 1). All four DPs explained total variance of 9.35% (4.37%, 1.93%, 1.61%, and 1.44%). DPs were categorized and ranked on the basis of a threshold factor loading value (>0.30). Each DP was named according to their corresponding factor loading values and dietary component structures. The first pattern comprising a total of ten food groups was named the plant-based DP (DP-1) because the highest factor loadings were exhibited by bamboo shoots and melons; mushroom and related products; carrots, roots, and tubers; dark-colored vegetables; and legumes and various beans. Other food groups in DP-1 included marine plants and kelp; nuts and nut products; animal organ meat and blood; general soy products and gluten pasta; and aquatic fish, shell, shellfish, and seafood. The second pattern was named the carnivore

DP (DP-2), which comprised the following six food groups from the highest to the lowest factor loadings: livestock lean meat; poultry meat; livestock lean meat; processed meat and meat products; herbs and spices; and salt. The third pattern was named the processed food DP (DP-3), which comprised the following six food groups: cake, pastry, and dumplings; salty buns and sweet buns; glutinous rice desserts and rhizome starch; pickled vegetables; deep water fish; and seafood products. Finally, the fourth pattern was named the dairy and non-dairy alternatives DP (DP-4), which comprised the following six food groups: milk and milk products; nondairy products, such as soy and rice milk; eggs; breakfast cereals and bread and related products; noodles and related products; and 100% pure juice and commercially available vegetable juice.

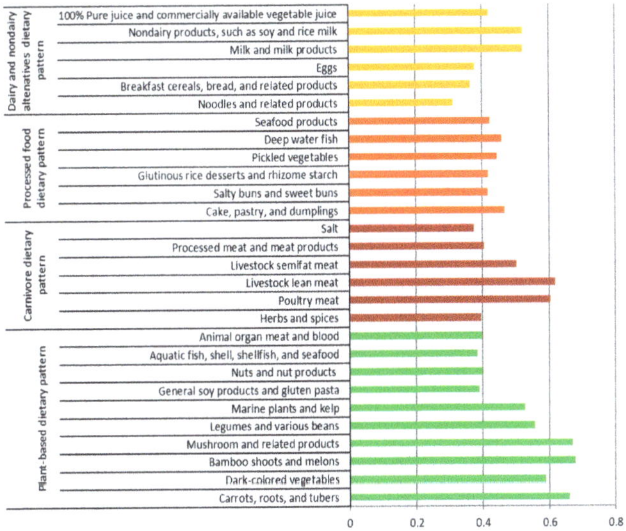

Figure 1. Factor loading of four dietary patterns identified by principal component analysis. The factor loadings of <0.30 were eliminated for simplification.

3.5. Association of DPs with Serum-Anemia-Related Biochemical Variables

Table 3 presents the association between plant-based DP (DP-1) and anemia-related biochemical variables. Serum ferritin levels in the crude model (model 1) were negatively (β: −0.06, 95% CI: −0.29, −0.01, $p \leq 0.05$) associated with DP-1, but after covariate adjustment, there was no significant association between serum ferritin levels and DP-1. In contrast, serum TIBC in model 1 (β: 0.09, 95% CI: 0.02, 0.10, $p \leq 0.001$) and serum vitamin D levels in all three models (model 1: β: 0.08, 95% CI: 0.02, 0.08, $p \leq 0.01$; model 2: β: 0.06, 95% CI: 0.00, 0.06, $p \leq 0.05$; model 3: β: 0.04, 95% CI: −0.00, 0.05, $p \leq 0.05$) were positively associated with DP-1.

As shown in Table 4, in all the three models, carnivore DP (DP-2) was correlated with the reduction in serum iron levels by 0.07–0.08 μmol/L (model 1: β: −0.08, 95% CI: −0.49, −0.10, $p \leq 0.01$; model 2: β: −0.07, 95% CI: −0.47, −0.07, $p \leq 0.01$; model 3: β: −0.08, 95% CI: −0.50, −0.11, $p \leq 0.01$). In addition, DP-2 was associated with the decrease in serum ferritin levels by 0.06 nmol/L (95% CI: −0.46, −0.04, $p \leq 0.05$) but the increase in serum TIBC levels by 0.08 μmol/L (95% CI: 0.02, 0.10, $p \leq 0.01$) in model 1. Changes in serum ferritin and TIBC levels were not significant after covariate adjustment. In all three models, serum vitamin D levels were positively associated with DP-2, and the increase in serum vitamin D ranged from 0.04 to 0.08 nmol/L (model 1: β: 0.08, 95% CI: 0.02, 0.10, $p \leq 0.01$; model 2: β: 0.06, 95% CI: 0.00, 0.08, $p \leq 0.05$; model 3: β: 0.04, 95% CI: −0.00, 0.07, $p \leq 0.05$).

Table 3. The association of plant-based dietary pattern with anemia-related biochemical variables in serum evaluated by the generalized linear regression analysis [1].

Variables	Model 1	Model 2	Model 3
	β (95% CI)	β (95% CI)	β (95% CI)
Hemoglobin (mmol/L)	−0.04 (−1.76, 1.50)	0.01 (−1.42, 1.85)	0.00 (−1.52, 1.13)
Iron (μmol/L)	−0.04 (−0.46, 0.08)	−0.03 (−0.45, 1.01)	−0.03 (−0.46, 0.09)
Ferritin (nmol/L)	−0.06 (−0.29, −0.01) *	−0.02 (−0.20, 0.07)	−0.02 (−0.19, 0.09)
TIBC (μmol/L)	0.09 (0.02, 0.10) ***	0.02 (−0.01, 0.03)	0.02 (−0.01, 0.03)
Transferrin saturation (%)	0.00 (−0.01, 0.01)	0.00 (−0.01, 0.01)	−0.00 (−0.01, 0.01)
Folate (nmol/L)	0.01 (−0.02, 0.03)	0.02 (−0.01, 0.03)	0.02 (−0.01, 0.03)
Vitamin B_{12} (pmol/L)	−0.04 (−0.36, 0.04)	−0.02 (−0.28, 0.11)	−0.02 (−0.27, 0.13)
Vitamin D (nmol/L)	0.08 (0.02, 0.08) **	0.06 (0.00, 0.06) *	0.04 (−0.00, 0.05) *

[1] The values of β and data in the parentheses indicate regression coefficient and 95% confidence interval (95% CI), respectively, after covariate adjustment in different models: model 1, crude model; model 2, adjusted for age, region of residence, parity, and trimester; and model 3, adjusted for age, region of residence, parity, trimester, and daily dietary intake, such as energy (kcal), carbohydrate (% of energy), protein (g and % of energy), fat (g and % of energy), iron (mg), folate (μg), and vitamin D (μg). * $p \leq 0.05$, ** $p \leq 0.01$, and *** $p \leq 0.001$. TIBC, total iron-binding capacity.

Table 4. The association of carnivore dietary pattern with anemia-related biochemical variables in serum evaluated by the generalized linear regression analysis [1].

Variables	Model 1	Model 2	Model 3
	β (95% CI)	β (95% CI)	β (95% CI)
Hemoglobin (mmol/L)	−0.03 (−1.82, 0.43)	−0.02 (−1.56, 0.74)	−0.02 (−1.60, 0.69)
Iron (μmol/L)	−0.08 (−0.49, −0.10) **	−0.07 (−0.47, −0.07) **	−0.08 (−0.50, −0.11) **
Ferritin (nmol/L)	−0.06 (−0.46, −0.04) *	−0.03 (−0.34, 0.06)	−0.03 (−0.32, 0.08)
TIBC (μmol/L)	0.08 (0.02, 0.10) **	0.02 (−0.01, 0.04)	0.02 (−0.01, 0.04)
Transferrin saturation (%)	0.01 (−0.02, 0.01)	−0.01 (−0.02, 0.01)	−0.02 (−0.02, 0.01)
Folate (nmol/L)	−0.02 (−0.05, 0.02)	−0.01 (−0.00, 0.00)	−0.00 (−0.03, 0.03)
Vitamin B_{12} (pmol/L)	0.00 (−0.29, 0.29)	0.02 (−0.18, 0.39)	0.01 (−0.21, 0.36)
Vitamin D (nmol/L)	0.08 (0.02, 0.10) **	0.06 (0.00, 0.08) *	0.04 (−0.00, 0.07) *

[1] The values of β and data in the parentheses indicate regression coefficient and 95% confidence interval (95% CI), respectively, after covariate adjustment in different models: model 1, crude model; model 2, adjusted for age, region of residence, parity, and trimester; and model 3, adjusted for age, region of residence, parity, trimester, and daily dietary intake, such as energy (kcal), carbohydrate (% of energy), protein (g and % of energy), fat (g and % of energy), iron (mg), folate (μg), and vitamin D (μg). * $p \leq 0.05$ and ** $p \leq 0.01$. TIBC, total iron-binding capacity.

The processed food DP (DP-3) did not exhibit any strong association with anemia-related biochemical biomarkers except vitamin B_{12} (Supplementary Table S3). Serum vitamin B_{12} levels were negatively associated with DP-3 in models 1 and 2 (model 1: β: −0.04, 95% CI: −1.44, 0.09, $p \leq 0.05$; model 2: β: −0.05, 95% CI: −1.48, 0.02, $p \leq 0.05$).

Table 5 presents the association between the dairy and nondairy alternatives DP (DP-4) and anemia-related biochemical variables. DP-4 was positively associated with serum TIBC in model 1 (β: 0.08, 95% CI: 0.02, 0.10, $p \leq 0.01$). Furthermore, the serum vitamin D level was only positively associated with DP-4 in models 1 and 2 (model 1: β: 0.05, 95% CI: 0.02, 0.09, $p \leq 0.05$; model 2: β: 0.04, 95% CI: −0.00, 0.08, $p \leq 0.05$).

3.6. Association of DPs with the Risk of Low-Anemia-Related Biomarkers

As shown in Table 6, the binomial logistic regression analysis revealed that the pregnant women with the highest consumption levels (T3) of plant-based DPs (DP-1) were associated with a reduced risk of low ferritin levels (OR: 0.73, 95% CI: 0.57, 0.94, $p \leq 0.05$) in model 1 compared with those with lower consumption levels (T1) of DP-1. However, there were no significant correlations between DP-1 and the risk of low serum ferritin levels after covariate adjustment. Additionally, the pregnant women with higher consumption levels (T2 and/or T3) of DP-1 were likely to have reduced risks of low folate and vitamin D levels compared with those with lower consumption levels (T1) of DP-1 in all the models.

Table 5. The association of dairy and nondairy alternatives dietary pattern with anemia-related biochemical variables in serum evaluated by the generalized linear regression analysis [1].

Variables	Model 1	Model 2	Model 3
	β (95% CI)	β (95% CI)	β (95% CI)
Hemoglobin (mmol/L)	−0.03 (−1.75, 0.33)	−0.03 (−0.30, 0.06)	−0.03 (−1.70, 0.41)
Iron (μmol/L)	−0.04 (−0.29, 0.05)	−0.03 (−0.30, 0.06)	−0.04 (−0.32, 0.04)
Ferritin (nmol/L)	−0.04 (−0.41, 0.03)	−0.02 (−0.30, 0.12)	−0.04 (−0.31, 2.00)
TIBC (μmol/L)	0.08 (0.02, 0.10) **	0.02 (−0.01, 0.05)	0.02 (−0.01, 0.05)
Transferrin saturation (%)	0.01 (−0.02, 0.02)	0.01 (−0.02, 0.02)	0.01 (−0.02, 0.02)
Folate (nmol/L)	0.03 (−0.02, 0.05)	0.04 (−0.01, 0.06)	0.04 (−0.01, 0.06)
Vitamin B_{12} (pmol/L)	−0.01 (−0.38, 0.24)	0.01 (−0.25, 0.35)	0.01 (−0.27, 0.34)
Vitamin D (nmol/L)	0.05 (0.02, 0.09) *	0.04 (−0.00, 0.08) *	0.03 (−0.01, 0.07)

[1] The values of β and data in the parentheses indicate regression coefficient and 95% confidence interval (95% CI), respectively, after covariate adjustment in different models: model 1, crude model; model 2, adjusted for age, region of residence, parity, and trimester; and model 3, adjusted for age, region of residence, parity, trimester, and daily dietary intake, such as energy (kcal), carbohydrate (% of energy), protein (g and % of energy), fat (g and % of energy), iron (mg), folate (μg), and vitamin D (μg). * $p \leq 0.05$ and ** $p \leq 0.01$. TIBC, total iron-binding capacity.

Table 6. Odds ratios (ORs) of low-anemia-related biochemical variables in serum across the tertiles of plant-based dietary pattern assessed by binomial logistic regression analysis [1].

Variables [2]	Plant-Based Dietary Pattern [3]					
	Model 1 OR (95% Confidence Interval)		Model 2 OR (95% Confidence Interval)		Model 3 OR (95% Confidence Interval)	
	T2	T3	T2	T3	T2	T3
Hemoglobin (mmol/L)	1.40 (0.44, 4.45)	1.00 (0.35, 2.87)	1.53 (0.47, 4.96)	0.94 (0.32, 2.77)	1.12 (0.32, 3.87)	0.65 (0.20, 2.04)
Iron (μmol/L)	0.98 (0.76, 1.25)	1.17 (0.91, 1.50)	0.98 (0.75, 1.27)	1.14 (0.88, 1.49)	0.96 (0.73, 1.25)	1.14 (0.87, 1.49)
Ferritin (nmol/L)	0.98 (0.76, 1.25)	0.73 (0.57, 0.94) *	0.92 (0.69, 1.22)	1.17 (0.87, 1.57)	0.89 (0.67, 1.20)	1.16 (0.86, 1.56)
TIBC (μmol/L)	1.00 (0.02, 1.28)	1.33 (0.04, 1.52)	1.07 (0.14, 1.48)	0.95 (0.12, 1.34)	1.06 (0.14, 1.48)	0.97 (0.12, 1.37)
Transferrin saturation (%)	1.06 (0.82, 1.36)	0.84 (0.65, 1.07)	1.04 (0.81, 1.34)	0.83 (0.65, 1.07)	1.03 (0.80, 1.33)	0.83 (0.64, 1.07)
Folate (nmol/L)	0.61 (0.44, 0.85) **	0.66 (0.48, 0.92) *	0.61 (0.42, 0.88) **	0.68 (0.47,0.98) *	0.60 (0.41, 0.87) **	0.69 (0.47, 1.00)
Vitamin B_{12} (pmol/L)	0.86 (0.64, 1.16)	1.01 (0.76, 1.35)	0.86 (0.64, 1.18)	0.95 (0.70, 1.29)	0.88 (0.67, 1.24)	1.04 (0.77, 1.42)
Vitamin D (nmol/L)	0.69 (0.52,0.92) *	0.75 (0.57, 0.99) *	0.68 (0.51, 0.91) *	0.81 (0.60, 1.08)	0.69 (0.52, 0.93) *	0.84 (0.62, 1.13)

[1] Three different models were performed in binomial logistic regression analysis: model 1, crude model; model 2, adjusted for age, region of residence, parity, and trimester; and model 3, adjusted for age, region of residence, parity, trimester, and daily dietary intake, such as energy (kcal), carbohydrate (% of energy), protein (g and % of energy), fat (g and % of energy), iron (mg), folate (μg), and vitamin D (μg). [2] Variables were divided into two levels on the basis of cutoff values in serum: hemoglobin, 6.52 mmol/L (10.5 g/dL); iron, 10.7 μmol/L (60 μg/dL); ferritin, 0.034 nmol/L (15 ng/mL); TIBC, 42.96 μmol/L (240 μg/dL); transferrin saturation, 16%; folate, 13.6 nmol/L (6 ng/mL); vitamin B_{12}, 149.8 pmol/L (203 pg/mL); and vitamin D, 75 nmol/L (30 ng/mL). [3] Dietary pattern scores were divided into tertiles: T1 (reference), 0.56–38.85; T2, >38.87–65.61; and T3 >65.85–436.82. * $p \leq 0.05$ and ** $p \leq 0.01$. TIBC, total iron-binding capacity.

As found in Table 7, the pregnant women with higher consumption levels (T3 and/or T2) of the carnivore DP (DP-2) were likely to have an increased risk of low iron levels in all the models. The pregnant women with higher consumption levels (T2) of DP-2 were associated with a decreased risk of low transferrin saturation (OR: 0.70, 95% CI: 0.54, 0.91, $p \leq 0.01$) in model 2. T2 and T3 of DP-2 were correlated with reduced risks of low serum vitamin B_{12} and vitamin D levels in the adjusted models.

The processed food DP (DP-3) did not exhibit any prominent associations with anemia-related biochemical biomarkers except serum vitamin D levels (Supplementary Table S4). The pregnant women with higher consumption levels (T2) of DP-3 were likely to have a reduced risk of low vitamin D levels in model 1 (OR: 0.71, 95% CI: 0.53, 0.95, $p \leq 0.05$) and model 2 (OR: 0.68, 95% CI: 0.51, 0.92, $p \leq 0.05$).

Table 8 demonstrates the associations between the dairy and nondairy alternatives DP (DP-4) and anemia-related biochemical variables. In Model 1, the pregnant women with the highest consumption levels (T3) of DP-4 were correlated with reduced risks of low serum TIBC (OR: 0.71, 95% CI: 0.54, 0.93, $p \leq 0.05$), low vitamin B_{12} (OR: 0.73, 95% CI: 0.54, 0.97, $p \leq 0.05$), and low vitamin D levels (OR: 0.72, 95% CI: 0.54, 0.96, $p \leq 0.05$).

After covariate adjustment, the pregnant women with the highest consumption levels (T3) of DP-4 were associated with decreased risks of low serum folate (models 2 and 3), low vitamin B_{12} (models 2 and 3), and low vitamin D (model 2).

Table 7. Odds ratios (ORs) of low-anemia-related biochemical variables in serum across the tertiles of carnivore dietary pattern assessed by binomial logistic regression analysis [1].

Variables [2]	Carnivore Dietary Pattern [3]					
	Model 1 OR (95% Confidence Interval)		Model 2 OR (95% Confidence Interval)		Model 3 OR (95% Confidence Interval)	
	T2	T3	T2	T3	T2	T3
Hemoglobin (mmol/L)	0.55 (0.18, 1.66)	1.00 (0.29, 3.48)	0.51 (0.17, 1.58)	1.03 (0.29, 3.68)	0.47 (0.14, 1.56)	0.93 (0.24, 3.54)
Iron (μmol/L)	1.36 (1.06,1.76) *	1.33 (1.03, 1.72) *	1.24 (0.95, 1.63)	1.33 (1.02, 1.74) *	1.30 (0.99, 1.72)	1.33 (1.02, 1.75) *
Ferritin (nmol/L)	1.29 (1.00, 1.66)	1.30 (1.00, 1.68)	1.24 (0.92, 1.66)	1.15 (0.86, 1.54)	1.24 (0.92, 1.67)	1.16 (0.86, 1.56)
TIBC (μmol/L)	0.83 (0.63, 1.08)	0.78 (0.59, 1.01)	0.92 (0.65, 1.28)	1.00 (0.14, 1.11)	1.00 (0.13, 1.27)	1.04 (0.14, 1.11)
Transferrin saturation (%)	0.86 (0.66, 1.10)	0.93 (0.72, 1.20)	0.84 (0.65, 1.08)	0.92 (0.71, 1.19)	0.70 (0.54, 0.91) **	0.93 (0.72, 1.21)
Folate (nmol/L)	1.18 (0.84, 1.68)	1.30 (0.92, 1.84)	1.15 (0.79, 1.69)	1.25 (0.85, 1.83)	1.15 (0.78, 1.70)	1.26 (0.86, 1.86)
Vitamin B_{12} (pmol/L)	0.85 (0.63, 1.14)	0.89 (0.67, 1.19)	0.56 (0.37, 0.84) **	0.54 (0.35, 0.82) **	0.68 (0.52, 0.90) **	0.25(0.17, 0.37) ***
Vitamin D (nmol/L)	0.69 (0.52, 0.92) *	0.55 (0.41, 0.74) ***	0.70 (0.52, 0.94) *	0.58 (0.43, 0.78) ***	0.70 (0.52, 0.95) **	0.59 (0.44, 0.80) **

[1] Three different models were performed in binomial logistic regression analysis: model 1, crude model; model 2, adjusted for age, region of residence, parity, and trimester; and model 3, adjusted for age, region of residence, parity, trimester, and daily dietary intake, such as energy (kcal), carbohydrate (% of energy), protein (g and % of energy), fat (g and % of energy), iron (mg), folate (μg), and vitamin D (μg). [2] Variables were divided into two levels on the basis of cutoff values in serum: hemoglobin, 6.52 mmol/L (10.5 g/dL); iron, 10.7 μmol/L (60 μg/dL), ferritin, 0.034 nmol/L (15 ng/mL); TIBC, 42.96 μmol/L (240 μg/dL); transferrin saturation, 16%; folate, 13.6 nmol/L (6 ng/mL); vitamin B_{12}, 149.8 pmol/L (203 pg/mL); and vitamin D, 75 nmol/L (30 ng/mL). [3] Dietary pattern scores were divided into tertiles: T1 (reference), 0.56–38.85; T2, >38.87–65.61; and T3 >65.85–436.82. * $p \leq 0.05$, ** $p \leq 0.01$, and *** $p \leq 0.001$. TIBC, total iron-binding capacity.

Table 8. Odds ratios (ORs) of low-anemia-related biochemical variables in serum across the tertiles of dairy and nondairy alternatives dietary pattern assessed by binomial logistic regression analysis [1].

Variables [2]	Dairy and Nondairy Alternatives Dietary Pattern [3]					
	Model 1 OR (95% Confidence Interval)		Model 2 OR (95% Confidence Interval)		Model 3 OR (95% Confidence Interval)	
	T2	T3	T2	T3	T2	T3
Hemoglobin (mmol/L)	0.63 (0.24, 1.65)	0.69 (0.35, 1.67)	0.73 (0.27, 1.95)	1.12 (0.72, 1.83)	0.61 (0.21, 1.78)	0.98 (0.41, 1.89)
Iron (μmol/L)	0.83 (0.65, 1.07)	0.90 (0.70, 1.16)	0.81 (0.62, 1.06)	0.84 (0.64, 1.10)	0.83 (0.63, 1.08)	0.85 (0.65, 1.12)
Ferritin (nmol/L)	0.91 (0.71, 1.17)	1.11 (0.86, 1.42)	0.91 (0.71, 1.17)	1.11 (0.86, 1.42)	0.85 (0.64, 1.15)	0.87 (0.64, 1.17)
TIBC (μmol/L)	1.03 (0.14, 1.26)	0.71 (0.54, 0.93) *	1.10 (0.15, 1.30)	0.94 (0.12, 1.24)	1.00 (0.16, 1.31)	0.95 (0.12, 1.25)
Transferrin saturation (%)	1.04 (0.81, 1.33)	0.96 (0.75, 1.23)	1.02 (0.79, 1.31)	0.95 (0.74, 1.22)	1.02 (0.79, 1.31)	0.96 (0.74, 1.24)
Folate (nmol/L)	0.72 (0.52, 1.01)	0.75 (0.53, 1.04)	0.80 (0.55, 1.15)	0.67 (0.47, 0.97) *	0.80 (0.55, 1.16)	0.67 (0.46, 0.98) *
Vitamin B_{12} (pmol/L)	0.80 (0.60, 1.07)	0.73 (0.54, 0.97) *	0.79 (0.59, 1.07)	0.63 (0.46, 0.85) **	0.81 (0.60, 1.10)	0.66 (0.48, 0.90) *
Vitamin D (nmol/L)	0.79 (0.60, 1.05)	0.72 (0.54, 0.96) *	0.79 (0.59, 1.06)	0.72 (0.54, 0.97) *	0.80 (0.60, 1.08)	0.75 (0.55, 1.02)

[1] Three different models were performed in binomial logistic regression analysis: model 1, crude model; model 2, adjusted for age, region of residence, parity, and trimester; and model 3, adjusted for age, region of residence, parity, trimester, and daily dietary intake, such as energy (kcal), carbohydrate (% of energy), protein (g and % of energy), fat (g and % of energy), iron (mg), folate (μg), and vitamin D (μg). [2] Variables were divided into two levels on the basis of cutoff values in serum: hemoglobin, 6.52 mmol/L (10.5 g/dL); iron, 10.7 μmol/L (60 μg/dL), ferritin, 0.034 nmol/L (15 ng/mL); TIBC, 42.96 μmol/L (240 μg/dL); transferrin saturation, 16%; folate, 13.6 nmol/L (6 ng/mL); vitamin B_{12}, 149.8 pmol/L (203 pg/mL); and vitamin D, 75 nmol/L (30 ng/mL). [3] Dietary pattern scores were divided into tertiles: T1 (reference), 0.56–38.85; T2, >38.87–65.61; and T3 >65.85–436.82. * $p \leq 0.05$ and ** $p \leq 0.01$. TIBC, total iron-binding capacity.

4. Discussion

4.1. Association of Serum Vitamin D with Other Serum-Anemia-Related Biomarkers

We showed that all anemia-related biochemical variables were significantly different across the tertiles of serum vitamin D levels in the pregnant women, except for transferrin saturation. Hence, pregnant women with higher serum vitamin D levels had higher serum Hb, iron, TIBC, folate, and vitamin B_{12} levels, which indicates better iron status. Similarly, Si et al. [24] found that plasma 25(OH) vitamin D levels were positively correlated with plasma Hb levels in each trimester of Chinese pregnant women. Additionally, Chinese pregnant women with vitamin D deficiencies (<50 nmol/L) in trimesters 1 and 2 were associated with an elevated risk of anemia compared with those without vitamin D deficiencies [24]. A cross-sectional study conducted in Vietnamese non-pregnant young women revealed that serum vitamin D levels, not dietary vitamin D intake, were positively associated with Hb levels, but not significantly correlated with anemia [26]. We also found that the pregnant women with higher serum vitamin D levels had lower serum ferritin levels, but the average ferritin levels were still within the normal range. A previous study demonstrated that serum 25(OH) vitamin D levels were not correlated with serum ferritin levels in Indonesian pregnant women in the first trimester; however, the pregnant women with insufficient (<75 nmol/L) or deficient (<50 nmol/L) 25(OH) vitamin D levels in the first trimester had a higher risk of developing anemia in the third trimester [46].

4.2. Association of DPs with Serum-Anemia-Related Biomarkers

Our findings from the linear regression analysis revealed that both the plant-based (DP-1) and carnivore (DP-2) DPs were negatively associated with serum ferritin levels in the crude mode, but positively correlated with serum vitamin D levels in all the models. In contrast, the processed food DP (DP-3) was negatively associated with serum vitamin B_{12} levels. The dairy and nondairy alternatives DP (DP-4) was positively correlated with serum TIBC and vitamin D levels. Consistently, our findings from the binomial regression analysis showed that both DP-1 and DP-2 were associated with a reduced risk of low serum vitamin D levels. DP-4 was correlated with decreased risks of low serum TIBC, folate, vitamin B_{12}, and vitamin D levels.

Plant-based foods (non-heme iron source) are rich in fiber, phytate, oxalate, and/or polyphenols which could chelate with iron as an inhibitor of iron bioavailability, and they have less iron absorption compared with heme iron food sources [47–49]; thus, the plant-based DP (DP-1) could be correlated with a reduction in serum ferritin levels. Our study demonstrated that DP-1 was correlated with reduced odds of low serum folate and vitamin D levels in pregnant women. Similarly, a previous study reported that pregnant women consuming an ovo-lacto vegetarian or a low-meat diet were likely to have a lower risk of folate deficiency compared with those consuming a Western diet [50]. Additionally, pregnant women consuming a vegetarian diet had significantly higher serum 1,25-$(OH)_2$ vitamin D levels compared with those consuming a nonvegetarian diet [51]. However, adults consuming a vegetarian diet or a plant-based diet were correlated with lower iron stores (lower serum ferritin levels) and a higher prevalence of anemia, probably due to the poor absorption of non-heme iron compared with those consuming a nonvegetarian diet [52,53].

Notably, the carnivore DP (DP-2) was associated with an increased risk of low serum iron levels in our study. However, a systematic review reported that the adults consuming a high intake of a carnivore/animal-based diet were positively correlated with iron status [54]. The possible reason for the association between DP-2 and low serum iron levels could be attributed to herbs and spices (such as chili paper, garlic, Thai leafy vegetables, shallot, tamarind, and turmeric) in DP-2, which are enriched in polyphenolic compounds and can hinder iron absorption by forming insoluble iron complexes [55]. We also found that DP-2 was correlated with reduced risks of low transferrin saturation, vitamin B_{12}, and vitamin D levels. Norwegian women (36–39 years old) consuming a reindeer meat DP were likely to have slightly higher transferrin saturation (mean: 28%) compared with those consuming a fish (mean: 26%), average (mean: 27%), fruit/vegetables (mean: 24%), or Western/marine DP (mean: 26%) [56]. Dutch pregnant women who consumed higher vitamin B_{12} intake from animal foods such as meat, fish, or dairy food which were rich in vitamin B_{12} were correlated with higher plasma vitamin B_{12} levels [57]. A previous study showed that Caucasian pregnant women in Ireland consumed dietary vitamin D primarily from meat, eggs, and breakfast cereals [58]. Meat was the predominant food group in DP-2, and the pregnant women with higher intakes of DP-2 presumably had better serum vitamin D statuses.

The processed food DP (DP-3) was negatively associated with serum vitamin B_{12} levels. The excessive thermal treatment of foods during food processing may be attributed to reduced vitamin B_{12} content in foods [59]. Additionally, high intakes of ultra-processed foods were correlated with decreased intakes of certain vitamins such as vitamin A, B_{12}, C, D, E, and niacin in adults [60].

After covariate adjustment, T3 of the dairy and nondairy alternatives DP (DP-4) was associated with reduced odds of low serum folate, vitamin B_{12}, and vitamin D levels. Consistent with our findings, Cifelli et al. [61] demonstrated that dairy and individual dairy foods were correlated with increased serum folate and vitamin B_{12} levels in a US population. Dairy food also provided rich sources of vitamins B_{12} [62] and D [63], which could significantly contribute to serum vitamin B_{12} and vitamin D levels.

Overall, we identified that plant-based, carnivore, and dairy and nondairy alternatives DPs were positively correlated with serum vitamin D levels and a reduced risk of low serum vitamin D. Serum vitamin D status could be affected not only by dietary patterns but also by exposure to sunlight or the use of sun protection [64]. Our previous study showed that among 1502 pregnant women in Taiwan, 69.6% women had sun exposure $\geq$10 min/d in the previous month, and 61.7% women had blood drawn in sunny months between June and November [65]. Additionally, dietary vitamin D intake had a greater impact on serum vitamin D levels in the women who lived in the northern part of Taiwan, whereas serum vitamin D levels were more greatly influenced by sunlight-related factors in those who lived in the southern or other parts of Taiwan [65]. These vitamin-D-associated DPs may reduce the risk of anemia in pregnant women, because these DPs were also negatively correlated with other anemia-related biochemical variables such as serum folate and vitamin B_{12}. A possible mechanism for the effect of vitamin D on anemia was its modulation in iron metabolism via the down-regulation of hepcidin [66,67]. Higher serum vitamin D levels could be beneficial for better iron statuses through reducing hepcidin at the transcriptional level and suppressing the expression of proinflammatory cytokines involved in iron imbalance [67]. Active vitamin D could down-regulate the production of endogenous hormone hepcidin, thereby improving iron release, iron recycling, and iron absorption [67], and further maintain iron status during pregnancy. A recent cross-sectional study reported that serum hepcidin levels were negatively associated with the consumption frequency of plant-based foods such as legumes, breakfast cereals, light-colored vegetables, and gourds and root vegetables in Taiwanese pregnant women [25]. In the present study, we did not analyze serum hepcidin, and further studies are necessary to identify whether vitamin-D-rich DP is correlated with serum hepcidin levels.

4.3. Strengths and Limitations

To the best of our knowledge, the present study pioneered the PCA-mediated identification method for the association of DPs with serum levels of vitamin D and iron biomarkers in Taiwanese pregnant women. PCA is commonly used in pragmatic analyses performed using correlation matrices of intake units to identify common DPs [68]. We used data from the Pregnant NAHSIT 2017–2019 and included pregnant women from different areas of Taiwan (northern, central, southern, and eastern). In addition, sociodemographic data (education and income levels) were also collected to complement our findings.

The present study has some limitations. First, because of the unavailability of data regarding serum vitamin C, hepcidin, and parathyroid hormone levels which could affect iron status, we could not assess the association of DPs with these biomarkers. Second, the use of the FFQ and self-reported data for body weight and height might have introduced biases, such as errors in overestimation or underestimation. To overcome or minimize the biases of the FFQ, we additionally obtained 24 h dietary recall data and used food pictures and measurement cups or spoons during data collection [69]. Third, we did not consider certain pathological conditions of pregnant women, such as morning sickness during the first trimester of pregnancy. Fourth, the data regarding dietary supplements and seasonality were limited. Finally, because of the cross-sectional study design, we could not establish any causal relationship among DPs, serum vitamin D levels, and iron status. Nevertheless, a correlation relationship was identified between DPs and serum levels of anemia-related biomarkers. Future cohort studies and randomized control trials are needed to overcome the aforementioned limitations.

5. Conclusions

This study is a novel attempt to identify the associations among DPs, serum vitamin D levels, and iron status in pregnant women. Plant-based (DP-1), carnivore (DP-2), and dairy and nondairy alternatives DPs (DP-4) are positively correlated with serum vitamin D levels. The medium intake of a plant-based DP (DP-1) is associated with higher levels of serum folate and vitamin D. The medium and high consumption of carnivore DP (DP-2) is correlated with higher levels of serum vitamin B_{12} and vitamin D. The high intake of dairy and nondairy alternatives DP (DP-4) is associated with higher levels of serum folate and vitamin B_{12}. However, we found no strong association between DPs and serum levels of Hb and iron status, except the negative correlation between the carnivore DP (DP-2) and serum iron levels. Thus, the medium intake of a vitamin D-rich diet such as a plant-based, carnivore, or dairy and nondairy alternatives DP is suggested to be beneficial for preventing anemia in pregnant women due to better statuses of serum folate, vitamin B_{12}, and vitamin D.

Supplementary Materials: The following supporting information can be downloaded at: https://www.mdpi.com/article/10.3390/nu15081805/s1. Table S1: Food groups and subgroups for dietary assessment; Table S2: Daily dietary intake of women across the tertiles of serum vitamin D levels (n = 1502); Table S3: The association of processed food dietary pattern with anemia-related biochemical variables in serum evaluated by the generalized linear regression analysis; Table S4: Odds ratios (ORs) of low-anemia-related biochemical variables in serum across the tertiles of processed food dietary pattern assessed by binomial logistic regression analysis.

Author Contributions: Conceptualization, A.D., Y.-C.C. and J.C.-J.C.; data curation, C.-H.B., J.-S.C., Y.-L.H. and F.-F.W.; formal analysis, A.D.; writing—original draft preparation, A.D., Y.-C.C. and J.C.-J.C.; writing—review and editing, J.C.-J.C.; supervision, Y.-C.C. and J.C.-J.C. All authors have read and agreed to the published version of the manuscript.

Funding: This study using the secondary data received no external funding.

Institutional Review Board Statement: The study was approved by the Joint Institutional Review Board of Taipei Medical University, Taiwan (approval number: N201707039; approval date: 7 November 2018) and conducted in accordance with the ethical principles of the Declaration of Helsinki.

Informed Consent Statement: All participants signed a consent form authorized by the team that conducted the Nationwide Nutrition and Health Survey in Pregnant Women in Taiwan.

Data Availability Statement: Data supporting the study findings are available from the database of Nationwide Nutrition and Health Survey in Pregnant Women in Taiwan. The data should be used for research purposes only. The study data are not publicly available.

Acknowledgments: We thank the Nationwide Nutrition and Health Survey in Pregnant Women (Taiwan) team for making their database available for our study.

Conflicts of Interest: The authors declare no conflict of interest.

References

1. Shah, T.; Khaskheli, M.S.; Ansari, S.; Lakhan, H.; Shaikh, F.; Zardari, A.A.; Warsi, J.; Rind, N.A.; Rind, K.H.; Shar, A.H. Gestational anemia and its effects on neonatal outcome, in the population of Hyderabad, Sindh, Pakistan. *Saudi J. Biol. Sci.* **2022**, *29*, 83–87. [CrossRef]
2. Imai, K. Parity-based assessment of anemia and iron deficiency in pregnant women. *J. Obstet. Gynecol.* **2020**, *59*, 838–841. [CrossRef] [PubMed]
3. World Health Organization. *Haemoglobin Concentrations for the Diagnosis of Anaemia and Assessment of Severity*; World Health Organization: Geneva, Switzerland, 2011.

4. Centers for Disease Control. CDC criteria for anemia in children and childbearing-aged women. *MMWR Morb. Mortal. Wkly. Rep.* **1989**, *38*, 400–404.
5. Anlaakuu, P.; Anto, F. Anaemia in pregnancy and associated factors: A cross sectional study of antenatal attendants at the Sunyani Municipal Hospital, Ghana. *BMC Res. Notes* **2017**, *10*, 402. [CrossRef] [PubMed]
6. Wedderburn, C.J.; Ringshaw, J.E.; Donald, K.A.; Joshi, S.H.; Subramoney, S.; Fouche, J.-P.; Stadler, J.A.M.; Barnett, W.; Rehman, A.M.; Hoffman, N.; et al. Association of maternal and child anemia with brain structure in early life in South Africa. *JAMA Netw. Open* **2022**, *5*, e2244772. [CrossRef]
7. Uta, M.; Neamtu, R.; Bernad, E.; Mocanu, A.G.; Gluhovschi, A.; Popescu, A.; Dahma, G.; Dumitru, C.; Stelea, L.; Citu, C.; et al. The influence of nutritional supplementation for iron deficiency anemia on pregnancies associated with SARS-CoV-2 infection. *Nutrients* **2022**, *14*, 836. [CrossRef]
8. Elema, T.B.; Yimam, K.B.; Waka, F.C.; Olana, B.N. Folate and vitamin B-12 status of anemic pregnant women and association to hemoglobin during antenatal care, 17–37 weeks in Ambo Hospital, Oromia, Ethiopia, a multi regression analysis of socio-economic and serum folate and vitamin B-12. *J. Nutr. Hum. Health* **2018**, *1*, 28–34. [CrossRef]
9. Behere, R.V.; Deshmukh, A.S.; Otiv, S.; Gupte, M.D.; Yajnik, C.S. Maternal vitamin B12 status during pregnancy and its association with outcomes of pregnancy and health of the offspring: A systematic review and implications for policy in India. *Front. Endocrinol.* **2021**, *12*, 619176. [CrossRef]
10. Finkelstein, J.L.; Fothergill, A.; Krisher, J.T.; Thomas, T.; Kurpad, A.V.; Dwarkanath, P. Maternal vitamin B12 deficiency and perinatal outcomes in Southern India. *PLoS ONE* **2021**, *16*, e0248145. [CrossRef]
11. Greenberg, J.A.; Bell, S.J.; Guan, Y.; Yu, Y.H. Folic acid supplementation and pregnancy: More than just neural tube defect prevention. *Rev. Obstet. Gynecol.* **2011**, *4*, 52–59.
12. Warner, M.J.; Kamran, M.T. *Iron Deficiency Anemia*; StatPearls Publishing: Tampa, FL, USA, 2017. Available online: https://www.ncbi.nlm.nih.gov/books/NBK448065/ (accessed on 7 November 2022).
13. Diana, A.; Purnamasari, D.M.; Rahmannia, S.; Luftimas, D.E.; Haszard, J.J.; Gibson, R.S.; Houghton, L.A. Multimicronutrient biomarkers are related to anemia during infancy in Indonesia: A repeated cross-sectional study. *Curr. Dev. Nutr.* **2019**, *3*, nzz022. [CrossRef] [PubMed]
14. Daru, J.; Colman, K.; Stanworth, S.J.; De La Salle, B.; Wood, E.M.; Pasricha, S.R. Serum ferritin as an indicator of iron status: What do we need to know? *Am. J. Clin. Nutr.* **2017**, *106*, 1634S–1639S. [CrossRef]
15. Crispin, P.; Stephens, B.; McArthur, E.; Sethna, F. First trimester ferritin screening for pre-delivery anaemia as a patient blood management strategy. *Transfus. Apher. Sci.* **2019**, *58*, 50–57. [CrossRef] [PubMed]
16. Rahman, S.M.; Siraj, M.S.; Islam, M.R.; Rahman, A.; Ekström, E.C. Association between maternal plasma ferritin level and infants' size at birth: A prospective cohort study in rural Bangladesh. *Glob. Health Action* **2021**, *1*, 1870421. [CrossRef] [PubMed]
17. Abu-Ouf, N.M.; Jan, M.M. The impact of maternal iron deficiency and iron deficiency anemia on child's health. *Saudi Med. J.* **2015**, *36*, 146–149. [CrossRef] [PubMed]
18. Li, N.; Zhao, G.; Wu, W.; Zhang, M.; Liu, W.; Chen, Q.; Wang, X. The efficacy and safety of vitamin C for iron supplementation in adult patients with iron deficiency anemia: A randomized clinical trial. *JAMA Netw. Open* **2020**, *3*, e2023644. [CrossRef]
19. Heffernan, A.; Evans, C.; Holmes, M.; Moore, J.B. The regulation of dietary iron bioavailability by vitamin C: A systematic review and meta-analysis. *Proc. Nutr. Soc.* **2017**, *76*, E182. [CrossRef]
20. Mogire, R.M.; Muriuki, J.M.; Morovat, A.; Mentzer, A.J.; Webb, E.L.; Kimita, W.; Ndungu, F.M.; Macharia, A.W.; Cutland, C.L.; Sirima, S.B.; et al. Vitamin D deficiency and its association with iron deficiency in African children. *Nutrients* **2022**, *14*, 1372. [CrossRef]
21. Smith, E.M.; Tangpricha, V. Vitamin D and anemia: Insights into an emerging association. *Curr. Opin. Endocrinol. Diabetes Obes.* **2015**, *22*, 432–438. [CrossRef]
22. Arabi, S.M.; Ranjbar, G.; Bahrami, L.S.; Vafa, M.; Norouzy, A. The effect of vitamin D supplementation on hemoglobin concentration: A systematic review and meta-analysis. *Nutr. J.* **2020**, *19*, 11. [CrossRef]
23. Qiu, F.; Li, R.; Gu, S.; Zhao, Y.; Yang, L. The effect of iron dextran on vitamin D_3 metabolism in SD rats. *Nutr. Metab.* **2022**, *19*, 47. [CrossRef]
24. Si, S.; Peng, Z.; Cheng, H.; Zhuang, Y.; Chi, P.; Alifu, X.; Zhou, H.; Mo, M.; Yu, Y. Association of vitamin D in different trimester with hemoglobin during pregnancy. *Nutrients* **2022**, *14*, 2455. [CrossRef] [PubMed]
25. Mayasari, N.R.; Bai, C.H.; Hu, T.Y.; Chao, J.C.; Chen, Y.C.; Huang, Y.L.; Wang, F.F.; Tinkov, A.A.; Skalny, A.V.; Chang, J.S. Associations of food and nutrient intake with serum hepcidin and the risk of gestational iron-deficiency anemia among pregnant women: A population-based study. *Nutrients* **2021**, *13*, 3501. [CrossRef] [PubMed]
26. Michalski, E.S.; Nguyen, P.H.; Gonzalez-Casanova, I.; Nguyen, S.V.; Martorell, R.; Tangpricha, V.; Ramakrishnan, U. Serum 25-hydroxyvitamin D but not dietary vitamin D intake is associated with hemoglobin in women of reproductive age in rural Northern Vietnam. *J. Clin. Transl. Endocrinol.* **2017**, *8*, 41–48. [CrossRef] [PubMed]
27. Wong, R.S.; Tung, K.T.S.; Chan, Y.W.K.; Chan, B.N.K.; Leung, W.C.; Yam, J.C.; Ip, P. Adequate dietary intake and vitamin D supplementation: A study of their relative importance in determining serum vitamin D and ferritin concentrations during pregnancy. *Nutrients* **2022**, *14*, 3083. [CrossRef]
28. Zhang, F.; Tapera, T.M.; Gou, J. Application of a new dietary pattern analysis method in nutritional epidemiology. *BMC Med. Res. Methodol.* **2018**, *18*, 119. [CrossRef]

29. Zang, J.; Luo, B.; Chang, S.; Jin, S.; Shan, C.; Ma, L.; Zhu, Z.; Guo, C.; Zou, S.; Jia, X.; et al. Validity and reliability of a food frequency questionnaire for assessing dietary intake among Shanghai residents. *Nutr. J.* **2019**, *18*, 30. [CrossRef]
30. Schwedhelm, C.; Iqbal, K.; Knüppel, S.; Schwingshackl, L.; Boeing, H. Contribution to the understanding of how principal component analysis–derived dietary patterns emerge from habitual data on food consumption. *Am. J. Clin. Nutr.* **2018**, *107*, 227–235. [CrossRef]
31. Jolliffe, I.T.; Cadima, J. Principal component analysis: A review and recent developments. *Philos. Trans. A Math. Phys. Eng. Sci.* **2016**, *374*, 20150202. [CrossRef]
32. Pfeiffer, C.M.; Looker, A.C. Laboratory methodologies for indicators of iron status: Strengths, limitations, and analytical challenges. *Am. J. Clin. Nutr.* **2017**, *106*, 1606S–1614S. [CrossRef]
33. Yamanishi, H.; Iyama, S.; Yamaguchi, Y.; Kanakura, Y.; Iwatani, Y. Total iron-binding capacity calculated from serum transferrin concentration or serum iron concentration and unsaturated iron-binding capacity. *Clin. Chem.* **2003**, *49*, 175–178. [CrossRef] [PubMed]
34. Shane, B. Folate status assessment history: Implications for measurement of biomarkers in NHANES. *Am. J. Clin. Nutr.* **2011**, *94*, 337S–342S. [CrossRef] [PubMed]
35. Karmi, O.; Zayed, A.; Baraghethi, S.; Qadi, M.; Ghanem, R. Measurement of vitamin B12 concentration: A review on available methods. *IIOAB J.* **2011**, *2*, 23–32.
36. Abdel-Wareth, L.; Haq, A.; Turner, A.; Khan, S.; Salem, A.; Mustafa, F.; Hussein, N.; Pallinalakam, F.; Grundy, L.; Patras, G.; et al. Total vitamin D assay comparison of the Roche Diagnostics "Vitamin D total" electrochemiluminescence protein binding assay with the Chromsystems HPLC method in a population with both D2 and D3 forms of vitamin D. *Nutrients* **2013**, *5*, 971–980. [CrossRef]
37. Health Promotion Administration, Ministry of Health and Welfare. *Taiwan's Obesity Prevention and Management Strategy*; Health Promotion Administration, Ministry of Health and Welfare: Taipei, Taiwan, 2018; p. 55.
38. Bellanger, R.A. Iron deficiency anemia in women. *US Pharm.* **2010**, *35*, 50–58.
39. Sukla, S.K.; Mohanty, P.K.; Patel, S.; Das, K.; Hiregoudar, M.; Soren, U.K.; Meher, S. Iron profile of pregnant sickle cell anemia patients in Odisha, India. *Hematol. Transfus. Cell Ther.* 2021; *in press*. [CrossRef]
40. Word Health Organization. *WHO Guideline on Use of Ferritin Concentrations to Assess Iron Status in Individuals and Populations*; World Health Organization: Geneva, Switzerland, 2020.
41. World Health Organization. *Archived: Iron Deficiency Anemia: Assessment, Prevention and Control*; World Health Organization: Geneva, Switzerland, 2001; pp. 47–62.
42. World Health Organization. *Serum and Red Blood Cell Folate Concentrations for Assessing Folate Status in Populations. Vitamin and Mineral Nutrition Information System*; World Health Organization: Geneva, Switzerland, 2015.
43. Holick, M.F.; Binkley, N.C.; Bischoff-Ferrari, H.A.; Gordon, C.M.; Hanley, D.A.; Heaney, R.P.; Murad, M.H.; Weaver, C.M.; Endocrine Society. Evaluation, treatment, and prevention of vitamin D deficiency: An Endocrine Society clinical practice guideline. *J. Clin. Endocrinol. Metab.* **2011**, *96*, 1911–1930. [CrossRef]
44. Kurniawan, A.; Hsu, C.-Y.; Rau, H.; Lin, L.-Y.; Chao, J. Dietary patterns in relation to testosterone levels and severity of impaired kidney function among middle-aged and elderly men in Taiwan: A cross-sectional study. *Nutr. J.* **2019**, *18*, 42. [CrossRef]
45. Szumilas, M. Explaining odds ratios. *J. Can. Acad. Child Adolesc. Psychiatry* **2010**, *19*, 227–229.
46. Judistiani, R.T.D.; Gumilang, L.; Nirmala, S.A.; Irianti, S.; Wirhana, D.; Permana, I.; Sofjan, L.; Duhita, H.; Tambunan, L.A.; Gurnadi, J.I.; et al. Association of colecalciferol, ferritin, and anemia among pregnant women: Result from cohort study on vitamin D status and its impact during pregnancy and childhood in Indonesia. *Anemia* **2018**, *2018*, 2047981. [CrossRef]
47. Perzia, B.M.; Ying, G.-S.; Dunaief, J.L.; Dunaief, D.M. Reduction in ferritin concentrations among patients consuming a dark-green leafy vegetable-rich, low inflammatory foods everyday (LIFE) diet. *Curr. Dev. Nutr.* **2022**, *6*, nzac095. [CrossRef] [PubMed]
48. Ma, Q.; Kim, E.-Y.; Lindsay, E.; Han, O. Bioactive dietary polyphenols inhibit heme iron absorption in a dose-dependent manner in human intestinal Caco-2 cells. *J. Food Sci.* **2011**, *76*, H143–H150. [CrossRef] [PubMed]
49. Piskin, E.; Cianciosi, D.; Gulec, S.; Tomas, M.; Capanoglu, E. Iron absorption: Factors, limitations, and improvement methods. *ACS Omega* **2022**, *7*, 20441–20456. [CrossRef]
50. Koebnick, C.; Heins, U.A.; Hoffmann, I.; Dagnelie, P.C.; Leitzmann, C. Folate status during pregnancy in women is improved by long-term high vegetable intake compared with the average western diet. *J. Nutr.* **2001**, *131*, 733–739. [CrossRef]
51. Specker, B.L.; Tsang, R.C.; Ho, M.; Miller, D. Effect of vegetarian diet on serum 1,25-dihydroxyvitamin D concentrations during lactation. *Obstet. Gynecol.* **1987**, *70*, 870–874. [PubMed]
52. Bhatnagar, R.S.; Padilla-Zakour, O.I. Plant-based dietary practices and socioeconomic factors that influence anemia in India. *Nutrients* **2021**, *13*, 3538. [CrossRef] [PubMed]
53. Pawlak, R.; Berger, J.; Hines, I. Iron status of vegetarian adults: A review of literature. *Am. J. Lifestyle Med.* **2018**, *12*, 486–498. [CrossRef]
54. Jackson, J.; Williams, R.; McEvoy, M.; MacDonald-Wicks, L.; Patterson, A. Is higher consumption of animal flesh foods associated with better iron status among adults in developed countries? A systematic review. *Nutrients* **2016**, *8*, 89. [CrossRef]
55. Tuntipopipat, S.; Zeder, C.; Siriprapa, P.; Charoenkiatkul, S. Inhibitory effects of spices and herbs on iron availability. *Int. J. Food Sci. Nutr.* **2009**, *60*, 43–55. [CrossRef]

56. Broderstad, A.R.; Melhus, M.; Brustad, M.; Lund, E. Iron stores in relation to dietary patterns in a multiethnic population: The SAMINOR study. *Public Health Nutr.* **2011**, *14*, 1039–1046. [CrossRef]
57. Denissen, K.F.M.; Heil, S.G.; Eussen, S.J.P.M.; Heeskens, J.P.J.; Thijs, C.; Mommers, M.; Smits, L.J.M.; van Dongen, M.C.J.M.; Dagnelie, P.C. Intakes of vitamin B-12 from dairy food, meat, and fish and shellfish are independently and positively associated with vitamin B-12 biomarker status in pregnant Dutch women. *J. Nutr.* **2019**, *149*, 131–138. [CrossRef] [PubMed]
58. McGowan, C.A.; Byrne, J.; Walsh, J.; McAuliffe, F.M. Insufficient vitamin D intakes among pregnant women. *Eur. J. Clin. Nutr.* **2011**, *65*, 1076–1078. [CrossRef] [PubMed]
59. Gille, D.; Schmid, A. Vitamin B12 in meat and dairy products. *Nutr. Rev.* **2015**, *73*, 106–115. [CrossRef] [PubMed]
60. Paula, W.O.; Gonçalves, V.S.S.; Patriota, E.S.O.; Franceschini, S.C.C.; Pizato, N. Impact of ultra-processed food consumption on quality of diet among Brazilian pregnant women assisted in primary health care. *Int. J. Environ. Res. Public Health* **2023**, *20*, 1015. [CrossRef]
61. Cifelli, C.J.; Agarwal, S.; Fulgoni, V.L., III. Association between intake of total dairy and individual dairy foods and markers of folate, vitamin B_6 and vitamin B_{12} status in the U.S. Population. *Nutrients* **2022**, *14*, 2441. [CrossRef]
62. Matte, J.J.; Britten, M.; Girard, C.L. The importance of milk as a source of vitamin B_{12} for human nutrition. *Anim. Front.* **2014**, *4*, 32–37. [CrossRef]
63. Polzonetti, V.; Pucciarelli, S.; Vincenzetti, S.; Polidori, P. Dietary intake of vitamin D from dairy products reduces the risk of osteoporosis. *Nutrients* **2020**, *12*, 1743. [CrossRef]
64. Dasgupta, A.; Saikia, U.; Sarma, D. Status of 25(OH)D levels in pregnancy: A study from the North Eastern part of India. *Indian J. Endocrinol. Metab.* **2012**, *16*, S405–S407. [CrossRef]
65. Huang, Y.-L.; Pham, T.T.M.; Chen, Y.-C.; Chang, J.-S.; Chao, J.C.-J.; Bai, C.-H. Effects of climate, sun exposure, and dietary intake on vitamin D concentrations in pregnant women: A population-based study. *Nutrients* **2023**, *15*, 1182. [CrossRef]
66. Pagani, A.; Nai, A.; Silvestri, L.; Camaschella, C. Hepcidin and anemia: A tight relationship. *Front. Physiol.* **2019**, *10*, 1294. [CrossRef]
67. Moran-Lev, H.; Weisman, Y.; Cohen, S.; Deutsch, V.; Cipok, M.; Bondar, E.; Lubetzky, R.; Mandel, D. The interrelationship between hepcidin, vitamin D, and anemia in children with acute infectious disease. *Pediatr. Res.* **2018**, *84*, 62–65. [CrossRef] [PubMed]
68. Thorpe, M.G.; Milte, C.M.; Crawford, D.; McNaughton, S.A. A comparison of the dietary patterns derived by principal component analysis and cluster analysis in older Australians. *Int. J. Behav. Nutr. Phys. Act.* **2016**, *13*, 30. [CrossRef] [PubMed]
69. Lyu, L.C.; Lin, C.F.; Chang, F.H.; Chen, H.F.; Lo, C.C.; Ho, H.F. Meal distribution, relative validity and reproducibility of a meal-based food frequency questionnaire in Taiwan. *Asia Pac. J. Clin. Nutr.* **2007**, *16*, 766–776. [PubMed]

nutrients

Article

Effect of Circadian Distribution of Energy and Macronutrients on Gestational Weight Gain in Chinese Pregnant Women

Wenjuan Xiong [1,†], Shanshan Cui [2,†], Jia Dong [3], Yuanyuan Su [1], Yu Han [1], Zhiyi Qu [1], Shihao Jin [1], Zhi Li [1], Lei Gao [1], Tingkai Cui [1] and Xin Zhang [1,*]

1 Department of Maternal, Child & Adolescence Health, School of Public Health, Tianjin Medical University, Tianjin 300070, China
2 Beijing Key Laboratory of Environmental Toxicology, School of Public Health, Capital Medical University, Beijing 100069, China
3 Department of Public Service, Tianjin Technician Institute of Mechanical & Electrical Technology, Tianjin 300350, China
* Correspondence: zhangxin@tmu.edu.cn
† These authors have contributed equally to this work.

Abstract: Gestational weight gain (GWG) may be affected by the timing of dietary intake. Previous studies have reported contradictory findings, possibly due to inconsistent characterizations of meal timing. We conducted a birth cohort study in Tianjin to determine the effect of daily energy and macronutrient distribution in mid and late pregnancy on GWG. Dietary intake information in the second and third trimesters used three 24-h dietary recalls, and meal timing was defined in relation to sleep/wake timing. The adequacy of GWG was assessed using recommendations from the Institute of Medicine guidelines. Pregnant women who had a relatively high average energy and macronutrient distribution in the late afternoon–early evening time window exhibited a greater GWG rate and a greater total GWG than that in morning time window during the third trimester ($\beta = 0.707$; $\beta = 0.316$). Carbohydrate intake in the morning of the second and third trimesters ($\beta = 0.005$; $\beta = 0.008$) was positively associated with GWG rates. Morning carbohydrate intake in the second trimester was also positively associated with total GWG ($\beta = 0.004$). Fat intake in the morning of the third trimester ($\beta = 0.051$; $\beta = 0.020$) was positively associated with the GWG rates and total GWG. Excessive GWG of Chinese pregnant women was related closely to eating behavior focused on the late afternoon–early evening and carbohydrate and fat intake in the morning during the second and third trimesters.

Keywords: energy; macronutrients; circadian distribution; gestational weight gain

Citation: Xiong, W.; Cui, S.; Dong, J.; Su, Y.; Han, Y.; Qu, Z.; Jin, S.; Li, Z.; Gao, L.; Cui, T.; et al. Effect of Circadian Distribution of Energy and Macronutrients on Gestational Weight Gain in Chinese Pregnant Women. *Nutrients* **2023**, *15*, 2106. https://doi.org/10.3390/nu15092106

Academic Editors: Louise Brough and Gail Rees

Received: 26 March 2023
Revised: 24 April 2023
Accepted: 26 April 2023
Published: 27 April 2023

1. Introduction

Optimal Gestational weight gain (GWG) is essential to ensure the health of both the mother and the baby. However, GWG above or below the recommended guidelines of the Institute of Medicine is related to adverse perinatal outcomes, including gestational hypertension, gestational diabetes, cesarean delivery, premature birth, macrosomia, and infant mortality, as well as long-term negative outcomes in the offspring, including childhood obesity and adiposity [1,2]. Abnormal GWG is currently a serious obstetric issue. For example, in the United States, weight gained is higher than the Institute of Medicine-recommended range in 48% of women giving birth to full-term singleton infants, with 21% gaining insufficient weight [3]. In China, inadequate and excessive weight gain account for 27.2% and 36.6%, respectively [4]. On average, maternal weight increases as pregnancy progresses. The fastest weight gain occurs in the second trimester, and the weight gain rate in the third trimester slightly decreases [5]. In the second and third trimesters, weight gained includes maternal fat accumulation, extravascular fluid, placenta, uterus, and fetus growth [6]. Therefore, it is necessary to simultaneously pay attention to the GWG during the second and third trimesters and explore the associated factors.

Emerging evidence suggests that the timing of food intake may affect weight gain. For instance, skipping breakfast, eating lunch late, and eating a large dinner have been associated with various indices of obesity [7]. Nevertheless, this subject has not been sufficiently studied in Chinese pregnant women, and one main methodological limitation is defining meal timing; conventional meal categories (i.e., breakfast, lunch, and dinner) and clock timing (external timing) to characterize meal timing may fail to accurately relate metabolic alterations in the context of the internal circadian rhythm [8]. Dim light melatonin onset is the recommended method for assessing the biological timing (internal circadian timing), which demands participants to stay in dim light conditions for a whole evening or more and undergo repeated blood or saliva collections to measure melatonin concentrations [9]. However, this method is unpractical for most epidemiological or clinical studies. A more practical approach to estimating the circadian time of food intake is to consider the timing of food intake relative to the sleep/wake cycle [10]. Moreover, changing an individual's meal timing in a real-world setting may be difficult, but changing the daily distribution of energy or macronutrients may be achievable. Therefore, in the present study, we investigated dietary intake and sleep/wake timing in the second and third trimesters to define mealtimes relative to sleep/wake timing. We examined the associations between individual daily energy and macronutrient distribution, macronutrient intake in different time windows, and GWG.

2. Materials and Methods

2.1. Study Design

Tianjin Maternal and Child Health Education and Service Cohort was a prospective cohort conducted at the Women and Children's Medical Care Center in Hebei and Heping districts of Tianjin, China, beginning in January 2018. The inclusion criteria for the cohort were: (1) age $\geq$ 18 years; (2) singleton pregnancy; (3) in the first trimester (8–13 weeks) at enrollment; and (4) no plan to move from Tianjin during the subsequent 4 years. The participants in this study were a subsample of this ongoing cohort. The exclusion criteria were (1) having no Chinese speaking or reading abilities; (2) an individual history of diabetes, hypertension, liver failure, renal failure, congestive heart failure, abnormal thyroid function, psychosis, or cancer; and (3) a positive test result for women of COVID-19, syphilis, human immunodeficiency virus, rubella, toxoplasmosis, varicella, or cytomegalovirus [11]. Accordingly, the present analysis included 149 pregnant women who had complete data on at least two of the three visits for the study and had not been locked down during pregnancy. Six of these women were excluded because their daily average energy intake was <500 kcal/d or >3500 kcal/d (first-trimester visit and second-trimester visit: n = 5; first-trimester visit, second-trimester visit, and third-trimester visit: n = 1). Finally, 143 pregnant women were included (first-trimester visit and second-trimester visit: n = 34; first-trimester visit and third-trimester visit: n = 16; first-trimester visit, second-trimester visit, and third-trimester visit: n = 92) and 234 complete pieces of data for the participants were collected between 2018 January to 2021 December.

2.2. Demographic Data and Covariates

In the first trimester, through face-to-face interviews, a self-administered questionnaire was used to collect the general demographic data of pregnant women, including age, educational level, employment status, and economic circumstances [12]. The height and weight within 1 month before pregnancy were self-reported. The pre-pregnancy body mass index (BMI) (weight (kg)/height(m)^2) was calculated using pre-pregnancy weight and height [11]. Physical activity was measured once per trimester: first trimester, 8–14 gestational weeks; second trimester, 16–27 gestational weeks; and third trimester, 28–37 gestational weeks. Physical activity evaluation was conducted by asking the participants whether they had performed any physical exertion and the duration of daily physical activity (0 = "0 h/d;" 1 = "$\leq$0.5 h/d;" 2 = ">0.5 h/d and $\leq$1.0 h/d;" 3 = ">1.0 h/d and $\leq$2.0 h/d;" and 4 = ">2.0 h/d"). Metabolic equivalents of the task were analyzed as reference thresholds of absolute intensities of the physical activities [13]. The pregnancy history, clinical history, gestational weight in each trimester, pre-delivery weight, and delivery condition were obtained from the women's medical documentation in the Women and Children's Medical Care Center.

2.3. Estimation of GWG

The evaluation indicators of GWG include total GWG across full pregnancy and the GWG rate in the second or third trimester.

First, the total GWG and the GWG rates were calculated as follows:

The total GWG = pre-delivery weight (kg) − pre-pregnancy weight (kg);

$$\text{The GWG rate} = \frac{\text{Weight at the last obstetrician visit(kg)} - \text{Weight at the first obstetrician visit(kg)}}{\text{Gestational age at the last obstetrician visit(w)} - \text{Gestational age at the first obstetrician visit(w)}}$$

Second, to evaluate the adequacy of GWG according to the Institute of Medicine recommendation [14], the value of GWG in participants with different pre-pregnancy BMIs was reassigned by the recommended value. When GWG was within the range of recommended value (adequate): Values = 1; when GWG was below or above the recommended value:

$$\text{Values} = \left(\frac{\text{GWG}}{\text{the recommended lower limit}} + \frac{\text{GWG}}{\text{the recommended upper limit}}\right)/2$$

Values > 1 represent excessive, values < 1 represent insufficient [15].

2.4. Three 24-h Dietary Recalls

Through a five-stage multiple-pass interviewing technique, three 24-h dietary recalls were conducted by trained researchers to assess the dietary intake in the second and third trimesters [16]. To further reduce recall bias and improve accuracy, the trained researchers explained the recording requirements of dietary recalls to pregnant women a few days before the survey. They suggested taking notes or photos of the food they consume [17]. Three 24-h dietary recalls were performed over consecutive days, including one on the weekend. The evaluation of dietary intake composition did not consider nutrient supplementation. The number of eating episodes was ascertained by the number of caloric events ≥50 kcal, with time intervals between food consumption ≥15 min. Additionally, meal clock timing for each eating episode was recorded. The intake of energy and macronutrients was calculated using the average of the three 24-h dietary recalls by the software Yingyangjisuanqi v2.7.6.10, with the Chinese database as a reference. Energy intakes <500 kcal/d or >3500 kcal/d were excluded from the analysis. Daily energy and macronutrient (carbohydrate, protein, and fat consumption) distribution was calculated as a percentage of total energy and macronutrient intake and divided into four time windows, as mentioned previously.

2.5. Sleep/Wake Time and Daily Time Windows

At each visit, pregnant women were required to report their usual wake time, bedtime, and sleep onset latency on weekdays. Daily food intake for the participants did not occur during the habitual sleep period on weekdays; therefore, the analysis of time windows was concentrated on the waking period. We divided the waking period into four time windows based on the relationship between the internal circadian time and the sleep/wake cycle [8,18]. The "morning" time window was defined as within 2 h after getting up. The "late morning–early afternoon" time window was defined as from 2 h after getting up to the middle of the waking period. The "late afternoon–early evening" time window was defined as from the middle of the waking period until 2 h before bedtime, and the "night" time window was defined as within 2 h before bedtime.

3. Statistical Analysis

Pregnant women were classified into mutually exclusive dietary patterns by latent profile analysis. Latent profile analysis could identify unobserved heterogeneity in multiple continuous response variables. The Akaike information criterion (AIC), Bayesian information criterion (BIC), and sample-size-adjusted BIC (aBIC) were used to determine the best-fitting latent profile model. Additionally, the Vuong, Lo, Mendell, and Rubin likelihood ratio test was used to determine whether adding an additional profile contributed to a significantly better-fitting model [19].

For continuous variables, the Shapiro–Wilk test was used to assess the distribution of variables. Data with parametric distribution are described as mean and standard deviation and were compared using the one-way analysis of variance or *t*-test. Data with nonparametric distribution are described as median and interquartile range and were compared using the Kruskal–Wallis or Mann–Whitney U tests. For categorical variables, data are described as numbers (percentages) and were compared using the chi-squared test or Fisher's exact test. Multiple comparisons were conducted using the Bonferroni post hoc test when necessary.

The Sample Wilcoxon Signed Rank Test was used to evaluate the adequacy of GWG in pregnant women with different dietary patterns. Spearman's correlation was used to explore correlations among macronutrient intake in different time windows and the GWG. Multiple Linear Regression Models (method = backward) were used to determine the effects of dietary patterns (independent variables) and macronutrient intake in different time windows (independent variables) on the adequacy of weight gain (dependent variable). Models were adjusted for age, educational level, employment status, household income, pregestational BMI, parity, the condition of gestational diabetes mellitus, gender of offspring, physical activity, daily sleep duration, time node of the time window, number of eating episodes, total energy intake, and gestational week of delivery. $p < 0.05$ was considered statistically significant. Statistical analyses were performed using SPSS version 24 and Mplus version 6.0.

4. Results

4.1. Dietary Patterns Based on Energy and Macronutrient Distribution

The model fit information for latent profile analysis model estimation based on one to five latent profiles is shown in Table S1. The Vuong, Lo, Mendell, and Rubin likelihood ratio test did not indicate that the data in the four-class model fit were significantly better than that in the three-class model ($p = 0.227$). However, as the number of latent profiles was raised, the values of AIC, BIC, and aBIC were reduced, and the entropy remained above 0.80. Based on the results of model fit tests, our research objective, and the goal of simplicity, the four-class model was identified as the best description of latent dietary profiles.

The four latent dietary profiles were characterized by average energy and macronutrient distribution in different time windows. Complete data of dietary recalls and sleep/wake time, 6.8% ($n = 16$, N = 234) were classified as having pattern 1, "high night distribution". This group had a relatively high average energy and macronutrient distribution in the night time window. A total of 40.6% ($n = 95$, N = 234) were classified as having pattern 2, "high late afternoon–early evening distribution". This group had relatively high average energy and macronutrient distribution in the late afternoon–early evening time window. Further, 31.2% ($n = 73$, N = 234) were classified as having pattern 3, "high late morning–early afternoon distribution," who had relatively high average energy and macronutrient distribution in the late morning–early afternoon time window, and 21.4% ($n = 50$, N = 234) were classified as having pattern 4, "high morning distribution," who had relatively high average energy and macronutrient distribution in the morning time window (shown in Figure 1).

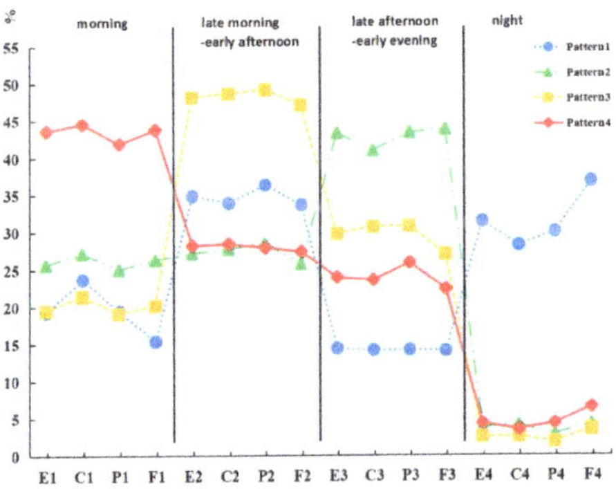

Figure 1. Average energy and macronutrient distribution of time windows in different dietary patterns. Latent profile analysis. E, energy; C, carbohydrate; P, protein; F, fat.

4.2. Participant Characteristics

The sociodemographic and anthropometric characteristics and the dietary pattern composition did not appear to differ meaningfully across subsequent analyses (shown in Table 1).

Table 1. The characteristics of participants.

Variables	The Second Trimester (n = 126)	The Third Trimester (n = 108)	The Second and Third Trimester (n = 92)		F/χ^2	p
	Mean ± SD/Median (IQR) or n (%)	Mean ± SD/Median (IQR) or n (%)	Mean ± SD/Median(IQR) Or n (%)			
Age (y)	30.85 ± 3.46	30.65 ± 3.63	30.88 ± 3.58		0.135	0.874
Level of education					0.328	0.988
High school or below	12 (9.52)	11 (10.19)	9 (9.78)			
College or university	101 (80.16)	88 (81.48)	75 (81.52)			
Master or higher	13 (10.32)	9 (8.33)	8 (8.70)			
Household income (thousand/y)					0.482	1.000
≤85	39 (30.95)	36 (33.33)	30 (32.61)			
≤180	60 (47.62)	48 (44.45)	43 (46.74)			
>180	27 (21.43)	24 (22.22)	19 (20.65)			
Unemployed					4.770	0.093
yes	15 (11.90)	14 (12.96)	4 (4.35)			
no	111 (88.10)	94 (87.04)	88 (95.65)			
Pregestational BMI (kg/m^2)	21.50 (4.94)	21.50 (4.95)	21.45 (5.14)			0.979
Parity					0.705	0.978
1	103 (81.75)	87 (80.56)	73 (79.35)			
2	22 (17.46)	20 (18.52)	18 (19.56)			
3	1 (0.79)	1 (0.92)	1 (1.09)			
Gestational weeks	39.00 (2.00)	39.00 (2.00)	39.00 (2.00)			0.908
Gender of offspring					0.074	0.964
male	58 (46.03)	51 (47.22)	44 (47.83)			
female	68 (53.97)	57 (52.78)	48 (52.17)			
Gestational diabetes mellitus			The second trimester	The third trimester	0.459	0.928
Yes	21 (16.67)	18 (16.67)	15 (16.30)	18 (19.57)		
No	105 (83.33)	90 (83.33)	77 (83.70)	74 (80.43)		
Dietary Pattern			The second trimester	The third trimester	5.684	0.771
1	10 (7.94)	6 (5.56)	10 (10.87)	3 (3.26)		
2	51 (40.48)	44 (40.74)	35 (38.04)	40 (43.48)		
3	39 (30.95)	34 (31.48)	31 (33.70)	32 (34.78)		
4	26 (20.63)	24 (22.22)	16 (17.39)	17 (18.48)		

BMI, Body mass index; SD, Standard deviation.

Age, household income, eating episodes, and time node of the "early evening/night" time window of the pregnant women differed meaningfully by dietary profile in the second trimester. Age and time node of the "early evening/night" time window of the pregnant women also differed meaningfully by dietary profile in the third trimester (shown in Table 2).

Table 2. The sociodemographic, anthropometric, chronobiological, and personal characteristics of participants by dietary profile.

Characteristic	Dietary Pattern in the Second Trimester					Dietary Pattern in the Third Trimester				
	1 (n = 10) Mean ± SD/Median (IQR) or n (%)	2 (n = 51) Mean ± SD/Median (IQR) or n(%)	3 (n = 39) Mean ± SD/Median (IQR) or n(%)	4 (n = 26) Mean ± SD/Median (IQR) or n (%)	p	1 (n = 6) Mean ± SD/Median (IQR) or n (%)	2 (n = 44) Mean ± SD/Median (IQR) or n (%)	3 (n = 34) Mean ± SD/Median (IQR) or n (%)	4 (n = 24) Mean ± SD/Median (IQR) or n (%)	p
Age (y)	30.78 ± 2.83	31.76 ± 3.53 [c]	29.62 ± 3.34 [b]	30.91 ± 3.34	**0.035**	26.73 ± 3.43 [bc]	30.88 ± 4.14 [a]	31.23 ± 3.12 [a]	30.37 ± 2.84	**0.039**
Level of education					0.841					0.515
High school or below	1 (10.00)	4 (7.84)	4 (10.26)	3 (11.54)		2 (33.33)	4 (9.09)	4 (11.76)	1 (4.17)	
College or university	9 (90.00)	43 (84.31)	30 (76.92)	19 (73.08)		4 (66.67)	37 (84.09)	27 (79.41)	20 (83.33)	
Master or higher	0 (0.00)	4 (7.84)	5 (12.82)	4 (15.38)		0 (0.00)	3 (6.82)	3 (8.82)	3 (12.50)	
Unemployed					0.447					0.074
yes	0 (0.00)	5 (9.80)	5 (12.82)	5 (19.23)		1 (16.67)	9 (20.45)	4 (11.76)	0 (0.00)	
no	10 (100.00)	46 (90.20)	34 (87.18)	21 (80.77)		5 (83.33)	35 (79.55)	30 (88.24)	24 (100.00)	
Household income(thousand/y)					**0.001**					0.215
≤85	3 (30.00)	14 (27.45)	10 (25.64)	12 (46.15)		4 (66.67)	15 (34.09)	12 (35.29)	5 (20.83)	
≤180	4 (40.00)	34 [c,d] (66.67)	15 [b] (38.46)	7 [b] (26.92)		1 (16.67)	23 (52.27)	13 (38.24)	11 (45.83)	
>180	3 (30.00)	3 [c] (5.88)	14 [b] (35.90)	7 (26.92)		1 (16.67)	6 (13.64)	9 (26.47)	8 (33.33)	
Pregestational BMI (kg/m^2)	22.32 ± 1.20	23.01 ± 0.49	21.18 ± 0.48	22.74 ± 0.74	0.087	21.37 ± 1.18	21.99 ± 0.53	22.37 ± 0.58	23.38 ± 0.71	0.380
Parity					0.694					0.974
1	7 (70.00)	40 (78.43)	33 (84.62)	23 (88.46)		5 (83.33)	36 (81.82)	27 (79.41)	19 (79.17)	
2	3 (30.00)	10 (19.61)	6 (15.38)	3 (11.54)		1 (16.67)	7 (15.91)	7 (20.59)	5 (20.83)	
3	0 (0.00)	1 (1.96)	0 (0.00)	0 (0.00)		0 (0.00)	1 (2.27)	0 (0.00)	0 (0.00)	
Gestational weeks	40.00 (2.00)	39.00 (2.00)	39.00 (2.00)	39.00 (2.00)	0.293	39.50 (1.00)	39.00 (2.00)	39.00 (2.00)	39.00 (2.00)	0.855
Gender of offspring					0.175					0.258
male	7 (70.00)	20 (39.22)	16 (41.03)	15 (57.69)		2 (33.33)	17 (38.64)	17 (50.00)	15 (62.50)	
female	3 (30.00)	31 (60.78)	23 (58.97)	11 (42.31)		4 (66.67)	27 (61.36)	17 (50.00)	9 (37.50)	
Gestational diabetes mellitus					0.935					0.476
Yes	1 (10.00)	8 (15.69)	7 (17.95)	5 (19.23)		2 (33.33)	6 (13.64)	7 (20.59)	3 (12.50)	
No	9 (90.00)	43 (84.31)	32 (82.05)	21 (80.77)		4 (66.67)	38 (86.36)	27 (79.41)	21 (87.50)	

Table 2. *Cont.*

Characteristic	Dietary Pattern in the Second Trimester					Dietary Pattern in the Third Trimester				
	1 (n = 10) Mean ± SD/Median (IQR) or n (%)	2 (n = 51) Mean ± SD/Median (IQR) or n(%)	3 (n = 39) Mean ± SD/Median (IQR) or n(%)	4 (n = 26) Mean ± SD/Median (IQR) or n (%)	p	1 (n = 6) Mean ± SD/Median (IQR) or n (%)	2 (n = 44) Mean ± SD/Median (IQR) or n (%)	3 (n = 34) Mean ± SD/Median (IQR) or n (%)	4 (n = 24) Mean ± SD/Median (IQR) or n (%)	p
Physical activity (MET)	32.40 ± 1.48	28.73 ± 1.21	30.14 ± 1.14	28.85 ± 1.18	0.492	27.42 ± 2.84	32.06 ± 1.46	30.75 ± 1.45	31.35 ± 2.09	0.482
Daily sleep duration (h)	470.20 ± 18.20	508.45 ± 11.37	521.41 ± 10.33	525.73 ± 10.05	0.144	549.17 ± 25.18	530.75 ± 12.97	531.29 ± 13.01	524.67 ± 15.84	0.928
Eating episodes	4.70 ± 0.67 [c,d]	4.10 ± 0.70	3.77 ± 0.77 [a]	3.92 ± 0.80 [a]	**0.004**	4.17 ± 1.33	4.25 ± 0.81	4.24 ± 0.70	4.00 ± 0.88	0.660
Time node of time window										
Morning/Late morning	09:05 ± 00:32	09:38 ± 01:00	09:49 ± 00:55	09:43 ± 00:58	0.621	10:12 ± 01:40	09:39 ± 00:49	09:41 ± 00:59	09:16 ± 00:51	0.178
Early afternoon/Late afternoon	14:25 ± 0:47 [b]	15:01 ± 0:47 [a]	15:33 ± 0:38	15:28 ± 0:53	**0.046**	14:57 ± 01:05	15:35 ± 00:38	15:33 ± 00:40	15:09 ± 00:52	0.362
Early evening/ Night	19:59 ± 01:24 [b,c]	21:09 ± 00:50 [a]	20:47 ± 00:42 [a]	20:43 ± 01:01	**0.006**	19:22 ± 01:07 [bcd]	20:56 ± 00:37 [a]	20:58 ± 00:51 [a]	20:29 ± 01:12 [a]	**0.004**
Daily energy and macronutrients										
Energy (kcal)	1761.00 (1160.09)	1379.33 (451.00)	1477.00 (1052.80)	1721.50 (647.33)	0.318	1487.33 (1008.32)	1659.33 (684.08)	1586.92 (474.00)	1472.00 (498.33)	0.721
Carbohydrate (g)	226.60 (176.89)	185.80 (111.81)	234.63 (158.00)	218.72 (146.41)	0.538	178.00 (211.11)	238.18 (101.34)	237.38 (84.51)	222.05 (80.33)	0.810
Protein (g)	77.79 (50.07)	62.47 (30.27)	62.53 (41.77)	77.15 (33.28)	0.315	75.28 (35.64)	72.52 (24.98)	80.80 (39.08)	62.83 (31.58)	0.235
Fat (g)	59.07 (71.44)	44.77 (28.4)	40.03 (27.53)	46.44 (32.04)	0.335	55.68 (37.21)	45.90 (30.73)	42.96 (28.73)	37.52 (17.77)	0.372

[a] Values were significantly different from pattern 1 (α level for statistical significance identified with Bonferroni correction). [b] Values were significantly different from pattern 2 (α level for statistical significance identified with Bonferroni correction). [c] Values were significantly different from pattern 3 (α level for statistical significance identified with Bonferroni correction). [d] Values were significantly different from pattern 4 (α level for statistical significance identified with Bonferroni correction). Significant tests shown in bold. BMI, Body mass index; MET, Metabolic equivalents of task; SD, Standard deviation.

Daily energy and macronutrient intake did not differ significantly by dietary profile in the second and third trimesters. The energy and macronutrient intake in different time windows differed significantly by dietary profile in the second and third trimesters (shown in Tables 3 and 4).

Table 3. The differences in energy and macronutrient intake during the second trimester between each dietary pattern.

Nutrient	Dietary Pattern in the Second Trimester				P Value
	1 (*n* = 10) Median (IQR)	2 (*n* = 51) Median (IQR)	3 (*n* = 39) Median (IQR)	4 (*n* = 26) Median (IQR)	
Energy and macronutrients intake in "morning" time window					
Energy (kcal)	278.50 (509.74)	379.33 (221.33) [d]	326.67 (218.67) [d]	728.67 (369.17) [b,c]	**<0.001**
Carbohydrate (g)	44.38 (80.55)	53.53 (37.24) [d]	45.90 (38.25) [d]	98.16 (77.74) [b,c]	**<0.001**
Protein (g)	12.52 (22.40)	16.80 (10.64) [d]	12.37 (8.09) [d]	26.52 (13.88) [b,c]	**<0.001**
Fat (g)	7.34 (15.64) [d]	10.10 (7.04) [d]	7.53 (9.26) [d]	18.05 (11.28) [a,b,c]	**<0.001**
Energy and macronutrients intake in "late morning–early afternoon" time window					
Energy (kcal)	505.00 (593.42)	407.00 (218.67) [c]	674.00 (441.69) [b,d]	456.00 (227.42) [c]	**<0.001**
Carbohydrate (g)	61.93 (99.33)	51.90 (35.80) [c]	96.93 (65.04) [b,d]	56.94 (34.00) [c]	**<0.001**
Protein (g)	30.50 (18.18)	17.60 (11.93) [c]	28.27 (19.96) [b,d]	19.47 (13.46) [c]	**<0.001**
Fat (g)	15.85 (20.92)	10.57 (9.30) [c]	19.53 (16.67) [b,d]	12.72 (18.78) [c]	**<0.001**
Energy and macronutrients intake in "late afternoon–early evening" time window					
Energy (kcal)	252.00 (395.38) [b]	603.67 (290.89) [a,c,d]	472.97 (385.00) [b]	385.84 (175.19) [b]	**<0.001**
Carbohydrate (g)	17.22 (58.32) [b]	78.97 (74.77) [a,c,d]	69.53 (45.17) [b]	50.07 (32.06) [b]	**<0.001**
Protein (g)	9.52 (16.88) [b,c]	26.57 (14.40) [a,d]	19.23 (16.30) [a]	19.13 (9.07) [b]	**<0.001**
Fat (g)	6.59(18.49) [b]	16.17 (15.10) [a,c,d]	9.90 (9.89) [b]	8.96 (9.54) [b]	**<0.001**
Energy and macronutrients intake in "night" time window					
Energy (kcal)	453.67 (535.25) [b,c,d]	21.00 (106.67) [a]	0.00 (36.00) [a]	78.50 (167.75) [a]	**<0.001**
Carbohydrate (g)	72.99 (87.08) [b,c,d]	2.43 (15.87) [a]	0.00 (4.90) [a]	7.98 (15.32) [a]	**<0.001**
Protein (g)	23.17 (30.44) [b,c,d]	0.23 (2.77) [a]	0.00 (0.93) [a]	2.77 (6.72) [a]	**<0.001**
Fat (g)	21.59 (25.21) [b,c,d]	0.10 (2.57) [a]	0.00 (0.77) [a]	0.82 (6.4) [a]	**<0.001**

[a] Values were significantly different from pattern 1 (α level for statistical significance identified with Bonferroni correction). [b] Values were significantly different from pattern 2 (α level for statistical significance identified with Bonferroni correction). [c] Values were significantly different from pattern 3 (α level for statistical significance identified with Bonferroni correction). [d] Values were significantly different from pattern 4 (α level for statistical significance identified with Bonferroni correction). Significant tests shown in bold. IQR, interquartile range.

In the second trimester, there were 14.3% (n =18) of pregnant women with insufficient GWG rates, 33.3% (n = 42) with adequate GWG rates, and 52.4% (n = 66) with excessive GWG rates. In the third trimester, there were 22.2% (n = 24) of pregnant women with insufficient GWG rates, 24.1% (n = 26) with adequate GWG rates, and 53.7% (n = 58) with excessive GWG rates. There were 23.9% (n = 22) of pregnant women with insufficient total GWG, 45.7% (n = 42) with adequate total GWG, and 30.4% (n = 28) with excessive total GWG.

4.3. The Adequacy of GWG in Pregnant Women with Different Dietary Patterns

Pregnant women with a high late afternoon–early evening distribution in the second (Median (IQR) = 1.31 (0.70), Z = 3.391, p = 0.001) and third trimesters (Median (IQR) = 1.34 (0.72), Z = 3.065, p = 0.002), pregnant women with high late morning–early afternoon distribution (Median(IQR) = 1.00(0.68), Z = 3.296, p = 0.001) in the second trimester, and pregnant women with high morning distribution in the second (Median(IQR) = 1.35 (0.81), Z = 2.838, p = 0.005) and third trimesters (Median (IQR) = 1.68 (1.14), Z = 2.374, p = 0.018) appeared to have excessive GWG rates. Pregnant women with a high late morning–early afternoon distribution in the second trimester (Median (IQR) = 1.00 (0.31), Z = 2.374, p = 0.018) appeared to have excessive total GWG (shown in Figure 2).

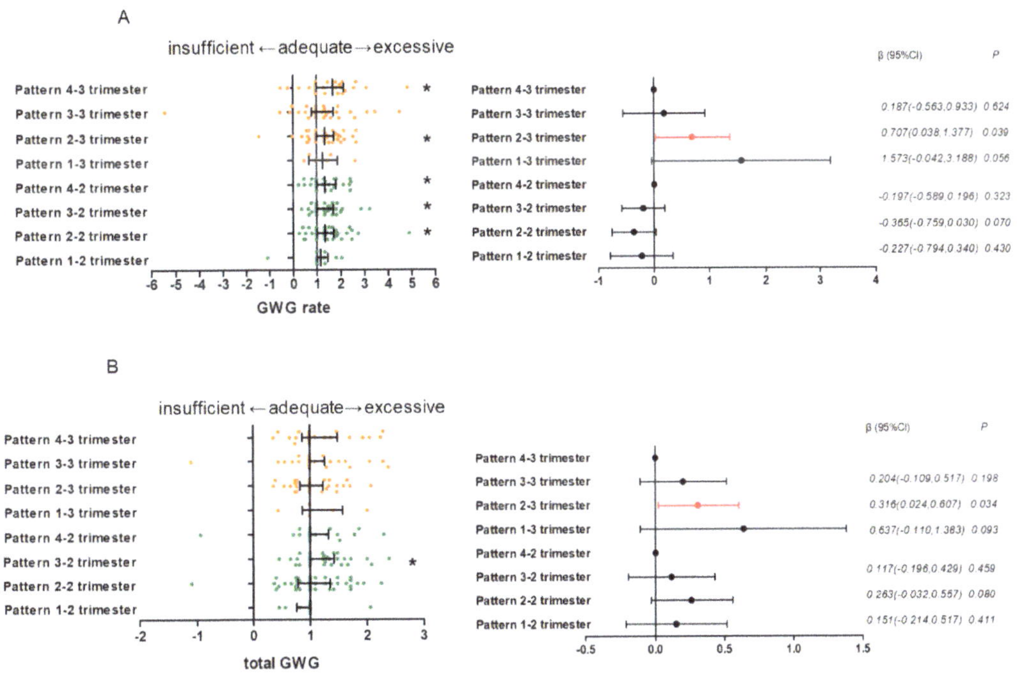

Figure 2. The effect of dietary patterns on GWG One Sample Wilcoxon Signed Rank Tests; Multiple Linear Regression Models (method = backward): (**A**) the effect of dietary patterns in the second and third trimesters on the adequacy of GWG rate; (**B**) the effect of dietary patterns in the second and third trimesters on the adequacy of total GWG * Values were significantly different from 1.

Table 4. The differences in energy and macronutrient intake during the third trimester between each dietary pattern.

Nutrient	Dietary Pattern in the Third Trimester				*p* Value
	1 (*n* = 6) Median (IQR)	2 (*n* = 44) Median (IQR)	3 (*n* = 34) Median (IQR)	4 (*n* = 24) Median (IQR)	
Energy and macronutrients intake in "morning" time window					
Energy (kcal)	440.67 (403.91)	389.84 (224.42) [d]	333.50 (222.00) [d]	633.67 (278.08) [b,c]	**<0.001**
Carbohydrate (g)	61.77 (81.58)	56.92 (28.73) [d]	48.18 (35.47) [d]	86.48 (56.23) [b,c]	**<0.001**
Protein (g)	21.85 (13.00)	17.65 (6.94) [d]	15.28 (12.29) [d]	25.40 (11.23) [b,c]	**<0.001**
Fat (g)	8.72 (9.29) [d]	10.70 (7.13) [d]	9.15 (8.81) [d]	19.12 (9.95) [a,b,c]	**<0.001**
Energy and macronutrients intake in"late morning–early afternoon" time window					
Energy (kcal)	550.67 (460.50)	454.00 (229.25) [c]	799.50 (282.25) [b,d]	436.84 (266.17) [c]	**<0.001**
Carbohydrate (g)	59.73 (92.64)	63.68 (35.83) [c]	107.85 (43.50) [b,d]	71.12 (50.54) [c]	**<0.001**
Protein (g)	23.17 (7.71)	19.93 (12.59) [c]	39.20 (22.83) [b,d]	15.33 (15.85) [c]	**<0.001**
Fat (g)	15.23 (19.43)	10.28 (14.11) [c]	20.22 (13.62) [b,d]	9.62 (10.77) [c]	**<0.001**
Energy and macronutrients intake in"late afternoon–early evening" time window					
Energy (kcal)	156.83 (364.83) [b]	714.00 (344.42) [a,c,d]	464.50 (287.59) [b]	373.67 (213.67) [b]	**<0.001**
Carbohydrate (g)	17.40 (64.83) [b]	91.91 (63.27) [a,c,d]	56.59 (39.93) [b]	56.02 (40.25) [b]	**<0.001**
Protein (g)	7.27 (13.52) [b,c]	29.29 (12.01) [a,d]	23.28 (14.47) [a]	20.02 (9.77) [b]	**<0.001**
Fat (g)	3.05 (10.92) [b]	16.95 (15.23) [a,c,d]	10.58 (11.83) [b]	8.55 (7.81) [b]	**<0.001**
Energy and macronutrients intake in "night" time window					
Energy (kcal)	491.00 (294.33) [b,c,d]	22.84 (127.33) [a]	16.67 (104.75) [a]	20.33 (97.83) [a]	**<0.001**
Carbohydrate (g)	57.93 (40.38) [b,c,d]	3.60 (17.28) [a]	2.85 (10.84) [a]	4.20 (10.26) [a]	**<0.001**

Table 4. *Cont.*

Nutrient	Dietary Pattern in the Third Trimester				p Value
	1 (n = 6) Median (IQR)	2 (n = 44) Median (IQR)	3 (n = 34) Median (IQR)	4 (n = 24) Median (IQR)	
	Energy and macronutrients intake in "morning" time window				
Protein (g)	23.97 (17.53) [b,c,d]	0.37 (3.55) [a]	0.33 (3.92) [a]	0.28 (3.88) [a]	**<0.001**
Fat (g)	24.58 (11.18) [b,c,d]	0.07 (3.36) [a]	0.08 (2.88) [a]	0.05 (4.20) [a]	**<0.001**

[a] Values were significantly different from pattern 1 (α level for statistical significance identified with Bonferroni correction). [b] Values were significantly different from pattern 2 (α level for statistical significance identified with Bonferroni correction). [c] Values were significantly different from pattern 3 (α level for statistical significance identified with Bonferroni correction). [d] Values were significantly different from pattern 4 (α level for statistical significance identified with Bonferroni correction). Significant tests shown in bold. IQR, interquartile range.

4.4. Correlations between Macronutrient Intake in Different Time Windows and the GWG

Fat consumption in the late afternoon–early evening of the second trimester was significantly positively correlated to the GWG rate of the second trimester (Spearman $\gamma = 0.192$, $p = 0.031$), fat consumption in the morning of the third trimester was significantly positively correlated to total GWG (Spearman $\gamma = 0.220$, $p = 0.022$) (shown in Figure 3).

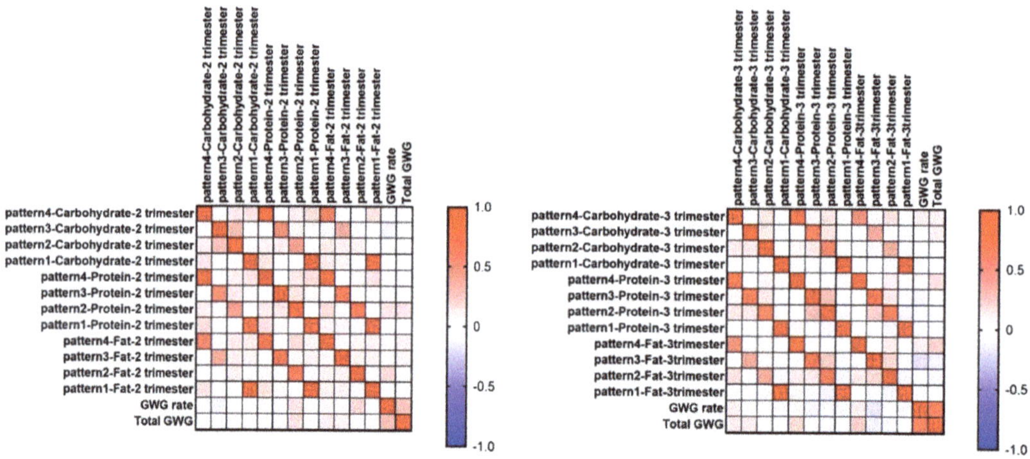

Figure 3. Correlations between macronutrient intake in different time windows and the GWG. Spearman's correlation.

4.5. Effect of Dietary Patterns and Macronutrient Intake in Different Time Windows on GWG

In the second trimester, carbohydrate (β (95% CI): 0.004 (0.000, 0.008); $p = 0.043$), fat (β (95% CI): 0.023 (0.010, 0.036); $p = 0.001$), and protein intake (β (95% CI): 0.015 (0.005, 0.026); $p = 0.005$) in the late afternoon–early evening time window, protein intake in the late morning–early afternoon time window (β (95% CI): 0.016 (0.006, 0.027); $p = 0.003$), and carbohydrate intake in the morning time window (β (95% CI): 0.005 (0.001, 0.010); $p = 0.018$) were positively associated with the GWG rates. Carbohydrate intake in the morning time window (β (95% CI): 0.004 (0.001, 0.007); $p = 0.005$) was positively associated with total GWG, and protein intake in the morning time window (β (95% CI): −0.014 (−0.026, −0.002); $p = 0.022$) were negatively associated with total GWG.

In the third trimester, fat intake in the late morning–early afternoon time window (β (95% CI): −0.023 (−0.044, −0.001); $p = 0.041$) and protein intake in the late afternoon–early evening (β (95% CI): −0.034 (−0.059, −0.010); $p = 0.007$) and morning time window (β (95% CI): −0.042(−0.073, −0.012); $p = 0.007$) were negatively associated with the GWG rates. Carbohydrate (β (95% CI): 0.008 (0.000, 0.016); $p = 0.037$) and fat (β (95% CI): 0.051 (0.017,

0.085); $p = 0.004$) intake in the morning time window was positively associated with the GWG rates. Pregnant women who had a relatively high average energy and macronutrient distribution in late afternoon–early evening time window exhibited a greater GWG rate than in morning time window (β (95% CI): 0.707(0.038, 1.377); $p = 0.039$) (shown in Figure 2). Protein intake in the late afternoon–early evening time window (β (95% CI): −0.013 (−0.024, −0.001); $p = 0.028$), carbohydrate intake in the late morning–early afternoon time window (β (95% CI): 0.004 (0.001, 0.007); $p = 0.014$), and fat intake in the morning time window (β (95% CI): 0.023 (0.011, 0.035); $p < 0.001$) were significantly associated with total GWG. Pregnant women who had a relatively high average energy and macronutrient distribution in late afternoon–early evening time window exhibited a greater total GWG than that in morning time window (β (95% CI): 0.316(0.024, 0.607); $p = 0.034$) (shown in Figure 2).

5. Discussion

To the best of our knowledge, the present study is the first to be conducted on Chinese pregnant women to investigate the effects of daily energy and macronutrient distribution on GWG during the second and third trimesters.

Our study findings showed that the proportion of pregnant women with an inadequate, adequate, or excessive trimester-specific mean rate of GWG (14.3%, 33.3%, 52.4% in the second trimester; 22.2%, 24.1%, 53.7% in the third trimester) and total GWG (23.9%, 45.7%, 30.4%) was approximately similar to some studies [4,20–22]. However, it differed from a large retrospective cohort study conducted with Chinese singleton pregnant women with gestational diabetes mellitus [23]. This large population-based study was conducted with Chinese singleton pregnant women who delivered between January 2011 and December 2017 in Beijing [24]. However, this could be due to the differences between populations, such as physical conditions and regional dietetic culture.

Though neither daily energy intake nor physical activity differed significantly across all dietary patterns in the present study, we found that pregnant women with the high late afternoon–early evening distribution in the second and third trimesters appeared to have excessive GWG rates; macronutrient (carbohydrate, fat, and protein) intake in the late afternoon–early evening time window of the second trimester was associated with greater GWG rates. Moreover, pregnant women who had a relatively high average energy and macronutrient distribution in late afternoon–early evening time window exhibited a greater GWG rate and a greater total GWG than in the morning time window during the third trimester. These findings are consistent with other studies conducted in pregnant women [15,25] and non-pregnant adults [8,26,27], which supported that higher intake in the evening was associated with a higher risk of weight gain. A potential mechanism may be associated with circadian changes in total energy expenditure, including resting metabolic rate and the thermic effect of food [28]. Randomized crossover trials reported that the endogenous circadian rhythm in the total energy expenditure of healthy adults peaked in the biological morning or early afternoon and was lower in the biological evening [29,30]. If the total energy expenditure was reduced, coupled with high energy-dense food intake, it might cause a positive energy balance in pregnant women as a contributing factor for excessive weight gained.

Additionally, we found that pregnant women with high late morning–early afternoon distribution in the second trimester with high morning distribution in the second and third trimesters experienced excessive GWG rates or excessive total GWG. Protein intake in the late morning–early afternoon time window of the second trimester, carbohydrate intake in the morning time window of the second trimester, carbohydrate intake in the late morning–early afternoon time window of the third trimester, and carbohydrate and fat intake in the morning time window of the third trimester was associated with greater GWG rates or greater total GWG. This finding is inconsistent with other studies conducted on pregnant women [15,25] and non-pregnant adults [8,26,27,31], which supported that higher morning or lunch intake was associated with a lower risk of weight gain. One possible reason is the difference between Chinese and Western food cultures. Taking breakfast as an example, nearly 90% of Chinese ingested cereals and tubers products (rich in carbohydrates), approximately 50% ingested vegetables, fruits, meat, fish, eggs, and milk, and only approximately 30% ingested beans and nuts [32]. In our study, participants with high morning distribution or high late morning–early afternoon distribution did not have a better diet quality for fruit components, milk, and nuts [33,34]. There is no significant difference in micronutrient intake across four dietary patterns (shown in Table S2). Much deep-fried food (rich in carbohydrates and fat) belongs to traditional Chinese breakfasts, such as dough sticks [35]. A previous study showed 4–8 weeks of overfeeding healthy adults with a high-fat breakfast resulted in 2–4 kg of weight gain [36], and a high-fat breakfast did not change satiety a few hours after breakfast [37]. Additionally, an increase of 1 g of carbohydrates was related to an increment of 17 g in weight during pregnancy. In comparison, 1 g of sugar was associated with an increase of 26 g of weight during pregnancy [38].

Interestingly, we found protein intake in the morning time window of the second trimester, protein intake in the late afternoon–early evening and morning time window of the third trimester, and fat intake in the late morning–early afternoon time window of the third trimester were negatively associated with the GWG rates or total GWG. This could be because foods high in protein are typically less energy dense. In healthy women, high-protein intake has a greater effect on satiety and appetite control and less subsequent food intake [39]. Though there is no significant difference in micronutrient intake across four dietary patterns, participants in our study were accustomed to eating food rich in monounsaturated and polyunsaturated fatty acids as snacks in the late morning–early afternoon time window. For instance, in nuts and yogurt, monounsaturated and polyunsaturated fatty acids have been found to contribute to weight loss and obesity prevention [40]. The total GWG was related more closely to eating behavior during the third trimester. This could be due to nonmonotonic fetal growth. However, the biparietal diameter and head circumference show an accelerated increase in the second trimester, while the abdominal circumference and estimated fetal weight velocity peak in the third trimester [41]. Another possible cause was the dietary counseling [42] after BMI monitoring in the second trimester; some pregnant women (65.2%, not shown in the result) in our study changed their dietary patterns after the second trimester.

This study has many strengths. First, we concurrently collected data about sleep timing and meal timing, which enabled us to establish an index indicating the circadian time of food intake. Second, we used a prospective design to assess multiple time points of sleep timing and dietary recalls, which reduced the potential effect of seasonal fluctuations in sleep timing and meal timing. Third, we considered the relationship between relative and absolute energy and macronutrient intake and GWG, since this is achievable in weight management during pregnancy. This study also has several limitations. The study was conducted on relatively healthy women in early pregnancy; therefore, the results of this study cannot be generalized to all pregnant women, especially those with high-risk pregnancies. A small sample size of pregnant women with higher night distribution hinders the observation of the association between the night distribution of energy and macronutrients and GWG. Moreover, a more detailed classification of nutrient consumption was not considered, such as saturated fatty acids, monounsaturated fatty acids, and polyunsaturated fatty acids. Future studies with more comprehensive investigations of sleep status and diet conditions in a larger population of pregnant women are needed.

6. Conclusions

Excessive GWG of Chinese pregnant women was related closely to eating behavior focused on the late afternoon–early evening time window and carbohydrate and fat intake in the morning during the second and third trimesters. Our findings emphasize that it is necessary to pay attention to Chinese pregnant women with high energy and macronutrient distribution in the late afternoon–early evening and adjust the macronutrient intake based on internal circadian timing for GWG management. Additionally, clinicians should provide more well-directed nutritional advice for pregnant women in different trimesters.

Supplementary Materials: The following supporting information can be downloaded at: https://www.mdpi.com/article/10.3390/nu15092106/s1, Table S1: Model fit information for latent profile analysis by number of estimated profiles; Table S2: The differences in micronutrient intake during the second and third trimester between each dietary pattern.

Author Contributions: Conceptualization, W.X.; Data curation, X.Z.; Formal analysis, W.X., S.C., J.D., Y.S., Y.H. and Z.Q.; Funding acquisition, S.C. and X.Z.; Investigation, W.X., J.D., Y.S., Y.H., Z.Q., S.J. and Z.L.; Methodology, W.X., L.G. and T.C.; Project administration, X.Z.; Supervision, X.Z.; Writing—original draft, W.X. and S.C.; Writing—review and editing, S.C. and X.Z. All authors have read and agreed to the published version of the manuscript.

Funding: This work was supported by grants from the National Natural Science Foundation of China (nos. 81973070, 82003449, and 82273655).

Institutional Review Board Statement: The present study was approved by the Institutional Review Board of Tianjin Medical University (TMUhMEC2017020) and was conducted in agreement with the ethical norms of the Declaration of Helsinki.

Informed Consent Statement: Written consent was obtained from the pregnant women involved in the study.

Data Availability Statement: The raw data analyzed in the present study will be available from the corresponding author on reasonable request.

Acknowledgments: We acknowledge the Women and Children's Medical Care Center in Hebei and Heping districts of Tianjin China. Special thanks to the pregnant women who agreed to participate in this study.

Conflicts of Interest: The authors have no conflict of interest to declare.

References

1. Champion, M.L.; Harper, L.M. Gestational Weight Gain: Update on Outcomes and Interventions. *Curr. Diabetes Rep.* **2020**, *20*, 11. [CrossRef] [PubMed]
2. LifeCycle Project-Maternal Obesity and Childhood Outcomes Study Group; Voerman, E.; Santos, S.; Inskip, H.; Amiano, P.; Barros, H.; Charles, M.A.; Chatzi, L.; Chrousos, G.P.; Corpeleijn, E.; et al. Association of Gestational Weight Gain With Adverse Maternal and Infant Outcomes. *JAMA* **2019**, *321*, 1702–1715. [PubMed]
3. Branum, A.M.; Sharma, A.J.; Deputy, N.P. Gestational weight gain among women with full-term, singleton births, compared with recommendations—48 states and the District of Columbia, 2015. *Morb. Mortal. Wkly. Rep.* **2016**, *65*, 1121.
4. Wang, J.; Duan, Y.F.; Pang, X.H.; Jiang, S.; Yin, S.A.; Yang, Z.Y.; Lai, J.Q. Gestational weight gain and optimal ranges in Chinese mothers giving singleton and full-term births in 2013. *Zhonghua Yu Fang Yi Xue Za Zhi* **2018**, *52*, 31–37. (In Chinese) [PubMed]
5. Chen, X.K.; Wen, S.W.; Fleming, N.; Demissie, K.; Rhoads, G.G.; Walker, M. Teenage pregnancy and adverse birth outcomes: A large population based retrospective cohort study. *Int. J. Epidemiol.* **2007**, *36*, 368–373. [CrossRef]
6. Cunningham, F.G. Maternal Physiology. In *Williams Obstetrics*, 24th ed.; McGraw Hill Education: New York, NY, USA, 2018; pp. 51–54.
7. Lopez-Minguez, J.; Gómez-Abellán, P.; Garaulet, M. Timing of Breakfast, Lunch, and Dinner. Effects on Obesity and Metabolic Risk. *Nutrients* **2019**, *11*, 2624. [CrossRef]
8. Xiao, Q.; Garaulet, M.; Scheer, F.A.J.L. Meal timing and obesity: Interactions with macronutrient intake and chronotype. *Int. J. Obes.* **2019**, *43*, 1701–1711. [CrossRef]
9. Reid, K.J. Assessment of Circadian Rhythms. *Neurol. Clin.* **2019**, *37*, 505–526. [CrossRef]
10. McHill, A.W.; Phillips, A.J.; Czeisler, C.A.; Keating, L.; Yee, K.; Barger, L.K.; Garaulet, M.; Scheer, F.A.; Klerman, E.B. Later circadian timing of food intake is associated with increased body fat. *Am. J. Clin. Nutr.* **2017**, *106*, 1213–1219. [CrossRef]
11. World Health Organization. Obesity: Preventing and managing the global epidemic. In *Report of a WHO Consultation*; World Health Organization: Geneva, Switzerland, 2000.
12. Suliga, E.; Rokita, W.; Adamczyk-Gruszka, O.; Pazera, G.; Cieśla, E.; Głuszek, S. Factors associated with gestational weight gain: A cross-sectional survey. *BMC Pregnancy Childbirth* **2018**, *18*, 465. [CrossRef]
13. Aadahl, M.; Jørgensen, T. Validation of a new self-report instrument for measuring physical activity. *Med. Sci. Sport. Exerc.* **2003**, *35*, 1196–1202. [CrossRef] [PubMed]
14. Rasmussen, K.M.; Yaktine, A.L. (Eds.) *Weight Gain during Pregnancy: Reexamining the Guidelines*; National Academy Press: Washington, DC, USA, 2009.

15. Gontijo, C.A.; Balieiro, L.C.T.; Teixeira, G.P.; Fahmy, W.M.; Crispim, C.A.; Maia, Y.C.P. Higher energy intake at night effects daily energy distribution and contributes to excessive weight gain during pregnancy. *Nutrition* **2020**, *74*, 110756. [CrossRef] [PubMed]
16. Conway, J.M.; Ingwersen, L.A.; Vinyard, B.T.; Moshfegh, A.J. Effectiveness of the US Department of Agriculture 5-step multiple-pass method in assessing food intake in obese and nonobese women. *Am. J. Clin. Nutr.* **2003**, *77*, 1171–1178. [CrossRef] [PubMed]
17. Ding, Y.; Yang, Y.; Li, F.; Shao, Y.; Sun, Z.; Zhong, C.; Fan, P.; Li, Z.; Zhang, M.; Li, X.; et al. Development and validation of a photographic atlas of food portions for accurate quantification of dietary intakes in China. *J. Hum. Nutr. Diet.* **2021**, *34*, 604–615. [CrossRef] [PubMed]
18. Lovato, N.; Micic, G.; Gradisar, M.; Ferguson, S.A.; Burgess, H.J.; Kennaway, D.J.; Lack, L. Can the circadian phase be estimated from self-reported sleep timing in patients with Delayed Sleep Wake Phase Disorder to guide timing of chronobiologic treatment? *Chronobiol. Int.* **2016**, *33*, 1376–1390. [CrossRef]
19. Tein, J.Y.; Coxe, S.; Cham, H. Statistical Power to Detect the Correct Number of Classes in Latent Profile Analysis. *Struct. Equ. Model. Multidiscip. J.* **2013**, *20*, 640–657. [CrossRef]
20. Wang, X.; Zhang, X.; Zhou, M.; Juan, J.; Wang, X. Association of pre-pregnancy body mass index, rate of gestational weight gain with pregnancy outcomes in Chinese urban women. *Nutr. Metab.* **2019**, *16*, 54. [CrossRef]
21. Wen, F.H.; Lee, C.F.; Lin, C.J.; Lin, H.M. Total gestational weight change and rate of change in pregnant Taiwanese women. *Taiwan J. Obstet. Gynecol.* **2019**, *58*, 196–200. [CrossRef]
22. Sun, Y.; Shen, Z.; Zhan, Y.; Wang, Y.; Ma, S.; Zhang, S.; Liu, J.; Wu, S.; Feng, Y.; Chen, Y.; et al. Effects of pre-pregnancy body mass index and gestational weight gain on maternal and infant complications. *BMC Pregnancy Childbirth* **2020**, *20*, 390. [CrossRef]
23. Fan, X.; Dai, J.; He, J.; Tian, R.; Xu, J.; Song, J.; Bai, J.; Liu, Y.; Zou, Z.; Chen, X. Optimal gestational weight gain in Chinese pregnant women with gestational diabetes mellitus: A large retrospective cohort study. *J. Obstet. Gynaecol. Res.* **2023**, *49*, 182–193. [CrossRef]
24. Zheng, W.; Huang, W.; Zhang, L.; Tian, Z.; Yan, Q.; Wang, T.; Li, G.; Zhang, W. Suggested Gestational Weight Gain for Chinese Women and Comparison with Institute of Medicine Criteria: A Large Population-Based Study. *Obes. Facts* **2021**, *14*, 1–9. [CrossRef] [PubMed]
25. Balieiro, L.C.T.; Gontijo, C.A.; Marot, L.P.; Teixeira, G.P.; Fahmy, W.M.; de Paiva Maia, Y.C.; Crispim, C.A. Is chronotype associated with dietary intake and weight gain during pregnancy? A prospective and longitudinal study. *Nutrition* **2022**, *94*, 111530. [CrossRef] [PubMed]
26. Kahleova, H.; Lloren, J.I.; Mashchak, A.; Hill, M.; Fraser, G.E. Meal Frequency and Timing Are Associated with Changes in Body Mass Index in Adventist Health Study 2. *J. Nutr.* **2017**, *147*, 1722–1728. [CrossRef]
27. Wang, J.B.; Patterson, R.E.; Ang, A.; Emond, J.A.; Shetty, N.; Arab, L. Timing of energy intake during the day is associated with the risk of obesity in adults. *J. Hum. Nutr. Diet.* **2014**, *27* (Suppl. S2), 255–262. [CrossRef] [PubMed]
28. Basolo, A.; Bechi Genzano, S.; Piaggi, P.; Krakoff, J.; Santini, F. Energy Balance and Control of Body Weight: Possible Effects of Meal Timing and Circadian Rhythm Dysregulation. *Nutrients* **2021**, *13*, 3276. [CrossRef] [PubMed]
29. Kräuchi, K.; Wirz-Justice, A. Circadian rhythm of heat production, heart rate, and skin and core temperature under unmasking conditions in men. *Am. J. Physiol.* **1994**, *267 Pt 2*, R819–R829. [CrossRef] [PubMed]
30. Morris, C.J.; Garcia, J.I.; Myers, S.; Yang, J.N.; Trienekens, N.; Scheer, F.A. The Human Circadian System Has a Dominating Role in Causing the Morning/Evening Difference in Diet-Induced Thermogenesis. *Obesity* **2015**, *23*, 2053–2058. [CrossRef]
31. Hermenegildo, Y.; López-García, E.; García-Esquinas, E.; Pérez-Tasigchana, R.F.; Rodríguez-Artalejo, F.; Guallar-Castillón, P. Distribution of energy intake throughout the day and weight gain: A population-based cohort study in Spain. *Br. J. Nutr.* **2016**, *115*, 2003–2010. [CrossRef]
32. Li, L.; Cao, W.; Xu, J.; Pan, H.; Yang, T.; Xu, P.; Gan, Q.; Hu, X.; Zhang, Q. Breakfast food varieties of children aged 6-17 in China from 2010 to 2012. *Wei Sheng Yan Jiu* **2019**, *48*, 395–398. (In Chinese)
33. Gontijo, C.A.; Balieiro, L.C.T.; Teixeira, G.P.; Fahmy, W.M.; Crispim, C.A.; Maia, Y.C.P. Effects of timing of food intake on eating patterns, diet quality and weight gain during pregnancy. *Br. J. Nutr.* **2020**, *123*, 922–933. [CrossRef]
34. Chatelan, A.; Castetbon, K.; Pasquier, J.; Allemann, C.; Zuber, A.; Camenzind-Frey, E.; Zuberbuehler, C.A.; Bochud, M. Association between breakfast composition and abdominal obesity in the Swiss adult population eating breakfast regularly. *Int. J. Behav. Nutr. Phys. Act.* **2018**, *15*, 115. [CrossRef] [PubMed]
35. An, K.J.; Liu, Y.L.; Liu, H.L. Relationship between total polar components and polycyclic aromatic hydrocarbons in fried edible oil. *Food Addit. Contam. Part A* **2017**, *34*, 1596–1605. [CrossRef] [PubMed]
36. Gupta, N.; Jensen, M.D. Clinical effects of high-fat meals and weight gain due to high-fat feeding. *Int. J. Obes.* **2012**, *2* (Suppl. S2), S51–S55. [CrossRef] [PubMed]
37. Smith-Ryan, A.E.; Hirsch, K.R.; Blue, M.N.M.; Mock, M.G.; Trexler, E.T. High-Fat Breakfast Meal Replacement in Overweight and Obesity: Implications on Body Composition, Metabolic Markers, and Satiety. *Nutrients* **2019**, *11*, 865. [CrossRef]
38. Diemert, A.; Lezius, S.; Pagenkemper, M.; Hansen, G.; Drozdowska, A.; Hecher, K.; Arck, P.; Zyriax, B.C. Maternal nutrition, inadequate gestational weight gain and birth weight: Results from a prospective birth cohort. *BMC Pregnancy Childbirth* **2016**, *16*, 224. [CrossRef]
39. Ortinau, L.C.; Hoertel, H.A.; Douglas, S.M.; Leidy, H.J. Effects of high-protein vs. high- fat snacks on appetite control, satiety, and eating initiation in healthy women. *Nutr. J.* **2014**, *13*, 97. [CrossRef]

40. Liu, R.; Chen, L.; Wang, Z.; Zheng, X.; Hou, Z.; Zhao, D.; Long, J.; Liu, J. Omega-3 polyunsaturated fatty acids prevent obesity by improving tricarboxylic acid cycle homeostasis. *J. Nutr. Biochem.* **2021**, *88*, 108503. [CrossRef]
41. Grantz, K.L.; Kim, S.; Grobman, W.A.; Newman, R.; Owen, J.; Skupski, D.; Grewal, J.; Chien, E.K.; Wing, D.A.; Wapner, R.J.; et al. Fetal growth velocity: The NICHD fetal growth studies. *Am. J. Obstet. Gynecol.* **2018**, *219*, 285.e1–285.e36. [CrossRef]
42. Abdel-Aziz, S.B.; Hegazy, I.S.; Mohamed, D.A.; Abu El Kasem, M.M.A.; Hagag, S.S. Effect of dietary counseling on preventing excessive weight gain during pregnancy. *Public Health* **2018**, *154*, 172–181. [CrossRef]

nutrients

MDPI

Article

Dietary Inflammatory Index during Pregnancy and Congenital Heart Defects

Jiaomei Yang [1,*], Qianqian Chang [1], Qiancheng Du [1], Shaonong Dang [1], Lingxia Zeng [1] and Hong Yan [1,2,3]

1 Department of Epidemiology and Health Statistics, School of Public Health, Xi'an Jiaotong University Health Science Center, Xi'an 710061, China; cqq20160820@stu.xjtu.edu.cn (Q.C.); duqiancheng@stu.xjtu.edu.cn (Q.D.); tjdshn@mail.xjtu.edu.cn (S.D.); tjzlx@xjtu.edu.cn (L.Z.); xjtu_yh2014@163.com (H.Y.)
2 Nutrition and Food Safety Engineering Research Center of Shaanxi Province, Xi'an 710061, China
3 Key Laboratory of Environment and Genes Related to Diseases, Xi'an Jiaotong University, Ministry of Education, Xi'an 710061, China
* Correspondence: violetyjm18@xjtu.edu.cn; Tel.: +86-029-8265-5104

Abstract: The relationship between diet-related inflammation during pregnancy and congenital heart defects (CHD) is unclear. This study attempted to investigate the association between the dietary inflammation index (DII) during pregnancy, reflecting the overall inflammatory potential of the maternal diet, and CHD in Northwest China. A case-control study with 474 cases and 948 controls was performed in Xi'an City, China. Eligible women awaiting delivery were recruited, and their dietary and other information during pregnancy was collected. Logistic regression models were applied to estimate the risk of CHD in association with DII. The maternal DII ranged from −1.36 to 5.73 in cases, and 0.43 to 5.63 in controls. Pregnant women with per 1 higher DII score were at 31% higher risk of fetal CHD (OR = 1.31, 95%CI = 1.14–1.51), and the adjusted OR (95%CI) comparing the pro-inflammatory diet group with the anti-inflammatory diet group was 2.04 (1.42–2.92). The inverse association of maternal DII score with CHD risk was consistent across various subgroups of maternal characteristics. Maternal DII in pregnancy had good predictive value for CHD in offspring, with the areas under the receiver operating characteristic curve higher than 0.7. These findings suggested that avoiding a pro-inflammatory diet in pregnancy should be emphasized in the prevention of CHD.

Keywords: dietary inflammatory index; congenital heart defects; pregnancy; Chinese

Citation: Yang, J.; Chang, Q.; Du, Q.; Dang, S.; Zeng, L.; Yan, H. Dietary Inflammatory Index during Pregnancy and Congenital Heart Defects. *Nutrients* **2023**, *15*, 2262. https://doi.org/10.3390/nu15102262

Academic Editors: Louise Brough, Gail Rees and Jose Lara

Received: 11 April 2023
Revised: 8 May 2023
Accepted: 9 May 2023
Published: 10 May 2023

1. Introduction

Congenital heart defects (CHD) are the most common congenital disorders globally, with the birth prevalence being 9.41‰ worldwide [1] and 9.00‰ in China [2]. It is estimated that millions of neonates are diagnosed with CHD every year worldwide [1], including 0.15 million in China [2]. CHD is the leading cause of infant morbidity and mortality from birth defects, and responsible for more than 0.26 million deaths globally [3], imposing great burdens on the family and society. The etiology for CHD is largely unknown, but previous research has shown that both genetic and environmental factors may contribute to CHD [4]. The major modifiable risk factors for CHD are generally accepted as maternal smoking, alcohol intake, dietary habits, and environmental exposures [4].

Previous studies have reported that maternal intakes of some nutrients, including folic acid, iron, selenium, zinc, and niacin, are associated with fetal CHD [5–8]. Maternal obesity, diabetes mellitus, and infection during pregnancy are reported to be associated with fetal cardiovascular development [9,10]. These maternal risk factors for CHD are associated with localized and systemic inflammatory cytokine milieu in the placenta and plasma [11]. One study has shown that whole blood cultures derived from mothers with CHD fetuses had higher levels of pro-inflammatory cytokines when activated with mitogen [11], emphasizing the importance of maternal inflammatory conditions in fetal cardiovascular development.

Pregnant women are usually in a low-grade systemic inflammation state due to physiological responses [12]. Diet plays a central role in the regulation of systemic inflammation through pro-inflammatory or anti-inflammatory components of foods and nutrients [13], and is also an important modifiable factor for the prevention of CHD [7,8,14–16]. Thus, it is important to investigate the association between pro-inflammatory diet in pregnancy and CHD to provide optimal recommendations for pregnant women to prevent fetal CHD. The Dietary Inflammatory Index (DII) is a literature-derived score for evaluating the overall inflammatory potential of a person's diet [13]. The DII was determined by peer-reviewed articles about the effect of diet on inflammatory biomarkers [13]. A higher DII score indicates that the diet is pro-inflammatory, while a lower DII score indicates that the diet is anti-inflammatory. The DII has been proven to be of value for the associations with health status in the general population [13], and has also been increasingly used as a predictor of pregnancy outcomes among pregnant women [17,18]. However, to our knowledge there has been no study assessing the association between DII during pregnancy and CHD risk. Previous studies have evaluated some maternal predictors in pregnancy for CHD [14,19,20], giving references for the early prediction of CHD. However, the predictive value of DII for CHD has not been assessed.

The present case-control study in Northwest China attempted to investigate the relationship between DII in pregnancy and CHD and assess the prediction value for DII on CHD.

2. Materials and Methods

2.1. Study Design and Participants

Between August 2014 and August 2016, we undertook a case-control study in six comprehensive hospitals in Xi'an City, Northwest China. These six hospitals have incorporated fetal echocardiography at 20th–24th gestational weeks into the routine prenatal ultrasound program to screen for CHD. The detailed study design has been reported previously [8,15,16]. Briefly, among pregnant women awaiting delivery in hospitals, those having fetuses with isolated CHD and no genetic malformation were included in the case group, and those having normal fetuses without any birth defects were included in the control group. Pregnant women with multiple pregnancies or diabetes were excluded because of potentially distinct etiologies. Qualified specialists in each hospital strictly enforced the standard criteria to diagnose birth outcomes. We also undertook a follow-up by telephone within one year after birth to confirm the diagnoses. We randomly selected controls in each hospital each month, and the ratio of the number of controls to cases included in the same hospital in the same month was 2:1. To detect a significant ($p < 0.05$) OR of 1.50 between high and low DII score groups with a statistical power of 80%, 305 cases and 610 controls would be required. A total of 474 cases and 948 controls with completed questionnaires were finally included in the analysis, meeting the sample size requirements.

The study was approved by the Xi'an Jiaotong University Health Science Center (No. 2012008). All participants provided informed consent before the survey.

2.2. Dietary Assessment and DII Score

We collected maternal diet information throughout pregnancy by face-to-face interviews while awaiting delivery using a semi-quantitative food frequency questionnaire (FFQ). The FFQ consists of 111 food items on the basis of a validated FFQ for pregnant women in Northwest China [21]. Women reported consumption frequency according to eight predefined categories and also recalled the portion sizes with the assistance of food portion images [22,23]. Maternal dietary habits tend to be stable throughout pregnancy [24]; thus, maternal diets throughout pregnancy are comparable with those in the 3rd–8th gestational week, the critical period of fetal cardiovascular development [7,8,15,16]. We applied the Chinese Food Composition Tables to derive maternal nutrient intakes during pregnancy [25,26].

We calculated the DII score using the methods described by Shivappa et al. [13]. We included 30 food parameters to calculate the DII score: 8 pro-inflammatory food parameters (energy, carbohydrate, total fat, protein, cholesterol, saturated fatty acid, vitamin B_{12}, and iron) and 22 anti-inflammatory parameters (fiber, monounsaturated fatty acid, polyunsaturated fatty acid, *n*-3 fatty acid, thiamin, riboflavin, vitamin B_6, folic acid, niacin, β-carotene, vitamin A, vitamin C, vitamin E, zinc, selenium, magnesium, caffeine, alcohol, garlic, onion, green/black tea, and pepper) that were available in the current study. We obtained the z-score by subtracting the "standard global mean" from the consumption amount recalled by each pregnant woman and dividing this value by the standard deviation. To minimize the "right skewness", this z-score was converted to a centered proportion. We then multiplied this proportion by the respective food parameter effect score according to the study by Shivappa et al. [13]. We finally summed all of the food-parameter-specific DII scores to create the overall DII score for each pregnant woman. In addition, we constructed a Mediterranean Diet Score (MDS) and a Global Diet Quality Score (GDQS) using the FFQ data according to the methods previously reported [14,27,28].

2.3. Covariates

Using a structured questionnaire, trained investigators collected the following covariates: (1) sociodemographic characteristics: maternal age, residence, education, work, and parity; (2) maternal health-related factors in early pregnancy: passive smoking, anemia, medication use, and iron/folate supplements use. Maternal age was grouped as two categories (<30 years/≥30 years). Residence included rural and urban areas. Maternal education was divided into two categories (junior high school or below/senior high school or above). Women with no paid employment outside their homes were classified as without employment, otherwise they were classified as in employment. Parity was categorized as two groups (0/≥1). The other covariates were treated as dichotomized factors (no/yes). Women with hemoglobin concentration <110 g/L in pregnancy were diagnosed with anemia.

2.4. Statistical Analysis

In univariate comparisons, the χ^2 test was adopted for categorical variable, and for continuous variables the Kruskal–Wallis test or Mann–Whitney U test was applied because of the non-normal distributions observed by the Shapiro–Wilk test. Considering the clustering in the design through hospitals, mixed logistic regression models were applied to evaluate ORs (95%CIs) for total CHD and CHD subtypes in association with maternal DII during pregnancy. The DII score was divided into three groups according to the 25th percentile and 75th percentile of the control distribution. The anti-inflammatory diet group was defined if the DII score was lower than the 25th percentile, the pro-inflammatory diet group was defined if the DII score was higher than the 75th percentile, and the intermediate group was defined if the DII score was in the range of the 25th percentile and 75th percentile. Potential confounders were controlled in the models if they were important priori confounders [4,8,29] and changed the estimates by more than 10% [30]. P for trend was calculated by including group specific median value in the model. Subgroup analyses were conducted according to maternal characteristics (maternal age, residence, education, occupation, parity, and maternal passive smoking, anemia, medication use, and iron/folate supplement use in early pregnancy). The interaction between maternal DII and each subgroup factors was tested by the likelihood ratio test comparing regression models with and without an interaction term. Sensitivity analyses were also conducted by dividing participants as three groups according to the tertiles of DII score in the control.

The receiver operating characteristic (ROC) curves were established to estimate the optimal cut-off values of DII during pregnancy for total CHD and CHD subtypes with the maximum Youden index. The areas under the ROC curves (AUCs) showed the accuracy of DII as a predictor for CHD. The AUC values indicated the predictive power as follows: >0.9, very good; >0.8, good; and >0.7, useful [31].

All analyses were conducted using the Stata software (version 15.0; StataCorp, College Station, TX, USA). Two-sided statistical significance was set at 0.05.

3. Results

3.1. Characteristics of the Study Participants

The distribution of DII scores in pregnancy among cases and controls is shown in Figure 1. The maternal DII ranged from −1.36 to 5.73 in cases, and 0.43 to 5.63 in controls. Pregnant women in the cases had a higher DII score than the controls ($p < 0.001$), with the medians (25th percentile, 75th percentile) being 4.83 (4.34, 5.23) and 4.63 (4.04, 5.08), respectively. The baseline characteristics of the three groups of maternal DII scores are displayed in Table 1. Among the cases, no difference in maternal characteristics existed among the three DII groups. Among the controls, participants in the intermediate group were more likely to be multipara, and mothers with higher DII score were more likely to take iron/folate supplements in early pregnancy. Maternal residence, education, occupation, parity, and maternal passive smoking, anemia, medication use, and iron/folate supplements use in early pregnancy were significantly different between cases and controls (all $p < 0.05$) (Table S1).

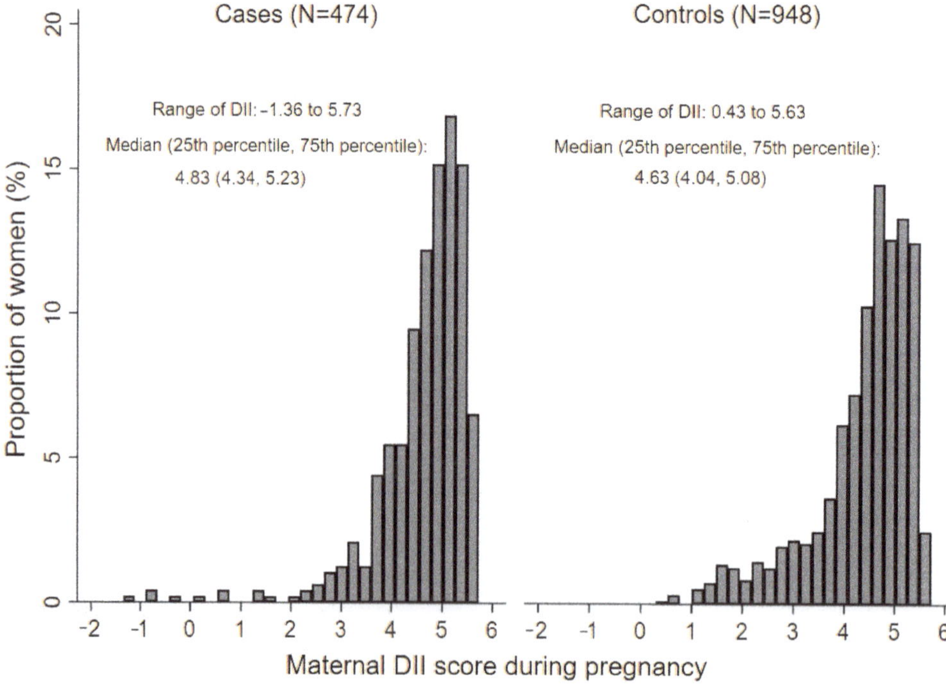

Figure 1. The distribution of DII scores during pregnancy among cases and controls. A significant difference in maternal DII was found between cases and controls by Mann–Whitney U test ($p < 0.001$). DII, Dietary Inflammatory Index.

Table 1. Characteristics of the study participants according to three groups of maternal DII scores during pregnancy.

	Cases (N = 474)				Controls (N = 948)			
	Anti-Inflammatory Diet Group [1] (N = 83)	Intermediate Group [1] (N = 218)	Pro-Inflammatory Diet Group [1] (N = 173)	p [2]	Anti-Inflammatory Diet Group [1] (N = 237)	Intermediate Group [1] (N = 477)	Pro-Inflammatory Diet Group [1] (N = 234)	p [2]
DII								
Range	−1.36 to 4.04	4.04 to 5.06	5.08 to 5.73		0.43 to 4.04	4.05 to 5.08	5.08 to 5.63	
Median (25th percentile, 75th percentile)	3.55 (2.88, 3.82)	4.66 (4.42, 4.86)	5.30 (5.20, 5.42)	<0.001	3.16 (2.35, 3.77)	4.63 (4.41, 4.84)	5.30 (5.21, 5.42)	<0.001
Sociodemographic characteristics, n (%)								
Maternal age ≥30 years	24 (28.9)	79 (36.2)	56 (32.4)	0.446	77 (32.5)	170 (35.6)	77 (32.9)	0.631
Rural residence	32 (38.6)	81 (37.2)	48 (27.7)	0.093	58 (24.5)	143 (30.0)	68 (29.1)	0.296
Maternal education, senior high school or above	50 (60.2)	136 (62.4)	93 (53.8)	0.218	195 (82.3)	377 (79.0)	193 (82.5)	0.427
Maternal occupation, in employment	42 (50.6)	112 (51.4)	86 (49.7)	0.948	185 (78.1)	388 (81.3)	174 (74.4)	0.096
Nulliparity	53 (63.9)	127 (58.3)	94 (54.3)	0.347	197 (83.1)	367 (76.9)	197 (84.2)	0.033
Maternal health-related factors in early pregnancy, n (%)								
Passive smoking	22 (26.5)	79 (36.2)	58 (33.5)	0.279	17 (7.2)	49 (10.3)	22 (9.4)	0.404
Anemia	8 (9.6)	39 (17.9)	33 (19.1)	0.146	27 (11.4)	48 (10.1)	28 (12.0)	0.713
Medication use	34 (41.0)	88 (40.4)	75 (43.4)	0.832	86 (36.3)	138 (28.9)	64 (27.4)	0.067
Iron/folate supplements use	59 (71.1)	171 (78.4)	133 (76.9)	0.401	204 (86.1)	423 (88.7)	219 (93.6)	0.027

DII, Dietary Inflammatory Index. [1] The anti-inflammatory diet group indicates the DII score lower than the 25th percentile of the control distribution, the pro-inflammatory diet group indicates the DII score higher than the 75th percentile of the control distribution, and the intermediate group indicates the DII score in the range of the 25th percentile and 75th percentile of the control distribution. [2] p values are from χ^2 test for categorical variables and from Kruskal–Wallis test for continuous variables.

3.2. Dietary Intakes and Dietary Quality Scores during Pregnancy among the DII Groups

Pregnant women with higher DII score in pregnancy showed lower intakes of main food groups, including grains and tubers, vegetables, fruits, dairy, legumes, meats, fish, eggs, and nuts, both in cases and controls (all $p < 0.001$) (Table 2). Pregnant women with higher DII scores also showed lower MDS and GDQS scores in the case and control groups (all $p < 0.001$) (Table 2). Compared with the controls, case mothers had higher intakes of grains and tubers but lower intakes of other main food groups (all $p < 0.001$), and also had lower MDS and GDQS scores (both $p < 0.001$) (Table S2). Participants with higher DII score during pregnancy reported lower intakes of energy, carbohydrate, total fat, protein, cholesterol, fiber, saturated fatty acid, monounsaturated fatty acid, polyunsaturated fatty acid, n-3 fatty acid, vitamins (thiamin (vitamin B_1), riboflavin (vitamin B_2), niacin (vitamin B_3), vitamin B_6, folic acid (vitamin B_9), vitamin B_{12}, β-carotene, vitamin A, vitamin C, and vitamin E), minerals (iron, zinc, selenium, and magnesium), garlic, onion, and pepper both in cases and controls (Table S3). Participants in the cases consumed lower intakes than the controls of all dietary components included in the DII calculation except carbohydrate, caffeine, alcohol, green/black tea, and pepper (Table S4).

Table 2. Food groups intake and dietary quality scores during pregnancy according to three groups of maternal DII scores during pregnancy.

	Cases (N = 474)				Controls (N = 948)			
	Anti-Inflammatory Diet Group [1] (N = 83)	Intermediate Group [1] (N = 218)	Pro-Inflammatory Diet Group [1] (N = 173)	p [2]	Anti-Inflammatory Diet Group [1] (N = 237)	Intermediate Group [1] (N = 477)	Pro-Inflammatory Diet Group [1] (N = 234)	p [2]
Food groups intake, median (25th percentile, 75th percentile), g/d								
Grains and tubers	352.0 (259.3, 463.6)	244.2 (204.1, 313.8)	186.1 (142.3, 241.3)	<0.001	335.8 (252.1, 440.5)	204.5 (159.9, 280.4)	133.2 (100.4, 163.0)	<0.001
Vegetables	823.8 (590.4, 1084.3)	365.3 (263.0, 448.0)	178.0 (119.5, 214.7)	<0.001	784.3 (548.6, 1340.6)	373.8 (260.8, 460.0)	178.5 (111.6, 214.7)	<0.001
Fruits	563.8 (347.9, 875.0)	327.4 (216.6, 483.5)	162.7 (107.5, 258.3)	<0.001	668.8 (405.6, 915.0)	343.6 (242.6, 490.7)	179.8 (132.9, 254.8)	<0.001
Dairy	128.6 (28.6, 214.3)	85.7 (14.1, 200.0)	14.3 (0, 85.7)	<0.001	172.3 (128.6, 278.6)	172.0 (85.7, 242.9)	100.0 (42.9, 200.0)	<0.001
Legumes	110.7 (60.7, 189.1)	49.9 (24.0, 94.4)	21.4 (8.8, 35.4)	<0.001	192.9 (106.1, 235.7)	78.6 (44.5, 128.6)	36.7 (25.0, 47.9)	<0.001
Meats	78.1 (35.2, 128.6)	38.0 (16.3, 78.6)	20.0 (10.0, 41.0)	<0.001	96.2 (49.1, 156.9)	57.1 (33.3, 92.1)	28.1 (22.1, 41.9)	<0.001
Fish	14.3 (4.0, 31.6)	6.7 (1.3, 17.1)	3.3 (0, 8.0)	<0.001	41.8 (18.3, 85.7)	17.3 (10.1, 33.7)	11.1 (6.7, 16.9)	<0.001
Eggs	25.7 (8.6, 50.0)	21.4 (4.3, 50.0)	21.4 (3.3, 39.3)	<0.001	39.3 (21.4, 50.0)	32.9 (21.4, 50.0)	22.4 (8.5, 50.0)	<0.001
Nuts	18.9 (8.1, 45.0)	12.6 (4.6, 34.0)	3.0 (1.3, 6.4)	<0.001	38.6 (14.1, 71.1)	12.9 (5.5, 33.8)	4.8 (3.3, 8.5)	<0.001

Table 2. *Cont.*

	Cases (N = 474)				Controls (N = 948)			
	Anti-Inflammatory Diet Group [1] (N = 83)	Intermediate Group [1] (N = 218)	Pro-Inflammatory Diet Group [1] (N = 173)	p [2]	Anti-Inflammatory Diet Group [1] (N = 237)	Intermediate Group [1] (N = 477)	Pro-Inflammatory Diet Group [1] (N = 234)	p [2]
Dietary quality scores, median (25th percentile, 75th percentile)								
MDS	6.0 (5.0, 7.0)	4.0 (3.0, 5.0)	2.0 (1.0, 3.0)	<0.001	7.0 (6.0, 7.0)	5.0 (4.0, 6.0)	2.0 (2.0, 3.0)	<0.001
GDQS	32.8 (29.5, 35.0)	29.3 (26.5, 31.8)	22.5 (20.5, 25.0)	<0.001	34.8 (32.8, 36.9)	31.5 (29.3, 33.5)	25.0 (23.0, 27.0)	<0.001

DII, Dietary Inflammatory Index; MDS, Mediterranean Diet Score; GDQS, Global Diet Quality Score. [1] The anti-inflammatory diet group indicates the DII score lower than the 25th percentile of the control distribution, the pro-inflammatory diet group indicates the DII score higher than the 75th percentile of the control distribution, and the intermediate group indicates the DII score in the range of the 25th percentile and 75th percentile of the control distribution. [2] p values are from Kruskal–Wallis test for continuous variables.

3.3. Association between Maternal DII during Pregnancy and CHD

The associations of maternal DII in pregnancy with the risks of total CHD, ventricular septal defects (VSD), and atrial septal defects (ASD) are displayed in Table 3. Compared with those in the anti-inflammatory diet group, mothers in the pro-inflammatory diet group had a higher risk of delivering fetuses with total CHD (OR = 2.04, 95%CI = 1.42–2.92), VSD (OR = 2.00, 95%CI = 1.25–3.19), and ASD (OR = 1.92, 95%CI = 1.22–3.03), with the tests for trend statistically significant (all $p < 0.05$). The risks of total CHD, VSD, and ASD were increased by 31% (OR = 1.31, 95%CI = 1.14–1.51), 29% (OR = 1.29, 95%CI = 1.07–1.55), and 25% (OR = 1.25, 95%CI = 1.04–1.50) for per 1 higher score of maternal DII in pregnancy, respectively.

Table 3. Associations between DII score during pregnancy and congenital heart defects.

	Anti-Inflammatory Diet Group [1]	Intermediate Group [1]	Pro-Inflammatory Diet Group [1]	p for Trend	Per 1 Higher Score
Total congenital heart defects					
$N_{cases}/N_{controls}$	83/237	218/477	173/234	474/948	474/948
Unadjusted OR (95%CI)	1	1.30 (0.97, 1.76)	2.11 (1.54, 2.90)	<0.001	1.32 (1.16, 1.50)
Adjusted OR (95%CI) [2]	1	1.25 (0.89, 1.74)	2.04 (1.42, 2.92)	<0.001	1.31 (1.14, 1.51)
Ventricular septal defects					
$N_{cases}/N_{controls}$	39/237	100/477	83/234	222/948	222/948
Unadjusted OR (95%CI)	1	1.26 (0.84, 1.90)	2.10 (1.37, 3.21)	0.001	1.30 (1.09, 1.55)
Adjusted OR (95%CI) [2]	1	1.17 (0.75, 1.81)	2.00 (1.25, 3.19)	0.007	1.29 (1.07, 1.55)
Atrial septal defects					
$N_{cases}/N_{controls}$	42/237	100/477	76/234	218/948	218/948
Unadjusted OR (95%CI)	1	1.18 (0.80, 1.75)	1.83 (1.21, 2.78)	0.009	1.24 (1.05, 1.47)
Adjusted OR (95%CI) [2]	1	1.13 (0.74, 1.73)	1.92 (1.22, 3.03)	0.011	1.25 (1.04, 1.50)

DII, Dietary Inflammatory Index. [1] The anti-inflammatory diet group indicates the DII score lower than the 25th percentile of the control distribution, the pro-inflammatory diet group indicates the DII score higher than the 75th percentile of the control distribution, and the intermediate group indicates the DII score in the range of the 25th percentile and 75th percentile of the control distribution. [2] Adjusted for total energy intake, sociodemographic characteristics (maternal age, residence, education, occupation, and parity), and maternal health-related factors in early pregnancy (passive smoking, anemia, medication use, and iron/folate supplements use).

Subgroup analyses showed that the risks of total CHD, VSD, and ASD in association with maternal DII during pregnancy did not alter by maternal characteristics including maternal age, residence, education, occupation, parity, and maternal passive smoking, anemia, medication use, and iron/folate supplement use in early pregnancy (Figures S1–S3). When dividing participants as three groups according to the tertiles of DII score in the control, compared with the lowest tertile group, the highest tertile group showed higher risks of total CHD (OR = 1.66, 95%CI = 1.22–2.28), VSD (OR = 1.55, 95%CI = 1.03–2.33), and ASD (OR = 1.48, 95%CI = 1.08–2.02), with the tests for trend significant (all $p < 0.05$) (Table S5).

3.4. The Prediction Value for Maternal DII during Pregnancy on CHD

The ROC for maternal DII in pregnancy in the prediction of total CHD, VSD, and ASD is shown in Figure 2. The ROC indicated that maternal DII in pregnancy were useful in predicting total CHD, VSD, and ASD, with the AUC to be 0.79 (0.76, 0.81), 0.78 (0.74, 0.82), and 0.77 (0.73, 0.80), respectively. The optimal DII cut-off values were 5.41 for total CHD (sensitivity: 67.3%, specificity: 77.3%), 5.31 for VSD (sensitivity: 66.7%, specificity: 79.0%), and 5.53 for ASD (sensitivity: 75.2%, specificity: 67.9%), respectively.

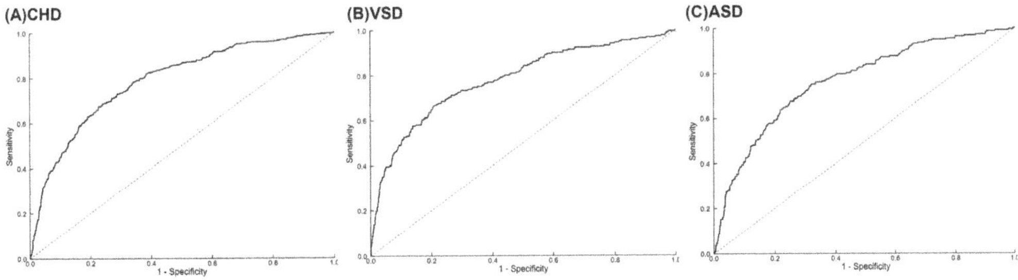

Figure 2. The ROC for Dietary Inflammatory Index in pregnancy in the prediction of (**A**) total congenital heart defects, (**B**) ventricular septal defects, and (**C**) atrial septal defects. ASD, atrial septal defects; CHD, congenital heart defects; ROC, receiver operating characteristic curves; VSD, ventricular septal defects. The dotted line refers to the reference line that results from random selection.

4. Discussion

In the current case-control study, we found that higher maternal DII scores, indicating a more pro-inflammatory diet, were associated with higher risks of total CHD and its subtypes in fetuses. These inverse associations of DII score in pregnancy with CHD were consistent across various subgroups of maternal characteristics. We also observed that maternal DII in pregnancy had good predictive value for total CHD and its subtypes. To our knowledge, this is the first study to report data on maternal DII in pregnancy and CHD.

Although there has been no study exploring the relationship between maternal DII in pregnancy and CHD, previous research has shown that maternal pro-inflammatory diet in pregnancy is associated with adverse birth outcomes, such as premature birth, low birth weight, and small for gestational age [17,32,33], which are closely related with birth defects. Moreover, several previous studies have reported CHD risk in association with dietary patterns and dietary quality indices during pregnancy [15,34,35], which share some similar dietary components as the DII. For example, the one-carbon-rich dietary pattern during pregnancy, which was high in fish and seafood, was observed to be associated with a lower risk of CHD [35], and the Mediterranean diet during pregnancy, which was high in whole grains, fruits, vegetables, legumes, nuts, and fish, and, high in olive oil but low in saturated lipids, low to moderate in dairy, and limited in red meat, was reported to reduce CHD risk [14,34]. These similar dietary components may explain why those dietary patterns and scores all showed potential health benefits for fetal cardiovascular development. Compared with other dietary scoring systems such as MDS and GDQS that were also reported to show good predictive value for CHD [14], the maternal DII score reflects the inflammation potential of one diet as a whole and has been shown in high relation with maternal cytokine levels such as TNF-α, IL-1β, IL-8, IL-6, IL-10, MCP-1, and C-reactive protein [36,37]. The DII is based on an extensive literature search on the effect of diet on inflammation and is independent on specific means or recommendations of food/nutrient intake [13], which is different from the MDS and GDQS. Considering the importance of maternal inflammatory conditions on fetal cardiovascular development, the DII provides an easy and noninvasive way to assess the dietary inflammatory potential as a predictor for CHD. Findings from the present study imply that it is important to incorporate the suggestion of avoiding a pro-inflammatory diet in routine pregnancy management practices to prevent fetal CHD.

Several mechanisms may explain the higher risk of fetal CHD associated with higher maternal DII during pregnancy. First, the deleterious effect of a pro-inflammatory diet in pregnancy on fetal CHD may come from the increased pro-inflammatory cytokines. One recent study reported that placental inflammatory monocytes of maternal origin could change the cardiac tissue structure by migrating the embryonic heart [38]. Second, the higher systemic inflammation due to higher DII may cause a stress response, further influencing the normal development of the fetal cardiovascular system [39]. Third, it is possible that dietary inflammatory potential during pregnancy participates in the regulation of gut microbiota [40], which was reported to influence fetal CHD [41]. Fourth, the observed relationship between DII and CHD may be partly due to the low dietary quality of a pro-inflammatory diet. Previous research has reported that a higher maternal MDS, indicating a higher dietary quality, was associated with a lower DII score [32] and lower risk of CHD [14,34]. In fact, the present study also showed lower MDS and GDQS scores in the pro-inflammatory diet group and in the case group.

Our study provides valuable evidence on the risk of CHD in association with maternal DII score during pregnancy. However, some limitations merit discussion. First, we cannot exclude recall bias because data in pregnancy was recalled by participants awaiting delivery, although previous research indicated that mothers could recall information in pregnancy well after years [42,43]. Second, we cannot exclude exposure misclassification because we gathered dietary data in the entire pregnancy rather than in the 3rd–8th gestational week, the critical period of fetal cardiovascular development. However, previous research has shown maternal dietary habits are usually stable throughout pregnancy [24]. Third, we cannot exclude selection bias because we did not include CHD fetuses who had died before delivery at term. Fourth, we cannot separately assess the relationships between DII and other CHD subtypes because of the limited sample size. Finally, we cannot rule out the possibility of residual confounders, and cannot uncover a real causal relationship because of the case-control design.

5. Conclusions

The present study suggested that a higher DII score during pregnancy, indicating a more pro-inflammatory diet, was associated with higher CHD risk. Furthermore, the maternal DII score in pregnancy had good predictive value for fetal CHD. Our results implied that avoiding a pro-inflammatory diet could be an interesting target for prevention strategies to reduce the incidence of CHD in Northwest China. Routine pregnancy management should emphasize the importance of reducing dietary inflammation to prevent fetal CHD. Further studies are warranted to investigate the validity of the DII as a predicator for CHD in other populations, and further understand the mechanisms associating dietary inflammation in pregnancy with fetal CHD.

Supplementary Materials: The following supporting information can be downloaded at: https://www.mdpi.com/article/10.3390/nu15102262/s1, Table S1: Characteristics of the study population among cases and controls; Table S2: Food groups intake and dietary quality scores during pregnancy among cases and controls; Table S3: Daily dietary components intake according to three groups of maternal DII during pregnancy; Table S4: Daily dietary components intake during pregnancy among cases and controls; Table S5: Associations between tertiles of maternal DII score during pregnancy and congenital heart defects; Figure S1: Subgroup analyses for the association between per 1 higher score of Dietary Inflammatory Index in pregnancy and the risk of total congenital heart defects; Figure S2: Subgroup analyses for the association between per 1 higher score of Dietary Inflammatory Index in pregnancy and the risk of ventricular heart defects; Figure S3: Subgroup analyses for the association between per 1 higher score of Dietary Inflammatory Index in pregnancy and the risk of atrial heart defects.

Author Contributions: J.Y. and H.Y. contributed to study concept and design; J.Y. and Q.C. drafted the initial manuscript; J.Y., Q.C., Q.D., S.D. and L.Z. conducted statistical analyses; J.Y., Q.C., Q.D., S.D. and L.Z. collected the data; J.Y., Q.C. and H.Y. revised the manuscript. All authors have read and agreed to the published version of the manuscript.

Funding: This work was supported by the National Natural Science Foundation of China (82103852, 81230016), Shaanxi Health and Family Planning Commission (Sxwsjswzfcght2016-013), and National Key Research and Development of China (2017YFC0907200, 2017YFC0907201).

Institutional Review Board Statement: The study was in accordance with the guidelines of the Declaration of Helsinki and approved by the ethics committee of Xi'an Jiaotong University Health Science Center (No. 2012008) on 3 March 2012.

Informed Consent Statement: Informed consent was obtained from all participants in the present study.

Data Availability Statement: The datasets in the current study are available from the corresponding author on reasonable request.

Acknowledgments: The authors are grateful to all mothers who participated in this study, all staff who coordinated field work, and all investigators who contributed to data collection.

Conflicts of Interest: The authors declare no conflict of interest.

References

1. Liu, Y.; Chen, S.; Zühlke, L.; Black, G.C.; Choy, M.K.; Li, N.; Keavney, B.D. Global birth prevalence of congenital heart defects 1970–2017: Updated systematic review and meta-analysis of 260 studies. *Int. J. Epidemiol.* **2019**, *48*, 455–463. [CrossRef] [PubMed]
2. Zhao, Q.M.; Liu, F.; Wu, L.; Ma, X.J.; Niu, C.; Huang, G.Y. Prevalence of Congenital Heart Disease at Live Birth in China. *J. Pediatr.* **2019**, *204*, 53–58. [CrossRef] [PubMed]
3. Global, regional, and national burden of congenital heart disease, 1990–2017: A systematic analysis for the Global Burden of Disease Study 2017. *Lancet. Child Adolesc. Health* **2020**, *4*, 185–200. [CrossRef] [PubMed]
4. Zhang, T.N.; Wu, Q.J.; Liu, Y.S.; Lv, J.L.; Sun, H.; Chang, Q.; Liu, C.F.; Zhao, Y.H. Environmental Risk Factors and Congenital Heart Disease: An Umbrella Review of 165 Systematic Reviews and Meta-Analyses with More Than 120 Million Participants. *Front. Cardiovasc. Med.* **2021**, *8*, 640729. [CrossRef]
5. Chen, H.; Zhang, Y.; Wang, D.; Chen, X.; Li, M.; Huang, X.; Jiang, Y.; Dou, Y.; Wang, Y.; Ma, X.; et al. Periconception Red Blood Cell Folate and Offspring Congenital Heart Disease: Nested Case-Control and Mendelian Randomization Studies. *Ann. Intern. Med.* **2022**, *175*, 1212–1220. [CrossRef]
6. Smedts, H.P.; Rakhshandehroo, M.; Verkleij-Hagoort, A.C.; de Vries, J.H.; Ottenkamp, J.; Steegers, E.A.; Steegers-Theunissen, R.P. Maternal intake of fat, riboflavin and nicotinamide and the risk of having offspring with congenital heart defects. *Eur. J. Nutr.* **2008**, *47*, 357–365. [CrossRef]
7. Yang, J.; Kang, Y.; Chang, Q.; Zhang, B.; Liu, X.; Zeng, L., Yan, H.; Dang, S. Maternal Zinc, Copper, and Selenium Intakes during Pregnancy and Congenital Heart Defects. *Nutrients* **2022**, *14*, 1055. [CrossRef]
8. Yang, J.; Kang, Y.; Cheng, Y.; Zeng, L.; Shen, Y.; Shi, G.; Liu, Y.; Qu, P.; Zhang, R.; Yan, H.; et al. Iron intake and iron status during pregnancy and risk of congenital heart defects: A case-control study. *Int. J. Cardiol.* **2020**, *301*, 74–79. [CrossRef]
9. Helle, E.; Priest, J.R. Maternal Obesity and Diabetes Mellitus as Risk Factors for Congenital Heart Disease in the Offspring. *J. Am. Heart Assoc.* **2020**, *9*, e011541. [CrossRef]
10. Ye, Z.; Wang, L.; Yang, T.; Chen, L.; Wang, T.; Chen, L.; Zhao, L.; Zhang, S.; Zheng, Z.; Luo, L.; et al. Maternal Viral Infection and Risk of Fetal Congenital Heart Diseases: A Meta-Analysis of Observational Studies. *J. Am. Heart Assoc.* **2019**, *8*, e011264. [CrossRef]
11. Blossom, S.J.; Rau, J.L.; Best, T.H.; Bornemeier, R.A.; Hobbs, C.A. Increased maternal cytokine production and congenital heart defects. *J. Reprod. Immunol.* **2013**, *97*, 204–210. [CrossRef]
12. Mor, G.; Cardenas, I.; Abrahams, V.; Guller, S. Inflammation and pregnancy: The role of the immune system at the implantation site. *Ann. N. Y. Acad. Sci.* **2011**, *1221*, 80–87. [CrossRef]
13. Shivappa, N.; Steck, S.E.; Hurley, T.G.; Hussey, J.R.; Hébert, J.R. Designing and developing a literature-derived, population-based dietary inflammatory index. *Public Health Nutr.* **2014**, *17*, 1689–1696. [CrossRef]
14. Yang, J.; Chang, Q.; Dang, S.; Liu, X.; Zeng, L.; Yan, H. Dietary Quality during Pregnancy and Congenital Heart Defects. *Nutrients* **2022**, *14*, 3654. [CrossRef]
15. Yang, J.; Cheng, Y.; Zeng, L.; Dang, S.; Yan, H. Maternal dietary diversity during pregnancy and congenital heart defects: A case-control study. *Eur. J. Clin. Nutr.* **2021**, *75*, 355–363. [CrossRef]
16. Yang, J.; Kang, Y.; Cheng, Y.; Zeng, L.; Yan, H.; Dang, S. Maternal Dietary Patterns during Pregnancy and Congenital Heart Defects: A Case-Control Study. *Int. J. Env. Res. Public Health* **2019**, *16*, 2957. [CrossRef]
17. de Freitas, N.P.A.; Carvalho, T.R.; Gonçalves, C.; da Silva, P.H.A.; de Melo Romão, L.G.; Kwak-Kim, J.; Cavalcante, M.B. The Dietary Inflammatory Index as a predictor of pregnancy outcomes: Systematic review and meta-analysis. *J. Reprod. Immunol.* **2022**, *152*, 103651. [CrossRef]
18. Sen, S.; Rifas-Shiman, S.L.; Shivappa, N.; Wirth, M.D.; Hébert, J.R.; Gold, D.R.; Gillman, M.W.; Oken, E. Dietary Inflammatory Potential during Pregnancy Is Associated with Lower Fetal Growth and Breastfeeding Failure: Results from Project Viva. *J. Nutr.* **2016**, *146*, 728–736. [CrossRef]
19. Liang, Y.; Li, X.; Hu, X.; Wen, B.; Wang, L.; Wang, C. A predictive model of offspring congenital heart disease based on maternal risk factors during pregnancy: A hospital based case-control study in Nanchong City. *Int. J. Med. Sci.* **2020**, *17*, 3091–3097. [CrossRef]

20. Qu, Y.; Deng, X.; Lin, S.; Han, F.; Chang, H.H.; Ou, Y.; Nie, Z.; Mai, J.; Wang, X.; Gao, X.; et al. Using Innovative Machine Learning Methods to Screen and Identify Predictors of Congenital Heart Diseases. *Front. Cardiovasc. Med.* **2021**, *8*, 797002. [CrossRef]
21. Cheng, Y.; Yan, H.; Dibley, M.J.; Shen, Y.; Li, Q.; Zeng, L. Validity and reproducibility of a semi-quantitative food frequency questionnaire for use among pregnant women in rural China. *Asia Pac. J. Clin. Nutr.* **2008**, *17*, 166–177. [PubMed]
22. Yang, J.; Cheng, Y.; Pei, L.; Jiang, Y.; Lei, F.; Zeng, L.; Wang, Q.; Li, Q.; Kang, Y.; Shen, Y.; et al. Maternal iron intake during pregnancy and birth outcomes: A cross-sectional study in Northwest China. *Br. J. Nutr.* **2017**, *117*, 862–871. [CrossRef] [PubMed]
23. Yang, J.; Dang, S.; Cheng, Y.; Qiu, H.; Mi, B.; Jiang, Y.; Qu, P.; Zeng, L.; Wang, Q.; Li, Q.; et al. Dietary intakes and dietary patterns among pregnant women in Northwest China. *Public Health Nutr.* **2017**, *20*, 282–293. [CrossRef] [PubMed]
24. Crozier, S.R.; Robinson, S.M.; Godfrey, K.M.; Cooper, C.; Inskip, H.M. Women's dietary patterns change little from before to during pregnancy. *J. Nutr.* **2009**, *139*, 1956–1963. [CrossRef] [PubMed]
25. Institute of Nutrition and Food Safety, China Center for Disease Control. *China Food Composition Book 2*; Peking University Medical Press: Beijing, China, 2005.
26. Institute of Nutrition and Food Safety, China Center for Disease Control. *China Food Composition Book 1*, 2nd ed.; Peking University Medical Press: Beijing, China, 2009.
27. Bromage, S.; Batis, C.; Bhupathiraju, S.N.; Fawzi, W.W.; Fung, T.T.; Li, Y.; Deitchler, M.; Angulo, E.; Birk, N.; Castellanos-Gutiérrez, A.; et al. Development and Validation of a Novel Food-Based Global Diet Quality Score (GDQS). *J. Nutr.* **2021**, *151*, 75s–92s. [CrossRef]
28. Mahmassani, H.A.; Switkowski, K.M.; Scott, T.M.; Johnson, E.J.; Rifas-Shiman, S.L.; Oken, E.; Jacques, P.F. Maternal diet quality during pregnancy and child cognition and behavior in a US cohort. *Am. J. Clin. Nutr.* **2022**, *115*, 128–141. [CrossRef]
29. Nie, X.; Liu, X.; Wang, C.; Wu, Z.; Sun, Z.; Su, J.; Yan, R.; Peng, Y.; Yang, Y.; Wang, C.; et al. Assessment of evidence on reported non-genetic risk factors of congenital heart defects: The updated umbrella review. *BMC Pregnancy Childbirth* **2022**, *22*, 371. [CrossRef]
30. Mickey, R.M.; Greenland, S. The impact of confounder selection criteria on effect estimation. *Am. J. Epidemiol.* **1989**, *129*, 125–137. [CrossRef]
31. Swets, J.A. Measuring the accuracy of diagnostic systems. *Science* **1988**, *240*, 1285–1293. [CrossRef]
32. Casas, R.; Castro-Barquero, S. Maternal Dietary Inflammatory Index during Pregnancy Is Associated with Perinatal Outcomes: Results from the IMPACT BCN Trial. *Nutrients* **2022**, *14*, 2284. [CrossRef]
33. Chen, L.W.; Aubert, A.M.; Shivappa, N. Associations of maternal dietary inflammatory potential and quality with offspring birth outcomes: An individual participant data pooled analysis of 7 European cohorts in the ALPHABET consortium. *PLoS Med.* **2021**, *18*, e1003491. [CrossRef]
34. Botto, L.D.; Krikov, S.; Carmichael, S.L.; Munger, R.G.; Shaw, G.M.; Feldkamp, M.L. Lower rate of selected congenital heart defects with better maternal diet quality: A population-based study. *Arch. Dis. Child. Fetal Neonatal Ed.* **2016**, *101*, F43–F49. [CrossRef]
35. Obermann-Borst, S.A.; Vujkovic, M.; de Vries, J.H.; Wildhagen, M.F.; Looman, C.W.; de Jonge, R.; Steegers, E.A.; Steegers-Theunissen, R.P. A maternal dietary pattern characterised by fish and seafood in association with the risk of congenital heart defects in the offspring. *BJOG Int. J. Obstet. Gynaecol.* **2011**, *118*, 1205–1215. [CrossRef]
36. Cui, T.; Zhang, J.; Liu, L.; Xiong, W.; Su, Y.; Han, Y.; Gao, L.; Qu, Z.; Zhang, X. Relationship between the Dietary Inflammatory Index Score and Cytokine Levels in Chinese Pregnant Women during the Second and Third Trimesters. *Nutrients* **2022**, *15*, 194. [CrossRef]
37. Pieczyńska, J.; Płaczkowska, S.; Pawlik-Sobecka, L.; Kokot, I.; Sozański, R.; Grajeta, H. Association of Dietary Inflammatory Index with Serum IL-6, IL-10, and CRP Concentration during Pregnancy. *Nutrients* **2020**, *12*, 2789. [CrossRef]
38. Ward, E.J.; Bert, S.; Fanti, S.; Malone, K.M.; Maughan, R.T.; Gkantsinikoudi, C.; Prin, F.; Volpato, L.K.; Piovezan, A.P.; Graham, G.J.; et al. Placental Inflammation Leads to Abnormal Embryonic Heart Development. *Circulation* **2023**, *147*, 956–972. [CrossRef]
39. Fisher, S.A.; Burggren, W.W. Role of hypoxia in the evolution and development of the cardiovascular system. *Antioxid. Redox Signal.* **2007**, *9*, 1339–1352. [CrossRef]
40. Zheng, J.; Hoffman, K.L.; Chen, J.S.; Shivappa, N.; Sood, A.; Browman, G.J.; Dirba, D.D.; Hanash, S.; Wei, P.; Hebert, J.R.; et al. Dietary inflammatory potential in relation to the gut microbiome: Results from a cross-sectional study. *Br. J. Nutr.* **2020**, *124*, 931–942. [CrossRef]
41. Wang, T.; Chen, L.; Huang, P.; Yang, T.; Zhang, S.; Zhao, L.; Chen, L.; Ye, Z.; Luo, L.; Qin, J. Association of maternal gut microbiota and plasma metabolism with congenital heart disease in offspring: A multi-omic analysis. *Sci Rep* **2021**, *11*, 5339. [CrossRef]
42. Bosco, J.L.; Tseng, M.; Spector, L.G.; Olshan, A.F.; Bunin, G.R. Reproducibility of reported nutrient intake and supplement use during a past pregnancy: A report from the Children's Oncology Group. *Paediatr. Perinat. Epidemiol.* **2010**, *24*, 93–101. [CrossRef]
43. Bunin, G.R.; Gyllstrom, M.E.; Brown, J.E.; Kahn, E.B.; Kushi, L.H. Recall of diet during a past pregnancy. *Am. J. Epidemiol.* **2001**, *154*, 1136–1142. [CrossRef] [PubMed]

nutrients

Article

Effects of a Mediterranean Diet Intervention on Maternal Stress, Well-Being, and Sleep Quality throughout Gestation—The IMPACT-BCN Trial

Irene Casas [1,†], Ayako Nakaki [1,2,†], Rosalia Pascal [1,3,4,†], Sara Castro-Barquero [1,5,6,*], Lina Youssef [1,2,7], Mariona Genero [1], Leticia Benitez [1,2], Marta Larroya [1,2], Maria Laura Boutet [1], Giulia Casu [1], Alex Gomez-Gomez [8], Oscar J. Pozo [8], Ivette Morilla [9], Anabel Martínez-Àran [9], Eduard Vieta [9], María Dolores Gómez-Roig [1,3,4], Rosa Casas [5,6], Ramon Estruch [5,6], Eduard Gratacos [1,2,10], Fàtima Crispi [1,2,10,‡] and Francesca Crovetto [1,3,4,‡]

1 BCNatal | Fetal Medicine Research Center (Hospital Clínic and Hospital Sant Joan de Déu), University of Barcelona, 08028 Barcelona, Spain
2 Institut de Recerca August Pi Sunyer (IDIBAPS), 08036 Barcelona, Spain
3 Primary Care Interventions to Prevent Maternal and Child Chronic Diseases of Perinatal and Development Origin, RD21/0012/0001, Instituto de Salud Carlos III, 28040 Barcelona, Spain
4 Institut de Recerca Sant Joan de Deu (IRSJD), 08950 Barcelona, Spain
5 Department of Internal Medicine Hospital Clinic, IDIBAPS, University of Barcelona, 08036 Barcelona, Spain
6 Centro de Investigación Biomédica en Red de Fisiopatología de la Obesidad y Nutrición (CIBEROBN), 28029 Madrid, Spain
7 Josep Carreras Leukaemia Research Institute, Hospital Clínic, University of Barcelona Campus, 08036 Barcelona, Spain
8 Integrative Pharmacology & Systems Neuroscience Group, IMIM (Hospital del Mar Medical Research Institute), 08003 Barcelona, Spain
9 Department of Psychiatry and Psychology, Hospital Clinic, Neuroscience Institute, IDIBAPS, University of Barcelona, CIBERSAM, 08035 Barcelona, Spain
10 Centre for Biomedical Research on Rare Diseases (CIBER-ER), 28029 Madrid, Spain
* Correspondence: sara.castro@ub.edu
† These authors contributed equally to this work.
‡ These authors also contributed equally to this work.

Citation: Casas, I.; Nakaki, A.; Pascal, R.; Castro-Barquero, S.; Youssef, L.; Genero, M.; Benitez, L.; Larroya, M.; Boutet, M.L.; Casu, G.; et al. Effects of a Mediterranean Diet Intervention on Maternal Stress, Well-Being, and Sleep Quality throughout Gestation—The IMPACT-BCN Trial. *Nutrients* **2023**, *15*, 2362. https://doi.org/10.3390/nu15102362

Academic Editor: Herbert Ryan Marini

Received: 19 April 2023
Revised: 10 May 2023
Accepted: 17 May 2023
Published: 18 May 2023

Abstract: Stress and anxiety are frequent occurrences among pregnant women. We aimed to evaluate the effects of a Mediterranean diet intervention during pregnancy on maternal stress, well-being, and sleep quality throughout gestation. In a randomized clinical trial, 1221 high-risk pregnant women were randomly allocated into three groups at 19–23 weeks' gestation: a Mediterranean diet intervention, a Mindfulness-Based Stress Reduction program, or usual care. All women who provided self-reported life-style questionnaires to measure their anxiety (State Trait Anxiety Inventory (STAI), Perceived Stress Scale (PSS)), well-being (WHO Five Well Being Index (WHO-5)), and sleep quality (Pittsburgh sleep quality index (PSQI)) at enrollment and at the end of the intervention (34–36 weeks) were included. In a random subgroup of 106 women, the levels of cortisol and related metabolites were also measured. At the end of the intervention (34–36 weeks), participants in the Mediterranean diet group had significantly lower perceived stress and anxiety scores (PSS mean (SE) 15.9 (0.4) vs. 17.0 (0.4), $p = 0.035$; STAI-anxiety mean (SE) 13.6 (0.4) vs. 15.8 (0.5), $p = 0.004$) and better sleep quality (PSQI mean 7.0 ± 0.2 SE vs. 7.9 ± 0.2 SE, $p = 0.001$) compared to usual care. As compared to usual care, women in the Mediterranean diet group also had a more significant increase in their 24 h urinary cortisone/cortisol ratio during gestation (mean 1.7 ± SE 0.1 vs. 1.3 ± SE 0.1, $p < 0.001$). A Mediterranean diet intervention during pregnancy is associated with a significant reduction in maternal anxiety and stress, and improvements in sleep quality throughout gestation.

Keywords: Mediterranean diet; pregnancy; anxiety; well-being; sleep quality

1. Introduction

The Mediterranean diet (MedDiet) has several positive effects on individual health: randomized trials demonstrated its contribution to improved cardiovascular profiles and reduced major cardiovascular events in individuals at risk of [1] diabetes, inflammatory-based disorders, cancer, and cognitive decline [2–4]. Additionally, there has been increasing interest of the effects of a MedDiet on mental health, stress, and quality of life in general [5]. The role of the diet, particularly the MedDiet, in the development of mental disorders, has become a recent research focus over the past decade [6]. Several studies evaluated the effect of a MedDiet intervention on the reduction in depressive symptoms and the improvement in quality of life in individuals with major depressive disorders [7,8]. In a secondary analysis of the PREvención con DIeta MEDiterránea (PREDIMED) study, a reduced risk in depression was observed in participants with type 2 diabetes allocated to the group receiving a MedDiet supplemented by nuts (hazard ratio 0.59 (95% confidence interval (CI) 0.36 to 0.98)) [9]. A recent review based on 37 studies confirmed the association between (poly)phenols consumption and the risk of depression, and a reduction in the severity of depressive symptoms [10]. Some authors hypothesized that a high-quality diet, rich in fiber, antioxidant dietary components and omega-3-polyunsaturated fatty acids, may be linked to a reduced risk of depression, anxiety, and stress [11], which could provide new potential methods for the treatment and prevention of mental disorders in general. Moreover, it has been described that a dysregulated redox signaling is a key factor in the pathophysiology of mental disorders, especially in depression, and increased reactive oxygen and nitrogen species were observed in these patients [12,13].

Stress and anxiety are frequent occurrences among pregnant women. Peripartum anxiety disorders are more prevalent than previously thought, as 1 in 5 women can suffer from them [14]. Mental disorders can appear before pregnancy, with a changing course during pregnancy and postpartum. These findings highlight the need for screenings for stress-related disorders and education by different health professionals from the early stages of pregnancy. Several studies have shown the effectiveness of non-pharmacological treatments in the improvement in stress and other mental disorders during pregnancy, such as mindfulness meditation, biofeedback, or exercise such as yoga [15]. However, there is paucity of data regarding the dietary approach to these conditions during pregnancy. Interestingly, a recent observational study revealed an association between the MedDiet and anxiety [16]. Moreover, the production of reactive oxygen and nitrogen species production, as well as individual antioxidant capacity, is influenced by several dietary factors. A dietary intervention promoting plant-based foods that are rich in antioxidants, such fruits, vegetables, extra-virgin olive oil, and whole-grain cereals, may modulate the individual antioxidant capacity, explaining the improvements in mental wellbeing [12]. Thus, randomized clinical trials are needed to establish the potential effects of dietary patterns on mental health, avoiding the confusion attributed to the co-occurrence of other lifestyle-related and sociodemographic factors.

During pregnancy, evidence has been provided regarding the potential beneficial effects that structured dietary interventions based on a MedDiet can have, not only on pregnant women [9,13,14], but also their offspring and the pregnancy itself. In a recent randomized clinical trial, pregnant individuals at high risk for small-for-gestational-age newborns (SGA) who followed a structured MedDiet intervention significantly reduced the incidence of newborns being born small (with birth weight below the 10th percentile) and other perinatal complications [17]. However, the influence of MedDiet on maternal wellbeing during pregnancy remains to be determined.

The present study aimed to evaluate the influence of a structured intervention during pregnancy based on a MedDiet on maternal stress and anxiety, mindful state, quality of life and sleep.

2. Materials and Methods

2.1. Study Design, Population and Ethics

Improving Mothers for a better PrenAtal Care Trial BarCeloNa (IMPACT BCN) was a parallel, unblinded randomized clinical trial conducted at BCNatal (Hospital Clínic and Hospital Sant Joan de Déu), a large referral center for maternal–fetal and neonatal medicine in Barcelona, Spain. Details of the trial are provided in the protocol of the study [18], approved by the Institutional Review Board (HCB-2016-0830) before any participant enrolment. All individuals who agreed to participate provided written informed consent before randomization. Participants were screened for eligibility during routine second trimester ultrasound scans (19–23.6 weeks of gestation) for being at high risk of developing an SGA newborn [19], and were randomly assigned 1:1:1, based on a computerized random number generator, to one of the three study groups: a MedDiet supplemented with extra-virgin olive oil and walnuts; a stress reduction intervention based on the Mindfulness-Based Stress Reduction (MBSR) program; or usual care without any intervention (control group). For this specific study, only women belonging to the group of MedDiet and usual care who provided lifestyle questionnaires were included. The trial was registered in ClinicalTrials.gov Identifier: NCT03166332.

2.2. Interventions and Measurements

2.2.1. Mediterranean Diet Program

The dietary intervention, adapted from the PREDIMED trial [20], aimed to change the general dietary pattern instead of focusing on changes in single foods or macronutrients. Participants were encouraged to increase their intake of whole-grain cereals ($\geq$5 servings/d); vegetables and dairy products ($\geq$3 servings/d); fresh fruit ($\geq$2 servings/d); and legumes, nuts, fish, and white meat ($\geq$3 servings/week), as well as increasing their olive oil use for cooking and dressings. To achieve a personalized goal, personal and individual recommendations were introduced to the participant's diet according to height, weight, culture, and dietary preferences. Dieticians conducted 30 min face-to-face interviews at enrollment and monthly until the end of intervention (34–36 weeks' gestation). Two weeks following each face-to-face visit, participants underwent telephone interviews. In addition, all participants received extra-virgin olive oil (2 L every month) and 15 g of walnuts per day (450 g every month) at no cost. Additional details of the intervention are provided elsewhere [18]. No intervention or advice regarding mental health, well-being, anxiety, stress, or sleep quality were provided to the participants allocated to the Mediterranean diet group.

2.2.2. Usual Care (Control Group)

Women randomized into this group received usual pregnancy care as per institutional protocols (no intervention), and lifestyle questionnaires were collected at enrollment and at the end of intervention (34–36 week's gestation). No intervention or advice regarding mental health, well-being, anxiety, stress, or sleep quality were provided to the participants allocated to the control group.

2.3. Outcomes

In this trial sub-analysis, the main aim was to investigate the influence of a Mediterranean diet intervention program during pregnancy on maternal stress, anxiety, well-being, mindful state, and sleep quality. Additionally, in a randomly selected subgroup of participants, the levels of cortisol, cortisone and other intermediate related metabolites were measured at the beginning and at the end of the intervention in 24 h urine samples.

2.4. Data Collection

The data of participants included in the study were anonymized and entered in an electronic case report form. Investigators collected maternal sociodemographic and clinical data.

All individuals included in the trial had a baseline visit (19–23 weeks of gestation) and a final visit (34–36 weeks of gestation) with a trained dietitian to assess their diet using a validated 151-item food-frequency questionnaire [21], 7-day dietary registry and the 17-item MedDiet adapted to pregnancy adherence score (score range: 0–17). All participants also provided self-report lifestyle questionnaires to measure their anxiety and stress (State-trait Anxiety Inventory (STAI) Anxiety and Personality [22], range 0–80); Perceived Stress Scale (PSS) [23], range 0–40; well-being (WHO Five Well Being Index (WHO-5) [24], range 0–100); mindful state (WHO Five Facet Mindfulness Questionnaire (FFMQ) [25], range 8–40 for the observation, description, awareness, and nonjudgmental facets, respectively, and range 7–35 for nonreactivity facet); sleep quality (Pittsburgh Sleep Quality Index (PSQI) [26], range 0–21). The questionnaires were carried out at enrollment (baseline punctuation) and at 34–36 weeks of gestation (final punctuation). Abnormal scores were considered the 75th percentile of the baseline scores of each questionnaire in the usual care group, except for the WHO-5 questionnaire, which presents a previously reported cut-off point that defines optimum mental well-being as a score greater than 52 [27].

2.5. Sample Collection

In a subgroup of randomly selected participants from each study group (excluding those receiving corticosteroid treatment), the 24 h urinary cortisone and cortisol metabolites were measured at the baseline and final assessment and analyzed by a validated method based on liquid chromatography-tandem mass spectrometry (LC-MS/MS) [28]. The activity of 11β-Hydroxysteroid Dehydrogenase Type 2 was estimated by the cortisone/cortisol ratio.

2.6. Statistical Analysis

Clinical data are presented as mean (standard deviation (SD) or standard error (SE)), median (interquartile range (IQR)) or number (percentage), as appropriate. The methods of statistical analyses used for the comparison of clinical and perinatal characteristics included Student's *t*-test, ANOVA or ANCOVA with baseline adjustments for continuous variables and X^2 test for categorical variables. Differences were considered significant when p-value < 0.05. Statistical analyses were performed using the Statistical Package for the Social Sciences statistical software package version 27 (SPSS Inc., Chicago, IL, USA).

3. Results

3.1. Study Population and Pregnancy Outcomes

Within these patients, after excluding those that did not provide lifestyle questionnaires to measure their anxiety and stress, mindful state and sleep quality, a population of 680 individuals was considered (n = 331 for Mediterranean diet, n = 349 for usual care), as reported in Figure 1.

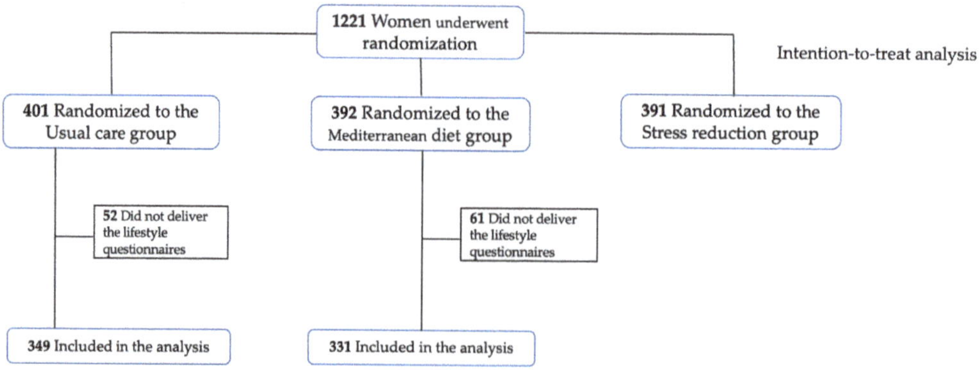

Figure 1. Flowchart of participants from the IMPACT BCN trial involved in the current study.

Baseline characteristics of the study population are shown in Table 1 with no differences between study groups. Pregnancy and perinatal outcomes are shown in Supplementary Table S1, with no significant differences between groups apart from the prevalence of SGA newborns, as reported in the main outcome of the trial [17].

Table 1. Baseline characteristics of women included in the study according to intervention groups ($n = 680$).

Characteristics	Usual Care $n = 349$	Mediterranean Diet $n = 331$	p Value
Age at recruitment (years)	37.1 (33.3–40.5)	37.3 (34.7–40.4)	0.28
Ethnicity			
White	281 (80.5%)	269 (81.3%)	0.80
Latin	50 (14.3%)	44 (13.3%)	0.70
Afro-American	6 (1.7%)	5 (1.5%)	0.83
Asian	6 (1.7%)	7 (2.1%)	0.70
Others	6 (1.7%)	6 (1.8%)	0.93
Socio-economic status [a]			
Low	20 (5.7%)	15 (4.5%)	0.48
Medium	106 (30.4%)	86 (26.0%)	0.20
High	223 (63.9%)	230 (69.5%)	0.12
BMI before pregnancy (Kg/m^2)	23.7 (4.8)	24.0 (4.7)	0.60
BMI > 30 kg/m^2 before pregnancy	39 (11.2%)	38 (11.5%)	0.90
Medical history before pregnancy			
Autoimmune disease	48 (13.8%)	39 (11.8%)	0.44
Thyroid disorders	20 (5.7%)	29 (8.8%)	0.13
Chronic hypertension	15 (4.3%)	8 (2.4%)	0.18
Diabetes Mellitus	12 (3.4%)	16 (4.8%)	0.36
Psychiatric disorders	11 (3.2%)	8 (2.4%)	0.56
Chronic kidney disease	5 (1.4%)	6 (1.8%)	0.70
Obstetric history			
Nulliparous	143 (41.0%)	145 (43.8%)	0.46
Previous placental disease	68 (19.5%)	66 (19.9%)	0.88
Previous preterm birth	9 (2.6%)	10 (3.0%)	0.73
Use of assisted reproductive technologies	92 (26.4%)	85 (25.7%)	0.84
Cigarette smoking during pregnancy	28 (8.0%)	22 (6.6%)	0.49
Alcohol intake during pregnancy	8 (2.3%)	4 (1.2%)	0.27
Drug consumption during pregnancy	1 (0.3%)	2 (0.6%)	0.77
Sports practice during pregnancy	78 (22.3%)	71 (21.5%)	0.94
Yoga or Pilates during pregnancy	73 (20.9%)	63 (19.0%)	0.54

BMI: Body mass index. Data are expressed as median (IQR) or mean (SD) or n (%). [a] socioeconomical status: low (never work or unemployed >2 years), medium (secondary studies and work), high (university studies and work).

3.2. *Effects of Mediterranean Diet on Stress, Anxiety, Well-Being, Sleep Quality and Mindful State*

3.2.1. Life-Style Questionnaires

Table 2 displays baseline and final life-style questionnaire scores on stress, anxiety, well-being, sleep quality, and mindful state between study groups, and Table 3 reports the percentage of high/poor scores at the final assessment. Perceived stress, anxiety and poor sleep quality increased throughout gestation in all study groups (Figure 2). At the end of the intervention, participants in the Mediterranean diet group showed significantly lower levels of perceived stress as compared to patients undergoing usual care, as shown in Figure 2A (mean difference −0.85 (−1.63 to −0.06), $p = 0.035$). Similarly, the Mediterranean diet group presented significantly lower final anxiety scores compared to the non-intervention group (mean 13.6 ± 0.4 SE vs. 15.8 ± 0.5, $p < 0.004$) (Figure 2B), with a lower frequency of high anxiety scores ($n = 58$, 17.9% vs. $n = 87$, 25.4%, $p = 0.020$), as reported in Table 3. Aligned with the previous findings, women's sleep quality improved following the Mediterranean diet intervention compared to controls (PSQI mean 7.0 ± 0.2 SE vs. 7.9 ± 0.2 SE, $p = 0.001$) (see Table 2 and Figure 2C).

Table 2. Changes in maternal anxiety, well-being, sleep quality, and mindful state evaluated at baseline and final evaluation according to intervention groups.

		Within-Group Mean Changes		p §	Between-Group Changes
		Usual Care $n = 349$	MedDiet $n = 331$		MedDiet vs. Usual Care Difference (95% CI)
Perceived stress scale score	Baseline †	16.3 ± 7.8	15.9 ± 7.6		
	Final ‡	17.0 ± 0.4 *	15.9 ± 0.4	0.035	−0.85 (−1.63 to −0.06)
State-trait Anxiety Inventory (anxiety)	Baseline †	14.1 ± 8.8	12.9 ± 8.3		
	Final ‡	15.8 ± 0.5 **	13.6 ± 0.4 *	0.004	−1.35 (−2.28 to −0.43)
State-trait Anxiety Inventory (personality)	Baseline †	15.8. ± 9.0	14.2 ± 7.9		
	Final ‡	15.8 ± 0.5	14.0 ± 0.5	0.100	−0.68 (−1.48 to 0.13)
WHO Five Well-being index	Baseline †	62.7 ± 17.3	67.5 ± 15.2		
	Final ‡	62.9 ± 0.9	66.6 ± 0.8	0.587	0.51 (−1.32 to 2.33)
Pittsburgh Sleep Quality Index	Baseline †	6.7 ± 2.4	6.4 ± 2.1		
	Final ‡	7.9 ± 0.2 **	7.0 ± 0.2 **	0.001	−0.73 (−1.15 to −0.31)
FFMQ 1: Observation	Baseline †	23.3 ± 5.9	24.2 ± 5.6		
	Final ‡	24.0 ± 0.3	24.6 ± 0.3	0.729	0.12 (−0.57 to 0.81)
FFMQ 2: Description	Baseline †	32.1 ± 5.5	32.7 ± 4.8		
	Final ‡	31.7 ± 0.3	32.4 ± 0.3	0.273	0.35 (−0.27 to 1.37)
FFMQ 3: Awareness	Baseline †	31.3 ± 6.0	31.3 ± 6.3		
	Final ‡	30.6 ± 0.4 *	30.0 ± 0.4 **	0.280	−0.51 (−1.43 to 0.41)
FFMQ 4: Non-judgmental	Baseline †	29.9 ± 5.6	30.1 ± 5.2		
	Final ‡	30.0 ± 0.3	30.0 ± 0.3	0.994	0.00 (−0.64 to 0.64)
FFMQ 5: Non-reactivity	Baseline †	22.5 ± 4.8	22.6 ± 4.8		
	Final ‡	22.9 ± 0.2	22.5 ± 0.3	0.091	−0.55 (−1.05 to 0.08)

MedDiet: Mediterranean diet; FFMQ Five Facet. Mindfulness questionnaire. † Baseline values are observed means ± SD. ‡ Final values are baseline-adjusted (least-squares) means ± SE and comparison among groups obtained with ANCOVA analysis. * $p < 0.05$ and ** $p < 0.001$ final from baseline comparison. § ANCOVA analysis.

Table 3. Frequency of women high maternal stress, poor well-being and sleep quality questionnaires score at final evaluation according to intervention groups.

Final Scores	Usual Care $n = 349$	Mediterranean Diet $n = 331$	p Value
Perceived Stress Scale score > p75	85 (24.4%)	80 (24.2%)	0.96
State-trait Anxiety Inventory (anxiety) score > p75 [a]	82 (23.9%)	75 (23.1%)	0.82
State-trait Anxiety Inventory (personality) score > p75 [a]	87 (25.4%)	58 (17.9%)	0.02
WHO Five Well-Being Index score < 52 [b]	95 (27.5%)	65 (19.8%)	0.02
Pittsburgh Sleep Quality Index score > p75 [c]	62 (21.8%)	44 (16.8%)	0.14

Data are expressed as n (%). High maternal stress/anxiety defined as Perceived Stress Scale and State-strait Anxiety Inventory scores above 75th percentile. Poor well-being defined as Five Well-Being Index score below 52. Poor sleep quality defined as Pittsburgh Sleep Quality score above 75th percentile. [a] Data available for 667 pregnancies. [b] Data available for 674 pregnancies. [c] Data available for 546 pregnancies.

Regarding the well-being questionnaire, 19.8% ($n = 65$) of women from the Mediterranean diet group presented with poor well-being as compared to 27.5% ($n = 95$) in the control group ($p = 0.02$), revealing better well-being (see Table 3 and Figure 3). No significant differences between groups were observed with the mindful state questionnaire (Table 2). Changes in key foods and nutrient intake during intervention are shown in Supplementary Tables S2 and S3.

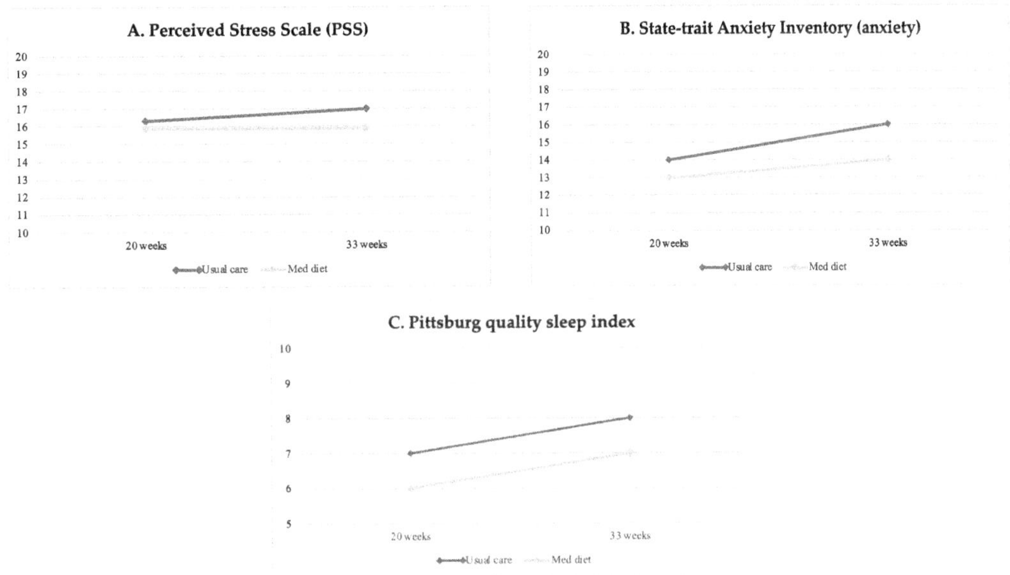

Figure 2. Changes in maternal stress (**A**), anxiety (**B**) and sleep quality (**C**) at baseline (20 weeks of gestation) and final (33 weeks) evaluation according to intervention groups.

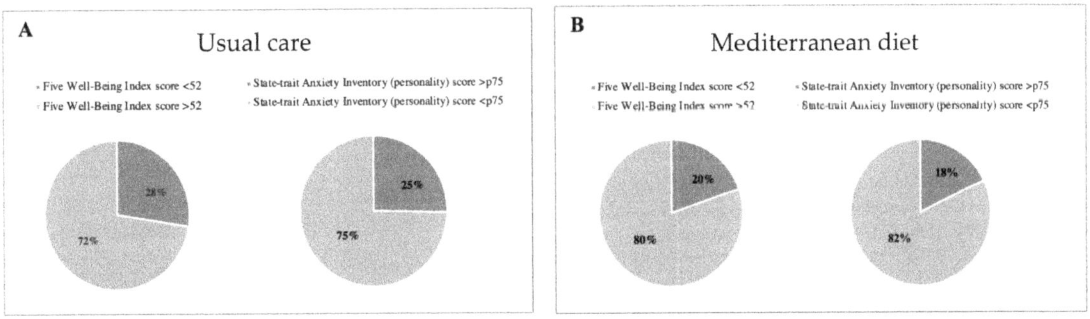

Figure 3. Percentage of high- vs. low-stress participants, and poor vs. good well-being (WHO-5) according to intervention groups. High stress is shown in dark grey color and defined as a State-trait Anxiety Inventory (STAI) personality score above 75th percentile in Usual care (**A**) and Mediterranean diet group (**B**). Poor well-being is shown in in dark grey color and defined as a Five Well-Being Index WHO score below 52.

3.2.2. Cortisol Assessment

The baseline 24 h urinary cortisone/cortisol ratio in 106 participants was similar between groups and increased during gestation. This increase was more pronounced in the Mediterranean diet group compared to usual care (mean 1.7± SE 0.1 vs. mean 1.3 ± SE 0.1, $p < 0.001$) (Table 4). At final assessment, Mediterranean diet participants showed higher levels of total cortisone concentration (mean 134.7± SE 8.3 vs. mean 111.5 ± SE 7.7, $p = 0.012$) and percentage (mean 2.9± SE 0.1 vs. mean 2.4 ± SE 0.1, $p = 0.002$), and lower levels of the 5β-tetrahydrocortisone/Cortisone (mean 16.8 ± SE 1.2 vs. mean 21.4 ± SE 1.4, $p = 0.032$) compared to the control group.

Table 4. Differences in urinary 24 h cortisol, cortisone and other related metabolites at baseline and final evaluation according to intervention group (n = 106).

		Within-Group Mean Changes		p §	Between-Group Changes
		Usual Care n = 52	MedDiet n = 54		MedDiet vs. Usual Care Difference (95% CI)
Total Cortisone/Total Cortisol	Baseline †	1.0 ± 0.6	1.2 ± 0.8		
	Final ‡	1.3 ± 0.1 **	1.7 ± 0.1 **	0.015	0.26 (0.05 to 0.47)
Total cortisol	Baseline †	89.9 ± 42.6	81.6 ± 36.1		
	Final ‡	89.8 ± 4.8	84.9 ± 5.3	0.619	2.66 (−7.83 to 13.16)
Total cortisol %	Baseline †	2.0 ± 0.8	2.0 ± 0.8		
	Final ‡	2.1 ± 0.1	2.0 ± 0.1	0.536	−0.08 (−0.33 to 0.17)
5β-tetrahydrocortisol	Baseline †	823.1 ± 419.3	734.4 ± 304.2		
	Final ‡	777.8 ± 54.6	766.3 ± 55.3	0.279	64.9 (−52.60 to 182.42)
5β-THF/Cortisol	Baseline †	10.0 ± 5.2	10.9 ± 5.0		
	Final ‡	9.1 ± 0.6	9.6 ± 0.7	0.774	0.19 (−1.13 to 1.52)
Total cortisone	Baseline †	85.6 ± 52.5	87.0 ± 50.1		
	Final ‡	111.5 ± 7.7 *	134.7 ± 8.3 **	0.012	24.3 (5.45 to 43.3)
Total cortisone %	Baseline †	1.9 ± 1.0	1.9 ± 0.7		
	Final ‡	2.4 ± 0.1 **	2.9 ± 0.1 **	0.002	0.47 (0.18 to 0.78)
5β-tetrahydrocortisone %	Baseline †	2185.2 ± 1189.3	1961.1 ± 973.2		
	Final ‡	2209.3 ± 171.2	2196.5 ± 184.4	0.627	111.0 (−336.96 to 558.99)
5β-THE/Cortisone	Baseline †	29.8 ± 15.5	26.3 ± 14.8		
	Final ‡	21.4 ± 1.4 **	16.8 ± 1.2 **	0.032	−3.39 (−6.49 to −0.30)

5β-THF/Cortisol: 5β-tetrahydrocortisol/Cortisol; 5β-THE/Cortisone: 5β-tetrahydrocortisone/Cortisone. † Baseline values are observed means ± SD. ‡ Final values are baseline-adjusted (least-squares) means ± SE and comparison among groups obtained with ANCOVA analysis. * $p < 0.05$ and ** $p < 0.001$ final from baseline comparison. § ANCOVA analysis.

4. Discussion

In this randomized clinical trial that involved pregnant women at high risk for an SGA newborn, an intervention based on MedDiet significantly reduced maternal anxiety and stress and improved well-being and sleep quality. These effects were revealed by self-reported stress questionnaires and biomarkers, as reflected by the increased estimated activity of a cortisol-deactivating enzyme.

Interest in mental health and care has grown exponentially in recent years and associations between healthy dietary patterns and mental health parameters have been reported. Jacka et al. conducted a randomized controlled trial to investigate the efficacy of a dietary intervention based on the MedDiet for the treatment of symptoms related to major depressive episodes in subjects with Major Depressive Disorder, independently of other factors such as physical activity, smoking habit, or weight loss [29]. The MedDiet group showed significantly greater improvements in symptoms of depression compared to the control group. In addition, other studies have evidenced that a lower incidence of depression incidence was significantly correlated with increasing adherence to MedDiet [7]. Additionally, in the PREDIMED study, a preventive effect for depression was found for the MedDiet in participants with type 2 diabetes [9]. Specifically, participants with type 2 diabetes allocated to the MedDiet supplemented with nuts group showed a 40% lower risk of depression compared to the control arm.

However, the evidence about the effects of dietary interventions on mental health during pregnancy is limited. Our study reveals that following the MedDiet during pregnancy is associated with a reduction in maternal anxiety/stress, together with an increase in the cortisol-deactivating enzyme. These findings are in line with previous data. In a recent study, Papandreou et al. conducted a randomized clinical trial with 40 pregnant women incorporating MedDiet recommendations into the Clinical Decision Support Systems, showing an improvement in nutritional status and reduction in health-related anxiety and depression [30]. Similarly, a longitudinal study with 152 pregnant women showed that higher adherence to the MedDiet was inversely associated with anxiety and directly associated with well-being [16]. Moreover, these associations were significant for some key foods of the MedDiet, specifically whole-grain cereals, fruits and vegetables, extra-virgin olive oil and nuts [16], food sources of dietary antioxidants whose consumption was encouraged during the intervention in our study. Aligned with our findings, other healthy dietary patterns promoting healthy foods not based on the MedDiet were associated with lower depression during pregnancy [31–33]. Nevertheless, in observational and cohort studies with pregnant women, some specific foods have been identified as protective against mental disorders (including depression and anxiety), including whole-grain cereals, fruits, and beans. In contrast, other foods are associated with higher risk, including ultra-processed foods such as pastries, red and processed meat, margarine, and artificial juices [16,34]. Additionally, it has been postulated that levels of depression tend to increase throughout pregnancy, highlighting the importance of structured dietary interventions to improve overall diet quality during pregnancy [33,35].

In addition to its beneficial effects on anxiety and stress, our study first demonstrates an improvement in maternal well-being and sleep quality with MedDiet. The association between higher MedDiet adherence and subjective well-being has been found in observational studies [36]. In the case of sleep quality, a longitudinal study with 150 pregnant women assessed the association between MedDiet adherence and the Pittsburgh Sleep Quality Index, showing an association between higher MedDiet adherence and better sleep quality at 16- and 34-week's gestation, results aligned with our findings [37]. It should also be considered the burden that women go through during pregnancy may affect their mental health; research often does not recognize the multiple competing demands on women, specifically during pregnancy. However, to our knowledge, the present study is the first randomized clinical trial with a structured intervention based on a MedDiet adapted to pregnancy to evaluate well-being and sleep quality.

Several biological mechanisms have been postulated regarding the relationship between diet and mental health. First, it should be noted that the MedDiet is an easy-to-follow dietary pattern and is not only a healthy diet but also promotes a healthy lifestyle, including cultural and lifestyle elements such as conviviality, seasonality, traditional recipes, physical activity, and culinary activities [38]. These behavioral changes related to lifestyle may also have a therapeutic benefit [29]. Second, the role of diet in mental health may be mediated by inflammatory and oxidative stress pathways [12,13], the modulation of gut microbiota [39] and brain plasticity [40]. A low production of brain-derived neurotrophic factor, a peptide implicated in synaptic plasticity and neuronal survival, has been observed in patients with depression [41]. Moreover, reduced brain-derived neurotrophic factor levels were observed in pregnant women with low sleep quality, as measured by the Pittsburgh Sleep Quality Index, compared to pregnant women with good sleep quality [42]. Interestingly, in a sub-group of the PREDIMED study, significantly higher plasma levels of brain-derived neurotrophic factor were observed in participants allocated to the MedDiet supplemented with nuts group compared to the control arm, whose secretion may be also modulated by diet [43]. The fatty acid profile of the MedDiet, rich in polyunsaturated fatty acids, may also promote mental health, as low polyunsaturated fatty acid intake (mainly omega-3 fatty acids) has been associated with several mental outcomes, including depression [44,45]. Thus, several dietary components, including nutrients and bioactive compounds, are required for healthy brain function and mental health, including the synergic effect between components. Therefore, dietary interventions promoting a healthy dietary pattern rather than a single nutrient may have greater benefits for mental health [46].

Important implications regarding the mental health of the mother may be expected, including a potential benefit during the postpartum period. Maternal mental health alterations, principally anxiety, are associated with several adverse outcomes for both the mother and the offspring, including postnatal depression, pre-term birth and the poor cognitive and behavioral development of the infants [47–50]. Additionally, the estimated prevalence of anxiety disorders across the perinatal period is around 21% [51]. Our results highlight the need for anxiety and stress screenings during pregnancy, nutritional education, and referrals for evaluation and treatment if necessary. Further research is needed to characterize the impact of the MedDiet on mental health during pregnancy, including the underlying mechanisms, specifically oxidative stress, and the potential benefits for the offspring's mental health. If confirmed, the MedDiet could become an early intervention strategy for the prevention of mental disorders [52].

The major strengths of the present study include a very well-characterized population of pregnant women who followed a structured intervention in a randomized clinical trial. Moreover, the use of different validated questionnaires with clinical applicability to assess mental stress, well-being and sleep quality provided rigor and validity to the results of the study, as well as the ability to analyze various stress-related biomarkers in a subgroup of patients with the aim of measuring stress in an empirical way. The use of validated questionnaires and biomarkers may mitigate the potential misclassification of self-reported data, along with the inherent risk of inaccuracies in the measurements.

The study has some limitations. Firstly, the trial was not designed for this purpose, although maternal stress, well-being and sleep quality were prespecified in the study protocol and assessed from the beginning of the study. Secondly, we were not able to assess long-term dietary intake, including measuring diet before pregnancy or the dietary changes from the beginning of the pregnancy. Most women were of white ethnicity and middle to high socio-economical level; hence, the results should not be extrapolated to other populations with different characteristics. These findings should be considered preliminary and require replication, including reseatch involving other study populations and an evaluation of the underlying mechanisms of action.

5. Conclusions

In conclusion, a MedDiet intervention significantly reduces maternal anxiety and stress, as well as improving well-being and sleep quality during gestation. Considering the increasing importance of the role of mental health during pregnancy, these findings might imply the promotion of a pregnancy-adapted MedDiet among pregnant women as a powerful public health strategy.

Supplementary Materials: The following supporting information can be downloaded at: https://www.mdpi.com/article/10.3390/nu15102362/s1, Table S1. Pregnancy and perinatal outcome of women included in the study; Table S2. Changes in dietary key foods' intake and Mediterranean diet adherence evaluated at baseline and final visits according to intervention groups; Table S3. Changes in nutrient intake and Mediterranean diet adherence evaluated at baseline and final visits according to intervention groups.

Author Contributions: Conceptualization, E.G., F.C. (Fàtima Crispi) and F.C. (Francesca Crovetto); methodology, R.C., F.C. (Fàtima Crispi), F.C. (Francesca Crovetto), E.V., R.E. and E.G.; validation, I.C., A.N., R.P., S.C.-B., L.Y., M.G., L.B., M.L., M.L.B., G.C., A.G.-G., O.J.P., I.M., A.M.-À., E.V., M.D.G.-R., R.C., R.E., E.G., F.C. (Fàtima Crispi) and F.C. (Francesca Crovetto).; formal analysis, I.C., F.C. (Francesca Crovetto), S.C.-B.; investigation, R.C., F.C. (Fàtima Crispi), F.C. (Francesca Crovetto), R.E., E.V. and E.G.; resources, E.G.; data curation, I.C., S.C.-B., F.C. (Francesca Crovetto), F.C. (Fàtima Crispi), R.E. and E.G.; writing—original draft preparation, I.C., A.N., R.P., S.C.-B. and F.C. (Francesca Crovetto); writing—review and editing, L.Y., M.G., L.B., M.L., M.L.B., G.C., A.G.-G., O.J.P., I.M., A.M.-À., E.V., M.D.G.-R., R.C., R.E., E.G. and F.C. (Fàtima Crispi); supervision, F.C. (Francesca Crovetto), F.C. (Fàtima Crispi) and S.C.-B.; funding acquisition, E.G. All authors have read and agreed to the published version of the manuscript.

Funding: The project was partially funded by a grant from "la Caixa" Foundation (LCF/PR/GN18/10310003 and LCF/BQ/DR19/11740018); Cerebra Foundation for the Brain Injured Child (Carmarthen, Wales, UK); AGAUR under grant 2017 SGR nº 1531; Instituto de Salud Carlos III (PI22/00684, INT21/00027, CM21/00058). S. Castro-Barquero has received support from Margarita Salas fellowship, University of Barcelona. L.Youssef was supported by the grant FJC2021-048123-I, funded by MCIN/AEI/10.13039/501100011033 and by the European Union "NextGenerationEU"/PRTR. L. Benitez was supported by a research grant from the Instituto de Salud Carlos III (CM21/00058). M.

Larroya has received support from Hospital Clínic Barcelona (Contracte Clínic de Recerca Emili Letang-Josep Font). F. Crovetto has received support from Centro de Investigaciones Biomédicas en Red sobre Enfermedades Raras (CIBERER).

Institutional Review Board Statement: The present study was approved by the Institutional Review Board (HCB-2016-0830) before any participant enrolment.

Informed Consent Statement: Informed consent was obtained from all subjects involved in the study.

Data Availability Statement: The datasets used and/or analyses during the current study are available from the corresponding author on reasonable request.

Acknowledgments: We thank the study participants for their personal time and commitment to this trial. We also thank all the medical staff, residents, midwives, and nurses of BCNatal, especially Annachiara Basso; Laura Segales; Marta Dacal; Marta Camacho; and Silvia Gomez, for their support in the recruitment, interventions, and data collection of the trial; Carlos Galante; and Tania Freitas, (Department of Internal Medicine, Hospital Clinic, Barcelona, Spain, Barcelona, Spain), for the support in the Mediterranean diet intervention; Georgina Badosa; and Amaia Helguera (Instituto esMindfulness, Barcelona, Spain), for their support in the stress-reduction intervention; we thank the Clinic-IDIBAPS Biobank for their valuable management of samples. CIBER OBN is an initiative of the Instituto de Salud Carlos III, Spain.

Conflicts of Interest: Ayako Nakaki reports personal fees from La Caixa Foundation (Doctoral INPhINIT—RETAINING, fellowship n LCF/BQ/DR19/11740018), during the conduct of the study. Eduard Vieta reports, outside the submitted work, personal fees from Abbott, Allergan, Angelini, Lundbeck, Sage, and Sanofi; grants from Dainippon Sumitomo, Ferrer, and Janssen. Ramon Estruch reports grants from Fundación Dieta Mediterránea, Spain and Cerveza y Salud, Spain; he reports personal fees for given lectures from Brewers of Europe, Belgium, Fundación Cerveza y Salud, Spain, Pernaud-Ricard, Mexico, Instituto Cervantes, Alburquerque, USA, Instituto Cervantes, Milan, Italy, Instituto Cervantes, Tokyo, Japan, Lilly Laboratories, Spain, and Wine and Culinary International Forum, Spain, and non-financial support to organize a National Congress on Nutrition. Eduard Gratacós reports, during the conduct of the study, grants from La Caixa Foundation, grants from Cerebra Foundation for the Brain Injured Child, and grants from AGAUR. Francesca Crovetto reports a personal fee from Centro de Investigaciones Biomédicas en Red sobre Enfermedades Raras, during the conduct of the study. The remaining authors declare no competing interests.

References

1. Salas-Salvadó, J.; Díaz-López, A.; Ruiz-Canela, M.; Basora, J.; Fitó, M.; Corella, D.; Serra-Majem, L.; Wärnberg, J.; Romaguera, D.; Estruch, R.; et al. Effect of a Lifestyle Intervention Program With Energy-Restricted Mediterranean Diet and Exercise on Weight Loss and Cardiovascular Risk Factors: One-Year Results of the PREDIMED-Plus Trial. *Diabetes Care* **2019**, *42*, 777–788. [CrossRef] [PubMed]
2. Valls-Pedret, C.; Sala-Vila, A.; Serra-Mir, M.; Corella, D.; De La Torre, R.; Martínez-González, M.Á.; Martínez-Lapiscina, E.H.; Fitó, M.; Pérez-Heras, A.; Salas-Salvadó, J.; et al. Mediterranean Diet and Age-Related Cognitive Decline: A Randomized Clinical Trial. *JAMA Intern. Med.* **2015**, *175*, 1094–1103. [CrossRef] [PubMed]
3. Schwingshackl, L.; Schwedhelm, C.; Galbete, C.; Hoffmann, G. Adherence to Mediterranean Diet and Risk of Cancer: An Updated Systematic Review and Meta-Analysis. *Nutrients* **2017**, *9*, 1063. [CrossRef] [PubMed]
4. Toledo, E.; Salas-Salvado, J.; Donat-Vargas, C.; Buil-Cosiales, P.; Estruch, R.; Ros, E.; Corella, D.; Fito, M.; Hu, F.B.; Aros, F.; et al. Mediterranean Diet and Invasive Breast Cancer Risk Among Women at High Cardiovascular Risk in the PREDIMED Trial: A Randomized Clinical Trial. *JAMA Intern. Med.* **2015**, *175*, 1752–1760. [CrossRef]
5. Ventriglio, A.; Sancassiani, F.; Contu, M.P.; Latorre, M.; Di Slavatore, M.; Fornaro, M.; Bhugra, D. Mediterranean Diet and Its Benefits on Health and Mental Health: A Literature Review. *Clin. Pract. Epidemiol. Ment. Health* **2020**, *16*, 156. [CrossRef]
6. Ventriglio, A.; Gentile, A.; Stella, E.; Bellomo, A. Metabolic Issues in Patients Affected by Schizophrenia: Clinical Characteristics and Medical Management. *Front. Neurosci.* **2015**, *9*, 297. [CrossRef]
7. Parletta, N.; Zarnowiecki, D.; Cho, J.; Wilson, A.; Bogomolova, S.; Villani, A.; Itsiopoulos, C.; Niyonsenga, T.; Blunden, S.; Meyer, B.; et al. A Mediterranean-Style Dietary Intervention Supplemented with Fish Oil Improves Diet Quality and Mental Health in People with Depression: A Randomized Controlled Trial (HELFIMED). *Nutr. Neurosci.* **2017**, *22*, 474–487. [CrossRef]
8. Cano-Ibáñez, N.; Serra-Majem, L.; Martín-Peláez, S.; Martínez-González, M.Á.; Salas-Salvadó, J.; Corella Piquer, M.D.; Lassale, C.; Martínez Hernandez, J.A.; Alonso-Gómez, Á.M.; Wärnberg, J.; et al. Association between the Prime Diet Quality Score and Depressive Symptoms in a Mediterranean Population with Metabolic Syndrome. Cross-Sectional and 2-Year Follow-up Assessment from PREDIMED-PLUS Study. *Br. J. Nutr.* **2022**, *128*, 1170–1179. [CrossRef]

9. Sánchez-Villegas, A.; Martínez-González, M.A.; Estruch, R.; Salas-Salvadó, J.; Corella, D.; Covas, M.I.; Arós, F.; Romaguera, D.; Gómez-Gracia, E.; Lapetra, J.; et al. Mediterranean Dietary Pattern and Depression: The PREDIMED Randomized Trial. *BMC Med.* **2013**, *11*, 208. [CrossRef]
10. Bayes, J.; Schloss, J.; Sibbritt, D. Effects of Polyphenols in a Mediterranean Diet on Symptoms of Depression: A Systematic Literature Review. *Adv. Nutr.* **2020**, *11*, 602–615. [CrossRef]
11. Taylor, A.M.; Holscher, H.D. A Review of Dietary and Microbial Connections to Depression, Anxiety, and Stress. *Nutr. Neurosci.* **2018**, *23*, 237–250. [CrossRef] [PubMed]
12. Moylan, S.; Berk, M.; Dean, O.M.; Samuni, Y.; Williams, L.J.; O'Neil, A.; Hayley, A.C.; Pasco, J.A.; Anderson, G.; Jacka, F.N.; et al. Oxidative & Nitrosative Stress in Depression: Why so Much Stress? *Neurosci. Biobehav. Rev.* **2014**, *45*, 46–62. [CrossRef] [PubMed]
13. Berk, M.; Williams, L.J.; Jacka, F.N.; O'Neil, A.; Pasco, J.A.; Moylan, S.; Allen, N.B.; Stuart, A.L.; Hayley, A.C.; Byrne, M.L.; et al. So Depression Is an Inflammatory Disease, but Where Does the Inflammation Come from? *BMC Med.* **2013**, *11*, 200. [CrossRef]
14. Fawcett, E.J.; Fairbrother, N.; Cox, M.L.; White, I.R.; Fawcett, J.M. The Prevalence of Anxiety Disorders During Pregnancy and the Postpartum Period: A Multivariate Bayesian Meta-Analysis. *J. Clin. Psychiatry* **2019**, *80*, 1181. [CrossRef] [PubMed]
15. Traylor, C.S.; Johnson, J.D.; Kimmel, M.C.; Manuck, T.A. Effects of Psychological Stress on Adverse Pregnancy Outcomes and Nonpharmacologic Approaches for Reduction: An Expert Review. *Am. J. Obstet. Gynecol. MFM* **2020**, *2*, 100229. [CrossRef] [PubMed]
16. Flor-Alemany, M.; Baena-García, L.; Migueles, J.H.; Henriksson, P.; Löf, M.; Aparicio, V.A. Associations of Mediterranean Diet with Psychological Ill-Being and Well-Being throughout the Pregnancy Course: The GESTAFIT Project. *Qual. Life Res.* **2022**, *31*, 2705–2716. [CrossRef]
17. Crovetto, F.; Crispi, F.; Casas, R.; Martín-Asuero, A.; Borràs, R.; Vieta, E.; Estruch, R.; Gratacós, E. Effects of Mediterranean Diet or Mindfulness-Based Stress Reduction on Prevention of Small-for-Gestational Age Birth Weights in Newborns Born to At-Risk Pregnant Individuals: The IMPACT BCN Randomized Clinical Trial. *JAMA* **2021**, *326*, 2150–2160. [CrossRef]
18. Crovetto, F.; Crispi, F.; Borras, R.; Paules, C.; Casas, R.; Martín, R.; Arranz, A.; Vieta, E.; Estruch, R.G.E. Mediterranean Diet, Mindfulness Based Stress Reduction and Usual Care during Pregnancy for Reducing Fetal Growth Restriction and Adverse Perinatal Outcomes: IMPACT BCN (Improving Mothers for a Better PrenAtal Care Trial Barcelona): A Study Protocol for Randomized Controlled Trial. *Trials* **2021**, *22*, 1–14.
19. Royal College of Obstetricians and Gynaecologist. The Investigation and Management of the Small for Gestational Age Fetus. *Green-Top Guidel.* **2013**, *31*, 1–34.
20. Estruch, R.; Ros, E.; Salas-Salvadó, J.; Covas, M.I.; Corella, D.; Arós, F.; Gómez-Gracia, E.; Ruiz-Gutiérrez, V.; Fiol, M.; Lapetra, J.; et al. Primary Prevention of Cardiovascular Disease with a Mediterranean Diet Supplemented with Extra-Virgin Olive Oil or Nuts. *N. Engl. J. Med.* **2018**, *378*, e34. [CrossRef]
21. Juton, C.; Castro-barquero, S.; Casas, R.; Freitas, T.; Ruiz-león, A.M.; Crovetto, F.; Domenech, M.; Crispi, F.; Vieta, E.; Gratacós, E.; et al. Reliability and Concurrent and Construct Validity of a Food Frequency Questionnaire for Pregnant Women at High Risk to Develop Fetal Growth Restriction. *Nutrients* **2021**, *13*, 1629. [CrossRef] [PubMed]
22. Spielberger, C.D.; Vagg, P.R. Psychometric Properties of the STAI: A Reply to Ramanaiah, Franzen, and Schill. *J. Pers. Assess.* **1984**, *48*, 95–97. [CrossRef] [PubMed]
23. Cohen, S.; Kamarck, T.; Mermelstein, R. A Global Measure of Perceived Stress. *J. Health Soc. Behav.* **1983**, *24*, 385–396. [CrossRef] [PubMed]
24. Bech, P.; Olsen, L.R.; Kjoller, M.; Rasmussen, N.K. Measuring Well-Being Rather than the Absence of Distress Symptoms: A Comparison of the SF-36 Mental Health Subscale and the WHO-Five Well-Being Scale. *Int. J. Methods Psychiatr. Res.* **2003**, *12*, 85–91. [CrossRef] [PubMed]
25. Baer, R.A.; Smith, G.T.; Hopkins, J.; Krietemeyer, J.; Toney, L. Using Self-Report Assessment Methods to Explore Facets of Mindfulness. *Assessment* **2006**, *13*, 27–45. [CrossRef] [PubMed]
26. Buysse, D.J.; Reynolds, C.F.; Monk, T.H.; Berman, S.R.; Kupfer, D.J. The Pittsburgh Sleep Quality Index: A New Instrument for Psychiatric Practice and Research. *Psychiatry Res.* **1989**, *28*, 193–213. [CrossRef]
27. Bonnín, C.M.; Yatham, L.N.; Michalak, E.E.; Martínez-Arán, A.; Dhanoa, T.; Torres, I.; Santos-Pascual, C.; Valls, E.; Carvalho, A.F.; Sánchez-Moreno, J.; et al. Psychometric Properties of the Well-Being Index (WHO-5) Spanish Version in a Sample of Euthymic Patients with Bipolar Disorder. *J. Affect. Disord.* **2018**, *228*, 153–159. [CrossRef]
28. Marcos, J.; Renau, N.; Casals, G.; Segura, J.; Ventura, R.; Pozo, O.J. Investigation of Endogenous Corticosteroids Profiles in Human Urine Based on Liquid Chromatography Tandem Mass Spectrometry. *Anal. Chim. Acta* **2014**, *812*, 92–104. [CrossRef]
29. Jacka, F.N.; O'Neil, A.; Opie, R.; Itsiopoulos, C.; Cotton, S.; Mohebbi, M.; Castle, D.; Dash, S.; Mihalopoulos, C.; Chatterton, M.L.; et al. A Randomised Controlled Trial of Dietary Improvement for Adults with Major Depression (the "SMILES" Trial). *BMC Med.* **2017**, *15*, 23. [CrossRef]
30. Papandreou, P.; Amerikanou, C.; Vezou, C.; Gioxari, A.; Kaliora, A.C.; Skouroliakou, M. Improving Adherence to the Mediterranean Diet in Early Pregnancy Using a Clinical Decision Support System; A Randomised Controlled Clinical Trial. *Nutrients* **2023**, *15*, 432. [CrossRef]
31. Huang, P.; Wei, D.; Xiao, W.; Yuan, M.; Chen, N.; Wei, X.; Xie, J.; Lu, J.; Xia, X.; Lu, M.; et al. Maternal Dietary Patterns and Depressive Symptoms during Pregnancy: The Born in Guangzhou Cohort Study. *Clin. Nutr.* **2021**, *40*, 3485–3494. [CrossRef] [PubMed]

32. Miyake, Y.; Tanaka, K.; Okubo, H.; Sasaki, S.; Furukawa, S.; Arakawa, M. Dietary Patterns and Depressive Symptoms during Pregnancy in Japan: Baseline Data from the Kyushu Okinawa Maternal and Child Health Study. *J. Affect. Disord.* **2018**, *225*, 552–558. [CrossRef]
33. Tokumitsu, K.; Tokumitsu, K.; Sugawara, N.; Sugawara, N.; Maruo, K.; Suzuki, T.; Shimoda, K.; Yasui-Furukori, N.; Yasui-Furukori, N. Prevalence of Perinatal Depression among Japanese Women: A Meta-Analysis. *Ann. Gen. Psychiatry* **2020**, *19*, 41. [CrossRef]
34. Paskulin, J.T.A.; Drehmer, M.; Olinto, M.T.; Hoffmann, J.F.; Pinheiro, A.P.; Schmidt, M.I.; Nunes, M.A. Association between Dietary Patterns and Mental Disorders in Pregnant Women in Southern Brazil. *Braz. J. Psychiatry* **2017**, *39*, 208. [CrossRef] [PubMed]
35. Fowles, E.R.; Stang, J.; Bryant, M.; Kim, S.H. Stress, Depression, Social Support, and Eating Habits Reduce Diet Quality in the First Trimester in Low-Income Women: A Pilot Study. *J. Acad. Nutr. Diet.* **2012**, *112*, 1619–1625. [CrossRef] [PubMed]
36. Moreno-Agostino, D.; Caballero, F.F.; Martín-María, N.; Tyrovolas, S.; López-García, P.; Rodríguez-Artalejo, F.; Haro, J.M.; Ayuso-Mateos, J.L.; Miret, M. Mediterranean Diet and Wellbeing: Evidence from a Nationwide Survey. *Psychol. Health* **2019**, *34*, 321–335. [CrossRef]
37. Flor-Alemany, M.; Nestares, T.; Alemany-Arrebola, I.; Marín-Jiménez, N.; Borges-Cosic, M.; Aparicio, V.A. Influence of Dietary Habits and Mediterranean Diet Adherence on Sleep Quality during Pregnancy. The GESTAFIT Project. *Nutrients* **2020**, *12*, 3569. [CrossRef]
38. Bach-Faig, A.; Berry, E.M.; Lairon, D.; Reguant, J.; Trichopoulou, A.; Dernini, S.; Medina, F.X.; Battino, M.; Belahsen, R.; Miranda, G.; et al. Mediterranean Diet Pyramid Today. Science and Cultural Updates. *Public Health Nutr.* **2011**, *14*, 2274–2284. [CrossRef]
39. Dash, S.; Clarke, G.; Berk, M.; Jacka, F.N. The Gut Microbiome and Diet in Psychiatry: Focus on Depression. *Curr. Opin. Psychiatry* **2015**, *28*, 1–6. [CrossRef]
40. Jacka, F.N.; Cherbuin, N.; Anstey, K.J.; Sachdev, P.; Butterworth, P. Western Diet Is Associated with a Smaller Hippocampus: A Longitudinal Investigation. *BMC Med.* **2015**, *13*, 215. [CrossRef]
41. Bocchio-Chiavetto, L.; Bagnardi, V.; Zanardini, R.; Molteni, R.; Gabriela Nielsen, M.; Placentino, A.; Giovannini, C.; Rillosi, L.; Ventriglia, M.; Riva, M.A.; et al. Serum and Plasma BDNF Levels in Major Depression: A Replication Study and Meta-Analyses. *World J. Biol. Psychiatry* **2010**, *11*, 763–773. [CrossRef] [PubMed]
42. Kriengtuntiwong, T.; Zaw, Y.H.; Taneepanichskul, N. Brain-Derived Neurotrophic Factor (BDNF) Depression and Subjective Sleep Quality in the First Trimester of Pregnancy Among Migrant Workers in Thailand. *J. Multidiscip. Healthc.* **2021**, 2549–2556. [CrossRef]
43. Sánchez-Villegas, A.; Galbete, C.; Martinez-González, M.A.; Martinez, J.A.; Razquin, C.; Salas-Salvadó, J.; Estruch, R.; Buil-Cosiales, P.; Martí, A. The Effect of the Mediterranean Diet on Plasma Brain-Derived Neurotrophic Factor (BDNF) Levels: The PREDIMED-NAVARRA Randomized Trial. *Nutr. Neurosci.* **2013**, *14*, 195–201. [CrossRef] [PubMed]
44. Sinn, N.; Milte, C.; Howe, P.R.C. Oiling the Brain: A Review of Randomized Controlled Trials of Omega-3 Fatty Acids in Psychopathology across the Lifespan. *Nutrients* **2010**, *2*, 128–170. [CrossRef]
45. Stahl, L.A.; Begg, D.P.; Weisinger, R.S.; Sinclair, A.J. The Role of Omega-3 Fatty Acids in Mood Disorders. *Curr. Opin. Investig. Drugs* **2008**, *9*, 57–64.
46. Parletta, N.; Milte, C.M.; Meyer, B.J. Nutritional Modulation of Cognitive Function and Mental Health. *J. Nutr. Biochem.* **2013**, *24*, 725–743. [CrossRef]
47. Nielsen-Scott, M.; Fellmeth, G.; Opondo, C.; Alderdice, F. Prevalence of Perinatal Anxiety in Low- and Middle-Income Countries: A Systematic Review and Meta-Analysis. *J. Affect. Disord.* **2022**, *306*, 71–79. [CrossRef]
48. Coelho, H.F.; Murray, L.; Royal-Lawson, M.; Cooper, P.J. Antenatal Anxiety Disorder as a Predictor of Postnatal Depression: A Longitudinal Study. *J. Affect. Disord.* **2011**, *129*, 348–353. [CrossRef] [PubMed]
49. Glasheen, C.; Richardson, G.A.; Fabio, A. A Systematic Review of the Effects of Postnatal Maternal Anxiety on Children. *Arch. Womens Ment. Health* **2010**, *13*, 61–74. [CrossRef] [PubMed]
50. Grigoriadis, S.; Graves, L.; Peer, M.; Mamisashvili, L.; Tomlinson, G.; Vigod, S.N.; Dennis, C.L.; Steiner, M.; Brown, C.; Cheung, A.; et al. A Systematic Review and Meta-Analysis of the Effects of Antenatal Anxiety on Postpartum Outcomes. *Arch. Womens Ment. Health* **2019**, *22*, 543–556. [CrossRef]
51. Dennis, C.L.; Falah-Hassani, K.; Shiri, R. Prevalence of Antenatal and Postnatal Anxiety: Systematic Review and Meta-Analysis. *Br. J. Psychiatry* **2017**, *210*, 315–323. [CrossRef] [PubMed]
52. Vieta, E.; Berk, M. Early intervention comes late. *Eur. Neuropsychopharmacol.* **2022**, *59*, 1–3. [CrossRef] [PubMed]

nutrients MDPI

Article

Dietary Intake of Pregnant Women with and without Inflammatory Bowel Disease in the United States

Barbara C. Olendzki [1,*], Bi-Sek Hsiao [2], Kaitlyn Weinstein [3], Rosemary Chen [3], Christine Frisard [1], Camilla Madziar [1], Mellissa Picker [3], Connor Pauplis [4], Ana Maldonado-Contreras [5] and Inga Peter [3]

1 Department of Population and Quantitative Health Sciences, University of Massachusetts Chan Medical School, Worcester, MA 01655, USA; christine.frisard@umassmed.edu (C.F.); camilla.madziar@umassmed.edu (C.M.)
2 Department of Nutrition, University of Massachusetts Amherst, Amherst, MA 01003, USA; bhsiao@umass.edu
3 Department of Genetics and Genomic Sciences, Icahn School of Medicine at Mount Sinai, New York, NY 10029, USA; kaitlyn.weinstein@mssm.edu (K.W.); rosemary.chen@mssm.edu (R.C.); mellissa.picker@mssm.edu (M.P.); inga.peter@mssm.edu (I.P.)
4 Department of Medicine, University of Massachusetts Chan Medical School, Worcester, MA 01655, USA; connor.pauplis@umassmed.edu
5 Department of Microbiology and Physiology Systems, University of Massachusetts Chan Medical School, Worcester, MA 01655, USA; ana.maldonado@umassmed.edu
* Correspondence: barbara.olendzki@umassmed.edu

Abstract: Background: Pregnancy is a vulnerable time where the lives of mother and baby are affected by diet, especially high-risk pregnancies in women with inflammatory bowel disease (IBD). Limited research has examined diet during pregnancy with IBD. Aims: Describe and compare the diet quality of pregnant women with and without IBD, and examine associations between dietary intake and guidelines during pregnancy. Methods: Three 24 h recalls were utilized to assess the diets of pregnant women with IBD (n = 88) and without IBD (n = 82) during 27–29 weeks of gestation. A customized frequency questionnaire was also administered to measure pre- and probiotic foods. Results: Zinc intake (p = 0.02), animal protein (g) (p = 0.03), and ounce equivalents of whole grains (p = 0.03) were significantly higher in the healthy control (HC) group than the IBD group. Nutrients of concern with no significant differences between groups included iron (3% IBD and 2% HC met the goals), saturated fat (only 1% of both groups met the goals), choline (23% IBD and 21% HC met the goals), magnesium (38% IBD and 35% HC met the goals), calcium (48% IBD and 60% HC met the goals), and water intake (49% IBD and 48% HC met the goals). Conclusions: Most pregnant women in this cohort fell short of the dietary nutrients recommended in pregnancy, especially concerning for women with IBD.

Keywords: diet; pregnancy; IBD; inflammatory bowel disease; dietary guidelines

Citation: Olendzki, B.C.; Hsiao, B.-S.; Weinstein, K.; Chen, R.; Frisard, C.; Madziar, C.; Picker, M.; Pauplis, C.; Maldonado-Contreras, A.; Peter, I. Dietary Intake of Pregnant Women with and without Inflammatory Bowel Disease in the United States. *Nutrients* **2023**, *15*, 2464. https://doi.org/10.3390/nu15112464

Academic Editors: Louise Brough and Gail Rees

Received: 2 May 2023
Revised: 20 May 2023
Accepted: 23 May 2023
Published: 25 May 2023

1. Introduction

Pregnancy is a critical time for the intergenerational transmission of health [1–4]. Pregnant women with active inflammatory bowel disease (IBD), a chronic disease characterized by inflammation of the gastrointestinal tract [5] are considered to be at higher risk of poor pregnancy outcomes such as preterm birth, low birthweight or small for gestational age (SGA), spontaneous abortion, and stillbirth, and comprise an increased percentage of Cesarean deliveries compared to women in remission or without IBD [6–9]. The prevalence of IBD has been increasing worldwide [5]; thus, improving the health of pregnant women with IBD is essential to decreasing their risk for adverse pregnancy outcomes.

A balanced perinatal diet can support optimal health for pregnant women and have a long-term impact on their offspring [10–13]. Patients with IBD are already prone to nutrition deficiencies due to factors such as restrictive diets, nutrient loss, drug–nutrient interaction, and decreased absorption from the ileum [14]. Furthermore, reduced oral intake and chronic inflammation increases nutrient needs among IBD patients [15,16]. Two reports have explored the diets of pregnant women in the Norwegian Mother and Child Cohort (MoBa). The first study found that compared to pregnant women without IBD, pregnant women with IBD were less likely to adhere to a traditional Norwegian dietary pattern characterized by a high intake of lean fish or fish products, potatoes, rice porridge, cooked vegetables, and gravy, and were more likely to adhere to a Western dietary pattern with higher intake of foods and beverages rich in sugar and saturated fats [17,18]. Moreover, pregnant women with IBD who did adhere to the traditional Norwegian diet had lower odds of having an SGA infant [17]. The second study found that pregnant women with IBD consumed a lower proportion of protein from dairy products compared to pregnant women without IBD. In this case, a reduced intake of protein from dairy was associated with a lower risk of having an SGA infant [18].

Maternal diet during pregnancy has also been linked to the infant microbiome composition, which is critical for the priming of a balanced immune system during early life [19]. Importantly, our team has demonstrated that infants born to women with IBD have less diverse microbiomes and higher levels of fecal calprotectin (a biomarker of intestinal inflammation) compared to the infants of women without IBD [4,20]. Along with emerging reports demonstrating the mediating role of the gut microbiota in the effectiveness of dietary interventions for IBD management [21,22], this finding suggests that improving dietary patterns during pregnancy may beneficially modify the microbiome composition, thereby promoting both maternal and infant health. This hypothesis is being explored by the MELODY (Modulating Early Life Microbiome through Dietary Intervention in Pregnancy) Trial [12].

Diet has been increasingly integrated into IBD management, and studies demonstrate the effectiveness of dietary interventions for inducing IBD remission [23–25]. In adults, the specific carbohydrate diet (SCD); the Mediterranean diet; the low fermentable oligosaccharides, disaccharides, monosaccharides, and polyols (low FODMAP) diet; and the anti-inflammatory IBD (IBD-AID) diet are among those that have shown efficacy in reducing disease activity and symptoms [23]. Yet, informational resources on nutrition for pregnant women with IBD are sparse. The USDA MyPlate website focuses on a variety of food groups with only broad suggestions of foods and meal plans specific to pregnancy and postpartum needs [26]. The 2014 and 2017 American College of Obstetricians and Gynecologists (ACOG) guideline statements seem focused on nutrients that may be obtained by taking a prenatal vitamin, rather than on whole foods [27,28]. The 2019 American Gastroenterological Association's Inflammatory Bowel Disease in Pregnancy Clinical Care Pathway report encourages nutrition consultation for specific nutrient deficiency and weight gain patterns in this population, but with few details on compliance to guidelines [29]. In keeping with these publications, pregnant women may hear only general advice from health care providers to take a prenatal vitamin, follow a healthy diet, limit caffeine intake, avoid alcohol and tobacco, and observe caution with seafood [30,31]. However, while a prenatal vitamin may be recommended in addition to a healthy diet, it cannot supply all the nutrients that are needed to promote healthy and low-risk pregnancies [32].

While diet can support IBD management, with the potential to positively benefit perinatal as well as longer-term health outcomes, little is known about the quality of dietary patterns among pregnant women with IBD in the United States (US), a country with a high prevalence of the disease. Therefore, the objectives of the current study are to describe the dietary patterns and diet quality of pregnant women with and without IBD living in the US, and to examine the associations between dietary patterns, diet quality, and dietary guidelines for pregnancy established by the Society for Obstetricians and Gynaecologists of Canada; the American College of Obstetricians and Gynecologists; the World Health Organization Guidelines; the Academy of Nutrition and Dietetics; the Royal College of Physicians of Ireland; the National Institutes of Health Daily Recommended Intake; and UpToDate [27,30].

2. Methods

We conducted a case–control study nested into our ongoing MELODY Trial, which is a prospective non-randomized diet intervention trial testing the effects of IBD anti-inflammatory diet (IBD-AID) during the third trimester of pregnancy on maternal IBD activity and microbiome composition in mothers and their babies [12]. Pregnant women with and without IBD were recruited nationwide for this trial. Study participants were identified by clinical research coordinators in outpatient gastrointestinal clinics; alternatively, pregnant women reached out if interested after seeing posts on the websites or Facebook accounts of the Crohn's and Colitis Foundation or the Center for Applied Nutrition at the University of Massachusetts. Written informed consent was obtained from all eligible participants. The current case–control study examines dietary assessments conducted at the 27th–29th weeks of gestation prior to any dietary intervention, between January 2019 and December 2022.

The study was approved by the Institutional Review Boards at each institution (IRB docket #H00016462 at the University of Massachusetts Chan Medical School and #18–01206 at the Icahn School of Medicine). The inclusion criteria included: pregnant women carrying a singleton pregnancy, and a documented IBD diagnosis or lack thereof (for healthy controls, HC). The diagnosis of IBD was based on the patient's history supported by clinical documentation. The exclusion criteria were an inability to provide informed consent, HIV/AIDS, multi-fetus pregnancy, fetal chromosomal or structural abnormalities, intrauterine growth restriction, active infection (including chorioamnionitis or sepsis), alcohol use disorder, renal disease, or a dietary regime that conflicts with the intervention diet. Additionally, pregnant IBD patients who had active perianal or extra-intestinal disease or were treated with antibiotic therapy or steroids at recruitment, as well as women scheduled for C-section prior to week 37, were excluded [12]. The final selection of participants is shown in Figure 1.

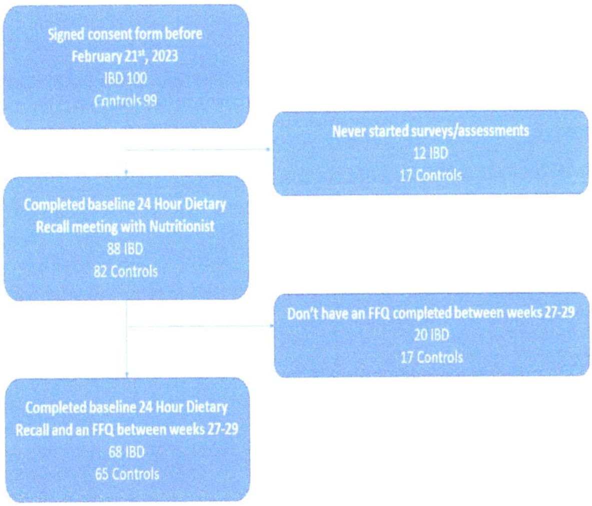

Figure 1. Participant Flow.

2.1. Dietary Assessment

We performed three 24 h dietary recalls (24 HRs) and a specially designed pre- and probiotic food frequency questionnaire for more detailed detection of food groups than provided by the 24 HR (IBD-AID FFQ) [33–38]. The 24 HR were performed using the University of Minnesota Nutrition Coordinating Center's (NCC) Nutrition Data System for Research (NDSR) software (current version: NDSR, 2022, updated yearly) as previously described [12,39,40]. Specifically, trained dietitians administered 24 HR on two weekdays and one weekend, by phone, between 27 and 29 weeks of pregnancy. The 24 HR also included assessments of dietary supplements. The IBD-AID FFQ was self-administered online using REDCap, as previously reported by us [12]. The dietary assessments were conducted from 2019 to 2022.

2.2. Dietary Quality Assessment

Diet quality was estimated from the 24 HR recalls using the standard Alternative Healthy Eating Index—2010 (or AHEI-2010) score (range: 0–110), with higher scores representing healthier diets [39,41,42], and the IBD-AID FFQ score (range: 0–26) [12,37,43]. The IBD-AID FFQ was developed by Barbara Olendzki and her team at the Center for Applied Nutrition, Umass Chan Medical School, and addresses a gap in the nutrition information available from the 24 HR recalls, particularly with regard to pre-and probiotic foods. We found construct validity in using the IBD-AID FFQ, as pre- and post-dietary intervention changes correlated with bacterial abundance and serum cytokine levels [43]. The beneficial foods of the IBD-AID FFQ were matched with the food categories of the validated Alternate Healthy Eating index-2010 or AHEI-2010 [44]. Namely, the IBD-AID FFQ assesses the intake of 15 food groups and components. Beneficial Nutrient Score is calculated from all components and ranges from 0 to 26. Raw Score = [prebiotic foods] + [probiotic foods] + [Beneficial Nutrient Score] − [adverse foods]. The standard score eliminates the negative values, so if the raw score is <0, then the standard score is 0. If the raw score is >0, then the standard score is the raw score. In addition, the IBD-AID FFQ measures prebiotic foods (>3 servings/day), probiotic foods (>2 servings/day), and foods associated with gastrointestinal symptoms and poor IBD outcomes, including: refined carbohydrates (<2 servings per day), lactose (0 servings), certain grains (wheat, corn; 0 servings/day), processed foods (0 servings per day) and foods high in saturated (<7% of calories) or trans fats (0 servings/day).

We scored each beneficial food component (to correlate with the AHEI) from non-adherence = 0, to perfect adherence = 26. Pre- and probiotic foods were scored separately, with a perfect score being >3 and >2 servings per day, respectively. The IBD-AID FFQ total score = (prebiotic foods + probiotic foods + beneficial foods) minus adverse foods, with higher scores representing higher servings of beneficial foods minus adverse foods.

2.3. Statistical Methods

The demographic characteristics were presented using means and standard deviations for continuous variables and compared between pregnant women with and without IBD using a two-sample *t*-test. The categorical variables were described using counts and proportions, with *p*-values calculated via a Fisher's exact test. To minimize the bias of a particular day where food intake is not typical, the reported servings were averaged across three 24 HR. The means and standard deviations summarized nutrients, components of interest from foods, and food group servings on the IBD-AID FFQ using two-sample *t*-tests quantifying between-group differences for normally distributed data and Wilcoxon rank sum tests for skewed outcome variables. The proportions and standard deviations described the proportion of participants who met the guidelines for nutrients at baseline, with chi-square tests measuring between-group differences.

3. Results

3.1. Participant Characteristics

The demographic characteristics of our study population, comprising 82 healthy controls (HC) and 88 participants with IBD (Crohn's disease (CD) = 80, and ulcerative colitis (UC) = 8), are presented in Table 1. On average, women were 34 ± 4 years of age, predominantly white (91%) and non-Hispanic (90%). Most were married (93%), had a 4-year college degree or greater (90%), were employed full-time (71%), and had a household annual income of more than USD 100,000 per year (72%). Most were non-smokers (90%) and took a daily prenatal vitamin (91%). There were no significant differences between HC and IBD participants, except in profession and religious affiliation. The proportion of women with IBD who identified as Jewish was higher than the in the HC cohort ($p < 0.001$). The women with IBD reported working in more scientific technical professions than the HC group, while HC women reported working in more skill-, craft-, and health-based professions compared to IBD participants ($p = 0.02$). The average disease duration of the IBD participants was 14 years for CD and 10 years UC. We found 89% remission for our CD patients (three did not complete this section of the form so 4% were N/A), and 88% remission for our UC patients.

Table 1. Demographic Characteristics of Healthy Controls vs. Pregnant Women with Inflammatory Bowel Disease at Baseline ($n = 170$).

	IBD $n = 88$	**Healthy Controls** $n = 82$	**Total**	***p*-Value**
	***n* (%)**	***n* (%)**	***n* (%)**	
Age—mean (SD)	33.7 (4.4)	34.4 (4.4)	34.0 (4.4)	0.32
Race				0.26
White	82 (94.3%)	70 (87.5%)	152 (91.0%)	
Black	2 (2.3%)	1 (1.3%)	3 (1.8%)	
Asian	1 (1.1%)	4 (5%)	5 (3.0%)	
Other	2 (2.3%)	5 (6.3%)	7 (4.2%)	
Hispanic or Latino descent				0.29
No	81 (93.1%)	70 (87.5%)	151 (90.4%)	
Yes	6 (6.9%)	10 (12.5%)	16 (9.6%)	
Jewish				<0.001 *
No	71 (88.8%)	49 (56.3%)	120 (71.9%)	
Yes	9 (11.3%)	38 (43.7%)	47 (28.1%)	
Marital status				0.85
Married	73 (91.3%)	82 (94.3%)	155 (92.8%)	
Single	3 (3.8%)	2 (2.3%)	5 (3.0%)	
Living with partner	3 (3.8%)	3 (3.4%)	6 (3.6%)	
Other	1 (1.3%)	0 (0.0%)	1 (0.6%)	
Education				0.38
High school graduate	0 (0.0%)	4 (4.6%)	4 (2.4%)	
Some college	5 (6.3%)	2 (2.3%)	7 (4.2%)	
Associate's degree	3 (3.8%)	4 (4.6%)	7 (4.2%)	
Bachelor's degree	24 (30.4%)	27 (31.0%)	51 (30.7%)	
Graduate or professional degree	46 (58.2%)	49 (56.3%)	95 (57.2%)	
Other	1 (1.3%)	1 (1.1%)	2 (1.2%)	
Work status				0.87
Employed full-time	55 (68.8%)	63 (72.4%)	118 (70.7%)	
Employed part-time	9 (11.3%)	10 (11.5%)	19 (11.4%)	
Homemaker (not looking for a job)	10 (12.5%)	6 (6.9%)	16 (9.6%)	
Disabled (unable to work)	1 (1.3%)	2 (2.3%)	3 (1.8%)	
Unemployed	3 (3.8%)	4 (4.6%)	7 (4.2%)	

Table 1. *Cont.*

	IBD *n* = 88	Healthy Controls *n* = 82	Total	*p*-Value
	n (%)	*n* (%)	*n* (%)	
Student	2 (2.5%)	2 (2.3%)	4 (2.4%)	
Type of work				0.02 *
Skill or craft	3 (7.5%)	6 (16.7%)	9 (11.8%)	
Scientific technical work	11 (27.5%)	1 (2.8%)	12 (15.8%)	
Service work	10 (25%)	10 (27.8%)	20 (26.3%)	
Health professional	16 (40%)	19 (52.8%)	35 (46.1%)	
Total annual household income				0.77
Less than USD 20,000	2 (2.8%)	0 (0.0%)	2 (1.5%)	
USD 20,000–USD 39,000	2 (2.8%)	1 (1.7%)	3 (2.3%)	
USD 40,000–USD 59,000	4 (5.6%)	1 (1.7%)	5 (3.8%)	
USD 60,000–USD 79,000	5 (7.0%)	5 (8.5%)	10 (7.7%)	
USD 80,000–USD 99,000	9 (12.7%)	8 (13.6%)	17 (13.1%)	
USD 100,000 or more	49 (69.0%)	44 (74.6%)	93 (71.5%)	
Smoking status				0.45
Non-smoker	70 (87.5%)	79 (91.9%)	149 (89.8%)	
Ex-smoker	10 (12.5%)	7 (8.1%)	17 (10.2%)	
Intake of prenatal vitamins				0.58
No	8 (10.3%)	6 (7.1%)	14 (8.6%)	
Yes	70 (89.7%)	79 (92.9%)	149 (91.4%)	
IBD medication				
Aminosalicylates	21 (23.8%)	NA		
Anti-TNF	28 (31.8%)	NA		
Immunomodulators	4 (4.5%)	NA		
Oral corticosteroids	6 (6.8%)	NA		
Ustekinumab	16 (18.1%)	NA		
Vedolizumab	9 (10.2)	NA		

IBD—inflammatory bowel disease. * p-value < 0.05.

The list of IBD-directed medications is provided in Table 1.

3.2. Nutrient Intake and Dietary Quality for Pregnant Women with and without IBD

In total, we collected 496 24 HR at 27 and 29 weeks of pregnancy for the 170 women included in the study.

We estimated diet quality using the AHEI-2010 (scored 0–110), which incorporates components of evidence-based recommendations to identify future risk of chronic disease [40,44]. Overall, the participants in the study had a higher dietary quality (66.6 in IBD group, 67.9 in HC group) compared to the average American (47.6 ± 10.8) [44,45]. There were no differences in dietary quality between pregnant women with and without IBD.

Table 2 presents the average nutrients and components of interest from foods sources, excluding any dietary supplements. On average, the intake of nutrients was comparable between pregnant women with and without IBD, with some notable exceptions. The percentage of calories from monounsaturated fatty acids (MUFAs), and the intake of eicosapentaenoic acid (EPA) and docosahexaenoic acid (DHA), were significantly higher in pregnant women with IBD than HC. Conversely, healthy control participants reported a significantly higher intake of animal protein (their total protein intake was similar), whole grains, lactose, and zinc. There were no differences in calories consumed per group (approximately 2000 kcals/day).

Table 2. Nutrients and Components of Interest from Foods in Pregnant Women with Inflammatory Bowel Disease vs. Healthy Controls.

	IBD (*n* = 88)		**Healthy Controls (*n* = 82)**		
Nutrients	**Mean**	**SD**	**Mean**	**SD**	***p*-Value**
Energy (kcal)	1994.6	461.1	2077.8	524.9	0.27
% Calories from Fat	37.8	6.8	36.3	6.9	0.16
% Calories from Carbohydrate	46.1	8.2	46.9	8.3	0.52
% Calories from Protein	16	3.5	16.56	4.6	0.36
% Calories from Alcohol	0.04	0.06	0.2	0.5	0.77
% Calories from SFA	12.5	3.3	12.8	3.2	0.57
% Calories from MUFA	14.0	3.6	12.8	3.1	0.03 *
% Calories from PUFA	8.0	2.2	7.5	2.0	0.14
Polyunsaturated to Saturated Fat Ratio	0.7	0.3	0.7	0.3	0.11
Animal Protein (g)	47.3	19.11	54.4	23.6	0.03 *
Vegetable Protein (g)	31.2	12.7	30.5	8.6	0.70
Total Dietary Fiber (g)	22.7	10.3	24.2	7.7	0.31
Soluble Dietary Fiber (g)	6.6	2.9	6.9	2.2	0.54
Insoluble Dietary Fiber (g)	16.0	8.0	17.2	6.1	0.27
Total Sugars (g)	97.3	37.8	102.0	42.7	0.44
Added Sugars (by Total Sugars) (g)	51.5	29.8	49.8	31.0	0.72
Glycemic Index (glucose reference)	58.4	4.6	57.9	4.1	0.45
Glycemic Load (glucose reference)	126.2	44.4	131.3	45.7	0.46
Total Grains (oz equivalents)	7.0	3.2	7.6	3.1	0.29
Whole Grains (oz equivalents)	1.6	1.3	2.1	1.6	0.03 *
Refined Grains (oz equivalents)	5.4	2.9	5.4	2.9	0.97
Lactose (g)	9.2	7.4	13.6	11.2	0.01
Sucrose (g)	44.5	21.4	45.1	23.7	0.87
Starch (g)	100.2	40.8	106.5	37.5	0.30
Total Folate (mcg)	431.0	153.7	460.4	143.0	0.20
Dietary Folate Equivalents (mcg)	537.0	217.2	583.5	218.6	0.17
Choline (mg)	359.7	145.5	354.0	128.5	0.79
Vitamin B-12 (cobalamin) (mcg)	4.1	2.3	4.3	2.0	0.66
Calcium (mg)	1033.9	354.3	1153.4	474.6	0.06
Magnesium (mg)	335.3	120.0	338.7	94.3	0.84
Iron (mg)	14.6	5.5	16.0	5.6	0.10
Zinc (mg)	10.5	3.8	11.8	3.8	0.02*
Copper (mg)	1.5	0.7	1.5	0.5	0.73

Table 4. Average Daily Food Group Servings of the IBD-AID Food Query.

		IBD (n = 68)		Healthy Controls (n = 65)		
Variable	**Number of Servings for Optimal Score**	**Mean Servings**	**SD**	**Mean**	**SD**	***p*-Value**
Prebiotic score [1]	≥3	6.3	5.4	4.7	10.2	<0.0001 *
Probiotics score [2]	≥2	1.6	1.8	1.6	3.4	0.80
Adverse foods score [3]	0	7.1	4.5	15.7	38.0	<0.0001 *
Vegetable score	5	3.6	3.2	4.5	13.0	0.6
Fruit score	3	2.1	1.9	2.2	2.2	0.92
Nuts, seeds, and oils score	2	2.0	2.2	1.8	2.6	0.89
Lean protein score [4]	4	2.4	2.0	3.4	12.5	0.04 *
Fiber/grains score [5]	3	6.3	6.3	2.8	5.2	<0.0001 *
Probiotic dairy score [2]	3	1.1	1.2	1.2	1.4	0.27
Non-caloric fluids score		6.7	3.5	7.2	3.6	0.45
Beneficial beverages score [6]	6	1.8	3.7	6.6	6.8	<0.0001 *
Condiments score		0.3	0.4	0.7	2.9	0.63
Alcohol score		0	0	0.4	3.0	0.47
Foods with unknown effects [7]		0.3	0.5	1.1	4.8	0.04
IBD FFQ Beneficial Nutrient Score [8]	26	15.6	5.0	14.0	4.6	0.04
IBD AID total raw score [9]		16.4	12.9	4.6	24.3	<0.0001 *
IBD AID total standard score [10]		16.9	12.3	8.4	7.1	<0.0001 *

IBD-AID—inflammatory bowel disease anti-inflammatory diet. * p-value < 0.05. [1] Prebiotics are foods containing fiber that feed commensal organisms. [2] Probiotics are fermented foods that contain live bacteria. [3] Adverse foods include ultra-processed foods and foods high in added sugars. N optimal adverse foods goal is zero servings per day and counts negatively toward total score. [4] Lean protein score includes beans/legumes, seafood, and poultry. [5] Fiber/grains include foods such as oats, barley, and miso. [6] Beneficial beverages include beverages such as those with added probiotics, non-dairy milks, homemade smoothies, no-sugar-added fruit and vegetable juices, coconut water, tea sweetened with honey, etc. [7] Foods with unknown effects have yet to be determined in research. [8] Beneficial Nutrient Score is calculated from all components and ranges from 0 to 26. [9] Raw Score = [prebiotic] + [probiotics] + [Beneficial Nutrient Score] − [adverse]. [10] The standard score eliminates the negative values, so if the raw score is <0, then the standard score is 0. If the raw score is >0, then the standard score is the raw score.

4. Discussion

The current study addresses the gap in knowledge about the diets of pregnant women with IBD through an analysis of baseline data from The MELODY Trial. We observed that pregnant women with and without IBD do not consume most of the nutrients and food components recommended during pregnancy by established government and research-based organizations.

Specifically, we found that although most women reported taking a prenatal supplement, in hopes of supplementing the inadequate intake of nutrients from food sources, pregnant women IBD and the HC group fell short of most nutrients recommended in pregnancy from food sources alone. Of particular concern in women with IBD are the dietary micronutrients zinc, iron, calcium, magnesium, choline, folate, B6, B12, water, and fiber [46–50]. Patients with IBD require additional assistance to compensate for increased nutritional needs and poor absorption, whereby simply adding the nutrient does not guarantee that it will be well absorbed in the body [51,52].

Iron needs increase during pregnancy, especially in women with IBD, who may struggle with significant inflammation, anemia, and dysbiosis, leading to poor cardiovascular outcomes and suboptimal gestational weight gain [12,53–57]. The recommended daily allowance for pregnant women is around 27 mg per day. Many factors can influence iron absorption in the body, such as certain nutrient–nutrient interactions, including nutrient inhibitors (such as calcium) and enhancers (i.e., ascorbic acid) [58]. Furthermore, non-heme iron, primarily found in plant sources, is less easily absorbed by the body than heme iron, primarily found in animal sources, so the recommended amount of iron for vegetarians and vegans is 1.8 times greater [59]. In this study, only 3% of women with IBD and 2% of the HCs met the dietary guideline for (animal-based) iron. It is estimated that between 36 and 90% of people with IBD have iron-deficient anemia (IDA) [47] and that 15–20% of pregnant people have IDA [60]. This can lead to worse disease outcomes for both mothers and infants [61]. It is important that pregnant women meet the dietary guidelines set for iron first through food consumption, subsequently adding supplements as the need is determined.

The adequate intake of fiber is 28 g per day [62]. Fiber is typically not found in prenatal vitamins but is an especially important dietary component during pregnancy. Adequate fiber intake during pregnancy is crucial and may help alleviate iron-induced constipation. It is also helpful for reducing certain problems during pregnancy, such as inflammation, gestational diabetes mellitus, and cardiovascular outcomes [63,64]. However, even among the general population, dietary fiber intake falls below the recommended 28 g per day [56]. A study using 2001–2014 National Health and Nutrition Examination Survey (NHANES) data found that pregnant, non-lactating women aged 20–40 (n = 1003) had a mean total daily intake of 17.3 g of dietary fiber [65]. Only 33% of pregnant women with IBD in our study achieved the recommended fiber intake of >28 g per day. One mechanism by which diet can provide protection from IBD is through the addition of plant-based, fiber-rich foods that promote short-chained fatty acid-producing bacteria, which have been shown to support mucosal barrier integrity [23]. Adequate fiber intake important not only for women's health during pregnancy [62,64,66–69], but also for preventing infant outcomes such as SGA, preterm birth, and fetal growth restriction [70].

Both groups were consuming an excess of foods with saturated fat, which can lead to an elevated risk of gestational diabetes [71]. Notably, the IBD group consumed less zinc and calcium than did the HC group. Low calcium and zinc intakes have been correlated with risk for poor outcomes for both mother and child [46,47,72]. Prenatal vitamins may not overcome a low dietary intake of these nutrients [73]. In our sample, predominantly white women with a college degree and who earned higher than the national average income consumes a fairly healthy diet before entering the study, which is why we do not see many significant between-group differences.

A recent study revealed that almost no supplements met nutritional needs in the doses that are required for pregnant women (without excess) [32]. Prenatal vitamins are recommended for pregnancy, especially to provide folic acid, EPA/DHA, iron, and vitamin D. Vitamins are, by definition, recommended to supplement the diet, not to replace the inclusion of the nutritious foods needed during pregnancy. Nutrients are digested and absorbed most effectively in the complex milieu of the foods themselves and the complementary enzymes and microbiota that facilitate absorption. Absorption is biologically complex, and simply adding a nutrient does not mean it will be well absorbed [51,52]. Therefore, many individuals with IBD require additional assistance to compensate for increased nutritional needs and poor absorption, as the nutritional needs of pregnancy for women with IBD may be uniquely challenging. Despite the excellent consensus recommendations by the International Organization for the Study of Inflammatory Bowel Diseases (IOIBD), there is no guidance for pregnancy with IBD or prenatal advice for the prevention of IBD. The IOIBD, based in large part on epidemiological studies, does not cover altering the textures of foods (such as pureeing fiber) for ease of absorption, one of many considerations that goes beyond the nutrients themselves and addresses malnutrition and malabsorption [74].

However, even with the limited existing evidence, healthcare providers appear to be inadequately counseling pregnant IBD patients on diet. Apart from referral to a dietitian for gestational diabetes, the prescription of dietary guidelines for pregnant women is lacking, increasing the risk for detrimental outcomes, especially for those with high-risk pregnancies.

Current data show that only 37% of pregnant IBD patients reported receiving education from any physician about IBD in pregnancy [75]. Even worse, only 10% of patients reported having received pregnancy-specific information from their gastroenterologists, and of those who received information, 48% found the information to be insufficient [75]. Yet, several studies have demonstrated that those women who receive dietary counseling during pregnancy eat more fruits and vegetables, promoting the healthy growth and development of the fetus [76–79], suggesting that more dietary interventions are needed.

This apparent lack of patient education is not due to physician ignorance regarding pregnancy and IBD. In fact, when assessed with the Crohn's and Colitis Pregnancy Knowledge Score (CCPKnow), 91.8% of physicians demonstrated very good knowledge, with gastroenterologists scoring the highest [75,80]. In contrast, only 10.3% of patients exhibited very good knowledge when assessed using the CCPKnow, with 44.8% demonstrating poor knowledge levels [80]. This discrepancy between physician and patient CCPKnow scores highlights the need for increased patient counseling, particularly from gastroenterologists, who exhibit the highest CCPKnow scores [80]. Healthcare providers should first evaluate pregnant individuals at risk of nutrient deficiency and excess, and subsequently provide evidence-based suggestions for supplementation [81]. Importantly, specific suggestions and menu plans with foods that contain essential nutrients and other components, such as fiber and pre-and probiotics, should be presented in actionable formats.

We acknowledge that the assessment of diet is prone to limitations, including self-report bias, under- or overestimation, memory bias, and weakness in the methodology. Further, we did not account for the influence of the environment, medication, dietary supplementation, or IBD activity status on nutrition, although most of our IBD patients were in remission. We conducted a large part of this study during the pandemic, when changes to food intake occurred, and this would have affected both arms of the study. This study is further limited to pregnant women in the United States of higher socioeconomic status, as they may have better access to medical care and foods that may not be generalizable to other groups and countries. However, our IBD and HC study groups were well-balanced regarding age, education, and income, suggesting that the reported differences (or lack thereof) in dietary intake are representative of this cohort.

5. Conclusions

While many women adhered to taking a prenatal supplement, both pregnant IBD participants and HC participants fell short of most dietary nutrients recommended in pregnancy through dietary sources alone, especially micronutrients and fiber. The consumption of animal protein, lactose, zinc, and whole grains was significantly lower in pregnant women with IBD compared to the HCs. Large epidemiological and dietary intervention studies are warranted to improve the nutritional recommendations for pregnant women with and without IBD while addressing malnutrition and malabsorption. Future research should consider pregnancy outcomes and the effects on offspring, and determine the causes of dietary deficiencies and excess, to ultimately inform and improve the quality of provider training and patient education, especially in the setting of IBD.

Author Contributions: Conceptualization, B.C.O., A.M.-C. and I.P.; methodology, B.C.O., A.M.-C., C.F. and I.P.; formal analysis, C.F.; investigation, B.C.O., B.-S.H., K.W., R.C., C.P., A.M.-C. and I.P.; resources, M.P., C.M., K.W., R.C., C.P. and B.-S.H.; data curation, C.M., M.P., K.W. and R.C.; writing—original draft preparation, B.C.O., A.M.-C. and I.P.; writing—review and editing, B.C.O., B.-S.H., K.W., R.C., M.P., C.M., C.F., C.P., A.M.-C. and I.P.; visualization, C.F.; supervision, B.C.O., A.M.-C., M.P., C.M. and I.P.; project administration, M.P.; funding acquisition, B.C.O., A.M.-C. and I.P. All authors have read and agreed to the published version of the manuscript.

Funding: We are grateful to our participants. The MELODY Trial is funded by The Leona M. and Harry B. Helmsley Charitable Trust.

Institutional Review Board Statement: The study was approved by the Institutional Review Boards of the Icahn School of Medicine at Mount Sinai (project identification code 18–01206) and the University of Massachusetts (project identification code H00016462).

Informed Consent Statement: Informed consent was obtained from all subjects involved in the study.

Data Availability Statement: The data presented in this study are available on request from the corresponding author. The data are not publicly available due to data privacy restrictions.

Conflicts of Interest: The authors declare no conflict of interest.

References

1. Barker, D.J. The fetal and infant origins of ad ult disease. *BMJ* **1990**, *301*, 1111. [CrossRef]
2. Calkins, K.; Devaskar, S.U. Fetal Origins of Adult Disease. *Curr. Probl. Pediatr. Adolesc. Health Care* **2011**, *41*, 158–176. [CrossRef] [PubMed]
3. Chen, T.; Liu, H.X.; Yan, H.Y.; Wu, D.M.; Ping, J. Developmental origins of inflammatory and immune diseases. *Mol. Hum. Reprod.* **2016**, *22*, 858–865. [CrossRef] [PubMed]
4. Torres, J.; Hu, J.; Seki, A.; Eisele, C.; Nair, N.; Huang, R.; Tarassishin, L.; Jharap, B.; Cote-Daigneault, J.; Mao, Q.; et al. Infants born to mothers with IBD present with altered gut microbiome that transfers abnormalities of the adaptive immune system to germ-free mice. *Gut* **2020**, *69*, 42–51. [CrossRef] [PubMed]
5. The global, regional, and national burden of inflammatory bowel disease in 195 countries and territories, 1990–2017: A systematic analysis for the Global Burden of Disease Study 2017. *Lancet Gastroenterol. Hepatol.* **2020**, *5*, 17–30. [CrossRef]
6. Bengtson, M.B.; Solberg, I.C.; Aamodt, G.; Jahnsen, J.; Moum, B.; Vatn, M.H. Relationships between inflammatory bowel disease and perinatal factors: Both maternal and paternal disease are related to preterm birth of offspring. *Inflamm. Bowel Dis.* **2010**, *16*, 847–855. [CrossRef]
7. Cornish, J.; Tan, E.; Teare, J.; Teoh, T.G.; Rai, R.; Clark, S.K.; Tekkis, P.P. A meta-analysis on the influence of inflammatory bowel disease on pregnancy. *Gut* **2007**, *56*, 830–837. [CrossRef]
8. Fonager, K.; Sørensen, H.T.; Olsen, J.; Dahlerup, J.F.; Rasmussen, S.N. Pregnancy outcome for women with Crohn's disease: A follow-up study based on linkage between national registries. *Am. J. Gastroenterol.* **1998**, *93*, 2426–2430. [CrossRef]
9. Kim, M.A.; Kim, Y.H.; Chun, J.; Lee, H.S.; Park, S.J.; Cheon, J.H.; Kim, T.I.; Kim, W.H.; Park, J.J. The Influence of Disease Activity on Pregnancy Outcomes in Women with Inflammatory Bowel Disease: A Systematic Review and Meta-Analysis. *J. Crohn's Colitis* **2021**, *15*, 719–732. [CrossRef]
10. Myles, I.A.; Fontecilla, N.M.; Janelsins, B.M.; Vithayathil, P.J.; Segre, J.A.; Datta, S.K. Parental dietary fat intake alters offspring microbiome and immunity. *J. Immunol.* **2013**, *191*, 3200–3209. [CrossRef]
11. Hu, J.; Agrawal, M.; Tarassishin, L.; Rendon, A.P.; Picker, M.; Hillenbrand, C.; Eisele, C.; Ching, J.Y.; Wong, Y.M.; Zhan, H.; et al. 609: Differential gut microbiota in pregnant women with and without inflammatory bowel disease and their offspring in hong kong and united states: The meconium study. *Gastroenterology* **2022**, *162*, S-154. [CrossRef]
12. Peter, I.; Maldonado-Contreras, A.; Eisele, C.; Frisard, C.; Simpson, S.; Nair, N.; Rendon, A.; Hawkins, K.; Cawley, C.; Debebe, A.; et al. A dietary intervention to improve the microbiome composition of pregnant women with Crohn's disease and their offspring: The MELODY (Modulating Early Life Microbiome through Dietary Intervention in Pregnancy) trial design. *Contemp. Clin. Trials Commun.* **2020**, *18*, 100573. [CrossRef] [PubMed]
13. Abu-Saad, K.; Kaufman-Shriqui, V.; Freedman, L.S.; Belmaker, I.; Fraser, D. Preconceptional diet quality is associated with birth outcomes among low socioeconomic status minority women in a high-income country. *Eur. J. Nutr.* **2021**, *60*, 65–77. [CrossRef] [PubMed]
14. Saksena, S.; Goyal, S.; Raheja, G.; Singh, V.; Akhtar, M.; Nazir, T.M.; Alrefai, W.A.; Gill, R.K.; Dudeja, P.K. Upregulation of P-glycoprotein by probiotics in intestinal epithelial cells and in the dextran sulfate sodium model of colitis in mice. *Am. J. Physiol. Gastrointest. Liver Physiol.* **2011**, *300*, G1115–G1123. [CrossRef] [PubMed]
15. Balestrieri, P.; Ribolsi, M.; Guarino, M.P.L.; Emerenziani, S.; Altomare, A.; Cicala, M. Nutritional Aspects in Inflammatory Bowel Diseases. *Nutrients* **2020**, *12*, 372. [CrossRef]
16. MacMaster, M.J.; Damianopoulou, S.; Thomson, C.; Talwar, D.; Stefanowicz, F.; Catchpole, A.; Gerasimidis, K.; Gaya, D.R. A prospective analysis of micronutrient status in quiescent inflammatory bowel disease. *Clin. Nutr.* **2021**, *40*, 327–331. [CrossRef]
17. Myklebust-Hansen, T.; Aamodt, G.; Haugen, M.; Brantsæter, A.L.; Vatn, M.H.; Bengtson, M.B. Dietary Patterns in women with Inflammatory Bowel Disease and Risk of Adverse Pregnancy Outcomes: Results from The Norwegian Mother and Child Cohort Study (MoBa). *Inflamm. Bowel Dis.* **2017**, *24*, 12–24. [CrossRef]
18. Bengtson, M.-B.; Haugen, M.; Brantsæter, A.L.; Aamodt, G.; Vatn, M.H. Intake of dairy protein during pregnancy in IBD and risk of SGA in a Norwegian population-based mother and child cohort. *BMC Gastroenterol.* **2020**, *20*, 28. [CrossRef]
19. Mirpuri, J. Evidence for maternal diet-mediated effects on the offspring microbiome and immunity: Implications for public health initiatives. *Pediatr. Res.* **2021**, *89*, 301–306. [CrossRef]

20. Kim, E.S.; Tarassishin, L.; Eisele, C.; Barre, A.; Nair, N.; Rendon, A.; Hawkins, K.; Debebe, A.; White, S.; Thjømøe, A.; et al. Longitudinal Changes in Fecal Calprotectin Levels Among Pregnant Women with and without Inflammatory Bowel Disease and Their Babies. *Gastroenterology* **2021**, *160*, 1118–1130.e1113. [CrossRef]
21. Alsharairi, N.A. The Therapeutic Role of Short-Chain Fatty Acids Mediated Very Low-Calorie Ketogenic Diet-Gut Microbiota Relationships in Paediatric Inflammatory Bowel Diseases. *Nutrients* **2022**, *14*, 4113. [PubMed]
22. Svolos, V.; Gkikas, K.; Gerasimidis, K. Diet and gut microbiota manipulation for the management of Crohn's disease and ulcerative colitis. *Proc. Nutr. Soc.* **2021**, *80*, 409–423. [CrossRef]
23. Maldonado-Contreras, A. Food as Treatment of Inflammatory Bowel Diseases. *Infect. Immun.* **2022**, *90*, e0058321. [CrossRef] [PubMed]
24. Lewis, J.D.; Sandler, R.S.; Brotherton, C.; Brensinger, C.; Li, H.; Kappelman, M.D.; Daniel, S.G.; Bittinger, K.; Albenberg, L.; Valentine, J.F.; et al. A Randomized Trial Comparing the Specific Carbohydrate Diet to a Mediterranean Diet in Adults with Crohn's Disease. *Gastroenterology* **2021**, *161*, 837–852.e9. [CrossRef] [PubMed]
25. Popa, S.L.; Pop, C.; Dumitrascu, D.L. Diet Advice for Crohn's Disease: FODMAP and Beyond. *Nutrients* **2020**, *12*, 3751. [CrossRef]
26. Pregnancy and Breastfeeding | MyPlate. Available online: https://www.myplate.gov/life-stages/pregnancy-and-breastfeeding (accessed on 20 March 2023).
27. Nutrition During Pregnancy. Available online: https://www.acog.org/en/womens-health/faqs/nutrition-during-pregnancy (accessed on 29 March 2023).
28. Whitaker, K.M.; Wilcox, S.; Liu, J.; Blair, S.N.; Pate, R.R. Provider Advice and Women's Intentions to Meet Weight Gain, Physical Activity, and Nutrition Guidelines During Pregnancy. *Matern. Child Health J.* **2016**, *20*, 2309–2317. [CrossRef]
29. Mahadevan, U.; Robinson, C.; Bernasko, N.; Boland, B.; Chambers, C.; Dubinsky, M.; Friedman, S.; Kane, S.; Manthey, J.; Sauberan, J.; et al. Inflammatory Bowel Disease in Pregnancy Clinical Care Pathway: A Report From the American Gastroenterological Association IBD Parenthood Project Working Group. *Gastroenterology* **2019**, *156*, 1508–1524. [CrossRef]
30. U.S. Department of Agriculture and U.S. Department of Health and Human Services. *Dietary Guidelines for Americans, 2020–2025*, 9th ed.; U.S. Department of Agriculture and U.S. Department of Health and Human Services: Washington, DC, USA, 2020.
31. Mercado, A.; Marquez, B.; Abrams, B.; Phipps, M.G.; Wing, R.R.; Phelan, S. Where Do Women Get Advice About Weight, Eating, and Physical Activity During Pregnancy? *J. Women's Health* **2017**, *26*, 951–956. [CrossRef]
32. Sauder, K.A.; Couzens, G.L.; Bailey, R.L.; Hockett, C.W.; Switkowski, K.M.; Lyall, K.; Kerver, J.M.; Dabelea, D.; Maldonado, L.E.; O'Connor, T.G.; et al. Selecting a dietary supplement with appropriate dosing for 6 key nutrients in pregnancy. *Am. J. Clin. Nutr.* **2023**, *117*, 823–829. [CrossRef]
33. Olendzki, B.; Procter-Gray, E.; Magee, M.F.; Youssef, G.; Kane, K.; Churchill, L.; Ockene, J.; Li, W. Racial Differences in Misclassification of Healthy Eating Based on Food Frequency Questionnaire and 24-H Dietary Recalls. *J. Nutr. Health Aging* **2017**, *21*, 787–798. [CrossRef]
34. Ma, Y.; Olendzki, B.C.; Pagoto, S.L.; Hurley, T.G.; Magner, R.P.; Ockene, I.S.; Schneider, K.L.; Merriam, P.A.; Hébert, J.R. Number of 24-hour diet recalls needed to estimate energy intake. *Ann. Epidemiol.* **2009**, *19*, 553–559. [CrossRef]
35. Bogle, M.; Stuff, J.; Davis, L.; Forrester, I.; Strickland, E.; Casey, P.H.; Ryan, D.; Champagne, C.; McGee, B.; Mellad, K.; et al. Validity of a Telephone-Administered 24-Hour Dietary Recall in Telephone and Non-Telephone Households in the Rural Lower Mississippi Delta Region. *J. Am. Diet. Assoc.* **2001**, *101*, 216–222. [CrossRef] [PubMed]
36. Gersovitz, M.; Madden, J.P.; Smiciklas-Wright, H. Validity of the 24-hr. dietary recall and seven-day record for group comparisons. *J. Am. Diet. Assoc.* **1978**, *73*, 48–55. [CrossRef] [PubMed]
37. Schatzkin, A.; Kipnis, V.; Carroll, R.J.; Midthune, D.; Subar, A.F.; Bingham, S.; Schoeller, D.A.; Troiano, R.P.; Freedman, L.S. A comparison of a food frequency questionnaire with a 24-hour recall for use in an epidemiological cohort study: Results from the biomarker-based Observing Protein and Energy Nutrition (OPEN) study. *Int. J. Epidemiol.* **2003**, *32*, 1054–1062. [CrossRef] [PubMed]
38. Casey, P.H.; Goolsby, S.L.P.; Lensing, S.Y.; Perloff, B.P.; Bogle, M.L. The Use of Telephone Interview Methodology to Obtain 24-hour Dietary Recalls. *J. Am. Diet. Assoc.* **1999**, *99*, 1406–1411. [CrossRef]
39. Varraso, R.; Chiuve, S.E.; Fung, T.T.; Barr, R.G.; Hu, F.B.; Willett, W.C.; Camargo, C.A. Alternate Healthy Eating Index 2010 and risk of chronic obstructive pulmonary disease among US women and men: Prospective study. *BMJ* **2015**, *350*, h286. [CrossRef]
40. McCullough, M.L.; Feskanich, D.; Stampfer, M.J.; Giovannucci, E.L.; Rimm, E.B.; Hu, F.B.; Spiegelman, D.; Hunter, D.J.; Colditz, G.A.; Willett, W.C. Diet quality and major chronic disease risk in men and women: Moving toward improved dietary guidance. *Am. J. Clin. Nutr.* **2002**, *76*, 1261–1271. [CrossRef]
41. Bernstein, C.N.; Burchill, C.; Targownik, L.E.; Singh, H.; Roos, L.L. Events within the First Year of Life, but Not the Neonatal Period, Affect Risk for Later Development of Inflammatory Bowel Diseases. *Gastroenterology* **2019**, *156*, 2190–2197.e2110. [CrossRef]
42. Mijatovic-Vukas, J.; Capling, L.; Cheng, S.; Stamatakis, E.; Louie, J.; Cheung, N.W.; Markovic, T.; Ross, G.; Senior, A.; Brand-Miller, J.C.; et al. Associations of Diet and Physical Activity with Risk for Gestational Diabetes Mellitus: A Systematic Review and Meta-Analysis. *Nutrients* **2018**, *10*, 698. [CrossRef]
43. Olendzki, B.; Bucci, V.; Cawley, C.; Maserati, R.; McManus, M.; Olednzki, E.; Madziar, C.; Chiang, D.; Ward, D.V.; Pellish, R.; et al. Dietary manipulation of the gut microbiome in inflammatory bowel disease patients: Pilot study. *Gut Microbes* **2022**, *14*, 2046244. [CrossRef]

44. Chiuve, S.E.; Fung, T.T.; Rimm, E.B.; Hu, F.B.; McCullough, M.L.; Wang, M.; Stampfer, M.J.; Willett, W.C. Alternative dietary indices both strongly predict risk of chronic disease. *J. Nutr.* **2012**, *142*, 1009–1018. [CrossRef]
45. Shan, Z.; Li, Y.; Baden, M.Y.; Bhupathiraju, S.N.; Wang, D.D.; Sun, Q.; Rexrode, K.M.; Rimm, E.B.; Qi, L.; Willett, W.C.; et al. Association Between Healthy Eating Patterns and Risk of Cardiovascular Disease. *JAMA Intern. Med.* **2020**, *180*, 1090–1100. [CrossRef] [PubMed]
46. Weisshof, R.; Chermesh, I. Micronutrient deficiencies in inflammatory bowel disease. *Curr. Opin. Clin. Nutr. Metab. Care* **2015**, *18*, 576–581. [CrossRef] [PubMed]
47. Hwang, C.; Ross, V.; Mahadevan, U. Micronutrient Deficiencies in Inflammatory Bowel Disease: From A to Zinc. *Inflamm. Bowel Dis.* **2012**, *18*, 1961–1981. [CrossRef] [PubMed]
48. Magavi, P.R.; Beeken, L.A.; Matro, R.; Ally, M.; Ferrari, M.J.; Konijeti, G.G. Incorporating Nutrition-Based Strategies into IBD Treatment. *Curr. Gastroenterol. Rep.* **2022**, *24*, 183–190. [CrossRef]
49. Massironi, S.; Viganò, C.; Palermo, A.; Pirola, L.; Mulinacci, G.; Allocca, M.; Peyrin-Biroulet, L.; Danese, S. Inflammation and malnutrition in inflammatory bowel disease. *Lancet Gastroenterol. Hepatol.* **2023**, *8*, 579–590. [CrossRef]
50. Li, X.; Hu, Y.; Shi, X.; Zhu, X.; Liu, F. Prevalence and relevant factors of micronutrient deficiencies in hospitalized patients with inflammatory bowel disease. *Nutrition* **2022**, *99–100*, 111671. [CrossRef]
51. Kilby, K.; Mathias, H.; Boisvenue, L.; Heisler, C.; Jones, J.L. Micronutrient Absorption and Related Outcomes in People with Inflammatory Bowel Disease: A Review. *Nutrients* **2019**, *11*, 1388. [CrossRef]
52. Chen, X.; Zhao, D.; Mao, X.; Xia, Y.; Baker, P.N.; Zhang, H. Maternal Dietary Patterns and Pregnancy Outcome. *Nutrients* **2016**, *8*, 351. [CrossRef]
53. Aparicio, E.; Jardí, C.; Bedmar, C.; Pallejà, M.; Basora, J.; Arija, V.; ECLIPSES Study Group. Nutrient Intake during Pregnancy and Post-Partum: ECLIPSES Study. *Nutrients* **2020**, *12*, 1325. [CrossRef]
54. Mousa, A.; Naqash, A.; Lim, S. Macronutrient and Micronutrient Intake during Pregnancy: An Overview of Recent Evidence. *Nutrients* **2019**, *11*, 443. [CrossRef] [PubMed]
55. Perry, A.; Stephanou, A.; Rayman, M.P. Dietary factors that affect the risk of pre-eclampsia. *BMJ Nutr. Prev. Health* **2022**, *5*, 118–133. [CrossRef]
56. Pretorius, R.A.; Palmer, D.J. High-Fiber Diet during Pregnancy Characterized by More Fruit and Vegetable Consumption. *Nutrients* **2020**, *13*, 35. [CrossRef] [PubMed]
57. Bengtson, M.B.; Aamodt, G.; Mahadevan, U.; Vatn, M.H. Inadequate Gestational Weight Gain, the Hidden Link Between Maternal IBD and Adverse Pregnancy Outcomes: Results from the Norwegian Mother and Child Cohort Study. *Inflamm. Bowel Dis.* **2017**, *23*, 1225–1233. [CrossRef] [PubMed]
58. Piskin, E.; Cianciosi, D.; Gulec, S.; Tomas, M.; Capanoglu, E. Iron Absorption: Factors, Limitations, and Improvement Methods. *ACS Omega* **2022**, *7*, 20441–20456. [CrossRef]
59. Petre, A. 21 Vegetarian Foods That Are Loaded with Iron. Available online: https://www.healthline.com/nutrition/iron-rich-plant-foods (accessed on 16 March 2023).
60. Gernand, A.D.; Schulze, K.J.; Stewart, C.P.; West, K.P., Jr.; Christian, P. Micronutrient deficiencies in pregnancy worldwide: Health effects and prevention. *Nat. Rev. Endocrinol.* **2016**, *12*, 274–289. [CrossRef]
61. Loveikyte, R.; Boer, M.; van der Meulen, C.N.; ter Steege, R.W.F.; Tack, G.; Kuyvenhoven, J.; Jharap, B.; Vu, M.K.; Vogelaar, L.; West, R.L.; et al. Anemia and Iron Deficiency in Outpatients with Inflammatory Bowel Disease: Ubiquitous Yet Suboptimally Managed. *J. Clin. Med.* **2022**, *11*, 6843. [CrossRef]
62. Sharaf, A.A.; Nguyen, G.C. Predictors of Cesarean Delivery in Pregnant Women with Inflammatory Bowel Disease. *J. Can. Assoc. Gastroenterol.* **2018**, *1*, 76–81. [CrossRef]
63. Leung, K.K.; Tandon, P.; Govardhanam, V.; Maxwell, C.; Huang, V. The Risk of Adverse Neonatal Outcomes with Maternal Inflammatory Bowel Disease: A Systematic Review and Meta-analysis. *Inflamm. Bowel Dis.* **2020**, *27*, 550–562. [CrossRef]
64. Mahadevan, U.; Sandborn, W.J.; Li, D.K.; Hakimian, S.; Kane, S.; Corley, D.A. Pregnancy outcomes in women with inflammatory bowel disease: A large community-based study from Northern California. *Gastroenterology* **2007**, *133*, 1106–1112. [CrossRef]
65. Bailey, R.L.; Pac, S.G.; Fulgoni, V.L., III; Reidy, K.C.; Catalano, P.M. Estimation of Total Usual Dietary Intakes of Pregnant Women in the United States. *JAMA Netw. Open* **2019**, *2*, e195967. [CrossRef]
66. Nørgård, B.; Hundborg, H.H.; Jacobsen, B.A.; Nielsen, G.L.; Fonager, K. Disease activity in pregnant women with Crohn's disease and birth outcomes: A regional Danish cohort study. *Am. J. Gastroenterol.* **2007**, *102*, 1947–1954. [CrossRef] [PubMed]
67. Kornfeld, D.; Cnattingius, S.; Ekbom, A. Pregnancy outcomes in women with inflammatory bowel disease–a population-based cohort study. *Am. J. Obs. Gynecol.* **1997**, *177*, 942–946. [CrossRef]
68. O'Toole, A.; Nwanne, O.; Tomlinson, T. Inflammatory Bowel Disease Increases Risk of Adverse Pregnancy Outcomes: A Meta-Analysis. *Dig. Dis. Sci.* **2015**, *60*, 2750–2761. [CrossRef]
69. Tandon, P.; Diong, C.; Chong, R.Y.; Nguyen, G.C. Regional Variation in Pregnancy Outcomes amongst Women in Inflammatory Bowel Disease: A Population-Based Cohort Study. *Can. J. Gastroenterol. Hepatol.* **2021**, *2021*, 3037128. [CrossRef] [PubMed]
70. Reijonen, J.K.; Tihtonen, K.M.H.; Luukkaala, T.H.; Uotila, J.T. Association of dietary fiber, liquid intake and lifestyle characteristics with gastrointestinal symptoms and pregnancy outcome. *Eur. J. Obstet. Gynecol. Reprod. Biol. X* **2022**, *16*, 100168. [CrossRef] [PubMed]

71. Hernandez, T.L.; Mande, A.; Barbour, L.A. Nutrition therapy within and beyond gestational diabetes. *Diabetes Res. Clin. Pract.* **2018**, *145*, 39–50. [CrossRef]
72. Zupo, R.; Sila, A.; Castellana, F.; Bringiotti, R.; Curlo, M.; De Pergola, G.; De Nucci, S.; Giannelli, G.; Mastronardi, M.; Sardone, R. Prevalence of Zinc Deficiency in Inflammatory Bowel Disease: A Systematic Review and Meta-Analysis. *Nutrients* **2022**, *14*, 4052. [CrossRef]
73. Marshall, N.E.; Abrams, B.; Barbour, L.A.; Catalano, P.; Christian, P.; Friedman, J.E.; Hay, W.W., Jr.; Hernandez, T.L.; Krebs, N.F.; Oken, E.; et al. The importance of nutrition in pregnancy and lactation: Lifelong consequences. *Am. J. Obs. Gynecol.* **2022**, *226*, 607–632. [CrossRef]
74. Levine, A.; Rhodes, J.M.; Lindsay, J.O.; Abreu, M.T.; Kamm, M.A.; Gibson, P.R.; Gasche, C.; Silverberg, M.S.; Mahadevan, U.; Boneh, R.S.; et al. Dietary Guidance From the International Organization for the Study of Inflammatory Bowel Diseases. *Clin. Gastroenterol. Hepatol.* **2020**, *18*, 1381–1392. [CrossRef]
75. Vieujean, S.; De Vos, M.; D'Amico, F.; Paridaens, K.; Daftary, G.; Dudkowiak, R.; Peyrin-Biroulet, L.; Danese, S. Inflammatory bowel disease meets fertility: A physician and patient survey. *Dig. Liver Dis.* **2023**. [CrossRef]
76. Piirainen, T.; Isolauri, E.; Lagstrom, H.; Laitinen, K. Impact of dietary counselling on nutrient intake during pregnancy: A prospective cohort study. *Br. J. Nutr.* **2006**, *96*, 1095–1104. [CrossRef]
77. Kominiarek, M.A.; Rajan, P. Nutrition Recommendations in Pregnancy and Lactation. *Med. Clin. N. Am.* **2016**, *100*, 1199–1215. [CrossRef] [PubMed]
78. Cox, J.T.; Phelan, S.T. Nutrition during pregnancy. *Obs. Gynecol. Clin. N. Am.* **2008**, *35*, 369–383. [CrossRef]
79. Ramakrishnan, U.; Imhoff-Kunsch, B.; Martorell, R. Maternal nutrition interventions to improve maternal, newborn, and child health outcomes. *Nestle Nutr. Inst. Workshop Ser.* **2014**, *78*, 71–80. [CrossRef] [PubMed]
80. Kashkooli, S.B.; Andrews, J.M.; Roberts, M.B.; Selinger, C.P.; Leong, R.W. Inflammatory bowel disease-specific pregnancy knowledge of gastroenterologists against general practitioners and obstetricians. *United Eur. Gastroenterol. J.* **2015**, *3*, 462–470. [CrossRef] [PubMed]
81. Girard, A.W.; Olude, O. Nutrition education and counselling provided during pregnancy: Effects on maternal, neonatal and child health outcomes. *Paediatr. Perinat Epidemiol.* **2012**, *26* (Suppl. 1), 191–204. [CrossRef]

nutrients

MDPI

Article

Is Health Education among the Decisive Factors for the Diet Quality of Pregnant Women in Poland?

Anna Demuth [1], Joanna Ratajczak [1,*], Urszula Czerniak [1] and Katarzyna Antosiak-Cyrak [2]

[1] Department of Anthropology and Biometry, Faculty of Sport Science, Poznan University of Physical Education, 61-871 Poznań, Poland; demuth@awf.poznan.pl (A.D.); czerniak@awf.poznan.pl (U.C.)
[2] Department of Swimming and Water Rescue, Poznan University of Physical Education, 61-871 Poznań, Poland; antosiak-cyrak@awf.poznan.pl
* Correspondence: jratajczak@awf.poznan.pl

Abstract: Health education (HE), an educational process that leads to increased nutritional awareness and improved health, is one of the factors influencing diet quality (DQ) during pregnancy. The aim was to evaluate the DQ of pregnant women and its determinants considering their HE. The study included 122 pregnant women aged 20–40 years. DQ was assessed using the Kom-PAN® questionnaire and the Pro-Healthy Diet Index (pHDI). Data collected included dietary habits, socio-demographic data, education level, place of residence, and maternal lifestyle-related characteristics, namely, pre-pregnancy weight, trimester of pregnancy, and pre-pregnancy and pregnancy physical activity (PA). Weekly energy expenditure was determined using the Polish version of the PPAQ questionnaire. HE at school more than tripled the odds of a higher DQ. Women in their second trimester were 54% more likely to have a higher DQ than women in their third trimester of pregnancy. Undertaking pre-pregnancy PA increased the odds of a higher DQ 2.5 times. Comparative analyses performed in a group of women with HE (HEG, n = 33) and without HE (nHEG, n = 89) showed better DQ in the former, but this was still unsatisfactory in health-promoting properties. The results obtained showed that the HE and trimester of pregnancy and pre-pregnancy Pa influenced DQ in pregnant women.

Keywords: pregnancy; health education; diet quality; diet quality determinants

Citation: Demuth, A.; Ratajczak, J.; Czerniak, U.; Antosiak-Cyrak, K. Is Health Education among the Decisive Factors for the Diet Quality of Pregnant Women in Poland? *Nutrients* **2023**, *15*, 2627. https://doi.org/10.3390/nu15112627

Academic Editors: Louise Brough and Gail Rees

Received: 28 April 2023
Revised: 1 June 2023
Accepted: 2 June 2023
Published: 4 June 2023

1. Introduction

Health and dietary behaviors before and during pregnancy consistently remain an important and ongoing area of research [1–3]. Epidemiological studies have highlighted the significance of assessing diet quality and its determinants as the consequences of inadequate nutrition expose not only women but also their children to poorer health outcomes for the rest of their lives [4].

Among the factors influencing diet quality in pregnant women age, socioeconomic and lifestyle variables are the most commonly reported factors [5,6]. Other factors include pre-pregnancy BMI, physical activity, smoking, and alcohol consumption [7–12] but also nutritional knowledge, which has been reported to play an important role in pregnancy and influencing dietary choices. Obesity and overweight are currently a serious problem among women of reproductive age. The Central Statistical Office in Poland shows that the percentage of women of reproductive age (20–39 years) with excessive body weight (BMI > 25 kg/m^2) increased from 25.8% to 31.3% between 2009 and 2019 [13]. Efforts to provide appropriate health education and care for pregnant women should be intensified due to the fact that almost one in three Polish women of reproductive age has problems with maintaining a healthy body weight.

Despite the proven link between maternal nutrition and pregnancy outcomes, many pregnant women do not follow the dietary recommendations. Moreover, behaviors such as a sedentary lifestyle and unhealthy eating habits are common among pregnant women worldwide, including Poland [14–19]. It has been indicated that such behaviors during pregnancy are caused by both non-adherence to the recommendations and insufficient health education and health promotion [20].

In Poland, health education is understood as a didactic and educational process in which pupils starting from primary school learn how to maintain and improve their own and other people's health, how to create a health-favorable environment, and, in the case of illness or disability, how to actively participate in its treatment, cope with its negative effects, and reduce its consequences [21]. An important part of health education in schools is the development of appropriate eating behaviors, by which pupils acquire competences in the knowledge of basic nutrients and their role in the body, the preparation and storage of food, the knowledge of diseases related to poor nutrition, the knowledge of labeling food packages, and the ability to prepare menus for different groups of people [22]. Health education also plays an important role in shaping health-promoting attitudes by practicing hygienic behaviors that are safe for health, as well as the use of prevention, the practice of physical activity, and the consolidation of knowledge about its benefits.

Researchers emphasize that the level of knowledge and awareness may influence the level of acceptance of educational messages, and, therefore, their effectiveness, which is why health education may be particularly important [23,24]. As schools play an important role in meeting the nutritional needs of children and adolescents and in shaping appropriate behavior [21], health education should already start at an early stage of education. Unfortunately, this type of education has not always been included in the compulsory school curriculum, Poland being an example. In Poland, health education was included in the core curriculum of general education for all types of schools only in 1997 [25]. However, it is not a separate school subject, but its content has been included in many subjects, e.g., biology, family life education, social studies, and safety education. An important step in the Polish education system was linking health education with physical education 2013. Since then, physical education has been playing a leading role in health education. According to the Education Law in Poland [26], a child's compulsory education starts at the beginning of the school year in the calendar year in which the child turns 7 and lasts until the end of primary school, no longer than until the age of 18. Therefore, all people who started primary school in 1997 or later have achieved the expected learning outcomes for health education. In contrast, people who started school before 1997 did not receive health education classes at school, and their knowledge about health behavior comes from a variety of sources.

So far, little attention has been paid to the impact of early health education on diet quality in pregnant women. Considering the importance of diet in pregnant women and studies assessing diet quality, the aim of this study was to evaluate the diet quality of pregnant women and identify its determinants with particular attention to health education.

2. Materials and Methods

2.1. Survey Design and Sample

The survey was conducted in Poznań in free birthing schools, i.e., where access is universal, and there is no extra cost for parents to attend. Due to the lack of official data on the percentage of pregnant women attending antenatal classes, the sample size was estimated based on the list of women attending the classes in three randomly selected birthing schools between September and December 2019. The total number of the women attending antenatal classes was 170, all of whom were asked to participate in the study. Slovin's formula (see below) was used to calculate the sample size with a 5% margin of error and 95% confidence interval [27]. The minimum number of the necessary sample size to meet the criteria listed above was 119. Of the total number of 170 women, 129 (75.9%) agreed to participate in the study, and 41 (24.1%) refused. In addition, seven of the women were excluded from the study due to incomplete questionnaire answers. Finally, 122 women were included in the study.

$$n = \frac{N}{1 + Ne^2}$$

n—sample size; N—population size; e—margin error.

The study took the form of a direct, individual questionnaire survey. The participants completed the questionnaire on their own. In case of any problems with understanding the questions, the interviewer was helpful in explaining the inaccuracies. The collected information included eating habits, sociodemographic data, i.e., age, level of education (university/secondary/vocational/primary), presence of health education in school, place of residence (urban/rural), and maternal lifestyle-related characteristics, i.e., pre-pregnancy weight, trimester of pregnancy, and pre-pregnancy and pregnancy physical activity (PA). In addition, the respondents were asked about the year in which they started primary school. This made it possible to distinguish two groups of women: with health education (i.e., women who started primary school education after 1997; HEG; n = 33) and without health education (i.e., women who started primary school education before 1997; nHEG; n = 89). The distinguished groups were further used for comparative analyses. The study was approved by the Bioethics Committee of the Poznan University of Medical Sciences (reference no. 878/19, 12 September 2019). All women gave written consent to participating in the study.

The KomPAN® questionnaire provided data on eating habits and enabled the calculation of the Pro-Healthy Diet Index (pHDI), which gave information on diet quality [28]. The index was the sum of the daily intakes (times/day) of 10 food groups with potentially beneficial outcomes: 1. wholemeal bread; 2. grains and coarse-ground groats; 3. milk (including flavored milk, cocoa, coffee with milk); 4. fermented milk beverages; 5. curd; 6. white meat; 7. fish; 8. legumes; 9. fruits; and 10. vegetables. Each respondent reported habitual consumption of the above-mentioned products by indicating one of the six frequency categories: never, 1–3 times a month, once a week, a few times a week, once a day, and a few times a day. Those categories were converted to daily frequency expressed as times/day: never (0), 1–3 times a month (0.06), once a week (0.14), a few times a week (0.5), once a day (1.0), and a few times a day (2.0). The pHDI values ranged from 0 to 100 points and were calculated using the formula below. The pHDI values in the range of 0–33 points were defined as low, in the range of 34–66 points as moderate, and in the range of 67–100 points as high. The higher the value, the greater the intensity of health-promoting properties in the diet and, therefore, the better quality of the diet [28].

$$\text{pHDI in points} = \frac{100}{20} \times \text{sum of the consumption of 10 food groups (times/day)}$$

The Polish version of PPAQ questionnaire enabled us to determine the weekly energy expenditure (MET hour/week^{-1}) [29]. The respondents self-assessed their physical activity levels by filling in a questionnaire consisting of 33 items grouped into the following activity categories: household/caregiving (15 items), occupational (5 items), sports/exercises (7–9 items), transportation (3 items), and inactivity (3 items). The declared duration of performance of particular tasks was assigned fixed numbers of minutes (0; 0.12; 0.50; 1.0; 2.0; 3.0) and then multiplied by the number of days of performance of the tasks per week. The obtained values were then multiplied by intensity (MET) in accordance with the guidelines in "Compendium of Physical Activities: an update of activity codes and MET intensities" [30], thus obtaining the energy expenditure measured in Metabolic Equivalent of Task (MET). The following levels of intensity were assigned to the different activities: sedentary < 1.5 METs; light 1.5–<3.0 METs; moderate $\geq$3.0–$\leq$6.0 METs; and vigorous > 6.0 METs. In addition, the respondents were asked if they had undertaken physical activity before pregnancy. The participants could choose between yes/no answers.

2.2. Analysis

All statistical analyses were performed using STATISTICA 13 (Dell Inc.; Tulsa, OK, USA, StatSoft Polska, Cracow, Poland, 2017). The threshold of statistical significance was set at $p \leq 0.05$. The distribution of the variables was tested using the Shapiro–Wilk test. For quantitative variables, arithmetic means and standard deviations (SD) were calculated. The median, lower, and upper quartiles were calculated for the frequency of consumption of 10 product groups. The Mann–Whitney (Z) test was used to test the significance of differences between the distinguished groups. The Chi-square test (χ^2) was used for comparative analysis of categorical variables. The Spearman's rank correlation coefficients (r) were used to assess the presence and strength of the associations between diet quality and consumption of selected food products, as well as sociodemographic data and maternal lifestyle-related variables. The interpretation of the correlation coefficients was as follows: weak (<0.3), moderate (0.3 to <0.5), strong (0.5 to <0.7), and very strong (≥0.7) correlation [31]. To identify the determinants of diet quality, multiple regression models were run with diet quality as the dependent variable. Only factors that were significantly correlated with diet quality were included in the models. Logistic regression analysis was used to assess the odds of having a higher-quality diet. The dependent variable was diet quality as assessed by the Pro-Healthy Diet Index (pHDI). The categorization of the two groups for the dependent variable in the logistic regression was based on pHDI values. Values $\leq$ 33 points were assigned to the "lower quality diet" category, whereas values > 33 points were assigned to the "higher quality diet" category. Odds ratios (ORs) and 95% confidence intervals (95% CI) were calculated.

3. Results

3.1. Group Characteristics

The characteristics of the participants are shown in Table 1. The mean age was 27.7 ± 3.7 years. The women from the health education group were younger than women in the group without health education (23.4 ± 1.5 vs. 29.3 ± 2.9; Z = −8.45; $p < 0.001$). The percentage of the women with a higher level of education was greater in nHEG than in HEG (76.4% vs. 54.6%; $\chi^2 = 6.58$; $p = 0.037$). The vast majority of participants had a higher level of education (70.5%) and lived in urban areas (68.9%). Of the participants, 49.2% were in their third trimester of pregnancy. The mean pre-pregnancy weight was 66.3 ± 14.3 kg. Undertaking physical activity before pregnancy was declared by 58.2% of the respondents. An assessment of the physical activity levels of the pregnant women showed that the highest energy expenditure was recorded for light and moderate intensity efforts ($\bar{x}$ =71.7 MET hour/week; $\bar{x}$ =72.9 MET hour/week), accounting for 37.5% and 38.2% of total physical activity, respectively.

3.2. Diet Characteristics

In the entire study group, the mean value of the pHDI was 26.3 ± 13.0 points. The women with health education had a higher value of the pHDI than the women without health education (HEG = 28.3 ± 12.7 points vs. nHEG = 20.9 ± 12.3 points; Z = 2.99; $p = 0.002$). There were no women with a high-quality diet in the whole study group; however, a moderate-quality diet was noted in 30.3% of the participants.

In general, fruit and vegetables were consumed with the greatest frequency (on average once a day), whereas fish and legumes were consumed least frequently (on average 1–3 times a month). The remaining products were consumed with an average frequency of once to several times a week (see Supplement Table S1). A comparative analysis showed significant differences in the frequency of consumption of wholemeal bread (Z = 2.72; $p = 0.007$), grains and coarse-ground groats (Z = 2.43; $p = 0.02$), legumes (Z = 1.97; $p = 0.049$), and fruits (Z = 2.21; $p = 0.03$). Each time, the nHEG group was characterized by a lower frequency of consumption of the above-mentioned products.

The correlations of health education with the pHDI and ten food products with beneficial health outcomes are shown in Table 2. Positive and significant correlations were found for all variables except milk consumption, fermented milk beverages, curd, and white meat.

Table 1. Characteristics of surveyed group.

Variables	Total n = 122	HEG n = 33	nHEG n = 89	*p*-Value
age (years)	27.7 ± 3.7	23.4 ± 1.5	29.3 ± 2.9	<0.001
educational level (%) (n)				
- primary	5.7 (7)	12.1 (4)	3.4 (3)	0.037
- vocational/secondary	23.8 (29)	33.3 (11)	20.2 (18)	
- university	70.5 (86)	54.6 (18)	76.4 (68)	
place of residence (%) (n)				
- rural	31.1 (38)	33.3 (11)	30.3 (27)	0.751
- urban	68.9 (84)	66.7 (22)	69.7 (62)	
trimester of pregnancy (%) (n)				
- I	9.8 (12)	18.2 (6)	6.7 (6)	0.161
- II	41.0 (50)	39.4 (13)	41.6 (37)	
- III	49.2 (60)	42.4 (14)	51.7 (46)	
pre-pregnancy weight (kg) (mean± SD)	66.3 ± 14.3	63.5 ± 13.8	67.3 ± 14.4	0.110
pre-pregnancy PA (%) (n)				
- no	41.8 (51)	54.5 (18)	37.1 (33)	0.082
- yes	58.2 (71)	45.5 (15)	62.9 (56)	
pregnancy PA (METs; mean ± SD)				
- total PA	191.0 ± 118.7	187.6 ± 156.8	192.4 ± 102.1	0.177
- sedentary (<1.5)	41.1 ± 31.6	41.2 ± 31.7	41.1 ± 31.5	0.977
- light PA (1.5–<3.0)	71.7 ± 38.9	69.2 ± 42.5	72.6 ± 37.6	0.536
- moderate PA (≥3.0–≥6.0)	72.9 ± 75.8	68.6 ± 92.8	74.6 ± 68.9	0.132
- vigorous PA (>6.0)	5.3 ± 22.3	8.6 ± 33.7	4.1 ± 16.2	0.762

HEG—group with health education; nHEG—group without health education; $p \leq 0.05$—a statistically significant value.

Table 2. Correlation coefficients of the health education with the pHDI and 10 food products with beneficial health outcomes.

	r	*p*-Value
1. pHDI	0.27	0.002
2. wholemeal bread	0.25	0.005
3. grains and coarse-ground groats	0.23	0.012
4. milk	0.10	0.269
5. fermented milk beverages	0.14	0.111
6. curd	0.16	0.082
7. white meat	0.14	0.112
8. fish	0.19	0.039
9. legumes	0.19	0.033
10. fruits	0.21	0.019
11. vegetables	0.18	0.044

$p \leq 0.05$—a statistically significant value.

3.3. Food Determinants of Diet Quality

Before testing the hypothesis concerning the food correlates of diet quality, the correlations between diet quality as the dependent variable and ten food products with a potentially beneficial effects on health were analyzed (Table 3). In each group, moderate but significant, strong, and very strong correlations between diet quality and the mentioned independent variables were found. In the group with health education, all variables were positively correlated with the diet quality. They were as follows: wholemeal bread (r = 0.58;

$p \leq 0.001$); grains and coarse-ground groats (r = 0.74; $p \leq 0.001$); milk (r = 0.60; $p \leq 0.001$); fermented milk beverages (r = 0.62; $p \leq 0.001$); curd (r = 0.62; $p \leq 0.001$); white meat (r = 0.35; $p = 0.001$); fish (r = 0.45; $p \leq 0.001$); legumes (r = 0.47; $p \leq 0.001$); fruits (r = 0.75; $p \leq 0.001$); and vegetables (r = 0.81; $p \leq 0.001$). In a group with no health education, no correlation was found for milk and white meat, whereas positive correlations for other food products were as follows: wholemeal bread (r = 0.50 $p = 0.002$); grains and coarse-ground groats (r = 0.42; $p = 0.009$); fermented milk beverages (r = 0.60; $p \leq 0.001$); curd (r = 0.37; $p = 0.02$); fish (r = 0.33; $p = 0.041$); legumes (r = 0.53; $p \leq 0.001$); fruits (r = 0.61; $p \leq 0.001$); and vegetables (r = 0.73; $p \leq 0.001$).

Table 3. Food correlates of diet quality in surveyed groups.

	Variables	HEG	nHEG
1.	wholemeal bread	0.58 *	0.50 *
2.	grains and coarse-ground groats	0.74 *	0.42 *
3.	milk	0.60 *	0.26
4.	fermented milk beverages	0.62 *	0.60 *
5.	curd	0.62 *	0.37 *
6.	white meat	0.35 *	0.28
7.	fish	0.45 *	0.33 *
8.	legumes	0.47 *	0.53 *
9.	fruits	0.75 *	0.61 *
10.	vegetables	0.81 *	0.73 *

HEG—group with health education; nHEG—group without health education. * a statistically significant correlation coefficient.

These significant variables were then included in the multiple regression model in order to assess which of them contributed most to explaining the variability in the diet quality in separate groups. According to the results obtained (Table 4), diet quality in the group with health education was determined by eight variables, i.e., vegetables, fermented milk beverages, milk, wholemeal bread, fruits, grains, coarse-ground groats, curd, and white meat. The model was significant and explained 99.6% of the variance in the diet quality $F(8.75) = 2297.2$; $p \leq 0.001$). The consumption of vegetables ($R^2 = 0.607$; $p \leq 0.001$) and fermented dairy drinks ($\Delta R^2 = 0.223$; $p \leq 0.001$) made the greatest contribution to the prediction of the dependent variable.

Table 4. Regression analysis of food determinants of diet quality in distinguished groups.

Variables	R^2	β	F	*p*-Value
Model 1: HEG	0.996		2297.2	<0.001
vegetables		0.28		<0.001
fermented milk beverages		0.16		<0.001
milk		0.23		<0.001
wholemeal bread		0.20		<0.001
fruits		0.22		<0.001
grains and coarse-ground groats		0.20		<0.001
curd		0.16		<0.001
white meat		0.06		<0.001
Model 2: nHEG	0.939		79.5	<0.001
vegetables		0.21		0.004
fermented milk beverages		0.34		<0.001
grains and coarse-ground groats		0.16		0.002
fruits		0.38		<0.001
legumes		0.25		<0.001
wholemeal bread		0.26		<0.001

$p \leq 0.05$—a statistically significant value.

In the group with no health education, six variables were included in the final diet quality model, i.e., vegetables, fermented milk beverages, grains and coarse-ground groats, fruits, legumes, and wholemeal bread. The model was significant and explained 93.9% of the variance in the dependent variable ($F(6.31) = 79.5$, $p \leq 0.001$). As in the previous model, vegetables and fermented dairy drinks had the largest contribution to the prediction of the dependent variable (respectively: $R^2 = 0.594$; $p \leq 0.001$; $\Delta R^2 = 0.179$; $p \leq 0.001$). The smallest, however still significant, contribution to explaining the variability of diet quality was made by wholemeal bread ($\Delta R^2 = 0.038$; $p \leq 0.001$).

3.4. Sociodemographic and Maternal Lifestyle-Related Determinants of Diet Quality

The first step in assessing the sociodemographic and maternal determinants of diet quality was to examine the correlations between diet quality as the dependent variable and all the variables listed in Table 1. Significant correlations were found for variables such as age ($r = 0.20$; $p = 0.026$), health education ($r = 0.27$; $p = 0.002$), educational level ($r = 0.20$; $p = 0.025$), trimester of pregnancy ($r = 0.31$; $p \leq 0.001$), pre-pregnancy PA ($r = 0.26$, $p = 0.003$), moderate PA ($r = 0.19$; $p = 0.039$), and vigorous PA ($r = 0.19$; $p = 0.035$). A regression model was then run with diet quality as the dependent variable. According to the results obtained (Table 5), diet quality was predicted by four variables, i.e., health education, trimester of pregnancy, moderate PA, and pre-pregnancy PA. The greatest contribution to the prediction of the dependent variable was made by health education ($\Delta R^2 = 0.069$; $p = 0.003$), followed by the trimester of pregnancy ($\Delta R^2 = 0.063$; $p = 0.028$). Then, moderate PA was added ($\Delta R^2 = 0.044$; $p = 0.013$), and, in the last step, pre-pregnancy PA was included ($\Delta R^2 = 0.032$; $p = 0.032$). The final model was significant and explained 20.8% of the variance of the diet quality ($F(4.17) = 7.69$; $p \leq 0.001$).

Table 5. Regression analysis of socio-demographic and maternal lifestyle-related determinants of diet quality.

Variable	R^2	β	F	*p* Value
	0.208		7.69	<0.001
health education		0.25		0.003
trimester of pregnancy		0.21		0.028
moderate PA		0.19		0.013
pre-pregnancy PA		0.18		0.032

$p \leq 0.05$—a statistically significant value.

3.5. The Odds Ratio of Higher-Quality Diet

A logistic regression analysis was performed to assess how the sociodemographic and maternal lifestyle-related predictors from Table 5 affected the odds of achieving a higher-quality diet (Figure 1). Unfortunately, due to lack of standards and cut-off points, a similar analysis could not be performed for moderate PA during pregnancy. The results showed that the presence of health education in the educational history of the surveyed participants more than tripled the odds of a higher-quality diet (OR = 3.14; 95% CI: 1.09–7.03; $p = 0.032$). The women in their second trimester were 54% more likely to have a higher-quality diet than the women in their third trimester of pregnancy (OR = 1.54; 95% CI: 1.23–2.17; $p = 0.046$). Undertaking PA before pregnancy increased the odds of a higher-quality diet by 2.5 times (OR = 2.51; 95% CI: 1.08–5.88; $p = 0.032$).

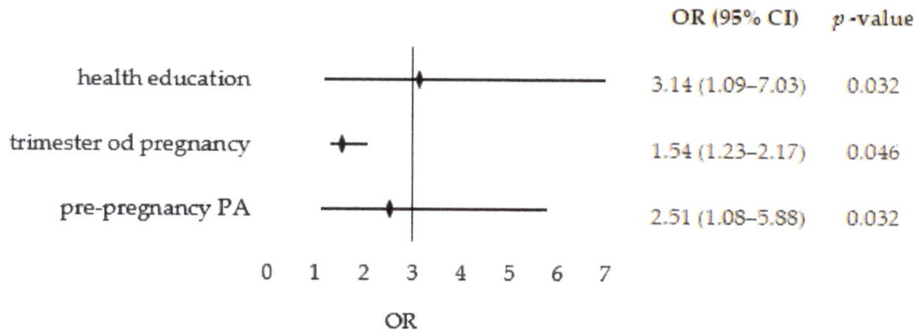

Figure 1. The odds ratio of a higher-quality diet.

4. Discussion

The literature indicates that pregnancy is an important time in a woman's life, contributing to changes in both her dietary habits and other health-related behaviors that are undertaken out of concern for her life and health and that of her baby [1,3,32]. Previous studies have shown a wide variation in the determinants of diet quality among pregnant women. In addition to social and cultural factors [24,33–36], nutritional knowledge and health education have also been indicated as factors influencing diet quality in pregnancy [35]. Therefore, the aim of this study was to assess the dietary quality of pregnant women and its determinants, with attention to health education as possible one.

Among the most commonly reported factors influencing the quality of pregnant women's diets are age and socioeconomic variables, including the education level, which is considered to be an awareness variable that significantly influences dietary decisions [8,9,12,37–40]. In turn, the presented study highlighted the particularly important role of health education, trimester of pregnancy, moderate PA, and pre-pregnancy PA in shaping dietary habits and diet quality. According to the literature, younger mothers have poorer diet quality because they have lower levels of education, lower socioeconomic status, and less life experience, unlike older women [1,37,41–47]. However, our own results show that women in the no health education group, despite being older and having achieved a university degree, had poorer diet quality than younger women without a higher education but with health education in the core curriculum. This suggests that diet quality does not depend as much on age and educational attainment but, to a large extent, on the health education provided as part of compulsory schooling for children up to the age of 18. Our further analysis showed that participation in compulsory health education more than tripled the odds of having a better diet. Sedentary lifestyles and unhealthy eating habits are known to be common among pregnant women [17], but our results show that women with healthier pre-pregnancy behaviors were also those with better diets during pregnancy. In contrast to McGowan and McAuliffe [48], our study showed a significant positive influence of pre-pregnancy and pregnancy PA on diet quality, with the pre-pregnancy PA increasing the odds of a higher-quality diet during pregnancy by a factor of 2.5. This confirms that physical activity is an important target for nutrition and health interventions. In the presented study, women in the second trimester of pregnancy had a healthier dietary profile than women in the third trimester. This is on the contrary to Fernández-Gómez et al. [49], but consistent with McGowan and McAuliffe [42], who reported the odds in predicting the likelihood of following a healthy dietary pattern in each trimester. In their study, higher levels of maternal education together with normal maternal BMI as well as the nationality were important predictors of following a healthy diet in the second trimester. This indicates that women with higher levels of education also are more likely to make positive changes in their diet. Although awareness of the positive effects of a healthy diet and physical activity on pregnancy outcomes has been reported to be a strong motivator for changing dietary behaviors [50,51], it is not always sufficient to maintain changes until the end of pregnancy. As shown by McGowan and McAuliffe [48], 69 out of 95 women continued the healthy dietary pattern into the third trimester. Therefore, there is a strong need for research to investigate the reasons why healthy dietary behaviors are not maintained during pregnancy.

A positive contribution of health education to dietary behaviors was also shown in the case of the Pro-Healthy Diet Index, which provides information on diet quality. The diets of women who received counselling and education on healthy eating and lifestyles were of better quality than those of women who did not receive adequate substantive support. In addition, health education was positively associated with the intake of wholemeal bread, grains and coarse-ground groats, fish, legumes, fruit, and vegetables but not with intakes of milk, fermented milk beverages, curd, or white meat. Our results differ from those obtained by Goodarzi-Khoigani et al. [52], who showed that health education was positively associated with the intake of vegetables and fish but not bread, legumes, dairy products, or fruit in the Japanese population.

Unfortunately, despite the positive contribution of health education to dietary behaviors and noticeable differences in the level of DQ and the frequency of consumption of selected groups of products, the diets of women with nutrition education were not in accordance with nutritional recommendations [53,54]. In the surveyed groups, the consumption of products with beneficial health effects was insufficient, which corresponds with the findings of other authors [14,16,18]. In general, the respondents consumed fruit and vegetables most frequently (once a day on average), which is significant, as they are the basis of a healthy diet in many nutritional recommendations, mainly because of the vitamins, minerals, and antioxidants they contain [55,56]. The remaining food products were consumed with an unsatisfactory frequency, and the identified dietary errors were particularly related to insufficient consumption of whole grain products (wholemeal bread, groats, oatmeal), fish, and legumes. Given the fact that whole grain products are a good source of fiber and have a positive impact on the prebiotic index [57,58], a well-balanced diet should be rich in these products. Unfortunately, only 16% of the women with health education met the recommendations of several servings of whole grain per day [57], compared to 9% of the women without health education. The recommended intake of 2–3 portions of fish per week was reported by 10% of the women with health education and only 3% of those without health education. The consumption of legumes was also low. However, this can be regarded as a positive outcome, especially if they had been eaten as raw sprouts (e.g., beansprouts). Similar to legumes, sprouts are a good source of protein [59] and also of health-maintaining nutrients such as glucosinolates, phenolics, and isoflavones [60]. However, it should be noted that sprouts also belong to a group with a high risk of Listeria monocytogenes infection [61], and, unlike maternal listeriosis infection, fetal or neonatal infection carries a high risk of fatal complications [62]. Therefore, pregnant women should limit their consumption of sprouts.

The results obtained indicate the positive impact of educational programs conducted in Polish schools aimed at implementing the principles of proper nutrition described by the healthy eating pyramid [54]. In the group of the women with health education, eight out of ten groups of products with potentially health-promoting properties determined the quality of the diet (i.e., vegetables, fermented milk beverages, milk, wholemeal bread, fruit, grains and coarse-ground groats, curd, and white meat). In turn, in the group without health education, the variety of food determinants of diet quality was smaller. Only six out of ten recommended products explained the variance in diet quality, i.e., vegetables, fermented milk beverages, grains and coarse-ground groats, fruit, legumes, and wholemeal bread. However, it should also be noted that the consumption of vegetables and fermented dairy drinks was one of the determining factors of diet quality in each studied group.

Previous studies have shown that women's compliance with recommendations increased when they were given detailed explanations on the importance of the recommended food products [23,24]. On the other hand, the lack of adequate knowledge about nutritional recommendations of those responsible for developing nutritional awareness have been identified as one of the barriers to changing dietary behaviors [63–65]. Therefore, it is possible that the results obtained in the present study are caused by inadequate health education in Polish schools, e.g., the content provided may be insufficient or not adapted to the age of the recipients, yet the individual non-adherence to the recommendations cannot be excluded.

Important clues for nutrition education also come from studies that indicate the preferred form of knowledge transfer. As was shown by Wise and Arcamone [66], among adolescents, the best way to learn about nutrition was to listen to teachers and health professionals. Unfortunately, it is not appreciated in Poland. Here, health education is provided only by schoolteachers, nor is it not a separate school subject, but it is implemented in a number of different subjects in the form of selected individual class topics. Crucially, partners and relatives are an important source of nutritional support for mothers and mothers-to-be [67]; in order to improve the quality of pregnant women's diets, it is also necessary to educate and increase knowledge about the positive or reinforcing effects of healthy nutrition also in the woman's immediate environment.

Limitations

This study has some strengths and limitations. The study included a group of women attending childbirth school, and access to health education was taken into account. The KomPAN® and PPAQ (Polish version) questionnaires used in the study have good relevance, and acceptable test–retest reliability of the test–retest, therefore, represent a reliable set of data. The PPAQ questionnaire has been adapted to the cultural conditions of many countries, including Poland, allowing international comparisons to be made regarding the level of AP of pregnant women. Furthermore, the study was conducted in the form of a direct questionnaire interview, which allowed us to better understand the questions and obtain more complete and reliable information about the dietary habits of the women surveyed. However, we are aware of some limitations. It was a cross-sectional study, in which diet quality was analyzed based on questions about general food consumption rather than questions about specific dietary components. Future research should include this type of data to gain full insight into the complex model of determinants of dietary quality. The Pro-Healthy Diet Index (pHDI) used to assess diet quality is based on the consumption of health-promoting products recommended in the Mediterranean diet and included in the healthy eating pyramid.

5. Conclusions

The present study highlighted the particularly important role of health education, trimester of pregnancy, moderate PA, and pre-pregnancy PA in shaping dietary habits and diet quality. We recommend that the proposed interventions for the nutritional education of women of reproductive age include not only nutritional aspects but also physical activity adapted to the gestational age and capabilities of the pregnant women. Appropriate adaptation of the interventions to the individual needs of the woman, her preferences, and, above all, her knowledge and health habits can effectively influence the modification of her dietary behavior during pregnancy. The present study also has practical implications. The results obtained can be used by institutions providing health education to preconceptional and pregnant women to develop an appropriate strategy aimed at raising awareness of the importance of proper nutrition during pregnancy and possibly changing inappropriate eating habits.

Supplementary Materials: The following supporting information can be downloaded at: https://www.mdpi.com/article/10.3390/nu15112627/s1, Table S1. Dietary characteristics of surveyed women.

Author Contributions: Conceptualization: A.D.; methodology: A.D., K.A.-C., J.R. and U.C.; formal analysis: A.D. and J.R.; investigation: K.A.-C.; writing—original draft preparation: A.D. and K.A.-C.; writing—review and editing: J.R., U.C., A.D. and K.A.-C.; project administration: A.D. and K.A.-C. All authors have read and agreed to the published version of the manuscript.

Funding: This research received no external funding.

Institutional Review Board Statement: The study was conducted according to the guidelines of the Declaration of Helsinki. The study protocol was reviewed and approved by bioethics committee at the Medical University of Karol Marcinkowski in Poznań (reference no. 878/19, 12 September 2019).

Informed Consent Statement: All participants provided written informed consent prior to their participation in this study.

Data Availability Statement: Data are available on request from the corresponding author.

Conflicts of Interest: The authors declare no conflict of interest.

References

1. Forbes, L.E.; Graham, J.E.; Berglund, C.; Bell, R.C. Dietary change during pregnancy and women's reasons for change. *Nutrients* **2018**, *10*, 1032. [CrossRef] [PubMed]
2. Harrison, C.L.; Lombard, C.B.; Teede, H.J. Understanding health behaviours in a cohort of pregnant women at risk of gestational diabetes mellitus: An observational study. *BJOG Int. J. Gynaecol. Obstet.* **2012**, *119*, 731–738. [CrossRef] [PubMed]
3. Olander, E.K.; Smith, D.M.; Darwin, Z. Health behaviour and pregnancy: A time for change. *J. Reprod. Infant. Psychol.* **2018**, *36*, 1–3. [CrossRef] [PubMed]
4. Chia, A.R.; Chen, L.W.; Lai, J.S.; Wong, C.H.; Neelakantan, N.; van Dam, R.M.; Chong, M.F. Maternal Dietary Patterns and Birth Outcomes: A Systematic Review and Meta-Analysis. *Adv. Nutr.* **2019**, *10*, 685–695. [CrossRef]
5. Teruel Camargo, J.; Taylor, M.K.; Gajewski, B.J.; Carlson, S.E.; Sullivan, D.K.; Gibbs, H.D. Higher Diet Quality in Latina Women during Pregnancy May Be Associated with Sociodemographic Factors. *Int. J. Environ. Res. Public Health* **2022**, *19*, 13895. [CrossRef]
6. Wesołowska, E.; Jankowska, A.; Trafalska, E.; Kałużny, P.; Grzesiak, M.; Dominowska, J.; Hanke, W.; Calamandrei, G.; Polańska, K. Sociodemographic, Lifestyle, Environmental and Pregnancy-Related Determinants of Dietary Patterns during Pregnancy. *Int. J. Environ. Res. Public Health* **2019**, *16*, 754. [CrossRef]
7. Cucó, G.; Fernández-Ballart, J.; Sala, J.; Viladrich, C.; Iranzo, R.; Vila, J.; Arija, V. Dietary patterns and associated lifestyles in preconception, pregnancy and postpartum. *Eur. J. Clin. Nutr.* **2006**, *60*, 364–371. [CrossRef]
8. Laraia, B.A.; Bodnar, L.M.; Siega-Riz, A.M. Pregravid body mass index is negatively associated with diet quality during pregnancy. *Public Health Nutr.* **2007**, *10*, 920–926. [CrossRef]
9. Gollenberg, A.; Pekow, P.; Markenson, G.; Tucker, K.L.; Chasan-Taber, L. Dietary behaviors, physical activity, and cigarette smoking among pregnant Puerto Rican women. *Am. J. Clin. Nutr.* **2008**, *87*, 1844–1851. [CrossRef]
10. Northstone, K.; Emmett, P.; Rogers, I. Dietary patterns in pregnancy and associations with socio-demographic and lifestyle factors. *Eur. J. Clin. Nutr.* **2008**, *62*, 471–479. [CrossRef]
11. Fowler, J.K.; Evers, S.E.; Campbell, M.K. Inadequate dietary intakes among pregnant women. *Can. J. Diet. Pract. Res.* **2012**, *73*, 72–77. [CrossRef] [PubMed]
12. Nash, D.M.; Gilliland, J.A.; Evers, S.E.; Wilk, P.; Campbell, M.K. Determinants of diet quality in pregnancy: Sociodemographic, pregnancy-specific, and food environment influences. *J. Nutr. Educ. Behav.* **2013**, *45*, 627–634. [CrossRef]
13. Central Statistical Office. Percentage of People Aged 15 and Over by Body Mass Index (BMI). 2020. Available online: https://stat.gov.pl/obszary-tematyczne/zdrowie/zdrowie/odsetek-osob-w-wieku-powyzej-15-lat-wedlug-indeksu-masy-ciala-bmi,23,1.html (accessed on 21 May 2023). (In Polish)
14. Deierlein, A.L.; Ghassabian, A.; Kahn, L.G.; Afanasyeva, Y.; Mehta-Lee, S.S.; Brubaker, S.G.; Trasande, L. Dietary Quality and Sociodemographic and Health Behavior Characteristics Among Pregnant Women Participating in the New York University Children's Health and Environment Study. *Front. Nutr.* **2021**, *8*, 639425. [CrossRef] [PubMed]
15. Antosiak-Cyrak, K.Z.; Demuth, A. A study of physical activity levels of pregnant women using the Polish version of Pregnancy Physical Activity Questionnaire (PPAQ-Pl). *Ginekol. Pol.* **2019**, *90*, 250–255. [CrossRef] [PubMed]
16. Pick, M.E.; Edwards, M.; Moreau, D.; Ryan, E.A. Assessment of diet quality in pregnant women using the Healthy Eating Index. *J. Am. Diet. Assoc.* **2005**, *105*, 240–246. [CrossRef]
17. Rojhani, A.; Ouyang, P.; Gullon-Rivera, A.; Dale, T.M. Dietary Quality of Pregnant Women Participating in the Special Supplemental Nutrition Program for Women, Infants, and Children. *Int. J. Environ. Res. Public Health* **2021**, *18*, 8370. [CrossRef]
18. Walsh, J.M.; McAuliffe, F.M. Impact of maternal nutrition on pregnancy outcome—Does it matter what pregnant women eat? *Best. Pract. Res. Clin. Obs. Gynaecol.* **2015**, *29*, 63–78. [CrossRef]
19. Yamashita, T.; Roces, R.E.D.; Ladines-Llave, C.; Tuliao, M.T.R.; Yamada, C.; Tanaka, T.; Shimazawa, K.; Iwamoto, S.; Matsuo, H. Dietary Intake Quality Is Affected by Knowledge and Dietary Intake Frequency among Pregnant Women in Muntinlupa, Philippines: A Cross-Sectional Study. *Int. J. Environ. Res. Public Health* **2021**, *18*, 12306. [CrossRef]
20. Kebbe, M.; Flanagan, E.M.; Sparks, J.R.; Redman, L.M. Eating Behaviors and Dietary Patterns of Women during Pregnancy: Optimizing the Universal 'Teachable Moment'. *Nutrients* **2021**, *13*, 3298. [CrossRef]
21. Ministry of Education and Science. Health Education. 2013. Available online: https://www.gov.pl/web/edukacja-i-nauka/edukacja-zdrowotna (accessed on 21 May 2023). (In Polish)

22. Wolny, B. *Edukacja Zdrowotna w Szkole. Poradnik dla Dyrektorów Szkół i Nauczycieli;* Ośrodek Rozwoju Edukacji: Warszawa, Poland, 2019.
23. Bloomingdale, A.; Guthrie, L.B.; Price, S.; Wright, R.O.; Platek, D.; Haines, J.; Oken, E. A qualitative study of fish consumption during pregnancy. *Am. J. Clin. Nutr.* **2010**, *92*, 1234–1240. [CrossRef]
24. De Jersey, S.J.; Nicholson, J.M.; Callaway, L.K.; Daniels, L.A. An observational study of nutrition and physical activity behaviours, knowledge, and advice in pregnancy. *BMC Pregnancy Childbirth* **2013**, *13*, 115. [CrossRef] [PubMed]
25. Woynarowska, B. Edukacja zdrowotna w szkole w Polsce. Zmiany w ostatnich dekadach i nowa propozycja. *Probl. Hig. Epidemiol.* **2008**, *89*, 445–452.
26. Education Law. Compulsory Schooling. Dz.U.2023.900 [In Polish]. 2023. Available online: https://sip.lex.pl/akty-prawne/dzu-dziennik-ustaw/prawo-oswiatowe-18558680/art-35?_ga=2.42963813.1518331979.1684747071-432803955.1684747070 (accessed on 21 May 2023).
27. Tejada, J.J.; Punzalan, J.R.B. On the misuse of Slovin's formula. *Philipp. Stat.* **2012**, *61*, 129–136.
28. Jeżewska-Zychowicz, M.; Gawecki, J.; Wadolowska, L.; Czarnocinska, J.; Galinski, G.; Kollajtis Dolowy, A.; Roszkowski, W.; Wawrzyniak, A.; Przybylowicz, K.; Stasiewicz, B.; et al. *KomPAN® Dietary Habits and Nutrition Beliefs Questionnaire and the Manual for Developing of Nutritional Data;* Gawecki, J., Ed.; The Committee of Human Nutrition, Polish Academy of Sciences: Olsztyn, Poland, 2020; Available online: http://www.knozc.pan.pl/ (accessed on 20 January 2023).
29. Krzepota, J.; Sadowska, D. Kwestionariusz aktywności fizycznej kobiet w ciąży—Wersja polska (PPAQ-PL). *Med. Ogólna Nauk. Zdrowiu* **2017**, *23*, 100–106. [CrossRef]
30. Ainsworth, B.E.; Haskell, W.L.; Whitt, M.C.; Irwin, M.L.; Swartz, A.M.; Strath, S.J.; O'Brien, W.L.; Bassett, D.R., Jr.; Schmitz, K.H.; Emplaincourt, P.O.; et al. Compendium of physical activities: An update of activity codes and MET intensities. *Med. Sci. Sport. Exerc.* **2000**, *32* (Suppl. S9), 498–504. [CrossRef]
31. Stanisz, A. Basics of korrelation and regression. In *Accessible Course of Statistics with Application of Statistica PL Using Medical Examples;* Basics Statistics; StatSoft: Kraków, Poland, 2007; Volume 1, pp. 203–219.
32. Szwajcer, E.; Hiddink, G.J.; Maas, L.; Koelen, M.; van Woerkum, C. Nutrition awareness before and throughout different trimesters in pregnancy: A quantitative study among dutch women. *Fam. Pract.* **2012**, *29*, i82–i88. [CrossRef] [PubMed]
33. Bandura, A. Health promotion by social cognitive means. *Health Educ. Behav.* **2004**, *31*, 143–164. [CrossRef]
34. Blondin, J.H.; LoGiudice, J.A. Pregnant women's knowledge and awareness of nutrition. *Appl. Nurs. Res.* **2018**, *39*, 167–174. [CrossRef]
35. Lee, A.; Newton, M.; Radcliffe, J.; Belski, R. Pregnancy nutrition knowledge and experiences of pregnant women and antenatal care clinicians: A mixed methods approach. *Women Birth* **2018**, *31*, 269–277. [CrossRef]
36. Lucas, C.; Charlton, K.E.; Yeatman, H. Nutrition advice during pregnancy: Do women receive it and can health professionals provide it? *Matern. Child. Health* **2014**, *18*, 2465–2478. [CrossRef]
37. Doyle, I.M.; Borrmann, B.; Grosser, A.; Razum, O.; Spallek, J. Determinants of dietary patterns and diet quality during pregnancy: A systematic review with narrative synthesis. *Public Health Nutr.* **2017**, *20*, 1009–1028. [CrossRef] [PubMed]
38. Arkkola, T.; Uusitalo, U.; Kronberg-Kippilä, C.; Männistö, S.; Virtanen, M.; Kenward, M.G.; Veijola, R.; Knip, M.; Ovaskainen, M.L.; Virtanen, S.M. Seven distinct dietary patterns identified among pregnant Finnish women—Associations with nutrient intake and sociodemographic factors. *Public Health Nutr.* **2008**, *11*, 176–182. [CrossRef]
39. Bojar, I.; Owoc, A.; Humeniuk, E.; Wierzba, W.; Fronczak, A. Inappropriate consumption of vitamins and minerals by pregnant women in Poland. *Ann. Agric. Environ. Med.* **2012**, *19*, 263–266. [PubMed]
40. Jardí, C.; Aparicio, E.; Bedmar, C.; Aranda, N.; Abajo, S.; March, G.; Basora, J.; Arija, V.; Study Group, T.E. Food Consumption during Pregnancy and Post-Partum. ECLIPSES Study. *Nutrients* **2019**, *14*, 2447. [CrossRef] [PubMed]
41. Bodnar, L.M.; Simhan, H.N.; Parker, C.B.; Meier, H.; Mercer, B.M.; Grobman, W.A.; Haas, D.M.; Wing, D.A.; Hoffman, M.K.; Parry, S.; et al. Racial or ethnic and socioeconomic inequalities in adherence to national dietary guidance in a large cohort of US pregnant women. *J. Acad. Nutr. Diet.* **2017**, *117*, 867–877. [CrossRef] [PubMed]
42. Bodnar, L.M.; Siega-Riz, A.M. A diet quality index for pregnancy detects variation in diet and differences by sociodemographic factors. *Public Health Nutr.* **2002**, *5*, 801–809. [CrossRef]
43. Delbaere, I.; Verstraelen, H.; Goetgeluk, S.; Martens, G.; De Backer, G.; Temmerman, M. Pregnancy outcome in primiparae of advanced maternal age. *Eur. J. Obstet. Gynecol. Reprod. Biol.* **2007**, *135*, 41–46. [CrossRef]
44. Emond, J.A.; Karagas, M.R.; Baker, E.R.; Gilbert-Diamond, D. Better diet quality during pregnancy is associated with a reduced likelihood of an infant born small for gestational age: An analysis of the prospective new hampshire birth cohort study. *J. Nutr.* **2018**, *148*, 22–30. [CrossRef]
45. Rifas-Shiman, S.L.; Rich-Edwards, J.W.; Kleinman, K.P.; Oken, E.; Gillman, M.W. Dietary quality during pregnancy varies by maternal characteristics in project viva: A US cohort. *J. Am. Diet. Assoc.* **2009**, *109*, 1004–1011. [CrossRef]
46. Shapiro, A.L.; Kaar, J.L.; Crume, T.L.; Starling, A.P.; Siega-Riz, A.M.; Ringham, B.M.; Glueck, D.H.; Norris, J.M.; A Barbour, L.; Friedman, J.E.; et al. Maternal diet quality in pregnancy and neonatal adiposity: The healthy start study. *Int. J. Obes.* **2016**, *40*, 1056–1062. [CrossRef]
47. Thomson, J.L.; Tussing-Humphreys, L.M.; Goodman, M.H.; Olender, S. Baseline demographic, anthropometric, psychosocial, and behavioral characteristics of rural, Southern women in early pregnancy. *Matern. Child. Health J.* **2016**, *20*, 1980–1988. [CrossRef] [PubMed]

48. McGowan, C.A.; McAuliffe, F.M. Maternal dietary patterns and associated nutrient intakes during each trimester of pregnancy. *Public Health Nutr.* **2013**, *16*, 97–107. [CrossRef] [PubMed]
49. Fernández-Gómez, E.; Luque-Vara, T.; Moya-Fernández, P.J.; López-Olivares, M.; Gallardo-Vigil, M.Á.; Enrique-Mirón, C. Factors Influencing Dietary Patterns during Pregnancy in a Culturally Diverse Society. *Nutrients* **2020**, *23*, 3242. [CrossRef] [PubMed]
50. Aittasalo, M.; Pasanen, M.; Fogelholm, M.; Kinnunen, T.I.; Ojala, K.; Luoto, R. Physical activity counseling in maternity and child health care—A controlled trial. *BMC Womens Health* **2008**, *8*, 14. [CrossRef] [PubMed]
51. Skouteris, H.; Hartley-Clark, L.; McCabe, M.; Milgrom, J.; Kent, B.; Herring, S.J.; Gale, J. Preventing excessive gestational weight gain: A systematic review of interventions. *Obes. Rev.* **2010**, *11*, 757–768. [CrossRef] [PubMed]
52. Goodarzi-Khoigani, M.; Baghiani Moghadam, M.H.; Nadjarzadeh, A.; Mardanian, F.; Fallahzadeh, H.; Mazloomy-Mahmoodabad, S. Impact of Nutrition Education in Improving Dietary Pattern During Pregnancy Based on Pender's Health Promotion Model: A Randomized Clinical Trial. *Iran. J. Nurs. Midwifery Res.* **2018**, *23*, 18–25. [CrossRef]
53. World Health Organization (WHO). *Healthy Diet*; World Health Organization: Geneva, Switzerland, 2018. Available online: https://www.who.int/publications/m/item/healthy-diet-factsheet394 (accessed on 20 March 2023).
54. IFN—Institute of Food and Nutrition, Pyramid of Healthy Nutrition and Physical Activity for Adults. 2019. Available online: https://ncez.pzh.gov.pl/aktywnosc-fizyczna/piramida-zdrowego-zywienia-i-aktywnosci-fizycznej-dla-osob-doroslych-2/ (accessed on 26 April 2023). (In Polish)
55. Skreden, M.; Bere, E.; Sagedal, L.R.; Vistad, I.; Øverby, N.C. Changes in fruit and vegetable consumption habits from pre-pregnancy to early pregnancy among Norwegian women. *BMC Pregnancy Childbirth* **2017**, *17*, 107. [CrossRef]
56. Slavin, J.L.; Lloyd, B. Health benefits of fruits and vegetables. *Adv. Nutr.* **2012**, *3*, 506–516. [CrossRef]
57. Prasadi, N.V.P.; Joye, I.J. Dietary Fibre from Whole Grains and Their Benefits on Metabolic Health. *Nutrients* **2020**, *12*, 3045. [CrossRef]
58. Tosh, S.M.; Bordenave, N. Emerging science on benefits of whole grain oat and barley and their soluble dietary fibers for heart health, glycemic response, and gut microbiota. *Nutr. Rev.* **2020**, *78*, 13–20. [CrossRef]
59. Semba, R.D.; Ramsing, R.; Rahman, N.; Kraemer, K.; Bloem, M.W. Legumes as a sustainable source of protein in human diets. *Glob. Food Sec.* **2021**, *28*, 100520. [CrossRef]
60. Miyahira, R.F.; Lopes, J.O.; Antunes, A.E.C. The Use of Sprouts to Improve the Nutritional Value of Food Products: A Brief Review. *Plant. Foods Hum. Nutr.* **2021**, *76*, 143–152. [CrossRef] [PubMed]
61. Xu, W.; Cater, M.; Gaitan, A.; Drewery, M.; Gravois, R.; Lammi-Keffe, C.J. Awareness of Listeria and high-risk food consumption behavior among pregnant women in Louisiana. *Food Control.* **2017**, *76*, 62–66. [CrossRef]
62. Barlik, M.; Seremak-Mrozikiewicz, A.; Drews, K. Listerioza w ciąży—Opis przypadku. *Ginekol. Pol.* **2014**, *85*, 309–313.
63. Bauer, P.W.; Broman, C.L.; Pivarnik, J.M. Exercise and pregnancy knowledge among healthcare providers. *J. Womens Health* **2010**, *19*, 335–341. [CrossRef]
64. Evenson, K.R.; Pompeii, L.A. Obstetrician practice patterns and recommendations for physical activity during pregnancy. *J. Womens Health* **2010**, *19*, 1733–1740. [CrossRef]
65. Burdick, L.; Mielke, G.I.; Parra, D.C.; Gomes, G.; Florindo, A.; Bracco, M.; Lobelo, F.; Simoes, E.J.; Pratt, M.; Ramos, L.R.; et al. Physicians', nurses' and community health workers' knowledge about physical activity in Brazil: A cross-sectional study. *Prev. Med. Rep.* **2015**, *2*, 467–472. [CrossRef]
66. Wise, N.J.; Arcamone, A.A. Survey of adolescent views of healthy eating during pregnancy. *MCN Am. J. Matern. Child. Nurs.* **2011**, *36*, 381–386. [CrossRef]
67. Thornton, P.L.; Kieffer, E.C.; Salabarría-Peña, Y.; Odoms-Young, A.; Willis, S.K.; Kim, H.; Salinas, M.A. Weight, diet, and physical activity-related beliefs and practices among pregnant and postpartum Latino women: The role of social support. *Matern. Child. Health J.* **2006**, *10*, 95–104. [CrossRef]

nutrients

MDPI

Article

Exposure to Phosphates and Nitrites through Meat Products: Estimation of the Potential Risk to Pregnant Women

Danijela Vranić [1], Jelena Milešević [2], Dejana Trbović [1], Mirjana Gurinović [2], Vladimir Koričanac [1], Milica Zeković [2], Zoran Petrović [1], Slavica Ranković [2] and Dragan Milićević [1,*]

[1] Institute of Meat Hygiene and Technology, Kaćanskog 13, 11040 Belgrade, Serbia; danijela.vranic@inmes.rs (D.V.); dejana.trbovic@inmes.rs (D.T.); vladimir.koricanac@inmes.rs (V.K.); zoran.petrovic@inmes.rs (Z.P.)

[2] Centre of Research Excellence in Nutrition and Metabolism, Institute for Medical Research, National Institute of Republic of Serbia, University of Belgrade, Tadeuša Košćuška 1, 11000 Belgrade, Serbia; jelena.milesevic@gmail.com (J.M.); mirjana.gurinovic@gmail.com (M.G.); zekovicmilica@gmail.com (M.Z.); slavica.rankovic.imr@gmail.com (S.R.)

* Correspondence: dragan.milicevic@inmes.rs

Abstract: Diet during pregnancy is one of the most important nutritional challenges associated with some risks for the mother and the fetus. For the first time, the study aims to estimate long-term (2018–2022) exposure to nitrate and phosphates in Serbian pregnant women, based on individual consumption data and accurate values measured in frequently consumed meat products. For this purpose, seven types of meat products, consisting of 3047 and 1943 samples, were collected from retail markets across Serbia, to analyze nitrites and phosphorus content, respectively. These data were combined with meat product consumption data from the Serbian National Food Consumption Survey to assess dietary intake of nitrites and phosphate. The results were compared with the acceptable daily intake (ADI) proposed by the European Food Safety Authority. The average dietary exposure (EDI) to phosphorus ranged from 0.733 mg/kg bw/day (liver sausage and pate) to 2.441 mg/kg bw/day (finely minced cooked sausages). Considering nitrite intake, the major sources were bacon (0.030 mg/kg bw/day) and coarsely minced cooked sausages (0.0189 mg/kg bw/day). In our study, average nitrite and phosphorus exposure in the Serbian pregnant women population are far below the EFSA recommendations (ADI 0.07 mg/kg bw/day and 40 mg/kg bw/day, respectively).

Keywords: food additives; nitrites; phosphates; pregnant women; meat products; exposure assessment

Citation: Vranić, D.; Milešević, J.; Trbović, D.; Gurinović, M.; Koričanac, V.; Zeković, M.; Petrović, Z.; Ranković, S.; Milićević, D. Exposure to Phosphates and Nitrites through Meat Products: Estimation of the Potential Risk to Pregnant Women. *Nutrients* **2023**, *15*, 2777. https://doi.org/10.3390/nu15122777

Academic Editor: Shannon L. Kelleher

Received: 19 April 2023
Revised: 1 June 2023
Accepted: 14 June 2023
Published: 16 June 2023

1. Introduction

Even though meat and meat products are one of the most important contributors of the modern diet, it is well known that the nutritional profile of processed meat has been perceived as unhealthy due to the high levels of saturated fatty acids, cholesterol [1], or components that could be considered with negative health impacts (sulfites, nitrites, and sodium). Moreover, elevated consumption of processed meat and red meat has been associated with cardiovascular diseases, colorectal, stomach, prostate, and pancreatic cancer [2]. According to an epidemiological study, processed meat has been classified as carcinogenic to humans (Group 1) while red meat is probably carcinogenic to humans (Group 2A) [3]. Because of this, there is growing interested in the processed meat industry to reduce food additives that could be considered unhealthy [4].

Nitrates and nitrites (E249–E252) are food additives of concern for humans' health because they may interact with secondary amines in the stomach, producing nitritesN-nitroso compounds (*N-NAs*), which could play a role in the carcinogenicity of processed meat [5,6]. Among meat products, cured meats often contain detectable levels of *N-NAs* mainly due to the use of nitrites as a preserving agent, additionally influenced by several processing factors (i.e., temperature, pH, and storage conditions) strongly linked by the presence of free amines, particularly biogenic amines [7].

Besides meat products, the occurrence of *N-NAs* has also been reported in other foods, such as processed vegetables, cereals, milk and dairy products, and alcoholic and non-alcoholic beverages, among others. Regarding other sources of *N-NAs* exposure, tobacco products (cigarettes, cigars) followed by products used in personal hygiene (cosmetics, hair products, lotions, shampoos, soaps, etc.) represent the important non-dietary exposure sources to *N-NAs* [6].

The high incidence of gastrointestinal cancer reported in the United Kingdom, Canada, Colombia, Chile, Japan, Denmark, and Italy has been correlated with elevated nitrite intake from food [8]. Moreover, nitrites and nitrates may cause methemoglobinemia, a blood disorder in which hemoglobin can carry oxygen but is unable to release it effectively to body tissues. It is also known that nitrites cross the placenta in pregnancy, causing methemoglobin formation in fetuses [9]. Some earlier studies have demonstrated the teratogenic effect of nitrites, emphasizing their toxicity and severe developmental defects on embryos or even spontaneous abortions [10]. An ADI is established for the additives that represent a concern for the consumers' health. The European Commission, according to the Scientific Opinion of the Panel on Food Additives and Nutrient Sources added to Food (ANS) using a Benchmark Dose (BMD) approach, recommended an ADI of 0.07 mg nitrite ion/kg bw per day [7].

On the other hand, phosphates are used as food additives (E338–E341, E343, E450–E452) to improve food quality. Excessive intake of phosphates via consuming processed meat products can lead to various adverse effects on human health inducing anionic imbalance. An association between high serum phosphate levels and cardiovascular morbidity and mortality in patients with chronic kidney disease and bone health complications has long been known [11]. Therefore, high phosphorus intake from additives should be considered as a potential public health concern. For this purpose, the Scientific Committee for Food [11] derived a group acceptable daily intake (ADI) for phosphates expressed as phosphorus of 40 mg/kg bw/day and concluded that this ADI does not have adverse effects on human health.

Maximum permitted levels of food additives are set at the international level by the WHO-FAO JECFA and the European Food Safety Authority (EFSA) with the aim to ensure that additives are used properly to minimize potential risks to human health. Furthermore, under the European Directive [12], all Member States are obligated to monitor intakes to ensure that consumers do not have an excessive intake of a given food additive, which could lead to a health hazard. The current Serbian legislation has restricted the concentration of residual $NaNO_2$ in processed meat to 100 and 150 mg/kg depending on the type of product [13,14], whereas regulations in Europe state that the maximum residual level (expressed as $NaNO_2$) amount of nitrites that may be added to the processed meat during manufacturing should be from 50 to 180 mg/kg, particularly for dry-cured meat products such as bacon (175 mg/kg), for dry non-heat-treated meat products (50 mg/kg), and for other dry-cured meat products such as dry-cured ham (100 mg/kg), with several exemptions [12,15]. In terms of phosphorus used as a food additive, the Serbian standard maximum limit for total phosphorus expressed as P_2O_5 in meat products is less than 8 g/kg [14] or $\leq$5 g/kg of added phosphorus [13].

Diet during pregnancy is one of the most important nutritional challenges that may be associated with some risks for the health of mothers and the development of the fetus. In this context, a healthy and balanced diet is of the utmost importance during pregnancy and is an ongoing task for health care. Although nitrates and nitrites alone are considered to have no or limited carcinogenic potential [16], there are major human health concerns raised regarding nitrite intake, due to their potential conversion to form *N-NAs*. Based on the literature data, on associations between dietary intake of meat products, nitrite content, and cancer, the genotoxic properties of the *N-NAs* have been extensively investigated [6,17]. The high and frequent consumption of meat products, containing harmful substances such as nitrites, increases the risk of colorectal cancer and thyroid tumor promotion and adversely affects reproductive outcomes (e.g., fetal loss, reduced number of litters and live births, and neonatal mortality). Moreover, some studies reported a correlation between excessive dietary nitrite intake and a higher risk of development of neural tube defects [18,19] or even pediatric brain tumors in offspring [20].

Considering above mentioned rational and following our previous nitrites and phosphate studies [21–23], this study objective was to, for the first time, estimate dietary intake of nitrate and phosphates in Serbian pregnant women, based on individual consumption data and accurate values measured in most consumed groups of meat products. In addition, as a predictive model, i.e., "worse-case" scenario, values at the MPL was used in order to determine the level of reaching or exceeding ADI values for these two additives in meat products as a measure of identifying potential risk.

2. Materials and Methods

2.1. Meat Products and Sample Preparation

In the present study, 3047 meat product samples obtained from different regions of the Serbian retail market for the purposes of official controls by veterinary inspectors or for self-monitoring purposes of the meat producers during 2018–2022 were analyzed for nitrite content. Samples were divided into seven groups, including 381 bacon, 244 dry meat, 406 coarsely minced cooked sausages, 822 dry fermented sausages, 747 finely minced cooked sausages, 87 liver sausage and pate, and 423 smoked meat products, produced by the Serbian meat industry or imported.

In the same period of investigation, a total of 1943 meat product samples were categorized into five groups including bacon (298), coarsely minced cooked sausages (405), finely minced cooked sausages (718), liver sausage and pate (86), and smoked meat products (436) were analyzed for phosphorous content.

All samples of meat products were kept at refrigeration temperature and analyzed within 48 h. If the analyses were not conducted within the same day, the samples were stored in a refrigerator at 4 °C until required for testing.

The analyzed samples were thawed and blended in a commercial kitchen blender unit (Homogenizator Blixer 2, Robot Coupe, Vincennes, France (2.9 L) 700 w, 3000 rpm). For each sample, two composite samples were prepared. All samples were then analyzed in duplicate.

2.2. Determination of Sodium Nitrite Content

The content of sodium nitrites-$NaNO_2$, which is usually added to meat products—was examined in meat products according to the standard ISO procedure [24]. A representative sample amount (~10 g) was measured in a 300 mL flask using an analytical balance (Mettler, AE 200, Columbus, OH, USA), followed by the addition of a solution of hydrous sodium borate, $Na_2B_4O_7{\cdot}10H_2O$ (50 g/L) and 100 mL deionized water at 70.0 ± 0.2 °C. Residual nitrite extraction was achieved by keeping the samples in a hot water bath, at the temperature of boiling, for 15 min, and every 5 min, flasks were shaken vigorously. After cooling, 2 mL of each Carrez solution (Carezz reagent I and Carezz reagent II) was added and mixed thoroughly. Samples were then diluted to 200 mL with deionized water. Samples were filtered through quantitative cellulose filters (pore size < 5 μm). Color generation was achieved by transferring an aliquot of the filtrate (25 mL) to a 100 mL volumetric flask and adding 10 mL of the sulfanilamide solution and then 6 mL conc. HCl. Flasks were stored in the dark for 5 min. Subsequently, 2 mL solution of *N*-naftil-1-ethylenediamine-chloride (0.25 g/250 mL) was added to each flask and moved to the dark for 3 min. Thereafter, samples were diluted to 100 mL. Absorbance was measured at 538 nm using a spectrophotometer (UV/VIS Spectrophotometer, Jenway 6405, East Lyme, CT, USA). A procedural blank was run with every batch of samples.

Calibration curves were generated using concentration levels ranging from 2.5 to 10 $NaNO_3$ μg mL^{-1}, Y = 0.0669X + 0.024: R^2 = 0.999. A recovery study of the analytical procedure was carried out by spiking several already analyzed samples with standard solutions, and recovery rates were found to be between 87% and 94%. The nitrite content is expressed as $NaNO_2$ ($mg \cdot kg^{-1}$), following c × 2000/m × V, where c is the concentration of $NaNO_2$ (μg/mL) from the calibration curve, m is the mass of sample (g) for analysis, and V is a volume of an aliquot of the filtrate used for spectrometric determination.

The limit of detection (LOD) was considered to take the same value as the limit of quantification (LOQ) (0.03 mg/kg).

2.3. Determination of Phosphorus Content

The total phosphorus content, expressed as P_2O_5 (g/kg), in examined meat products was determined according to the standard ISO procedure [25]. The total phosphorus content, expressed as P_2O_5 (g/kg), in examined meat products was determined according to the standard ISO procedure [25]. In brief, a ~5 g portion of samples (measured using an analytical balance (Mettler, AE 200, USA)) was ashed at the maximum temperature of 500 °C in a muffle furnace (LE 14/11/R7, Nabertherm, Lilienthal, Germany). On completion of the digestion, the white ash was dissolved by heating with dilute nitric acid (1 + 1, *v*/*v*) and quantitatively transferred to a 100 mL flask. Then, made up by the addition of deionized water, and after mixing, the solution was then filtered, and the first 5 to 10 mL were discarded.

Aliquots (20 mL) of the treated solution were pipetted into 100 mL volumetric flasks and mixed thoroughly with 30 mL ammonium heptamolybdate solution 50 g/L. The resulting solution was then diluted to the volume with deionized water. After 15 min at room temperature, the absorbance was read against a reagent blank at 430 ± 2 nm using a UV-visible spectrophotometer (UV/VIS Spectrophotometer, Jenway 6405).

The standard curve was determined under the same conditions as those for the samples using potassium dihydrogen phosphate as a standard (10–60 P_2O_5 μg/mL; $Y = 0.0187X - 0.0096$: $R^2 = 0.9999$). A recovery study of the analytical procedure was carried out by spiking several already analyzed samples with standard solutions, and recovery rates were found to be between 89% and 95%. The total phosphorus content is expressed as P_2O_5 (g/kg), following c/20 m, where c is the concentration of P_2O_5 (μg/mL) from the calibration curve and m is the mass of the sample (g) for analysis.

The LOD was estimated at 0.0024 g/kg, while the LOQ for phosphorus as P_2O_5 was 0.081 g/kg.

2.4. Meat Products Consumption Data

The National Food Consumption Survey on adults including pregnant women, in compliance with the EFSA EU Menu methodology [26], was conducted between 2017 and 2022 and included a total of 145 pregnant women. EFSA EU Menu methodology considers the use of set of questionnaires: a general questionnaire on sociodemographic and anthropometric characteristics of the participants, an age-appropriate Food Propensity Questionnaire (FPQ), that is used to determine the frequency of food groups' consumption in a year, and a twice-repeated 24 h dietary recall. All the data are collected in the required format following the EU Menu framework, to provide harmonious and standardized data collection in all countries in Europe [27]. The consumed portion sizes were estimated based on natural units, household measures, packaging information, and a validated national Food Atlas for Portion Size Estimation [28]. The study was conducted in four geographical regions of Serbia (Belgrade, Vojvodina, Southeast Serbia, and West Serbia).

In this study, the following data were used: anthropometric characteristics of the participants, i.e., age, body weight, and height measurements, and intake data of meat products. This study assessed the consumption of meat products (per meat product type and on average) in a pregnant population. Consumed meat products were categorized into seven categories which were defined according to the actual Serbian Regulation on the quality of meat products [14]. The study group age is divided into two groups, to better describe characteristics of the population and age distribution, but is later not correlated in the exposure assessments, as both age groups belong to the same, adult population groups in the reference values—ADI and EDI—by the EFSA.

2.5. Exposure Assessment and Risk Characterization

According to the European Commission [29], there are three types of approaches to estimate the dietary exposure from food additives that pose a concern to human health:

(1) Tier 1: Estimation of the theoretical maximum daily intake by combining the maximum quantity of food and drinks that can be consumed by an individual with the maximum permitted level (MPL) of an additive.
(2) Tier 2: The use of individual consumption data multiplying with the MPL of the selected additives.
(3) Tier 3: The use of an individual Food Consumption Database (FCD) combined with the accurate measured values of selected additives.

The estimated daily intake (EDI) of nitrite and phosphate additives from processed meat by pregnant women included in this study was calculated using the Tier 3 approach, by combining data on individual food consumption patterns in pregnant women (g/day) with data on the levels of this type of additive in the investigated samples and division by the population's average body weight (Table 1). Additionally, the mean value regarding the body weight of the investigated population of pregnant women obtained in our study is in accordance with EFSA recommendations, where a body weight of 70 kg should be used as the default for the European adult population [30].

Table 1. Baseline characteristics of study participants.

Age	N	Body Weight (kg)					
		P25	**P50**	**P75**	**P95**	**Mean ± SD**	**Range (Min–Max)**
18–29	60	62.0	70.0	75.7	89.9	70.3 ± 11.2^{A}	50–107.1
30–43	85	64.2	71.0	78.0	97.6	72.9 ± 13.9^{A}	50–141
Total	145	63.1	70.5	76.9	93.8	71.8 ± 12.9	50–141
Meat Product		Distribution of processed meat daily intake of the pregnant s population (g/day).					
Bacon		10.7	25.0	48.5	74.5	30.8 ± 21.7^{A}	2.9–75.8
Dry meat		34.6	50.0	72.7	100.0	54.0 ± 27.8	12.8–125
Coarsely minced cooked sausages		35.0	50.0	100.0	100.0	64.0 ± 35.1	20–100
Dry fermented sausages		30.0	45.1	53.9	236.4	65.4 ± 64.2	25–240
Finely minced cooked sausages		46.8	72.5	137.5	152.0	84.8 ± 46.3^{B}	36.6–152
Liver sausage and pate		28.8	42.5	50.0	72.5	42.0 ± 15.8	25–75
Smoked meat products		17.1	25.0	47.5	170.0	37.6 ± 39.7^{A}	10–200
Average		22.45	41.69	55.02	150	49.58 ± 40.7	2.96–240

N—number of participants; Means with different superscripts in the same column are significantly different ($p < 0.05$).

In addition to the abovementioned method, the exposure assessment included certain assumptions of the worst-case scenario, so two levels of consumption were considered—mean and high consumer (P95 percentile)—assuming the maximum use level of these compounds defined by Serbian regulation [13,14] in meat processing combined with individual consumption data (Tier 2). For risk characterization, obtained results were then compared with the ADI values established by the European Union [7,11]. Relative contributions of processed meat products to the dietary intake of nitrites and phosphorus for pregnant women was expressed as a percentage of the ADI established at 0.07 mg/kg body weight/day and 40 mg/kg body weight/day, for nitrites and phosphorus, respectively. Taking into consideration adaptive changes in phosphorus metabolism that occur during pregnancy and lactation, the ADI for adults (40 mg/kg bw/day) could be also applied to pregnant and lactating women [31].

As international guidelines recommend [32] when calculating dietary exposure, all non-detected results, i.e., below the LOD or the LOQ, are known as left-censored. According to this guidance, for dietary exposure assessments where less than 60% of the results were left-censored, middle-bound (all non-detected results to the LOD/2) exposure scenarios were considered [32].

2.6. Statistical Analysis

Data were analyzed using Minitab statistical software version 17 (Minitab Ink., Coventry, UK). The results are presented in the form of descriptive statistics (mean ± standard deviation—SD) and their distribution (percentiles, and ranges). The normality of the distribution of the of the data were checked using by Kolmogorov–Smirnov normality test. One-way analysis of variance (ANOVA) followed by Tukey's test was used to compare the dietary intake of phosphorous and nitrites among different meat products. The level of significance was set at $p < 0.05$.

3. Results

The mean and range of baseline characteristics of participants included in this study are presented in Table 1. The mean weight of the pregnant women included in this survey ranged from 70.34 ± 11.21 kg to 72.92 ± 13.93 kg (average 71.85 ± 12.90 kg). No statistically significant difference ($p > 0{,}05$) was observed between these two ages group of pregnant women in body weight. Regarding meat consumption, based on 145 participants interviewed, the highest average value of meat product consumption obtained in our research was for finely minced cooked sausages (84.83 ± 46.33 g/day), followed by dry fermented sausages (65.44 ± 64.22 g/day), while the lowest consumption was for bacon (30.84 ± 21.77 g/day). A statistically significant difference ($p < 0.05$) was found between the daily intake of bacon and finely minced cooked sausages and between the daily intake of finely minced cooked sausages and smoked meat products.

The mean, median, and 95th percentile levels of residual nitrites ($NaNO_2$ and NO_2^-) and phosphorus (P_2O_5 and P^-) in examined processed meat products over the period of 2018–2022 are summarized in Tables 2 and 3. Nitrites were detected in 2443 (80%) of the total of 3047 analyzed meat product samples (Table 2). The results obtained in our study reveal that nitrite concentration varied with the type of meat product. The highest level of occurrence (99%) and mean residual level of nitrites, expressed as $NaNO_2$, was detected in finely minced cooked sausages (38.72 ± 20.52 mg/kg), followed by coarsely minced cooked sausages (31.86 ± 23.30 mg/kg), while the lowest incidence (45%) and mean residual level of nitrite, as $NaNO_2$, was detected in dry fermented sausages (1.44 ± 2.35 mg/kg). The average concentration of nitrites in the analyzed meat products was 19.56 ± 22.83 mg/kg. These results are far below the national Serbian or EU-regulated limit of 150 mg/kg [12,13]. In the current study, only one sample of smoked meat products exceeded the maximum permitted level of nitrites (data not shown). There were no statistically significant differences ($p > 0.05$) between the mean residual level of nitrite in bacon and liver sausage and pate, between dry meat and liver sausage and pate, and between dry meat and dry fermented sausages.

Phosphorus was detected in all analyzed meat product samples (1943) (Table 3). The average concentration of phosphorus, expressed as P_2O_5, in the analyzed meat products was 5.03 ± 1.37 g/kg within the range of 0.27 to 10.64 g/kg. The highest mean concentration and level of phosphorus, as P_2O_5, was found in smoked meat products (6.16 ± 1.38 g/kg and 10.64 g/kg, respectively), followed by coarsely minced cooked sausages (5.23 ± 1.14 g/kg and 9.92 g/kg, respectively), while the lowest mean concentration was found in liver sausage and pate (2.87 ± 0.95 g/kg). The results obtained in this study imply that the level of phosphorus in a total of 34 (1.7%) of the examined samples (except bacon and liver sausages and pate) exceeded the maximum permitted limit (MPL) of <8 g/kg as defined by the Serbian regulation [14] (Table 3).

Table 2. Ranges of residual nitrite levels expressed as $NaNO_2$ and nitrite ion (NO_2^-), consumption of processed meat products (g/day), dietary exposure to nitrite (mg/kg bw/day), and relative contributions of processed meat products to nitrite exposure.

Meat Product	*N*	*n* (%)	Mean ± SD	P50	P95	Range (Min–Max)	ADC (g/day)	EDI (mg/kg bw/Day)		Contribution to ADI (%)	
			$NaNO_2$(NO_2^-)(mg/kg)				Mean ± SD	Mean	P95	Mean	P95
Bacon	318	296 (93.1)	14.16 ± 17.72 ^{A} (9.44 ± 11.81)	6.61 (4.40)	53.20 (35.47)	<0.03–100.38 (<0.03–66.92)	30.84 ± 21.77 ^{A}	0.0041	0.0094	5.79	13.45
Dry meat	244	168 (69.0)	4.86 ± 10.96 ^{B,C} (3.24 ± 7.31)	1.61 (1.07)	22.44 (14.96)	<0.03–97.30 (<0.03–64.87)	54.07 ± 27.88	0.0024	0.0056	3.49	7.99
Coarsely minced cooked sausages	406	396 (97.5)	31.86 ± 23.30 ^{E} (21.24 ± 15.53)	29.70 (19.80)	71.14 (47.43)	<0.03–113.51 (<0.03–75.67)	64.00 ± 35.07	0.0189	0.0296	27.03	42.23
Dry fermented sausages	822	372 (45.0)	1.44 ± 2.35 ^{C} (0.96 ± 1.57)	0.53 (0.35)	5.97 (3.98)	<0.03–24.88 (<0.03–16.59)	65.44 ± 64.22	0.0009	0.0032	1.26	4.54
Finely minced cooked sausages	747	742 (99.0)	38.72 ± 20.52 ^{F} (25.82 ± 13.68)	39.25 (26.17)	70.98 (47. 32)	<0.03–106.16 (<0.03–70.77)	84.83 ± 46.33 ^{B}	0.0305	0.0546	43.54	78.02
Liver sausage and pate	87	69 (79.0)	8.49 ± 8.49 ^{A,B} (5.66 ± 5.55)	5.21 (3.47)	25.55 (17.03)	<0.03–30.39 (<0.03–20.26)	42.00± 15.85	0.0033	0.0053	4.73	7.60
Smoked meat products	423	400 (94.5)	23.94 ± 23.21 ^{D} (15.96 ± 15.47)	19.06 (12.71)	68.92 (45.95)	<0.03–180.25 (<0.03–120.17)	37.61 ± 39.76 ^{A}	0.0084	0.0311	11.94	44.43
Average	3047	2443 (80.0)	19.56 ± 22.83 (13.04 ± 15.22)	7.62 (5.08)	63.36 (42.24)	<0.03–180.25 (<0.03–120.17)	49.58 ± 40.74	0.0098	0.0198	13.07	28.32

N—total number of analyzed samples; *n*-number of samples that contained nitrites (%); Nitrite ion content (66.65% of $NaNO_2$); Means values with different superscripts in the same column are statistically significantly different ($p < 0.05$); ADC–average daily consumption of meat products (g/day); EDI—estimated daily intake (mg/kg bw/day); ADI—acceptable daily intake of nitrite ion (NO_2^-) (0.07 mg/kg bw/day) [7]; LOQ—limit of quantification = 0.03 mg/kg.

Table 3. Range of phosphorus levels (P_2O_5 and P), consumption of processed meat products (g/day), dietary exposure to phosphorus (mg/kg bw/day), and relative contributions of processed meat products to phosphorus exposure.

Meat Product	*N*	Mean ± SD	P50	P95	Range (Min–Max)	Above MPL (%)	ADC (g/day)	EDI (mg/kg bw/Day)		Contribution to MTDI (%)	
		P_2O_5 (P^-), (g/kg)					Mean ± Sd	Mean	P95	Mean	P95
Bacon	298	4.40 ± 1.28 ^{A} (1.92 ± 0.48)	4.38 (1.91)	6.72 (2.93)	1.10–7.95 (0.48–3.47)		30.84 ± 21.77 ^{A}	0.82	1.92	2.06	4.79
Coarsely minced cooked sausages	405	5.23 ± 1.14 ^{B} (2.28 ± 0.50)	5.12 (2.23)	7.31 (3.19)	2.25–9.92 (0.98–4.33)	7 (1.7)	64.00 ± 35.07 ^{c}	2.04	3.18	5.09	7.95
Finely minced cooked sausages	718	4.74 ± 0.91 ^{C} (2.07 ± 0.40)	4.63 (2.02)	6.20 (2.71)	1.12–9.22 (0.49–4.02)	6 (0.8)	84.83 ± 46.33 ^{B}	2.44	4.37	6.10	10.93
Liver sausage and pate	86	2.87 ± 0.95 ^{D} (1.25 ± 0.41)	2.77 (1.21)	4.08 (1.78)	0.27–7.96 (0.12–3.47)		42.00 ± 15.85	0.73	1.18	1.83	2.95
Smoked meat products	436	6.16 ± 1.38 ^{E} (2.69 ± 0.60)	6.12 (2.67)	7.98 (3.48)	1.01–10.64 (0.44–4.04)	21 (5.0)	37.61 ± 39.76 ^{A}	1.41	5.24	3.52	13.09
Average	1943	5.03 ± 1.37 (2.19 ± 0.60)	4.88 (2.13)	7.67 (3.35)	0.27–10.64 (0.12–4.64)	34 (1.7)	45.94 ± 38.09	1.49	3.18	3.72	7.94

N—total number of analyzed samples; P content was 43.64% of P_2O_5; MPL—maximum permitted level ($\leq$8 g/kg); Means with different superscripts in the same column are significantly different ($p < 0.05$); ADC—average daily consumption of meat products (g/day); EDI—estimated daily intake (mg/kg bw/day); MTDI—maximum tolerable daily intake of phosphorus (P) (40 mg/kg bw/day) [11].

Exposure (mean, median, and 95th percentile) and the contribution of meat products to the daily nitrite intake of the pregnant women considered in this study are presented in Table 2 and Figure 1. Overall, dietary nitrite exposure at the mean and 95th percentile did not exceed the ADI for nitrite (0.07 mg/kg bw/day) [7] (Table 2). The main contributors to dietary exposure to nitrites were finely minced cooked sausages (43.54%), followed by coarsely minced cooked sausages (28%) and smoked meat products (12%), while the contribution of other groups was less than 10% (Figure 1).

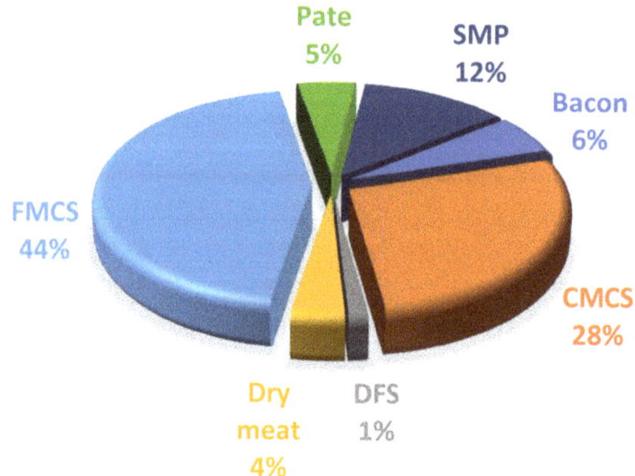

Figure 1. Relative contributions (%) of processed meat products to nitrite daily intake; CMCS—coarsely minced cooked sausages; DFS—dry fermented sausages; FMCS—finely minced cooked sausages; SMP—smoked meat products.

The main meat product contributing to dietary exposure to phosphates in our study was found to be finely minced cooked sausages, accounting for 33%, followed by coarsely minced cooked sausages (27%), smoked meat products (19%), bacon (11%), and liver sausage and pate (10%) (Figure 2). Hence, mean and 95th percentile exposure to phosphates in our study is far below this ADI (40 mg/kg bw/day) [11] (Table 3).

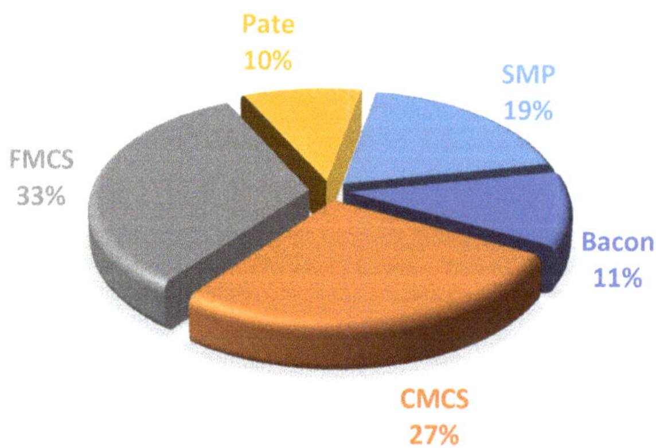

Figure 2. Relative contributions (%) of processed meat products to phosphorus daily intake; CMCS—coarsely minced cooked sausages; FMCS—finely minced cooked sausages; SMP—smoked meat products.

The results for the estimated daily intake and the relative percent contribution of each meat product included in this study to nitrite and phosphate exposure, combining individual consumption data with the MPL of the nitrite and phosphate additives (Tier 2 approach), are presented in Tables 4 and 5. The major contributors to excess nitrite ADI are finely minced cooked sausages, followed by dry fermented sausages and coarsely minced cooked sausages, at 168.62%, 130.11%, and 127.25%, respectively (Table 4).

Table 4. Scenario 2. Dietary exposure to nitrites by using actual national food consumption data and MPLs (Tier 2).

Meat Product	Daily Consumption of Meat Products (g/Day)			$NaNO_2$ (NO_2^-) (mg/kg)	EDI (mg/kg bw/Day)			Contribution to ADI (%)		
	Mean ± SD	P50	P95		Mean	P50	P95	Mean	P50	P95
Bacon	30.84 ± 21.77	25.00	74.55	150 * (100)	0.043	0.035	0.100	61.32	49.71	142.48
Dry meat	54.07 ± 27.88	50.00	100.00		0.075	0.070	0.173	107.51	99.41	246.46
Coarsely minced cooked sausages	64.00 ± 35.07	50.00	100.00		0.059	0.070	0.139	127.25	99.41	198.83
Dry fermented sausages	65.44 ± 64.22	45.10	236.40		0.091	0.063	0.329	130.11	89.62	470.03
Finely minced cooked sausages	84.83 ± 46.33	72.50	152.00		0.118	0.101	0.212	168.67	144.15	302.22
Liver sausage and pate	42.00 ± 15.85	42.50	72.50		0.058	0.059	0.094	83.51	84.50	134.21
Smoked meat products	37.61 ± 39.76	25.00	170.00		0.052	0.035	0.195	74.78	49.70	278.36
Average	49.58 ± 40.74	41.69	150.00		0.075	0.101	0.177	107.59	88.07	253.23

* MPL—maximum permitted level of $NaNO_2$ (150 mg/kg); EDI—estimated daily intake (mg/kg bw/day); ADI—acceptable daily intake of nitrite ion (NO_2^-) (0.07 mg/kg bw/day) [7].

Table 5. Scenario 2. Dietary exposure to phosphorus by using actual national food consumption data and MPLs (Tier 2).

Meat Product	Daily Consumption of Meat Products (g/Day)			P_2O_5 (P^-) (g/kg)	EDI (mg/kg bw/Day)			Contribution to MTDI (%)		
	Mean ± SD	P50	P95		Mean	P50	P95	Mean	P50	P95
Bacon	30.84 ± 21.77	25.00	71.70	≤8 * (3.49)	1.500	1.215	3.482	3.75	3.04	8.70
Coarsely minced cooked sausages	64.00 ± 35.07	50.00	100.00		3.110	2.430	4.860	7.77	6.07	12.15
Finely minced cooked sausages	84.83 ± 46.33	72.50	152.00		4.122	3.523	7.390	10.30	8.81	18.46
Liver sausage and pate	42.00 ± 15.85	42.50	67.50		2.041	2.065	3.280	5.10	5.16	8.20
Smoked meat products	37.61 ± 39.76	25.00	140.00		1.830	1.215	6.803	4.57	3.04	17.01
Average	45.94 ± 38.09	36.50	150.70		2.520	2.089	5.162	6.30	5.22	12.90

* MPL—maximum permitted level for phosphorus (≤8 g/kg); MTDI—maximum tolerable daily intake of phosphorus (P) (40 mg/kg bw/day) [11].

Concerning exposure to phosphates, in the worst-case scenario (Tier 2 approach), the meat products identified as the main contributor to phosphate intake were finely minced cooked sausages (10.30%), followed by coarsely minced cooked sausages (7.77%) and liver sausage and pate (5.10%) (Table 5). This is because these meat products were consumed in large quantities.

4. Discussion

The present study provides new information about pregnant women's exposure to food-grade additives—nitrites and phosphorus via meat products. Pregnant women are considered more vulnerable to chemicals, particularly to ones which have carcinogenic and teratogenic properties because exposure occurs during the development of an embryo or fetus. Although nitrate and nitrites alone are considered to have no or limited carcinogenic potential [16], there are major human health concerns raised regarding nitrite intake, due to their potential conversion to form *N-NAs*. Based on the literature data, on associations between dietary intake of meat products, nitrite content, and cancer, the genotoxic properties of the *N-NAs* have been extensively investigated [6,17]. Although the primary sources of dietary nitrates and nitrites are vegetables, nitrates/nitrites from animal sources were attributable to an increase in cancer risk for the presence of amines, amides, and amides and heme iron that favor the increased production of *N-NAs* carcinogens. Consequently, there is a trend to reduce or eliminate these compounds in meats [33].

The present study showed a wide range of nitrite levels within and between the meat products at 0.05–180.25 mg/kg and is comparable to those reported by Nurul Farhanah Haji Abd Hamid [34] at 0.5–140.6 mg/kg. However, the mean and P95 residual nitrite levels in analyzed samples were below the maximum permitted limit specified by Serbian or EU regulations (150 mg/kg) [12,13]. These findings are consistent with previously reported nitrites content in sausages by Bajčić et al. [35] and Vranić et al. [22] at 0.65–36.60 mg/kg and 1.86–40.35 mg/kg (mean 12.96 mg/kg), respectively.

The dry fermented sausage samples were found to have the lowest amount of nitrites at 1.44 $\pm$ 2.35, followed by dry meat (4.86 $\pm$ 10.96 mg/kg), and these values were much lower compared to the other types of sausages. These findings are unexpected because the shorter shelf life was valid for coarsely or finely minced cooked sausage products, which were mostly less than 90 days, hence a lower amount of nitrate and nitrite additives were necessary to add. In this study, the highest health risks regarding nitrite intake by consuming meat products are in finely minced cooked sausages followed by coarsely minced cooked sausages (mean 0.0305 mg/kg bw/day and 0.0189 mg/kg bw/day, respectively). Consumption of finely minced cooked sausages at 152 g/day recorded in our study is of high concern, contributing to 0.054 mg/kg bw/day or 78.02% of the nitrite ADI (0.07 mg/kg bw/day), while the least risk was from dry fermented sausages with a level of 0.0009 mg/kg bw/day or 1.26% of the nitrite ADI.

Phosphorus is an essential nutrient, occurring in foods of animal origin as a natural component and an approved ingredient added during food processing. Thus, JECFA proposed to assign a "maximum tolerable daily intake" (MTDI) rather than an ADI. The phosphorus EDI ranged from 0.733 to 2.445 mg/kg bw/day, representing 1.83 and 6.10% of the ADI specified by the EFSA [11]. The major contributor to phosphorus intake for pregnant women was finely minced cooked sausage (33% of phosphorus intake) and coarsely minced cooked sausage (27% of phosphorus intake) consumption. In both scenarios, the exposure does not exceed the ADI of 40 mg/kg bw per day (Tables 3 and 5). However, ADI did not apply to populations with chronic kidney disease (CKD) or cardiovascular disease (CVD), considered a vulnerable population group. Thus, assessment of the EDI for those who consume phosphorus-rich food products regularly was important.

Although most authorized food additives are used at a lower level than the MPL, to ensure a high level of consumer protection, in addition we created a worst-case scenario for our risk assessment. The Tier 2 approach included certain assumptions of the worst-case scenario assuming the maximum use level of these food additives defined by the EU Regulation [12] in meat processing and the mean and highest percentile (95th percentile) of food-intake consumers. The Tier 2 intake estimates for nitrites and phosphorus are presented in Tables 4 and 5. The differences between the results of nitrites and phosphates exposure obtained with two different exposure scenarios (Tier 2 and Tier 3 approaches) were significant. As expected, in the Tier 2 approach, exposure was considerably above the ADI. The major contributors to exceeding the ADI of nitrites and phosphates in this approach were finely minced cooked sausages, dry fermented sausages, and coarsely minced cooked sausages. These results could be explained by the fact that they were consumed in high quantities.

The strength of this study is in the fact that this exposure assessment determines a realistic dietary intake of nitrites and phosphorus additives based on data from national food consumption surveys and the concentrations of nitrites and phosphorus in each meat product measured analytically as practiced by EFSA [29]. From a broader perspective, these findings could be accepted as the most accurate reflection of current industry practices in Serbia. Furthermore, they complement and confirm the findings on nitrites and phosphorus content, obtained from laboratory analysis of meat products previously reported by the authors [21–23,35]. Bearing in mind that this provides new information about the dietary intake of nitrate and phosphates in Serbian pregnant women, using the method proposed by EFSA [29], the present survey has a lot of strengths and emphasizes the importance of monitoring the added amounts of food additives and why dietary exposure assessment must be continued.

Considering the wide range of nitrites and phosphorus concentration levels within the meat products, we are aware of some limitations of our study. Thus, further study is necessary to consider the brand loyalty scenario. Very comprehensive studies revealed that consumers always tend to buy products of a given brand, which could have a higher concentration of additives than others [36]. Another limitation of this study lies in the circumstance that data on pregnancy state (trimesters) was not collected and correlation with exposure to observed additives could not be performed. This should be considered in the design of exposure studies in pregnancy in the future.

The results of our study are not easily compared with others. To the best of our knowledge, so far, no studies on the exposure to nitrites and phosphorus by meat products in pregnant women were identified. In our study, the consumption of several meat product types exceeds the recommended intake ($\leq$50 g/day) [37]. Consumption of industrially processed meat products, high in calories, fats, and salt with additives such as nitrites, has a cumulative detrimental effect on the overall health of pregnant women, i.e., an unnecessary increase in weight, swelling, water retention in the body, and can increase the risk of high blood pressure in pregnancy and the occurrence of preeclampsia. Balancing the diet with a wider variety of (less processed) foods could help consumers of this kind reduce their intake of nitrosamines.

5. Conclusions

Our study revealed that the population of pregnant women in Serbia is not at risk of exceeding the ADI for nitrites or phosphates from the consumption of processed meat. Furthermore, food-grade additive nitrites and phosphates as currently used in industry practices in Serbia do not result in excessive exposure to the populations of pregnant women, even at the highest food consumption level (95%). Despite this, these results should be interpreted with caution, as other dietary sources of nitrites and phosphorus must be considered. Results in our study confirm that the Tier 2 approach can lead to overestimated exposure to additives, because the measured level of nitrites and phosphates was far below the MPL in meat products. Although we used the representative National Food Consumption Database, it is reasonable to assume that eating habits tend to change over the years. Therefore, it is mandatory to establish monitoring systems for the use and intake of food additives to ensure that the ADI is not exceeded. The application of nitrites should be decreased and controlled. For this reason, a further investigation into the presence of *N-NAs* in food of animal origin will be of great interest. Besides this, the study demonstrates the need for community work on raising awareness and constant education on healthy nutrition during pregnancy that includes information on the detrimental effects that additives can have on infants and offers advice on alternative healthier dietary options.

Author Contributions: Conceptualization, D.M.; methodology, D.M., J.M., M.G. and D.V.; software, D.M., J.M. and M.Z.; validation, D.V., D.T. and Z.P.; formal analysis, D.V., J.M. and V.K.; investigation, D.V., J.M., M.Z. and S.R.; data curation, D.V. and Z.P.; writing—original draft preparation, D.M. and J.M.; writing—review and editing, D.M., J.M. and M.G.; visualization, D.M.; supervision, M.G.; project administration, M.G.; funding acquisition, D.M.; J.M. and M.G. All authors have read and agreed to the published version of the manuscript.

Funding: This study was supported by the Ministry of Science, Technological Development and Innovation, Republic of Serbia, Grant No. 451-03-47/2023-01/200050 and 451-03-47/2023-01/200015 from 03.02.2023.

Institutional Review Board Statement: The study was conducted in accordance with the guidelines laid down in the Declaration of Helsinki and all procedures involving human subjects were approved by the Institute for Medical Research Ethics Committee in Serbia on 8 December 2017 (EO 123/2017).

Informed Consent Statement: Informed consent was obtained from all subjects involved in the study.

Data Availability Statement: Results attained in this study are included in the manuscript. Individual data are not available due to official legal, organizational and data security policies, and ethical restrictions.

Acknowledgments: Authors declare gratitude to Agnes Kadvan for the support in data processing and other IT issues.

Conflicts of Interest: The authors declare no conflict of interest.

References

1. Bechthold, A.; Boeing, H.; Schwedhelm, C.; Hoffmann, G.; Knüppel, S.; Iqbal, K.; De Henauw, S.; Michels, N.; Devleesschauwer, B.; Schlesinger, S.; et al. Food groups and risk of coronary heart disease, stroke, and heart failure: A systematic review and dose-response meta-analysis of prospective studies. *Crit. Rev. Food Sci. Nutr.* **2019**, *59*, 1071–1090. [CrossRef] [PubMed]
2. Boada, L.D.; Henriquez-Hernandez, L.A.; Luzardo, O.P. The impact of red and processed meat consumption on cancer and other health outcomes: Epidemiological evidences. *Food Chem. Toxicol.* **2016**, *92*, 236–244. [CrossRef] [PubMed]
3. IARC. Monographs on the Evaluation of Carcinogenic Risks to Humans. Consumption of red meat and processed meat. *IARC Work. Group* **2015**, *114*, 6–13.
4. Font-i-Furnols, M.; Guerrero, L. Consumer preference, behavior and perception about meat and meat products: An overview. *Meat Sci.* **2014**, *98*, 361–371. [CrossRef]
5. Habermeyer, M.; Roth, A.; Guth, S.; Diel, P.; Engel, K.-H.; Epe, B.; Fürst, P.; Heinz, V.; Humpf, H.-U.; Joost, H.-G.; et al. Nitrate and nitrite in the diet: How to assess their benefit and risk for human health. *Mol. Nutr. Food Res.* **2015**, *59*, 106–128. [CrossRef]
6. EFSA CONTAM Panel (EFSA Panel on Contaminants in the Food Chain); Schrenk, D.; Bignami, M.; Bodin, L.; Chipman, J.K.; Del Mazo, J.; Hogstrand, C.; Hoogenboom, L.; Leblanc, J.-C.; Nebbia, C.S.; et al. Scientific Opinion on the risk assessment of N-nitrosamines in food. *EFSA J.* **2023**, *21*, e07884. [CrossRef]
7. EFSA ANS Panel (EFSA Panel on Food Additives and Nutrient Sources added to Food); Mortensen, A.; Aguilar, F.; Crebelli, D.; Domenico, A.; Dusemund, B.; Frutos, M.J.; Galtier, P.; Gott, D. Scientific Opinion on the re-evaluation of potassium nitrite (E 249) and sodium nitrite (E 250) as food additives. *EFSA J.* **2017**, *15*, 4786.
8. Honikel, K.O. The use and control of nitrate and nitrite for the processing of meat products. *Meat Sci.* **2008**, *78*, 68–76. [CrossRef]
9. Gruener, N.; Shuval, H.; Behroozi, K.; Cohen, S. Methemoglobinemia induced by transplacental passage of nitrites in rats. *Bull. Environ. Contam. Toxicol.* **1973**, *9*, 44–48. [CrossRef]
10. Keshari, V.; Adeeb, B.; Simmons, A.E.; Simmons, T.W.; Diep, C.Q. Zebrafish as a Model to Assess the Teratogenic Potential of Nitrite. *J. Vis. Exp.* **2016**, *108*, 53615.
11. EFSA FAF Panel (EFSA Panel on Food Additives and Flavourings); Younes, M.; Aquilina, G.; Castle, L.; Engel, K.-H.; Fowler, P.; Frutos Fernandez, M.J.; Furst, P.; Gürtler, R.; Husøy, T.; et al. Scientific Opinion on the re-evaluation of phosphoric acid—phosphates—di-, tri- and polyphosphates (E 338–341, E 343, E 450–452) as food additives and the safety of proposed extension of use. *EFSA J.* **2019**, *17*, 5674. [CrossRef]
12. EC Regulation (EC) No 1333/2008 of the European Parliament and of the Council of 16 December 2008 on food additives. *OJL* **2008**, *186*, 27.
13. Official Gazette of the Republic of Serbia. *Regulation on the Food Additives 53/2018*; 2018.
14. Official Gazette of the Republic of Serbia. *Regulation on the Quality of Ground Meat, Meat Preparations and Meat Products 50/2019*; 2019.
15. European Parliament, Council of the European Union. Directive 2006/52/EC of the European Parliament and of the Council of 5 July 2006 amending Directive 95/2/EC on food additives other than colours and sweeteners and Directive 94/35/EC on sweeteners for use in foodstuffs. *OJL* **2006**, *204*, 10–22. Available online: https://eur-lex.europa.eu/legal-content/EN/TXT/PDF/?uri=CELEX:32006L0052 (accessed on 22 January 2023).
16. Grosse, Y.; Baan, R.; Straif, K.; Secretan, B.; El Ghissassi, F.; Cogliano, V. WHO International Agency for Research on Cancer Monograph Working Group. Carcinogenicity of nitrate, nitrite, and cyanobacterial peptide toxins. Original Text. *Lancet Oncol.* **2006**, *7*, 628–629. [CrossRef] [PubMed]
17. Efenberger-Szmechtyk, M.; Nowak, A.; Czyzowska, A. Plant extracts rich in polyphenols: Antibacterial agents and natural preservatives for meat and meat products. *Crit. Rev. Food Sci. Nutr.* **2021**, *61*, 149–178. [CrossRef]
18. Brender Jean, D.; Olive, J.M.; Felkner, M.; Suarez, L.; Marckwardt, W.; Hendricks, K. Dietary Nitrites and Nitrates, Nitrosatable Drugs, and Neural Tube Defects. *Epidemiology* **2004**, *15*, 330–336. [CrossRef]
19. Manassaram, B.D.M.; Backer, L.C.; Moll, D.M. A review of nitrates in drinking water: Maternal exposure and adverse reproductive and developmental outcomes. *Environ. Health Perspect.* **2006**, *114*, 320–327. [CrossRef]
20. Pogoda, J.; Preston-Martin, S. Maternal cured meat consumption during pregnancy and risk of paediatric brain tumour in offspring: Potentially harmful levels of intake. *Public Health Nutr.* **2001**, *4*, 183–189. [CrossRef]
21. Milicevic, D.; Vranic, D.; Koricanac, V.; Petrovic, Z.; Bajcic, A.; Betic, N.; Zagorac, S. The intake of phosphorus through meat products: A health risk assessment. In Proceedings of the 61st International Meat Industry Conference, Zlatibor, Serbia, 26–29 September 2021; Volume 854. [CrossRef]

22. Vranic, D.; Koricanac, V.; Milicevic, D.; Djinovic-Stojanovic, J.; Geric, T.; Lilic, S.; Petrovic, Z. Nitrite content in meat products from the Serbian market and estimated intake. In Proceedings of the 61st International Meat Industry Conference, Zlatibor, Serbia, 26–29 September 2021; Volume 854. [CrossRef]
23. Milešević, J.; Lilić, S.; Vranić, D.; Zeković, M.; Borović, B.; Glibetić, M.; Gurinović, M.; Milićević, D. Dietary Intake of Salt from Meat Products in Serbian Population. *Int. J. Environ. Res. Public Health* **2023**, *20*, 4192. [CrossRef]
24. *ISO 2918:1999*; Meat and Meat Products—Determination of Nitrite Content (Reference Method). ISO: Geneva, Switzerland, 1996.
25. *ISO 13730:1996*; Meat and Meat Products—Determination of Total Phosphorus Content—Spectrometric Method. ISO: Geneva, Switzerland, 1996.
26. EFSA. Guidance on the EU Menu methodology. *EFSA J.* **2014**, *12*, 3944. [CrossRef]
27. Zekovic, M.; Gurinovic, M.; Milesevic, J.; Kadvan, A.; Glibetic, M. National Food Consumption Survey among 10–74 Years Old Individuals in Serbia. *EFSA Support. Publ.* **2022**, *19*, 7401E. [CrossRef]
28. Nikolić, M.; Milešević, J.; Zeković, M.; Gurinović, M.; Glibetić, M. The Development and Validation of Food Atlas for Portion Size Estimation in the Balkan Region. *Front. Nutr.* **2018**, *5*, 1–8. [CrossRef]
29. EFSA. Panel on Food Additives and Nutrient Sources added to Food (ANS); Guidance for submission for food additive evaluations. *EFSA J.* **2012**, *10*, 2760. Available online: www.efsa.europa.eu/efsajournal (accessed on 22 January 2023). [CrossRef]
30. EFSA Scientific Committee. Guidance on selected default values to be used by the EFSA Scientific Committee, Scientific Panels and Units in the absence of actual measured data. *EFSA J.* **2012**, *10*, 2579. [CrossRef]
31. EFSA NDA Panel (EFSA Panel on Dietetic Products, Nutrition and Allergies). Scientific Opinion on Dietary Reference Values for phosphorus. *EFSA J.* **2015**, *13*, 4185. [CrossRef]
32. EFSA. Management of left-censored data in dietary exposure assessment of chemical substances. *EFSA J.* **2010**, *8*, 1557.
33. Karwowska, M.; Kononiuk, A. Nitrates/Nitrites in Food—Risk for Nitrosative Stress and Benefits. *Antioxidants* **2020**, *9*, 241. [CrossRef]
34. Hamid, N.F.H.A.; Khan, M.M.; Lim, L.H. Assessment of nitrate, nitrite and chloride in selected cured meat products and their exposure to school children in Brunei Darussalam. *J. Food Compos. Anal.* **2020**, *91*, 103520. [CrossRef]
35. Bajcic, A.; Petronijevic, R.; Katanic, N.; Trbovic, D.; Betic, N.; Nikolic, A.; Milojevic, L. Evaluation of the content and safety of nitrite utilisation in meat products in Serbia in the period 2016–2018. *Meat Technol.* **2018**, *59*, 102. [CrossRef]
36. Mancini, F.R.; Paul, D.; Gauvreau, J.; Volatier, J.L.; Vin, K.; Hulin, M. Dietary exposure to benzoates (E210–E213), parabens (E214–E219), nitrites (E249–E250), nitrates (E251–E252), BHA (E320), BHT (E321) and aspartame (E951) in children less than 3 years old in France. *Food Addit. Contam. Part A Chem. Anal. Control Expo. Risk Assess.* **2015**, *32*, 293–306. [CrossRef]
37. World Cancer Research Fund/American Institute for Cancer Research. Diet, Nutrition, Physical Activity and Cancer: A Global Perspective. Continuous Update Project Expert Report. 2018. Available online: https://dietandcancerreport.org (accessed on 18 January 2023).

MDPI
St. Alban-Anlage 66
4052 Basel
Switzerland
www.mdpi.com

Nutrients Editorial Office
E-mail: nutrients@mdpi.com
www.mdpi.com/journal/nutrients

www.ingramcontent.com/pod-product-compliance
Lightning Source LLC
Chambersburg PA
CBHW061440210926
51850CB00008B/1566
* 9 7 8 3 0 3 6 5 9 5 7 2 6 *